From the
Finland Station

From the Finland Station

The Graying of Revolution in the Twentieth Century

THEODORE S. HAMEROW

Basic Books, Inc., Publishers

NEW YORK

Grateful acknowledgment is made for permission to reprint:

Extended quotation from *Time*, February 2, 1959. Copyright 1959 Time Inc. Reprinted by permission.

Extended quotation from *Fanshen: A Documentary of Revolution in a Chinese Village* by William Hinton. Copyright © 1966 by William Hinton. Reprinted by permission of Monthly Review Foundation.

Library of Congress Cataloging-in-Publication Data
Hamerow, Theodore S.
    From the Finland station : the graying of revolution in the
twentieth century / Theodore S. Hamerow.
        p.   cm.
    Includes bibliographical references.
    ISBN 0–465–02575–7
    1. History, Modern—20th
century.   2. Revolutions—History—20th
    century.   3. History, Military—20th century.   I. Title.
    D445.H32   1990
909.82—dc20   89–43092
                                                                        CIP

To N.

CONTENTS

Disappointments and defections
The corruptions of power
The corruptions of powerlessness
From the Communist Manifesto *to* Animal Farm

The moderation and virtue of a single character [George Washington] has probably prevented this revolution from being closed, as most others have been, by a subversion of that liberty it was intended to establish.

—THOMAS JEFFERSON
April 16, 1784

PREFACE

Some fifty years ago, while still a college student, I came across a book that captivated me completely, as it captivated so many other members of my generation. Crane Brinton's *Anatomy of Revolution*, a comparative study of the English Revolution of the 1640s, the American Revolution, the French Revolution, and the Russian Revolution, was written with such grace and elegance, such discernment and understanding, that I found it irresistible. The author sought to invest his findings with a quasi-scientific objectivity, to underpin his conclusions with a rigorous methodology; but the enormous popularity of the work rested primarily on his urbanity and sophistication, on the analytical sharpness of his mind, and the polished smoothness of his style. As with all important ventures in scholarship, what gave the book its significance was not technique but insight.

Though clearly influenced by Brinton, my own work is nevertheless different from his in important respects. It does not pretend to match his elegance and urbanity, his cool detachment and worldly skepticism. But I do feel that the time has come to examine in comparative perspective some of the revolutions that have taken place in various parts of the world since his day. Those he had studied were, with the exception of the Russian Revolution, largely political in nature. They sought to shift the locus of dominance from one powerful group in society to another, replacing a less representative with a more representative system of government. Although they produced important changes in the structure of the community, they did not attempt to redefine the fundamental relationships of property and power. They aimed rather at an alteration in the pattern of politics. The revolutions of the twentieth century, on the other hand, have been concerned to a much higher degree with the interaction of economic interests and social classes. They have dealt more directly and rigorously with the distribution of wealth and authority. They have therefore been more drastic in their methods and more radical in their objectives. Their ultimate goal has been nothing less than the transformation of human behavior.

This aspect of the revolutionary movements of the twentieth century has been obscured to some extent by the vague use of the term "revolution." It has been applied, for example, to the process by which colonial peoples have succeeded in freeing themselves from the political control of the imperialist powers. But the liberation of the Third World has not led as a rule to any fundamental alteration in its economic or social institutions. Rather, it has meant generally the substitution of a native for a foreign elite, the replacement of an alien ascendancy with a domestic patriciate. The underlying disparities in wealth and power have remained to a large extent unchanged. Nor do I think that the establishment after the Second World War, under pressure from the Soviet Union, of Communist dictatorships in Eastern Europe can properly be called a revolution. It represents instead the imposition by external force of new allegiances and institutions on reluctant, fractious societies. I have sought rather to examine those revolutions occurring in my lifetime that have been indigenous and spontaneous, that have been a popular response to the failings of the *ancien régime*, and that have been inspired by the exciting vision of a new social order. In short, my book deals with deep-rooted insurrectionary movements seeking to alter the structure of property and authority.

I have tried to analyze the nature of such movements by comparing the revolutions taking place during the twentieth century in Russia, China, Cuba, and Vietnam. Though occurring in widely scattered parts of the world, among peoples with entirely different historical and cultural traditions, they seem to me to display a striking resemblance. They are alike in the words they utter, the strategies they employ, the objectives they pursue, and the institutions they establish. The resemblance between them is, in fact, so great that it could not be the result of pure chance. It must reflect an underlying similarity of motivation and purpose. My intention in writing this book has been to describe that similarity.

I make no claim that my findings represent ineluctable laws of revolutionary change. Nor do I pretend to have discovered a fundamental principle of insurrectionary entropy, some unvarying pattern of radical dictatorship. Historiography is strewn with the debris of failed attempts to impose a grand design on the past or to predict the future on the basis of some quasi-scientific theory of historical development. And yet basic similarities in several distinct revolutions point to tendencies and probabilities in all revolutions. Not every new order will inevitably follow the model of Russia, China, Cuba, and Vietnam, but there is a good chance that it will. That assertion does not seem to me excessive.

Since my linguistic knowledge is limited to the major West European languages, I have had to restrict my research to the primary materials and secondary works available in those languages. Fortunately, the scholarly literature in English, French, and German is considerable, and the major works of the important revolutionary leaders of the twentieth century have all been translated. It would no doubt have been better if I could also read Russian, Chinese, and Vietnamese. Yet to wait until I had mastered them all would have meant abandoning the project altogether. I therefore decided to forge ahead, fully aware of my linguistic shortcomings, but reasonably confident that I had at least examined the most significant historical materials. After all, scholarship is in most cases a compromise between what would be ideally desirable and what is realistically attainable.

I also visited each of the countries whose revolutions I was studying. My purpose was not to meet with government officials or party leaders in order to ask them what they were trying to accomplish. I had a fairly good idea of what they might tell me. I wanted rather to capture the flavor of life under the new order, to observe the everyday experiences, and to understand the satisfactions and frustrations of ordinary members of a revolutionary society. The foreign traveler in Havana who, during a casual walk, is approached by black marketeers offering him many more pesos for his dollars than the government bank, gains an insight into the new Cuba that no official guide will provide. The American tourist in Ho Chi Minh City who is greeted by the pedicab drivers in front of his hotel with a suggestively cheerful "Hi, Joe! Long time no see" will gather that the pleasures that had provided consolation to an earlier generation of American visitors are not entirely unknown in Communist Vietnam. This kind of historical insight cannot be found in libraries, archives, or interviews with prominent bureaucrats. It must be sought elsewhere.

The title of my book derives from Edmund Wilson's classic *To the Finland Station*, published in 1940, which sought to analyze the revolutionary movement in Europe up to the time when Lenin, returning from exile, reached the Finland Station in Saint Petersburg on April 16, 1917. I, on the other hand, have tried to examine what happens to a revolution after its Lenin has arrived, seized power, and started to build a new social system.

Finally, I want to thank some of my friends and colleagues—Maurice Meisner, Alfred E. Senn, and Thomas E. Skidmore—who read the manuscript in its entirety and offered suggestions for its improvement. Since they are recognized authorities on the history of the countries I examined, I relied on them to alert me to obvious errors in my work—to incorrect dates, misspelled names, or dubious statistics. But more than that, I asked them to comment on my analyses and interpretations, my arguments and conclusions. Although their advice was most valuable, I must confess that, with an author's obstinacy, I did not always follow it. In any case, they should not be held responsible for any errors of opinion or judgment that may appear in the book. Above all, they should not be held responsible for the implicit contention that some of the worst oppressions can be imposed in the name of freedom, some of the greatest offenses can be committed for the sake of justice, and some of the harshest cruelties can be rationalized as instruments of humaneness. That contention is mine alone.

Madison, Wisconsin
March 1989

CHAPTER 1

The Decline of Established Authority

The Mythology of Power

To say that the process of revolution begins with an erosion of the legitimacy of an existing political and social order may seem only a truism. Every system of public authority rests ultimately on an intricate fabric of beliefs, myths, and fictions designed to justify its exercise of power. There are also, to be sure, instruments of coercion such as the police, judiciary, bureaucracy, and army, whose function is to enforce the obedience of the subject to the established regime. But no form of government can endure by compulsion alone. A substructure of ideas and allegiances must also exist that helps make the status quo appear equitable or at least impregnable. Those who have been entrusted with the task of instilling loyalty to the old order claim that it embodies the collective experience and historic tradition of the community. Opposition to its will, on the other hand, is portrayed as a rejection of the most solemn civic duties and pieties. Hence established authority tends to assume a quasi-religious character. Its tone is sacerdotal, its mission sacred. The perception of the status quo as possessing mystical or magical qualities, as endowed with powers beyond the grasp of ordinary mortals, remains essential for its survival. Without this hold on the minds of those on whose obedience it depends, an established system of government becomes vulnerable to revolution.

Popular faith in the sanctity of the old order is generally reinforced by arguments regarding its benevolence. The overthrow of traditional authority will allegedly lead to mob rule, to violence and destruction, and to government by doctrinaires and rabble-rousers. There will be greater oppression and exploitation, greater inefficiency and corruption. The moral foundations of the community will be undermined; a war of all against all will ravage society. Anarchy and chaos await the nation that dares reject legitimate, anointed authority.

The existing regime, on the other hand, is portrayed as being committed to gradual but steady progress. It avoids dangerous experiments and foolhardy adventures. Respecting the inherited traditions of the community, it seeks to achieve the well-being of all without violating the rights of any. It may perhaps still have weaknesses and imperfections, but it is clearly improving. Social evils that may have escaped the attention of the authorities will eventually be perceived and rectified. Patience and faith in the goodwill of established authority will in time be rewarded with constructive, lasting reform. While the seductive promises of those who seek to subvert legitimate government may sometimes mislead the unwary, sober, deliberate reflection is bound to lead to a recognition that progress can be achieved only within the framework of traditional institutions.

Such is the classical rhetoric of the status quo. Ordinarily it is accepted without much question. Most people share the pieties of the established order. The few who remain skeptical feel constrained by circumstances to adopt an attitude of acquiescence or resignation. In private they may express doubt regarding the nature of the existing regime, but they feel powerless before its might. What good will it do to voice their complaints? "You can't fight city hall" is a bit of folk wisdom known in every culture. And from the point of view of those in authority, obedience arising from impotence is almost as good as compliance arising from conviction. Whatever the motives of the governed, their submission to the established system of government is essential for its survival.

The Erosion of Hieratic Legitimacy

But then, at some point in the emergence of a revolutionary situation, a process of civic demythologization begins that strips the old order of its hieratic character. The mystical assumptions on which it had rested come to be questioned and rejected. The emperor, the multitude now starts to whisper, is not really wearing new clothes; he is naked and slightly ridiculous. What had been accepted as sacred suddenly seems only too human. And once demystification of the status quo sets in, the established order is in trouble. The fabric of myths and fictions on which it had depended gradually unravels; the quasi-religious foundation of its authority, which had appeared so strong, starts to wobble. The process of revolution, in other words, originates in a fundamental change in collective mental perception. For without a popular conviction that those who rule possess powers that are in some sense magical or preternatural, no system of government can long endure.

What accounts for this sudden loss of a legitimacy that had for generations been accepted without question? What are the factors that deprive the *ancien régime* of the authority derived from a faith in its thaumaturgical nature? This is a complex question. It leads not only to a scrutiny of the shortcomings of the established system, but to an examination of the aspirations of the revolutionaries who seek to create a new social order.

To those directing the assault against traditional authority, the answer seems obvious. The existing regime is responsible for its own misfortunes. It has been overthrown by its avarice and oppression, its selfishness and cruelty. It has exploited the lower classes, battening on their poverty and ignorance. It has imprisoned its opponents, while lavishing wealth and preferment on its supporters. Behind its professions of high moral purpose lurks only an insatiable appetite for money and power. The litany of complaints against the old order is long and bitter. But its gist is that while the masses toil and hunger, the ruling elite leads a life of riotous profligacy. Is it any wonder then that the people, aroused from their torpor, finally rise up? Once the veil of officially sanctioned superstitions has fallen, once the powers that be stand revealed in all their wickedness, the masses are bound to turn against their exploiters. The *ancien régime* falls because its inner corruption can no longer be disguised.

This analysis of the source of revolutionary movements, however, though by no means implausible, fails to stand up under closer examination. The old order may indeed be as selfish and tyrannical as its critics contend. It admittedly remains ruthless and repressive down to the hour of its final collapse. It continues to persecute its adversaries, suppressing their newspapers, breaking up their meetings, and imprisoning their followers. Despite promises of a more equitable system of administration, it continues to wink at nepotism and corruption. Those who have been the beneficiaries of the status quo go on receiving its favors; those who have been its beasts of burden go on toiling. The established system is simply incapable of breaking with tradition, habit, and ingrained prejudice. All it can do is disguise the maintenance of an oligarchical form of authority behind a show of benevolence and progress.

Yet although the *ancien régime* on the eve of the revolution may not be much better than in the past, it is as a rule no worse. Corruption and greed are no more blatant than in its heyday. On the contrary, sensing the approach of a crisis, the old order often seeks to defend itself by the appearance or even the reality of reform. There are proclamations pledging political liberalization and economic improvement. Government will become more compassionate, justice more evenhanded, and administration more efficient. Nor do the authorities stop with mere declarations. They make efforts, though timidly and hesitantly, to carry out some of their promises. Advisory committees and consultative assemblies are appointed to propose needed changes in the established system. Regulations for recruiting members of the bureaucracy are made a little less restrictive. Censorship of the press is partly relaxed; some expressions of disaffection come to be tacitly tolerated. There are even attempts, by and large not very effective, to improve the economic position of the small farmer and the factory worker.

Only a generation earlier such reforms would have been greeted as a major step toward the improvement of society. Yet now that they have finally come, in response to a growing clamor for change, they are dismissed as timid and inadequate. The point is that the spread of dissatisfaction with established authority cannot be explained by its growing oppressiveness or venality. It may in fact be more tolerant or conscientious than before. But it has lost its hieratic character, its sacerdotal validation. The legitimacy of the status quo has suddenly dissipated. It is not a change in the objective political conditions that accounts for the decline of the old order, but a change in the subjective perception of those conditions. Revolution originates in people's minds.

Material Conditions
and Civic Discontents

Economic privation is not the key factor in the downfall of established authority any more than political repression. Insurrectionary rhetoric, to be sure, dwells on the sufferings of the lower classes, on their toil, hunger, squalor, and poverty. It paints vivid pictures of emaciated children, of their exhausted fathers and despairing mothers. Nor should these pictures be dismissed as only figments of the revolutionary imagination. There is in fact widespread privation among the masses, more than enough to arouse the indignation of middle-class social reformers. Yet material circumstances are no worse than in the past; indeed, they may be somewhat better. The overthrow of the old order occurs typically in an expanding rather than contracting economy, under a rising rather than declining standard of living. Progress may be slow or uneven or intermittent, but there is undeniably progress. What makes the economic situation seem intolerable is not deteriorating conditions but rising expectations. The way of life of the lower classes may be getting better, but it is not getting better as fast as they feel it should. Disparities in wealth that had once been accepted as natural and unalterable now begin to seem unjust. In economics as in politics, it is the demythologization of traditional institutions and relationships that accounts for the fall of the *ancien régime*.

Leon Trotsky, the sharpest analytical mind produced by the revolutionary movements of the twentieth century, openly acknowledged this primacy of perception over actuality in the decline of established authority. "In reality the mere existence of privations is not enough to cause an insurrection," he maintained. "If it were, the masses would always be in revolt. It is necessary that the bankruptcy of the social regime, being conclusively revealed, should make these privations intolerable, and that new conditions and new ideas should open the prospects of a revolutionary way out." Once a new order has been established, moreover, once its claim to power has been perceived as morally valid, "those same masses will prove capable of enduring doubled and tripled privations" in its defense. What turns the lower classes against traditional authority is not their suffering but that their suffering has ceased to appear justifiable.[1]

An examination of economic conditions on the eve of the overthrow of the old order reveals in fact an expanding productivity and a rising standard of living. There is certainly little evidence of any decline in national income. The economy of czarist Russia at the outbreak of the First World War, for example, though still backward in comparison with Western Europe, was making impressive gains in both industry and agriculture. Production of coal rose from 9,100,000 metric tons in 1895 to 16,160,000 in 1900, 18,670,000 in 1905, 25,430,000 in 1910, and 36,050,000 in 1913, an increase of 296 percent in eighteen years. The output of pig iron rose from 1,455,000 metric tons in 1895 to 2,937,000 in 1900, then dropped to 2,736,000 in 1905 in the wake of military defeat and revolutionary upheaval; but by 1910 it had climbed back to 3,047,000, and in 1913 it reached 4,641,000—an increase for the entire period of 219 percent. The output of crude steel rose from 879,000 metric tons in 1895 to 2,216,000 in 1900, 2,266,000 in 1905, 3,314,000 in 1910, and 4,918,000 in 1913, a spectacular increase of 459 percent. The combined index of Russian industrial production, which had stood at 44 in 1895, reached 63 in 1900, dropped slightly to 61 in 1905, and then climbed again rapidly to 86 in 1910 and 100 in 1913.

The gains in agricultural output, though not as impressive, were substantial enough to support rapid urbanization in the European provinces of the empire. The wheat crop rose from 8,400,000 metric tons in 1895 to 9,200,000 in 1900, 12,800,000 in 1905, and 16,500,000 in 1909. Comparisons with subsequent years are hard to make, because the territory covered by the official statistics expanded shortly before the First World War to include the trans-Ural region. But for the period 1895–1909 the increase was 96 percent. The production of rye went from 19,600,000 metric tons in 1895 to 22,700,000 in 1900, then fell sharply to 17,700,000 in 1905, before climbing once more to 22,000,000 in 1909. Though it failed to regain the level of 1900, the overall increase was 12 percent. There was less fluctuation in the barley crop: 4,900,000 metric tons in 1895, 4,500,000 in 1900, 6,400,000 in 1905, and 8,900,000 in 1909, a combined growth of 82 percent.

And the potato crop, traditionally a staple in the diet of the lower classes, rose without interruption from 21,100,000 metric tons in 1895 to 25,300,000 in 1900, 27,600,000 in 1905, and 31,500,000 in 1909, a combined growth of 49 percent. The impression created by all these figures is of a vigorous and expanding economy, experiencing the usual growing pains of rapid industrialization, but still capable of providing the population with an improving standard of living. There is certainly nothing here to suggest the widespread impoverishment that is sometimes assumed to be a precondition of a successful revolution.[2]

The Cuban economy just before Castro's victory appeared as sound as the Russian on the eve of the First World War. There was the same increase in output, the same growth of investment, the same rise in national income. The 1950s, despite a mild recession in the middle of the decade, were probably the most prosperous period in the history of the country. According to a United Nations report, the index of agricultural production, the island's leading economic sector, rose from 95 in 1949–50 to 106 in 1950–51 and 107 in 1951–52, reaching 124 in 1952–53. It then fell to 102 in 1953–54 and 1954–55, and to 97 in 1955–56, yet by 1956–57 it had climbed back to 101, and in 1957–58 stood at 115.

To be sure, the output of sugar, the chief component of Cuba's foreign trade, declined from 5,800,000 tons in 1951 and 7,200,000 tons in 1952 to 5,200,000 in 1953, 4,900,000 in 1954, and 4,500,000 in 1955. But then it started to grow again to 4,700,000 in 1956 and, in 1957, just as the guerrillas were beginning their struggle in Sierra Maestra, production reached 5,700,000. Because of an increase in price, moreover, the value of sugar exports recovered more rapidly than the volume of production. Earnings at first dropped from 672,000,000 dollars in 1951 to 578,000,000 in 1952, 529,000,000 in 1953, and 432,000,000 in 1954. In 1955, however, an upswing began. The figure for that year was 473,000,000 dollars; for 1956, 524,000,000. By 1957 income from sugar exports reached 680,000,000, exceeding the peak of six years before. Everything seemed to point to continuing economic growth.

It is therefore not surprising that throughout the decade investors continued to put their money into Cuban agriculture and industry, confident that the island's economic future was secure. Gross private investment in fixed capital fell at first from 269,000,000 pesos in 1951 to 258,000,000 in 1952 and 200,000,000 in 1953. In 1954, however, it recovered to 221,000,000 and then reached new highs of 273,000,000 in 1955, 328,000,000 in 1956, and 375,000,000 in 1957, 39 percent above the 1951 figure.

Statistics on the net national income of Cuba, though somewhat less favorable, seemed to support the investors' confidence. The total rose from 2,015,000,000 pesos in 1951 to 2,084,000,000 in 1952, before dropping sharply to 1,784,000,000 in 1953. But a year later a sustained recovery began: 1,827,000,000 pesos in 1954, 1,907,000,000 in 1955, 2,086,000,000 in 1956, and 2,345,000,000 in 1957. The index of net national income climbed from 97 in 1951 to 100 in 1952, fell to 86 in 1953, climbed again to 88 in 1954 and 92 in 1955, reached 100 in 1956, and peaked at 113 in 1957.

All calculations and measures of the island's economic prospects thus appeared to justify the optimistic tone of the United Nations report: "During 1957, Cuba's economic activity attained the highest level registered since the war. According to provisional estimates, the gross product at current prices was 11 percent more than in 1956, when the economy had already regained the peak level reached in 1952. If price rises are taken into account, the growth of the gross product in real terms may be estimated at rather over 8 percent." It was especially heartening that whereas in the previous two years public investment had been the main bulwark of the Cuban economy, "the principal factor stimulating expansion in 1957 was the marked increment in export earnings, accruing chiefly from a rise in sugar prices on the international free market. Sugar production expanded 19.7 percent, while its value rose 46.8 percent."[3]

By the time this report was published in 1959, Castro was already in power. So much for the contention that economic stagnation leads to revolution, while economic growth is a safeguard of the status quo. But what about the view that it is not the amount of national wealth but its distribution that is the key factor in the decline of the *ancien régime*? Does not a pronounced inequality in income between the affluent few and the impoverished many breed discontent that is bound to lead to a political upheaval? This line of reasoning, though seemingly more plausible and persuasive, is not always valid either. It may appear superficially credible, since revolutions occur typically in agrarian societies where there is a striking disparity between aristocratic *latifundia* and small peasant holdings. Yet an examination of economic conditions in countries on the verge of mass insurrection fails to reveal any direct connection between the concentration of landownership and the intensity of political disaffection.

The situation in Russia illustrates this point. The apportionment of land to the peasantry under the terms of the emancipation legislation of the 1860s was at least as generous as in Central or even Western Europe. Of the roughly 10,000,000 former serfs who participated in the redistribution of landed property, 81 percent received holdings of more than 2 hectares, and 53 percent holdings of more than 3 hectares. The size of the allotments varied considerably, to be sure. Those who had been state peasants received on an average close to 10 hectares, while those who had been serfs on the noble *latifundia* received not quite 4. Yet even the latter figure compares favorably with the holdings of most French farmers during the nineteenth century. In some parts of Russia the peasantry did very well indeed. The average family allotment on the lower Volga was between 34 and 36 hectares, and in the black soil belt it was about 16. The former serfs, moreover, succeeded through purchase in increasing the land in their possession by roughly 15 percent between 1877 and 1905. By the time of the First World War, the peasants owned approximately 82,000,000 hectares or 52 percent of the total, while the great landlords retained not quite 77,000,000.

Thus the real losers in the reorganization of Russian agriculture were not the *muzhiks* but the large property owners. Weak, indolent, and inefficient, most could not cope with the complexities of a competitive, capitalistic form of husbandry. "Formerly we kept no accounts and drank champagne," one of them complained to a British visitor. "Now we keep accounts and content ourselves with beer." Unable to adapt to new economic realities, many aristocratic proprietors were forced to sell part or all of their estates to middle-class or peasant purchasers. The nobility lost about 13 percent of their land by 1877, 24 percent by 1887, 35 percent by 1897, 48 percent by 1905, and 59 percent by the time of the Bolshevik revolution. Roughly half of it went directly to small farmers, and the other half to urban investors who generally leased it in turn to the land-hungry peasantry.

The prosperous real-estate developer *Lopahin* in Chekhov's *The*

Cherry Orchard, who eventually succeeds in acquiring the estate on which his father had once worked as a serf, embodies the rising class of agricultural capitalists shrewd enough to seize the opportunities created by free enterprise in rural property. *Madame Ranevskaya* and her brother *Leonid Andreyevich*, on the other hand, represent the charming, prodigal, and doomed Russian gentry sinking into genteel poverty. Thus the diffusion of landownership had become an economic reality in Russia long before the First World War. The statistical evidence shows that disparities in the size of agricultural holdings were diminishing rather than increasing. What the Bolsheviks did when they came to power was not to initiate the expropriation of the nobility, but to accelerate and complete a process of dispossession that had been going on for two generations.[4]

The pattern of landownership in Vietnam during the 1930s reinforces the conclusion that there is little direct connection between the concentration of property and the intensity of opposition to the established order. Although striking inequalities existed in the distribution of land, differences among the major regions of the country in the disparity of wealth show little correlation with the level of revolutionary activity. In Cochin China in the south, for example, fewer than 3 percent of all the proprietors of riceland had holdings of more than 50 hectares, yet they owned 45 percent of the total. Another 26 percent of the proprietors, those with holdings between 5 and 50 hectares, owned 37 percent. Those whose holdings were below 5 hectares, on the other hand, although they constituted almost 72 percent of all proprietors, owned only 15 percent of the area devoted to rice cultivation. Communal lands accounted for no more than 3 percent of the total. The considerable extent of absentee landlordism in Cochin China, moreover, can be inferred from government statistics showing that fewer than 65 percent of the proprietors were directly involved in farming their land.

In Tonkin in the north the concentration of agricultural wealth, though significant, was not nearly so pronounced. Fewer than 1 percent of all the proprietors of riceland owned holdings of more than 50 hectares, and what they owned amounted to only 20 percent of the total. Those with holdings between 5 and 50 hectares, constituting about 8 percent of the proprietors, had another 20 percent. And the nearly 91 percent of proprietors with holdings of less than 5 hectares owned 40 percent of the land devoted to rice cultivation. Another 20 percent was held as communal property. And there were virtually no absentee landlords, since almost 99 percent of the proprietors were directly involved in working the land. The economic and social differences between northern and southern Vietnam during the colonial era were thus substantial.

On the face of it, Cochin China should have been more hostile to the *ancien régime* than Tonkin—more willing to employ violence in order to bring about its overthrow. For while in the north the small proprietors, those with holdings of less than 5 hectares, owned individually or collectively about 60 percent of the area devoted to growing rice, the staple of the nation's agriculture, in the south the percentage was only 18. Yet in fact the opposite was the case. It was in Tonkin that armed resistance against the restoration of colonial rule began after the Second World War. It was here that the establishment of an independent Vietnamese state was proclaimed, that the French forces were defeated, and that the strategy for reunifying the country under a Communist regime originated. In the south, on the other hand, foreign political influence remained strong long after the achievement of independence in Tonkin. The tie to Western countries was more enduring in Cochin China, the defense of traditional institutions more vigorous, and the opposition to communism more determined. The degree of concentration of property seemed to have little effect on the attitude of the masses toward the old order.[5]

But is not the standard of living really the key to the emergence of a revolutionary situation? Is not the decisive factor a decline in the material well-being of a majority of the population? Granted that the total amount of wealth in society cannot be used as a measure of the economic condition of the lower classes. Not even the distribution of wealth is an accurate yardstick, since owners of considerable property may find their income shrinking, while propertyless laborers are enjoying steady employment and rising wages. But surely the level of consumption of goods by the masses—in other words, the standard of living—must have a significant effect on their loyalty to established authority. If a chicken on Sunday in the pot of every French peasant is a token of political stability, according

to Henry IV, does it not follow that hunger and privation are portents of revolution?

This line of reasoning has a certain compelling inner logic. It
seems to make sense to assume that attitudes toward government
are shaped by the economic environment in which people live.
Every politician under a system of free elections knows that hard
times mean trouble at the polls for the party in power. Hence it
appears reasonable that under an authoritarian form of rule the dissatisfactions that might otherwise be expressed in votes for the opposition will be channeled toward revolutionary thoughts and
deeds.

The argument is all the more persuasive because it is almost irrefutable. Of all the measures of national welfare, none is more elusive, more difficult to determine, than the standard of living. There
are satisfactory statistical techniques for ascertaining the amount or
distribution of national wealth. How are we to decide, however,
whether the lower classes are better or worse off than in the past?
Even if we measure changes in their diet, in the clothes they wear,
the dwellings they inhabit, or the amusements they pursue, are we
justified in averaging these figures across the entire population to
obtain an accurate measure of the standard of living?

The point is that at any given time there are some groups in society that are thriving, while other groups are enduring poverty.
There are always some workers who manage to win higher wages
and shorter hours, while other workers are suffering hunger and
privation. There are always some peasants who are enlarging their
holdings at the expense of other peasants who are sinking into a
landless rural proletariat. By emphasizing one or another of these
groups, almost any generalization regarding material conditions
can be defended, almost any contention concerning the relationship between the standards of living and the outbreak of revolution can be supported. Even if it could be shown that a majority of
the population is experiencing an improvement in its economic situation, can it not then be argued that the crucial factor is the disaffection of a decisive minority, of factory workers or unskilled
laborers, of small peasants or landless farmhands? Indeed, are not
all revolutions made by organized, determined minorities rather
than amorphous and indecisive majorities? The question is so

broad and complex, so open to subjective judgment, that no universally acceptable answer is attainable.

And yet a few tentative conclusions regarding the connection between the economic condition of the lower classes and the popular appeal of insurrectionary movements may be reached even on the basis of an incomplete body of statistical data. It does appear that, by and large, there is no deterioration in the material welfare of the lower classes in a prerevolutionary situation, and at times there is in fact a substantial improvement. Not enough reliable information on the standard of living of the masses in China in the 1900s or in Vietnam in the 1930s is available, but the statistics for Russia and Cuba, though far from comprehensive, generally support this judgment.

The economic situation in the last decades of czarism, especially the condition of the lower classes, is admittedly hard to assess. Detailed data on the consumption of food, the availability of housing, or the quality of clothing simply do not exist. There were many workers, to be sure, especially in large industrial enterprises like the well-known Putilov works in Saint Petersburg, who succeeded through strike activity or collective bargaining in obtaining a significant increase in real earnings. But there were many others—master artisans, skilled handicraftsmen, and small shopowners—who were going under in the struggle against big business and mechanized production. Nor can those wretched residents of the flophouse in Gorky's *The Lower Depths* be dismissed as creations of a playwright's dramatic fancy. Many peasants took advantage of the agrarian reforms introduced in 1906 to withdraw their holdings from collective village ownership, to enlarge them through purchase or lease, and to form a class of prosperous, independent farmers. But many others collapsed under the burden of heavy taxation, land shortage, and inefficient cultivation. To escape disaster, they too would sometimes withdraw their land from the *obshchina*, the peasant commune, only to find themselves forced in the end to sell it to the more affluent *kulaks*. Having lost what little they had, they became propertyless rural laborers or drifted to the big cities in search of employment as unskilled workers. Thus in rural communities, as in urban centers, the success of some groups among the lower classes was being built on the failure of others.

In the face of such contradictory evidence, can any generalization be made about the economic condition of the Russian masses? Despite inadequacies in the statistical data, virtually all scholars agree that the standard of living was rising. The Canadian economist James Mavor, after studying the situation in Russia at first hand, wrote just before the First World War that life for the rural population, comprising more than four-fifths of all inhabitants, was clearly getting better. "It must be allowed that, especially during the years immediately preceding the Russo-Japanese War, the position of the peasantry, though bad, had distinctly improved." The prosperity of the *kulaks*, the well-to-do farmers, was one of the significant features of the period. "The growth of this class was facilitated by the Peasants' Bank and its presence as an important fraction of the village population is noticed in all the reports from the districts of which details have been given." It seemed, moreover, that "while the village proletariat had not been similarly prosperous, while they had been undergoing exploitation at the hands of landowners and rich peasants alike, they had nevertheless succeeded owing to the economical conditions of the years from about 1900 to 1905 [when harvests were good], in forcing their wages somewhat upwards."

Further economic advances resulted from the growing militancy of the rural population. "The policy of strikes which the peasants adopted in 1905 was successful up to a certain point," according to Mavor. "They [later] lost some of the advantages which they gained during the disturbances, but they did not lose all of them. Their wages remained somewhat higher than they were before the agrarian movement began, and their rents were somewhat lower." It was obvious that "under these conditions contracts for land and for wages must be at least slightly more favourable to the peasants than they were formerly, and that thus the sacrifices made in the agrarian movement were not wholly fruitless."[6]

In the years since the appearance of Mavor's study, writers dealing with economic conditions in czarist Russia have almost without exception concurred with his general conclusion. Those in sympathy with the Bolshevik revolution have tended to be more grudging in their acknowledgment that the standard of living was improving before the First World War. They have usually emphasized the continuing disparities in income between the upper and the lower classes, between industrialists and landowners on one side and workers and peasants on the other. But even they have conceded that the masses were on the whole better off in 1914 than in 1894 or 1904. Those critical of the new order in Russia, on the other hand, have dwelt on the achievements of the prerevolutionary period, not necessarily out of sympathy with czarism, but because of their disapproval of Bolshevik policies. They have maintained that many of the gains claimed by the Soviet system were in the making long before the revolution. In any case, both sides agree that the standard of living in the final years of the *ancien régime* was in all likelihood improving.

Such a judgment is admittedly based in part on deduction and guesswork. But there is one indirect measure of national welfare that is unambiguous on this point. To the extent that popular literacy reflects a degree of economic well-being, there can be little doubt of the direction in which the standard of living was moving. In the last two decades of czarism, Russia made rapid advances toward the elimination of illiteracy. Though still far behind Western Europe, it had embarked on an ambitious program to narrow the gap. The rate of literacy for the population of European Russia rose from not quite 23 percent in 1897 to 33 percent in 1920. Progress was most rapid among the young, particularly young men. The proportion of literates among recruits into the Russian army, the group regarding which the statistical data is most complete, shows a steady improvement from 32 percent in 1890 to 39 in 1895, 49 in 1900, 56 in 1905, 65 in 1910, and 68 in 1913. In twenty years the percentage of illiteracy among the conscripts had been reduced by about half.

This improvement was the result of a concerted effort by the regime to expand primary instruction. Government expenditures on elementary education rose from 7,226,000 rubles in 1890 to 15,971,000 in 1900 and 42,882,000 in 1911, an overall increase of 493 percent. Between 1898 and 1911 the number of schools grew 27 percent, from 78,699 to 100,295; the number of teachers 31 percent, from 154,652 to 203,273; and the number of pupils 47 percent, from 4,203,246 to 6,180,510. The advance continued up to and beyond the outbreak of the First World War. According to a report of the Ministry of Public Education which dealt with primary instruction under its direct jurisdiction, excluding religious or nondenominational private institutions, the number of schools increased 32 percent between 1911 and 1915, the number of pupils 36 percent, and the number of teachers 39 percent. The authorities hoped to reach the goal of general and compulsory elementary education by the year 1922. In view of the progress made during the preceding two decades, that did not seem unrealistic. War and revolution meant that a new regime achieved universal schooling in Russia, but only at about the same time that czarism probably would have under conditions of peace and stability. As George F. Kennan has argued, "one simply cannot accept the thesis that the old regime kept the Russian people in darkness to the end and that a revolution was necessary in 1917 to correct the situation."

Equally significant are the statistics regarding changes in secondary and higher education. For what they reveal is not rigidity or uniformity in the class origin of students entering high schools and universities, but a steady broadening of social status. They make it clear that accessibility to advanced learning in prerevolutionary Russia was rapidly expanding.

To begin with, a substantial growth occurred in the number of those attending secondary schools, from 159,000 in 1880 to 631,000 in 1914, an increase of nearly 300 percent. The change in the family background of the pupils was even more surprising. In 1881 about 48 percent of those attending the classical "Gymnasia" for boys came from the gentry or bureaucracy, 19 percent were the sons of workers or craftsmen, and 8 percent the sons of peasants. In 1914 only 32 percent came from the gentry or bureaucracy, 27 percent from families of workers or craftsmen, and 22 percent from the peasantry. In the less prestigious "Real Schools," the shift in the class origins of the student population was still more pronounced. In 1882 roughly 41 percent of the pupils came from the gentry or bureaucracy, 20 percent from families of workers or craftsmen, and 12 percent from the peasantry. By 1914 the proportions had become almost completely reversed: barely 23 percent from the gentry or bureaucracy, 30 percent from families of workers or craftsmen, and 32 percent from families of peasants. It becomes apparent that on the eve of the old order's collapse, the social foundation of secondary education was being steadily democratized.

The same pattern of increasing accessibility to advanced learning is discernible in the Russian universities. There was swift growth in the total number of students from 9,344 in 1881 to 34,538 in 1912, about 270 percent. But equally remarkable was a change in the family background of the students. In 1880 some 47 percent came from the gentry or bureaucracy, 12 percent from families of workers or craftsmen, and only 3 percent from the peasantry. By 1914 the class basis of higher education had undergone a striking transformation. Now no more than 36 percent of the students came from the gentry or bureaucracy, while 24 percent came from families of workers or craftsmen, and close to 15 percent from the peasantry. In other words, well before the revolution, university students of lower-class origin had begun to outnumber those of upper-class background. The preponderance of the former was even more pronounced in the state schools of technology. Here the proportions at the outbreak of the First World War were less than 25 percent for the gentry or bureaucracy, 32 percent for the sons of workers or craftsmen, and 22 percent for the peasantry.

All in all, then, Russia in the last years of czarism does not give the impression of a stagnant, oppressed, or demoralized society groaning under the yoke of autocracy. On the contrary, distinct evidence exists of an improvement in the standard of living, a rise in popular literacy, growing access to higher education, and increasing social mobility. The common contention that it is impoverishment that breeds rebelliousness simply does not stand up under a careful scrutiny of conditions during the last years of the *ancien régime* in Russia.[7]

An examination of the economic situation in Cuba before the Castro revolution points to a similar conclusion. Little tangible support can be found for the view that the fall of the old order was the result of a deterioration in the standard of living. In fact, Cuba during the 1950s ranked near the top among the twenty nations of Latin America by virtually every statistical measure of material welfare. The island was fifth in per capita income, just behind the small group of states with the most advanced economy: Argentina, Uruguay, Chile, and Venezuela. Per capita income, to be sure, is not always an accurate reflection of the standard of living, since a high concentration of wealth may blur disparities among occupational groups and social classes. All the other indexes of well-being, however, also suggest a relatively wide diffusion of prosperity in Cuba. The literacy rate of 78 percent was exceeded only by Argentina, Uru-

guay, and Chile. The death rate of 15 per thousand, among the small-
est in Latin America, continued to lag behind Argentina and Uruguay with 10 each, but it was equal to Chile's and far ahead of
Venezuela's. Life expectancy at birth, between fifty-six and sixty-
two years, was the third or fourth highest. Taken in combination,
these statistics reinforce the impression of a rising standard of living
for most of the country's population.

Particularly significant was the widespread availability of those
bourgeois conveniences and amenities that characterize a vigorous,
modernizing economy. There was 1 automobile for every 39 or 40 inhabitants in Cuba, while in Argentina the ratio was only 1 to 60, in
Mexico 1 to 91, and in Brazil 1 to 158. There was 1 radio for every 5 or 6
inhabitants, second only to Argentina, with 1 for every 3. There was 1
telephone for every 38 inhabitants, the fourth highest rate in Latin
America. A report published by UNESCO dealing with material
conditions in various nations of the region concluded that during
the period of the Batista dictatorship "the economic indexes placed
Cuba in the middle upper group with Venezuela and immediately
below [the group] composed of Argentina, Uruguay, and Chile. This
favourable, though unbalanced, economic situation applies to a
population of which a considerable number are foreigners, 72.8 percent are white; 12.4 percent Negro; and 14.5 percent mulatto. If to
this is added a good literacy index (an illiteracy of only 20 or 25 percent), the Cuban situation at the time of the [Castro] revolution appears favourable."

What made the situation unstable, according to the report, was
"the social imbalance existing between the urban and the rural population." The general prosperity of the island had largely bypassed
the hamlets and villages of the countryside. The industrial worker in
Cuba had long been more inclined toward trade unionism than political activism, and labor organizations, whether led by Communists or anticommunists, had in the course of time won enough
concessions from employers to make him a member of a relatively
well-to-do class. But for the rural worker, especially the unskilled
farm laborer, the standard of living remained low. Heavily dependent on a single crop, sugarcane, and often unable to find more than
seasonal employment, many inhabitants of the countryside constituted a depressed agricultural proletariat whose impoverishment

seemed all the more abysmal in contrast to the prosperity of the large urban centers.

Although it is difficult to measure the rural standard of living exactly, a few indirect indexes of the poverty of the countryside exist. Whereas in the cities the rate of illiteracy was less than 12 percent, in the villages it was almost 42. What information there is about housing, sanitation, and health services points to a similar disparity. The per capita income in 1953 for the nonagricultural labor force was estimated at 1,600 dollars. For the agricultural labor force, on the other hand, the figure, though not precisely ascertainable, was low enough to reduce the overall average to 430 dollars. Here lay the great weakness of the economic situation under the Batista regime.

Yet the dimensions of the problem must not be exaggerated. Among the countries experiencing a social revolution during the twentieth century, Cuba was unique in being largely urbanized. Only about 45 percent of the population lived in the countryside, a lower proportion than anywhere else in Latin America except the four countries of the economic elite: Argentina, Uruguay, Chile, and Venezuela. The percentage of the labor force engaged in farming was even smaller, less than 42, again the fifth lowest in Latin America. Of the roughly 819,000 people employed in agriculture in 1953, moreover, about a fourth consisted of owners or renters of farms who could in many cases be categorized as middle or upper class. All in all, the economy of Cuba on the eve of Castro's revolution was thriving and expanding. There may have been disparities or tensions arising out of uneven growth, out of the contrast between advanced and backward sectors of production. There is little evidence, however, of a decline in the standard of living even among workers employed in agriculture. Their problem was stagnation rather than deterioration. And for most Cubans times had never been better than in the 1950s, the last years of the old order.[8]

From Economic Modernization
to Social Disequilibrium

But if there is no direct connection between the standard of living and the level of political disaffection, between the distribution of wealth or income and the degree of civic loyalty, are we to infer that material conditions have little effect on a country's vulnerability to revolution? Not quite. In fact a discernible dependence of politics on economics is to be found in all revolutionary situations, though it is too subtle and indirect to be measured by the volume or diffusion of wealth. It seems to lie rather in a process of far-reaching change in economy and society that social scientists generally call "modernization."

What characterizes this process is the adoption of radically new techniques of production and distribution. Industry becomes rationalized and liberalized through the introduction of technological innovation, the concentration of labor, the intensification of investment, the emergence of large-scale enterprise, the decline of the handicraft system, and the rise of an urban working class dependent on the demands of a capitalistic mode of production. Economic relationships tend to become more abstract, more detached and depersonalized, loosening the ties of piety and tradition characteristic of a preindustrial way of life. Increasing competitiveness leads to a decomposition or disintegration of established social classes and economic groups; it begins to separate those who are able to adapt to new forms of entrepreneurship from those who continue to cling to familiar institutions and customs. The transition to a more rational and efficient mode of production thus generates tensions in society that form a potential threat to the existing political order.

The changes that modernization initiates in agriculture are equally destabilizing. A similar tendency emerges to shift from subsistence to market cultivation, to adopt a more rational and efficient form of production. Small farmers, unable to compete with large landowners or middle-sized proprietors, are increasingly reduced to sharecroppers or agricultural laborers. Traditional class relationships in the countryside, essentially patriarchal in nature, based on a sense of reciprocal obligations or responsibilities, are increasingly replaced by the impersonal nexus of the marketplace with its ethos of wage payments and commercial transactions. The result is bound to be social disequilibrium. The old hierarchical order in rural society gradually declines. Abstract calculations of profit and advantage begin to compete with precepts of paternal or filial loyalty. The modernization of agricultural production, moreover, with its emphasis on specialized large-scale cultivation of a few crops, usually for the export market, not only intensifies the social and economic cleavage between large landowners and small farmers or rural laborers, but creates divisions within the peasantry as well. It separates those who recognize and exploit the possibilities of a more rational form of husbandry from those for whom agricultural innovation means bewilderment and vulnerability. In farming as in manufacturing, economic modernization initiates a process of social readjustment that can prove a grave threat to the *ancien régime*.

The erosion of traditional relationships among classes and interests is generally accompanied by a weakening of the social controls over conduct that are designed to reinforce acceptance of the status quo. For one thing, rationalization of the economy results in a substantial movement of population from country to city. And for the masses of displaced rustics, urbanization means a profound change in their way of life, affecting not only forms of employment but attitudes, ideas, and allegiances. The peasant who has left his village is no longer under the supervision of the representatives of authority —clergymen, teachers, landlords, and bureaucrats—whose task is to encourage loyalty to the established order. In the new, impersonal urban environment, norms of civic behavior that had been accepted without question in the rural community cease to be prescriptive or even enforceable. The result is a gradual loss of faith in tradition that in time turns into skepticism regarding the status quo. Common popular assumptions concerning the justice or immutability of the existing structure of power and wealth come to be questioned and rejected. Urbanization thus has the effect of instilling in the masses a belief in the possibility of a different order of society without privation or exploitation. Out of the rootlessness of city life emerges an awareness of the power inherent in collective civic action, an awareness dangerous to the *ancien régime*.

Even in the countryside a gradual unraveling takes place in the network of traditions on which the status quo rests. As economic relationships become more impersonal, as ties between various groups in rural society come to be based on calculations of profit and loss, acceptance of the established hierarchy of class and status starts to weaken. The sense of solidarity within the peasantry erodes as well, as some villagers learn how to prosper at the expense of others, and the gulf between thriving *kulaks* and landless rural laborers widens. The same economic innovations that make possible a more efficient form of cultivation also weaken the framework of rural society. There is growing resentment among the lower classes directed not only against great landowners, who seem increasingly exploitive and grasping, but also against middle-sized peasant entrepreneurs for whom rationalization of the rural economic structure provides an opportunity to enlarge their holdings. Changes in agriculture essential for greater efficiency, in other words, have the effect of undermining the foundation of loyalties on which the stability of village society depends. The improvement in material well-being that characterizes the old order on the eve of its downfall, the improvement by which it seeks to justify its policies, helps in fact to erode the social base of its power.

Most important, the process of modernization leads to a significant rise in the level of education of the masses, with the unintended result of promoting skepticism regarding the legitimacy of established authority. In preindustrial society the bulk of the population is almost invariably illiterate, its view of state and community shaped by officially nurtured myths and traditions. The exclusion of the lower classes from organized secular learning is in part a result of the limited financial resources of the state. There simply is not enough revenue, after expenditures for the primal government functions of defense and administration, to support a system of popular elementary education. But that is not the only reason for the inaccessibility of formal schooling. The *ancien régime* also believes that it would be inexpedient to teach the masses to read and write. They might be exposed to subversive ideas; they might begin to question the structure of wealth and power. In short, popular education could prove a threat to the status quo.

This is the view expressed in the words attributed to Catherine the Great of Russia regarding a proposal by the governor of Moscow for the establishment of a primary school: "We must not in any way provide instruction for the lower class of people. If they were to know as much as you and I, *Monsieur le maréchal*, they would no longer want to obey us, as they obey us today." Although the statement may in fact be apocryphal, it accurately reflects the attitude of those in authority in preindustrial society toward general elementary education.[9]

The rationalization of the economy, however, forces the *ancien régime* to overcome its distrust of universal schooling. There is still the fear that once learning ceases to be a monopoly of the well-to-do, the lower classes will become discontented and rebellious. But there is also the recognition that only a literate labor force can acquire the technical skills required by a modern, industrializing economy. A truck driver has to be able to read road signs; an electrician must know how to multiply and divide. Thus economic necessity compels the old order to establish a system of popular elementary education which it knows to be a potential social threat.

The authorities try to minimize the risk by restricting the kind of knowledge made available to the masses. Whereas children of the upper classes receive an education in which study of the classics, philosophy, and mathematics represents a conspicuous consumption of learning untainted by relevance to an occupational pursuit, the curriculum of the common elementary school is limited to the three R's, religious instruction, and the promotion of civic loyalty. These differences in the content of instruction are meant to perpetuate differences in the structure of society.

The consequences of a growing literacy, however, cannot be easily controlled. For many workers and peasants the ability to read and write does in fact reinforce an acceptance of the status quo. But for others elementary schooling leads to insights far beyond the officially prescribed bounds of piety and patriotism. They begin to doubt time-honored customs and traditions, to question established economic relationships and social institutions. They learn from books, pamphlets, and newspapers that the system of authority under which they live has not been divinely ordained or instituted. In other countries the common man enjoys greater comfort, opportunity, and influence. Why cannot their own government do as much for the people? Why is it not as efficient and benign as the government of France or Germany, England or America? The destabilizing effect of popular literacy, moreover, is magnified by new technological advances in the means of communication, first the radio and then television. Now the political horizon of those still unable to read begins to broaden through listening to a loudspeaker or looking at a screen. And as the written word ceases to be the sole means of acquiring organized secular knowledge, the last remaining controls of the old order over the loyalty of the lower classes start to disintegrate.

The Twilight of the Ancien Régime

The most important consequence of this intellectualizing process is the awakening of doubt regarding the status quo. For once the old order has become demythologized, once it has been deprived of its legitimation, nothing it does seems right. Its deficiencies and injustices, patiently endured for centuries, are suddenly felt to be intolerable. Its reforms and improvements are measured not by the criterion of past experience, but by a comparison with the advanced countries of the West. The regime finds itself assailed by popular criticism which, no matter what policy the authorities adopt, grows louder and more threatening.

A revolution of expectations thus prepares the way for a revolution of deeds. This helps explain why successful insurrectionary movements occur not under a declining but under a stable or rising standard of living. The modernizing process that makes possible an improvement in the economic condition of the lower classes also tends to undermine the civic faith supporting the authority of the old order. Revolutionary situations, to put it another way, originate in people's minds, not in their material circumstances. A social system, however oppressive or corrupt, can endure as long as its claim to a divinely or historically sanctioned exercise of power is accepted by the lower classes. But once their acquiescence erodes, once there is a perception that the established order is not providentially ordained, the ancien régime is in jeopardy. Yesterday it could do nothing wrong; today it can do nothing right. Fearful of drowning in the sea of disaffection, it struggles, flails, calls for help, promises to reform, only to be overwhelmed in the end by a rising tide of insurrection.

This pattern can be perceived, with varying degrees of distinctness, in each of the major social revolutions of the twentieth century. It is least discernible in the Chinese uprising of 1911 that led to the overthrow of the Ch'ing dynasty. The economy of the country was still in a preindustrial stage of development, the agricultural sector accounting for about two-thirds of the gross national product. The handicraft system, moreover, continued to dominate the production of manufactured goods. It is in fact this backwardness of the economic structure that helps explain the limited scope of the uprising in its early stages. For the revolt against the Manchus was initially little more than a spontaneous coup d'état, an unpremeditated change of dynasty. It was a contest for the control of government rather than a social revolution. Only two decades later did the modernization of economy and society advance far enough to transform a conflict over political power into a class struggle. The change was a measure of the extent and intensity of economic rationalization in China following the downfall of the imperial government.

Yet even in the last years of the *ancien régime* there were signs of a weakening of the social structure that prefigured the momentous developments of the 1920s and 1930s. The incipient decline of the handicraft system, a characteristic feature of a modernizing economy, could already be seen in the growth of production by domestic textile mills, their share of the consumption of cotton yarn rising from almost nothing in 1871–80 to nearly 18 percent in 1901–10, and in the increase in the share of imports during the same period from about 11 to almost 19 percent of the consumption of cotton cloth. Between 1895 and 1913, moreover, at least 549 private or semigovernmental mechanized enterprises in manufacture and mining were founded by native industrialists with a combined initial capitalization of 120,288,000 Chinese dollars. By the time of the revolution there were approximately 116 companies owned by Chinese and 40 owned by foreigners that employed 500 or more workers each, with a total of 130,985 workers in the former category and 109,410 in the latter. Here were the beginnings of an industrial urban proletariat in China. And finally, an embryonic modern financial system could be seen emerging in the establishment of 16 modern banks between 1896 and 1911, among them the important Imperial Bank of China and Hu Pu Bank. All these innovations were as yet far too modest to be described as rationalization or modernization. But in combination they portended a transformation of the economy that a generation later turned a political rebellion into a social conflict.[10]

The classic symptoms of a revolutionary situation are much more clearly discernible in Russia on the eve of the Bolshevik seizure of power. For one thing, the policy of hothouse industrialization on which the czarist regime embarked at the end of the nineteenth century had by the time of the First World War significantly altered the country's economy. Not only the volume of manufactured goods but the size of the industrial labor force had grown with great rapidity. The number of workers employed in factories had risen from 1,318,000 in 1887 to 2,609,000 in 1908, an increase of 98 percent. The value of factory output had risen even more swiftly, from 1,334,500,000 to 4,909,000,000 rubles, an increase of 268 percent, reflecting the growing mechanization and efficiency of manufacture. The tempo of economic change, moreover, accelerated after the opening of the twentieth century, the index of industrial production climbing from 24 in 1885 to 60 in 1899 and 100 just before the First World War. Between 1900 and 1913 the value of factory output in fifty provinces of European Russia rose 93 percent, from 861,700,000 to 1,665,000,000 rubles. Even in constant prices the increase was 74 percent, while on a per capita basis, despite the growth of population, it amounted to an impressive 46 percent.

Achievements of such magnitude would have been impossible without a substantial demographic movement from village to city. Given the vast size of the population, the extent of urbanization may appear rather modest. The proportion of all inhabitants living in cities rose from not quite 11 percent in 1885 to a little over 13 percent in 1914. But the growth of the large industrial metropolis was much more rapid. Between 1897 and 1914, the population of Saint Petersburg increased 67 percent, of Moscow 70 percent, of Kiev 110 percent, of Tiflis 93 percent, and of Baku 108 percent. Only a few years later these cities were to become important centers of revolutionary militancy.

Economic and social change in the countryside was less dramatic but equally disruptive. The emancipation of the peasantry in the 1860s had initiated a process of disintegration in the village community which was intensified after 1906 by the Stolypin decrees authorizing the withdrawal of holdings from the *obshchina*. The result was an aggravation of the tensions within rural society. The land hunger which had been undermining the cohesiveness of the peasant class by separating prosperous *kulaks* from impoverished farm laborers now led more and more villagers to seek security in individual proprietorship. By the beginning of 1916, no fewer than 2,478,000 households, about 24 percent of the total in forty provinces of European Russia, had obtained direct title to their land, and another 747,000 were awaiting registration of their applications. Some 1,200,000 households, moreover, had consolidated their holdings, and 103,364 of them had already left the village and, with the aid of government subsidies, had established homes on their newly acquired farms. The traditional village community, in other words, was in a process of dissolution long before the Bolsheviks came to power.

Finally, the spread of literacy, in the countryside as well as the city, exposed the masses to radical political and social ideas. By the time the war broke out in 1914, more than two-thirds of the army recruits could read. And this meant that the lower classes were now increasingly influenced by radical criticism of the policies and institutions of the old order. All the economic, social, and cultural preconditions for a successful revolution could thus be found in Russia during the last years of the *ancien régime*.[11]

The problems facing Vietnamese society before the Second World War were in important respects similar to those with which Russian society had to grapple before the First World War. There was the same tension arising out of the transition from a subsistence to a market form of agriculture. There was the same growing disparity between the successful large landowner and the propertyless farm laborer. And there was the same eroding foundation of the traditional village community. But whereas in Russia the rural problem was aggravated by demographic pressure, by a rapid increase in the number of people struggling to find a livelihood in farming, in Vietnam it was not the shortage but the distribution of landed property that was at the heart of the agrarian question. Although the population of the countryside was steadily growing, new soil brought under cultivation would have been more than enough to absorb the increase. It was largely devoted, however, to raising a few staple crops for the foreign market, which brought profit to the large estates owned by French *colons* or native landlords, but did little to help the small independent farmer.

This tendency toward a capitalistic organization of husbandry was clearly reflected in the statistics on the cultivation and marketing of rice between 1880, when colonial rule over Vietnam was being established, and 1937, when it was about to end. During that period of nearly sixty years, the population of Cochin China grew 267 percent, from 1,679,000 to 4,484,000. The rice-producing area in the region, on the other hand, expanded 421 percent, from 522,000 to 2,200,000 acres. But the largest proportionate increase was recorded in the exports of rice from the port of Saigon, 545 percent, from 284,000 to 1,548,000 tons. Here was a paradigm of the modernization of Vietnamese agriculture.

The rising importance of a few lucrative export crops, above all rice, but later also maize and rubber, encouraged the growth of *latifundia* at the expense of the small peasant proprietor. Land absorbed by the estates came mostly from areas that had remained uncultivated, but it was also increasingly acquired from impoverished, debt-ridden farmers. For these declassed villagers there was little opportunity for alternative forms of employment. Competition from France had retarded the growth of Vietnamese industry, which was unable to absorb the surplus population of the countryside. Although the statistics of the colonial administration are incomplete and not always reliable, it appears that the labor force in manufacture and commerce was less than 300,000 out of a total of 18,972,000 inhabitants.

Nor could native handicrafts, which had in the past supplemented the income of many rural families, protect them any longer against a modernizing economy. The spinning of cotton fiber continued in some villages in northern Annam, but in Tonkin it was becoming increasingly rare. The weaving of fabrics from native raw silk, moreover, was declining in the face of competition from manufactured finer textiles made mostly from Chinese silk. And handicraft production of sugar faced growing difficulties because of the large mechanized refineries such as the *Société des Sucreries et Raffineries de l'Indochine*. For the peasant proprietor who had lost his holding, there was no alternative but to become a tenant farmer or sharecropper on the land that had once been his, or to seek employment on the rubber plantations in the *terres rouges* of the interior.

On the eve of the Second World War, the French scholar Charles

Robequain, though not unsympathetic to the colonial regime, expressed concern about the disintegration of Vietnamese rural society. The economic policy of the government had led to the emergence of a "proletariat," he wrote, that "might be defined as including all those people who either own no land or have too little for their livelihood." Aggravating the problem of shrinking landownership was the "uprootedness" or "detribalization" of the peasantry. The displaced farmer forced to become a wage earner "no longer has any direct contact with his employer, who is almost always a foreigner, and of a different race." Now he is usually a member of a gang of laborers, "in which he feels as if he were only a number, or an interchangeable part, at the service of an unseen, anonymous power. Separated from his traditional surroundings, he feels that he is only a cog in an incomprehensible machine—an experience totally foreign to his ordinary concept of life. Cut off from the framework of his community and family, he woefully endures his spiritual loneliness."

To Robequain this was a disturbing development. "The fact remains that [Vietnamese] society today includes a considerable floating population, which is constantly increasing and tends to stray further and further from the traditional bonds, if not of the tribe, at least of the community." The process of disintegration was as yet only gradual. "Nevertheless, it is going on and is a not unimportant element in the country's economic and political life."

Vietnam thus seems to come closest to supporting the common contention that social revolution is engendered by poverty, oppression, and exploitation. Yet even here a danger exists of overstating the bleakness of the situation, of overlooking signs of modest but significant progress. The assimilated native landed patriciate and the educated urban bourgeoisie, prominent in business, bureaucracy, and the professions, can perhaps be dismissed as only small, parasitic social strata being rewarded for their collaboration with colonialism. But the technological, sanitary, and educational advances —the construction of highways, railroads, sewers, reservoirs, hospitals, and classrooms—had, indirectly at least, a beneficial effect on the way of life of the lower classes. Although illiteracy remained high, elementary education continued to grow, especially in the last years of the old order. The school population, which had been no more than 70,000 in 1924, rose to 378,000 in 1930 and 854,000 in 1944. There is little evidence, moreover, that the general standard of living was declining. On the contrary, it seems likely that at the outbreak of the Second World War most Vietnamese were measurably better off than their parents had been a generation earlier.

"The average standard of living of the Indo-Chinese has risen in fifty years," Robequain concluded in 1939. "The size of the increase cannot be computed exactly, but after learning the reminiscences of old-timers and comparing the descriptions given by early travellers and white missionaries with the picture we see today in the Indo-Chinese countryside, there can be no doubt about it." Obviously, the uprising against colonial rule that broke out a few years later could not have been the result of increasing privation.[12]

The most persuasive refutation of the immiserization theory of revolution, however, can be found in Cuba. Here was a country with an expanding, modernizing economy, a prosperous and growing middle class, a strong and assertive labor movement, and a steadily rising standard of living. For most people life had never been better than just before Castro's seizure of power. It was not impoverishment but dislocation or disequilibrium that led to the downfall of the *ancien régime*. In Cuba as in Vietnam, though not nearly on the same scale, economic rationalization had generated a strong tendency toward crop specialization, export agriculture, and the concentration of property. Big companies began to expand at the expense of small peasant holdings, so that by the 1920s the *centrales*, estates owned by the sugar mills, were reported to have control over about 20 percent of the total area of the island. The *colonos*, on the other hand, the independent cane growers, were increasingly reduced to suppliers or tenants of the large corporations, many of them foreign. The pattern of Cuban rural dislocation was thus similar to the Vietnamese. The danger to the old order lay in the disintegration of a traditional peasant society, a disintegration obscured by the prosperity of the urban economy. In the desolate villages of the interior, there was little of that glitter and excitement that was attracting thousands of American tourists to the night life of Havana.

During his visit to Cuba immediately after the Second World War, the sociologist Lowry Nelson noted the harsh existence of the countryside:

As we rode horseback . . . toward San Blas, my guide and friend, Jesús Martínez Moreno, kept pointing out to me the miserable habitations of the *precaristas*, the squatters who have settled on other people's land, and he would say, "Very bad!"—an overworked phrase, I thought, in his limited English vocabulary. "Very bad!" were the *bohíos*, the peasant houses, with their dirt floors, thatched roofs, and improvised walls of bark from royal palm trees. "Very bad" were the trails over which we rode, where in places the horses sank almost to their bellies in mud during the rainy season. "Very bad" were the naked children, their swollen stomachs testifying to an unbalanced diet and infection from parasitic worms—in rural Cuba parasitism is practically universal. "Very bad" was the evidence of great poverty everywhere on the part of large numbers of people, the absence of schools, medical care, and up-to-date methods of agriculture. "Very bad" also, in my friend's eyes, were the large concentrations of land in the hands of a few, and the politicians who took for themselves money which should have been spent for the benefit of the people.

It was destabilization of the peasant economy rather than general impoverishment that led to the collapse of the Batista dictatorship.[13]

Modernization, however, is only a necessary, not a sufficient condition of social revolution. It facilitates but does not cause the downfall of the old order. Otherwise every industrializing nation would have its Bolshevik uprising, every society experiencing agrarian dislocation would produce a Mao, Castro, or Ho Chi Minh. The *ancien régime*, even after it has become demythologized, even after it has lost its sanctification, is still able to exercise power as long as it continues to be perceived as impregnable. Fear can prove almost as effective as awe in helping to maintain the status quo. The structure of authority is in serious danger only when some grave national crisis shows it to be ineffectual and impotent.

Lenin recognized this central role of a major political or economic failure in undermining the old order. "The fundamental law of revolution, which has been confirmed by all revolutions," he wrote in 1920 in *"Left-Wing" Communism—An Infantile Disorder*, "is as follows: for a revolution to take place it is not enough for the exploited and oppressed masses to realize the impossibility of living in the old way, and demand changes; for a revolution to take place it is essential that

the exploiters should not be able to live and rule in the old way."
Here is the crux of a revolutionary situation. "It is only when the
'*lower classes*' *do not want* to live in the old way and the '*upper
classes*' *cannot carry on in the old way* that the revolution can triumph." To put it differently, "revolution is impossible without a
nation-wide crisis (affecting both the exploited and the exploiters). It
follows that, for a revolution to take place, it is essential . . . that the
ruling classes should be going through a government crisis, which
draws even the most backward masses into politics . . . , weakens the
government, and makes it possible for the revolutionaries to rapidly
overthrow it."[14]

The crisis that transforms the amorphous discontent of a destabil-
ized society into organized disaffection is generally a defeat in war.
Thereby the *ancien régime* shows itself incapable of performing the
primal function of government, defense of the nation. Failure in a
test of strength against a foreign enemy reveals its inner weakness. It
is now perceived as not only unjust but feeble and indecisive. Those
who have submitted to it out of fear are emboldened to challenge its
authority. Popular discontent, all the more intense for having been
so long suppressed, finally explodes in an outburst of violence and
destructiveness that overwhelms the old order. The regime pays the
price for military failure by succumbing to the forces of revolution.
Thus in China the humiliating outcome of the war with Japan in
1894–95 and the weakness of the government in yielding to the demands of the foreign powers after the Boxer Rebellion prepared the
way for the uprising of 1911. In Russia the defeat of the czarist armies
at the hands of the Japanese in 1904–1905 and of the Germans in
1914–17 led to the Bolshevik revolution. And in Vietnam the inability
of the French authorities to prevent an occupation by Japan during
the Second World War encouraged the outbreak of a struggle for independence in 1945. There is an obvious connection between inadequacy in war and susceptibility to revolution.

The effect of military defeat is usually intensified or sometimes
replaced by resentment against foreign financial influence. The
perception of alien control of the national economy can do almost
as much to weaken loyalty to established authority as the experience of hostile invasion. Both tend to undermine popular confidence in the *ancien régime*. In China the success of the Great

Powers in establishing "spheres of interest" and obtaining important economic concessions aggravated dissatisfaction with Manchu rule. In Russia the dependence of the economy on loans provided by foreign financiers, mostly French, British, and German, fostered the suspicion that foreign capitalists were dictating policy to the czar's government. In Vietnam political opposition to the colonial system was reinforced by the subordination of native industry and agriculture to the interests of France. And in Cuba the dominant role of American capital nourished a sense of bitterness at the government's subservience. Although the island had never suffered military defeat, its vulnerability to alien political pressure and its dependence on investments from abroad deeply offended patriotic pride. The inability of the established system to defend the national interest against foreign intrusion thus hastens the erosion of public confidence.

The *ancien régime* does not go to its destruction meekly, however. Recognizing that it is in danger, it tries to counter hostile criticism by adopting a strategy combining force with conciliation. On the one hand, it applies all the instrumentalities of repression at its disposal in a desperate effort to retain power. The government's opponents are hounded, arrested, imprisoned, tortured, and sometimes executed. Their meetings are prohibited, their newspapers are suppressed, their parties are dissolved. The official means of coercion, moreover, are frequently reinforced by the extralegal activities, which the authorities encourage, of loyal organizations comprising ardent patriots, religious zealots, ultranationalists, and archconservatives. In its struggle to survive, the old order can be ruthless and cruel.

Hand in hand with the attempt to crush the opposition by force, however, generally comes a policy of trying to allay discontent by the promise or even the introduction of reform. Whether motivated by expediency or conviction, the *ancien régime* in its last hour tries to initiate a program of major civic improvement. The judiciary is to become more equitable, the police more responsible, the bureaucracy less arbitrary, the crown less autocratic. Most important, there is to be a measure of self-government including an elected legislature, a party system, an uncensored press, and a legal opposition. This sudden conversion of the established system to the principles of constitutionalism is greeted by its opponents with derision as only an attempt to cling to power by a show of repentance. But whatever its motives, the government is now prepared to promulgate changes in official policy which a decade earlier would have been unthinkable. Never is the old order as open to innovation and modernization as on the eve of its downfall.

The "Hundred Days" of the reform movement in China in the summer of 1898, for example, led to a revision of the examination system for the civil service, the establishment of a "Metropolitan University" in Peking, the requirement of monthly budgetary reports to improve state finances, and an announcement by the emperor of a readiness "to open his palace for discussing changes of government structure." The program was cut short by a nativistic reaction under the empress dowager, but ten years later it reemerged with the promulgation of the "Principles of the Constitution" to go into effect in 1916. In the meantime provincial assemblies met in the fall of 1909 to consider ways of improving the established system of government and administration. In Russia the wave of popular unrest that followed defeat in the war against Japan resulted in the "October Manifesto" of 1905 establishing for the first time a national parliament with extensive legislative authority. And the following year an important agrarian reform made possible the withdrawal of peasant land from communal village control and the establishment of a class of small independent farmers. In Vietnam the defeat of the Japanese in the Second World War led to an attempt by the authorities in Paris to reestablish their domination by armed force, but at the same time there was a promise that the country would become part of the French Union with a federal government of its own and a national legislature empowered to decide budgetary questions. An abortive revolution from above thus usually precedes and facilitates a victorious revolution from below.

But neither force nor conciliation can now save the old order. Whatever it does is wrong. Its repressive measures are denounced as evidence of cruelty and injustice; they only create martyrs for the cause of radicalism. Its civic reforms are dismissed as signs of weakness; they embolden the opponents of the system to even greater defiance. Arrests and executions cease to intimidate; improvements and concessions are outstripped by rising expectations. It is too late for either brute force or sweet reason. Deprived of its legitimation, divested of its invincibility, the *ancien régime* rushes frantically back and forth, flounders and thrashes, threatens and cajoles, only to stumble in the end to its destruction at the hands of the triumphant revolution.

CHAPTER 2

The Emergence
of a Revolutionary Movement

The Party and the Masses

Once the old order has fallen, its overthrow is attributed by the victors to some vast impersonal force beyond human control. There was something ineluctable or foreordained about its fate, they contend. Its oppressiveness could simply no longer be endured. The masses, responding to changing material conditions, had finally risen against their exploiters in a spontaneous uprising culminating in the establishment of a new social system. Those who had led the resistance against established authority may deserve recognition for defying its might, but they were only the instruments of an inevitable historical process. Their function was not to initiate or even direct the struggle against the *ancien régime*. It was to fulfill an immanent revolutionary purpose shaped by the interests of the lower classes. There is an element of predestination in this view of revolution, something almost Calvinistic about its inevitability, with class struggle replacing providential design as the source of change in history.

In his account of the revolution in Russia, written some fifteen years after the Bolsheviks seized power, Trotsky reflected this radical faith in the unpremeditated action of the lower classes as the wellspring of insurrectionary movements. "In all critical moments the masses intervene 'spontaneously'—in other words, obeying only their own inferences drawn from political experience, and their as yet officially unrecognized leaders," he wrote. "Assimilating this or

that premise from the talk of agitators, the masses on their own volition translate its conclusions into the language of action." Thus the
Bolsheviks, after the fall of czarism early in 1917, were not yet able to
lead the campaign for the eight-hour day. They were not yet able to
summon the workers to the April demonstration. They were not yet
able to call the armed proletariat into the streets early in July. "Only
in October," after the lower classes had shown the way, "will the
party finally fall in step and march out at the head of the masses, not
for a demonstration, but for a revolution."

In short, those who seem to be leading are really following; those
who seem to be obeying are actually commanding. The success of
the uprising depends not on the men who appear to direct its course,
but on material conditions shaping the outlook of the masses. "The
immediate causes of the events of a revolution are changes in the
state-of-mind of the conflicting classes. The material relations of society merely define the channel within which these processes take
place. Changes in the collective consciousness have naturally a
semi-concealed character. Only when they have attained a certain
degree of intensity do the new moods and ideas break to the surface
in the form of mass activities which establish a new, although again
very unstable social equilibrium." The revolutionary process is spontaneous but impersonal; it is almost mechanical or predetermined.
The decline of the old order, as portrayed after its defeat, is ordained
by historical laws that neither supporters nor opponents can alter.[1]

But prior to the overthrow of the *ancien régime*, as long as the issue
remains undecided, the radical view of the respective roles of the activists and the masses is quite different. There is not as yet much talk
about the spontaneous insurrectionary zeal of the lower classes. The
emphasis rests rather on the need for planning and organizing. Less
importance is attached to the dialectical laws of history and more to
the tactics of the leaders of the opposition. In the heat of battle between the old and the new order, there is no time to wait for the un-
folding of the inner logic of the revolutionary process. The moment
urgently requires plans, choices, decisions, and commands. The axi-
oms of radical theory must therefore be subordinated to the imperatives of insurrectionary practice. And that means that in the
relationship between organized activists and broad masses, the former assume the dominant role.

In the summer of 1943, for example, while the war against Japan was still going on and a renewed struggle with the Kuomintang was becoming increasingly likely, Mao Tse-tung wrote for the Central Committee of the Communist Party of China a series of observations "Concerning Methods of Leadership." He reiterated the conventional radical view that revolutionaries can achieve nothing without the guidance of the lower classes. "However active the leading group may be, its activity will amount to fruitless effort by a handful of people unless combined with the activity of the masses." But unless the masses have forceful leadership, they will only waste their energies. They need a disciplined party to give them purpose and direction. "If the masses alone are active without a strong leading group to organize their activity properly, such activity cannot be sustained for long, or carried forward in the right direction, or raised to a high level."

The lower classes are not always wise or bold or selfless, Mao suggested. Generally they are composed in any given place of three parts: "the relatively active, the intermediate and the relatively backward." Those whose task it is to guide them "must therefore be skilled in uniting the small number of active elements around the leadership and must rely on them to raise the level of the intermediate elements and to win over the backward elements." The activists should not simply wait to be carried along by the revolutionary ardor of the proletariat. Their function is rather to organize the underlying amorphous discontent of the workers and peasants.

Mao did not reject the teachings of radical orthodoxy regarding the dialectical nature of revolution. He continued to avow his belief in the lower classes as the chosen instrument of historical change. But the lower classes alone could not fulfill their predestined purpose. They needed a leadership that would both direct and be directed by them. There had to be a mutually reinforcing relationship between them. "In all the practical work of our Party, all correct leadership is necessarily 'from the masses, to the masses.'" This means, according to Mao, that the activists must "take the ideas of the masses (scattered and unsystematic ideas) and concentrate them (through study turn them into concentrated and systematic ideas), then go to the masses and propagate and explain these ideas until the masses embrace them as their own, hold fast to them and translate them into action, and test the correctness of these ideas in such action. Then once again concentrate ideas from the masses and once again go to the masses so that the ideas are persevered in and carried through." This process has to be repeated over and over again "in an endless spiral," so that the ideas will become "more correct, more vital and richer each time." The "Marxist theory of knowledge" leads logically to a recognition of the crucial need for interaction between party and proletariat.[2]

To Lenin even this view of the revolutionary process would have seemed vague or transcendent. Struggling to build an effective socialist movement in backward Russia, he harbored few illusions about the spontaneous insurrectionary ardor of the impoverished masses. For him, all talk about the need to wait for the diffusion of radical ideas among workers and peasants only meant delaying the overthrow of the established order. There was nothing autonomous about the course of historical change. Uprisings did not occur simply as a result of the dictates of the Marxian dialectic. They had to be planned and organized. "There is much talk of spontaneity," he wrote in 1902 in *What Is to Be Done?*

> But the *spontaneous* development of the working-class movement leads to its subordination to bourgeois ideology . . . ; for the spontaneous working-class movement is trade-unionism, . . . and trade-unionism means the ideological enslavement of the workers by the bourgeoisie. Hence, our task, the task of Social-Democracy, is *to combat spontaneity, to direct* the working-class movement from this spontaneous, trade-unionist striving to come under the wing of the bourgeoisie, and to bring it under the wing of revolutionary Social-Democracy.

Behind his rejection of the autonomy of the revolutionary process was the conviction that the proletariat on its own is incapable of defending the interests of the exploited groups in society.

Lenin was quite explicit on this point. Without the guidance of a disciplined revolutionary party, the masses can never rise above mere bread-and-butter demands. Instead of fighting to overthrow the established order, they will simply try to improve their position within it. "The history of all countries shows that the working class, exclusively by its own effort, is able to develop only trade-union consciousness, i.e., the conviction that it is necessary to combine in unions, fight the employers, and strive to compel the government to pass necessary legislation, etc." It is therefore illusory to think that the masses can galvanize or inspire the party. On the contrary, it is the party which must learn to use the masses as an instrument of social change. The proletariat can only be the means, never the source, of its own liberation.

For Lenin, therefore, the central role in a successful revolution had to be assumed by a small, disciplined party capable of winning for the lower classes the social justice that they themselves could never achieve. What the struggle required was not *élan* but organization, not mystical faith but sober calculation. Hence only the party could provide effective leadership for the apathetic proletariat.

According to his strategy, "a small, compact core of the most reliable, experienced, and hardened workers, with responsible representatives in the principle districts and connected by all the rules of strict secrecy with the organization of revolutionaries, can, with the widest support of the masses . . . , perform *all* the functions of a trade-union organization, in a manner, moreover, desirable to Social-Democracy. Only in this way can we secure the *consolidation* and development of a *Social-Democratic* trade-union movement, despite all the gendarmes." To rely on the insurrectionary ardor of the lower classes, on the other hand, would only lead to defeat. "If we begin with the solid foundation of a strong organization of revolutionaries, we can ensure the stability of the movement as a whole and carry out the aims both of Social-Democracy and of trade unions proper." But "if we begin with a broad workers' organization, which is supposedly most 'accessible' to the masses (but which is actually most accessible to the police), we shall achieve neither the one aim nor the other; we shall not eliminate our rule-of-thumb methods, and, because we remain scattered and our forces are constantly broken up by the police, we shall only make trade unions of the [reformist] type the more accessible to the masses."

Lenin summarized his view of how an effective socialist party must be built in a series of theses or propositions emphasizing the need for discipline and selectivity. First of all, "no revolutionary movement can endure without a stable organization of leaders maintaining continuity." Second, "the broader the popular mass drawn spontaneously into the struggle, which forms the basis of the movement and participates in it, the more urgent the need for such an organization must be," since it is then much easier "for all sorts of demagogues to side-track the more backward sections of the masses." Third, "such an organization must consist chiefly of people professionally engaged in revolutionary activity." Fourth, "in an autocratic state, the more we *confine* the membership of such an organization to people who are professionally engaged in revolutionary activity and who have been professionally trained in the art of combating the political police, the more difficult it will be to unearth the organization." And finally, the more selective the party, "the *greater* will be the number of people from the working class and from the other social classes who will be able to join the movement and perform active work in it."

But where is the revolutionary organization to find a dedicated cadre of fighters for the liberation of the masses? In theory, they ought to come from the most intelligent and progressive members of the working class. Thereby the proletariat will become the means of its own salvation. The party should therefore make every effort to recruit and train talented workers for positions of leadership in the socialist movement. "A worker-agitator who is at all gifted and 'promising' *must not be left* to work eleven hours a day in a factory," Lenin argued. "We must arrange that he be maintained by the Party; that he may go underground in good time; that he change the place of his activity, if he is to enlarge his experience, widen his outlook, and be able to hold out for at least a few years in the struggle against the gendarmes." As their movement broadens and deepens, "the working-class masses [will] promote from their ranks not only an increasing number of talented agitators, but also talented organizers, propagandists, and 'practical workers' in the best sense of the term." Ultimately, workers will train workers for the revolution, proletarians will lead proletarians to victory.

All of that lay in the future, however. For the time being, the Russian masses, oppressed and ignorant, could not provide the activists needed to wage war against the established order. The revolutionary movement was therefore forced to seek its most talented recruits elsewhere. Lenin expressed agreement with the views recently published by the German socialist theoretician Karl Kautsky regarding the need to enlist members of the propertied classes in the struggle for the emancipation of the proletariat. The latter had maintained that since socialist consciousness can originate only in "profound scientific insight," it follows that "present-day economic science" is as much a precondition of a socialist form of production as "present-day technology." Yet the working class can create neither one nor the other, however hard it may try, for both arise out of the "present-day social process." The bearer of science and scholarship is not the proletariat but the "bourgeois intelligentsia." Indeed, modern socialism originated among some members of this group, and "only through them was it communicated to intellectually gifted proletarians, who are now in turn introducing it into the class struggle of the proletariat, wherever conditions permit." In other words, "socialist consciousness is . . . something which was introduced into the class struggle of the proletariat from outside, not something which arose out of it indigenously."

Lenin concurred. Economic conditions in Russia really left him little choice. The industrial proletariat was still too weak and uneducated to provide the shock troops to defeat czarism. He insisted, to be sure, that everything must be done to attract members of the working class to the socialist movement. He confessed that "we are directly *to blame* for doing too little to 'stimulate' the workers to take this path, common to them and to the 'intellectuals,' of professional revolutionary training, and for all too often dragging them back by our silly speeches about what is 'accessible' to the 'average workers,' etc." And yet he was forced to concede that for the time being the revolutionary cause could not do without converts and sympathizers in the enemy camp. "The theory of socialism . . . grew out of the philosophic, historical, and economic theories elaborated by educated representatives of the propertied classes, by intellectuals. By their social status, the founders of modern scientific socialism, Marx and Engels, themselves belonged to the bourgeois intelligentsia." The party would have to continue to rely on recruits from the well-to-do until the masses developed greater social awareness.

Lenin thus rejected the view that the dialectical process of historical change would spontaneously engender revolutionary militancy among the lower classes. Only the party was capable of providing leadership in the struggle against established authority. The masses could be no more than followers in the struggle for their liberation.[3]

The Social Structure
of the Radical Vanguard

A comparative examination of major revolutions in the twentieth century reveals that generally they follow Lenin's strategy of elite radicalism rather than Trotsky's theory of spontaneity or Mao's concept of synergism. Once the new order has been established, to be sure, its leaders pay homage to the masses for guiding the party. But as long as the struggle is still going on, the key role is invariably assumed by a small, determined cadre of revolutionaries composed mostly of disaffected members of the privileged strata in society. It is this group that succeeds in articulating the incoherent discontent of the masses, molding it into an effective political weapon. Although the radicals do not create the conditions leading to the downfall of the *ancien régime*, they succeed in exploiting its inadequacy to undermine its power. The masses on their own are unable to go beyond occasional demonstrations or sporadic riots expressing purely local grievances. Only through the party are their vague longings shaped into a systematic program of civic and social reconstruction. Without a hard core of militants, the dissatisfactions of the lower classes cannot become transformed into an organized insurrectionary movement.

The salient features of the revolutionary party are similar in all countries experiencing a fundamental social conflict. To begin with, as long as its chances of success seem remote, the organization remains weak and isolated, without much popular appeal or proletarian support. Only when the old order enters its mortal crisis, when the foundation of pieties on which it depends starts to totter, does the radical opposition cease to be a conspiratorial faction and become a mass party. It is therefore unable as a rule to play a major part in the overthrow of the *ancien régime*. Its importance emerges generally after the existing structure of authority has already been weakened and the struggle for succession has begun. At this point the party, no longer clandestine or isolated, with growing support among the lower classes, starts to compete in the contest for power against more moderate political organizations. In other words, it usually assumes a key role not in the destruction of the old order but in the creation of the new.

Secondly, the doctrines of the revolutionary party, though attracting followers among all strata of society, appeal disproportionately to members of the classes that are not victims but beneficiaries of the existing system. To put it another way, many of those who join the movement and most of those who achieve a position of leadership belong by income, education, and status to privileged groups in the social hierarchy. Clearly, what draws them to the cause of revolution is not the personal experience of privation or exploitation. On the contrary, they could normally expect to achieve a comfortable position within the established order, as their parents and grandparents had done. Their conversion to a radical ideology, usually some form of socialism, entails a major sacrifice of rewards. By breaking with traditional loyalties and values, they exchange a life of ease for the hunted existence of rebels. They dedicate themselves to a struggle not for but against their social class.

Finally, since entry into a revolutionary organization means the abandonment of private ambitions and gratifications, most members join at an early stage in life. They may not achieve a leading position until middle age; but the decision to enter the movement comes as a rule in their twenties or even teens. Those who have already acquired professional rewards, economic advantages, and family obligations find it difficult, however much they deplore the injustices of the established order, to sacrifice everything for a revolutionary ideal. They may sympathize with the opposition, but they rarely join it. The radical party is therefore to a disproportionate extent composed of young people, many of them students or recent graduates, children of affluent parents, who reject the opportunities offered them by the existing system. Their selfless commitment to a prophetic vision of the good society gives the movement a toughness and tenacity out of all proportion to its size.

This characterization of the revolutionary party emerges from a comparative study of its size and composition in several countries experiencing a violent transition from an old to a new social order. In the case of the Russian Revolution, the membership of the Bolshevik organization in January 1917, just before the fall of czarism, when it still had to operate underground, while many of its leaders were still imprisoned or exiled, was not quite 24,000—and even this figure is only a guess—in a nation of about 160,000,000. By the end of April, after the emperor had abdicated and the party came out into the open, the number rose to 79,000. In the next few months it continued to grow rapidly, so that by August there were about 200,000 members. No figures are available for November, when the Bolsheviks came to power, but the size of the party must have increased substantially since the late summer. While membership had thus expanded tenfold in less than a year, it was nevertheless surprisingly low in relation to the total population of Russia.

Data on the social composition of the Bolshevik organization are even sparser. Yet it is clear that whatever lower-class support the party had came primarily from the factory and the army. Its following among peasants actually working on the land, as opposed to those in uniform, was negligible. Although the proportion of industrial workers joining the movement was greater, it remained relatively quite small. According to the replies to a questionnaire received from 25 towns at the time of the party's sixth congress in August 1917, the percentage of Bolsheviks among factory employees varied from 1 to 12 percent, the average being 5 percent.

There is more information on the leadership of the organization than on its rank and file. Of the 267 delegates to the sixth congress, 171 provided autobiographical data showing that their average age was twenty-nine. Almost all had worked for years in the socialist movement as organizers, propagandists, secretaries, or committee members. No fewer than 94, some 55 percent of those responding, had received a secondary or higher education, while only 72 of them, or 42 percent, were listed as workers or soldiers by occupation. In short, more than half of the leaders for whom some personal information is available appear to have come from well-to-do families and to be classifiable as "intellectuals."

This general pattern conforms to the results of a study completed about a decade later of 163 prominent Communists in the Soviet Union. The men and women whose careers were examined had by then achieved positions of leadership under the new order, but their participation in the radical movement had started long before the Bolshevik victory. To begin with, almost all of them, over 95 percent, had engaged in some revolutionary activity by the time they were twenty-six, and nearly 80 percent had done so by the time they were twenty-one. Indeed, their initial act of disobedience against established authority had typically occurred about two years before they joined the party. While the ages of seventeen and eighteen were the most common for their first revolutionary deed, nineteen and twenty were the most frequent for their formal entry into the movement. All in all, over 50 percent of those in the sample were twenty or younger when they joined a radical party, and over 82 percent were twenty-five or less. The precocious political commitment of the Bolshevik elite is unmistakable. Whoever had not joined the movement by his middle twenties was not likely to achieve a leading position after its rise to power.

Data regarding the social origin of the Communist leaders reinforce the impression that urban intellectuals of middle-class background play a disproportionate role in the revolutionary party. First of all, although only about 13 percent of all Russians lived in cities around the turn of the century, communities of over 50,000 produced more than 38 percent of those in the sample, while communities of over 10,000 produced more than 50 percent. Towns and villages with a population up to 2,500, on the other hand, produced 43 percent, those between 2,501 and 5,000 less than 3 percent, and those between 5,001 and 10,000 less than 4. Bolshevism was largely an urban movement in an overwhelmingly rural society.

Not only that, the educational level of the Communist leaders suggests that a high proportion came from well-to-do families. More than 60 percent had studied at a university, although of these barely half had graduated. Some claimed that they had been expelled for revolutionary activity or for membership in a radical student organization. Another 15 percent had received a secondary education in a "Gymnasium" or its equivalent, without continuing at an institution of higher learning. Only about 23 percent had not gone beyond elementary school. Thus under the new order, as under the old, advanced education was in general a prerequisite for a position of leadership.

But the most direct evidence regarding the social composition of the revolutionary vanguard comes from data regarding the occupational status of the fathers of those in the sample. Only 19 percent were peasants and 21 percent workers, although the two classes together comprised more than 90 percent of the Russian population. The leaders whose fathers had been members of the learned professions, on the other hand—teachers, clergymen, doctors, lawyers, editors, engineers, and "intellectuals"—accounted for about 17 percent of the total, almost the same percentage as the peasantry. The children of teachers alone constituted over 9 percent. And then there were various other pursuits or occupations indicating a relatively high level of prestige and affluence: 12 percent of the fathers were minor government officials and clerks, 8 percent were proprietors of estates or factories, another 8 percent were described simply as "very wealthy," 6 percent were nobles, 4 percent businessmen, 2 percent important government officials, and 2 percent officers in the armed forces, including a general. It becomes apparent that the propertied classes under the *ancien régime* in Russia furnished the major part of the revolutionary elite that helped bring about its overthrow.[4]

A similar conclusion emerges from an examination of the social origin of the leadership of the two major political movements in China, the Kuomintang and the Communist party, which contended for power for nearly three decades after the downfall of the imperial government. A study published shortly after the victory of the Communists compared the class composition of the Central Executive Committee of the Kuomintang between 1924 and 1945 with that of the Politburo of the Communist party during roughly the same period. Although the available biographical data cover only part of the membership of the two groups, the samples are large enough to make an informed comparison possible. As a point of reference, the study also included an analysis of the family background of 23 leaders of the old order, men prominent during the last years of the Ch'ing dynasty from 1890 to 1911. The results are highly illuminating.

The most significant finding is the essential similarity in the social composition of the leadership of the autocratic imperial regime, the reformist Kuomintang, and the radical Communist party. That important officials under the old order would generally come from a background of wealth and status was only to be expected, and in fact the results of the study support this assumption. Of the 23 men in the sample, 7 were born into families of scholars and officials, 3 were sons of minor civil servants, another 3 came from the imperial family, 2 were sons of merchants, and 1 was the son of an army officer. Only 2 of them had risen from the lower classes. The first was the son of a peasant, while the second had started out as an outlaw, but had then entered the imperial army and won rapid promotion. There is no information on the social origin of the other 5 members of the group.

More surprising is the evidence of little difference in the class composition of the political elites of the old imperial order and the new republican one, whether in the Kuomintang or the Communist party. For one thing, there is the similarity in their family background. The leadership of each came almost exclusively from a thin upper layer of the population of China. Its members were generally sons of scholars, officials, landlords, and merchants. To be sure, a noticeable shift had occurred under the republic in the family origin of the ruling elite from the aristocratic and bureaucratic classes to the noveau riche strata of society: compradors, businessmen, landlords, and even wealthy peasants. But essentially there was little change in the social and economic exclusivity of the groups from which the governments and parties of China during the first half of the twentieth century recruited their leadership.

A study comparing the occupations of the fathers of 47 members of the Central Executive Committee of the Kuomintang with those of the fathers of 24 members of the Politburo of the Communist party shows that almost 49 percent of the former and over 33 percent of the latter belonged to the highest levels of the social hierarchy; that is, they were wealthy landlords, scholars, officials, and merchants. Nearly 45 percent of the former and about 42 percent of the latter belonged to the middle strata. They were small landowners, local merchants, and wealthy peasants. As for the lower classes—poor peasants and industrial workers—they accounted for only 6 percent of the Kuomintang sample and 25 percent of the Communist party sample. The pattern was by and large similar to that of the old imperial regime. After the fall of the Manchus, as before, at least 75 percent of the political leaders came from groups in society comprising, at most, 10 percent of the population.

This conclusion is further reinforced by an examination of the level of education of 261 members of the Kuomintang Central Executive Committee and 29 members of the Communist party Politburo. Over 99 percent of the former and about 93 percent of the latter had studied at an institution of higher learning. But since attendance at a university was so costly that, as a rule, only members of well-to-do families could afford it, the extent of advanced education in the two samples clearly suggests a background of comfort and affluence. This seems to apply to the Communists almost as much as to the Kuomintang Nationalists. The only major difference was that 86 percent of the former had studied abroad, while for the latter the percentage was 52. Does this mean that attendance at a foreign institution of learning exposed Chinese students to more radical ideas than those they encountered at home? Or does it suggest that students favoring revolutionary change were more frequently inclined or forced to pursue their education in Europe, America, and Japan? In any case, it is obvious that those vying for political power under the republic, whether moderates or radicals, recruited their elites from among the propertied and educated.

Yet there were also significant differences between them. Although in its administrative structure each organization relied heavily on leaders from the privileged classes, the radical movement was by background and orientation much more rural. A comparison of 45 members of the Kuomintang Central Executive Committee with 23 members of the Communist party Politburo shows that the fathers of 38 percent of the former and 65 percent of the latter were landlords or peasants, while the fathers of 62 percent of the former and 35 percent of the latter were scholars, officials, merchants, and workers. This difference in the occupational and environmental origin of the two political elites is especially important in light of the strategy that the radicals adopted in their struggle for power. The typical Communist leader was the son of an affluent landowner or well-to-do peasant, whereas the typical leader of the Kuomintang was likely to be the son of a merchant or civil servant. The success of the Communist party in gaining the support of the masses of the countryside becomes more understandable in light of the largely rural background of its bureaucracy.

Secondly, the radicals in China, like those in Russia, were a distinctly youthful political group. To be sure, the leadership of the Kuomintang, which had also arisen out of a revolutionary move-

ment, was relatively young as well; but the elite of the Communist
party was measurably and consistently younger. Between 1921 and
1931 the average age of the Kuomintang Central Executive fluctuated
between 42.6 and 44.6, while the average age of the Communist
party Politburo fluctuated between 27.3 and 33.4. After that both
leaderships began to grow older, as each organization became increasingly institutionalized and bureaucratized. The disparity between them, however, never disappeared. On the eve of the Second
World War the average age was 48.9 for the Nationalists and 39.3 for
the Communists. And in 1945, as the two prepared for their final test
of strength, the average age for the Kuomintang elite was 54.9 and
for the Communist party elite 48.9. In other words, there was a difference of about ten years between them almost throughout the
three decades of their struggle. Only toward the end did it gradually
begin to diminish.

Finally, the Chinese Communists, like the Russian Bolsheviks,
were a highly selective organization—disciplined, dedicated, and
very small. Though seeking to win a mass following, they restricted
membership in the party to the most gifted and committed. From
the time of its founding in 1921 to its fourth congress in 1925, the
number never exceeded 1,000. It then climbed to nearly 58,000 early
in 1927, but dropped again to 10,000 later that year after the break
with the Kuomintang. A steady recovery followed, so that by 1933,
just before the "Long March," the party had about 300,000 members. Its migration to the north amid bitter fighting against the Nationalist forces reduced the number once more to 40,000 in 1937. The
struggle against Japan led to a third recovery, even more rapid than
the previous two, the membership reaching 763,000 in 1941 and
853,000 in 1944. By the time the Second World War ended, the figure
was over 1,200,000. Still, in a country of around 450,000,000 people,
the Communist party remained a small organization, almost as
small proportionately as the Bolsheviks had been when they seized
power. Like Lenin, Mao hoped to enlist the masses in the revolutionary struggle; but he restricted its leadership to a select group of disciplined militants.[5]

Much less is known about the elite of the political movement that
established the Castro regime in Cuba. Yet the available data reveal
a striking similarity to the radical vanguard in Russia and China

with regard to social origin, age distribution, and numerical size. It is clear, to begin with, that the leaders of the revolution against Batista came largely from a background of middle-class affluence. Soon after the victory of the new order, Che Guevara admitted that those who had initiated the struggle were without exception the sons of well-to-do families: "None of us, none of the first group which arrived in the *Granma*, who settled in the Sierra Maestra, and learned to respect the peasant and the worker living with him, had a peasant or working-class background." An examination of the class composition of the militant core of the rebel forces supports this contention. It was made up primarily of revolutionary intellectuals, almost all of them of bourgeois origin. There were lawyers, like Fidel Castro himself and Osvaldo Dorticós; students, like Raúl Castro and Fauré Chomón; doctors, like Faustino Pérez and René Vallejo; and teachers, like Frank País. Only here and there in this radical elite of wealth and education could be found an occasional member of the urban unemployed such as Camilo Cienfuegos or Ephigenio Almejeiras.

A similar distribution of occupations characterized the cabinet formed by Castro shortly after his accession to power. Of the 18 members, 8 were lawyers, 3 were students, and the rest had followed a variety of miscellaneous middle-class pursuits: professor, architect, mayor, engineer, naval captain, medical worker, and holder of an advanced degree in philosophy. All had attended a university, some in the United States; all had come from affluent families; all had become or aspired to become members of the learned professions. The youngest was twenty-nine years old and the oldest fifty-three, the average being 34.9. The distribution of ages, backgrounds, and occupations thus conforms closely to the typical pattern of the young, educated, well-to-do intelligentsia that contributes disproportionately to the revolutionary elite in all countries.

As for the size of the militant cadre, Castro's movement rose to power so rapidly that no clearly organized party structure had emerged before the old order collapsed. Victory was achieved in large measure through improvisation and rule of thumb. In this regard the revolutionary struggle in Cuba differed from that of the Bolsheviks in Russia or the Communists in China, who had to endure a long period of conflict before their final triumph. Yet ample evidence exists that the Cuban radical elite was relatively even smaller than the Russian or

Chinese. Only 81 men sailed with Castro on the ramshackle *Granma* at the end of 1956 to initiate the uprising against the Batista dictatorship. No more than 12 remained after the first disastrous encounter with government troops. The insurrectionary forces then began to gain strength, especially after demonstrating that they could hold out indefinitely in the mountains of the Sierra Maestra. But many of the new recruits were politically ambivalent, halfhearted, and not always reliable, their commitment depending to a considerable extent on the fortunes of war. Those who were ready to fight through thick and thin never numbered more than a few thousand in a population of close to six million. The vanguard of activists that helped put Castro in power was proportionally no larger than that which made possible the victory of Lenin and Mao.[6]

Finally, the uprising in Vietnam, in the north as well as south, was led by a radical cadre which in its class origin closely resembled the Russian, Chinese, and Cuban. There was the same pattern of young men and women from affluent families rejecting social position and comfortable livelihood for the revolutionary cause. A study commissioned by the American government of the background of the leaders of the Viet Minh, the League for the Independence of Vietnam, which fought against the French after the Second World War, concluded that most were Communists who had been active in the movement since the late 1920s. "Many of these were highly educated intellectuals and professional people, all thoroughly familiar with French culture and generally schooled in Western ways, either having lived abroad for many years or having attended Western schools. As to social origins, most Vietminh leaders were from middle or lower-middle-class families and several came from an aristocratic mandarin background."

According to the data published in 1953 by the Dang Lao Dong, the Communist Workers party of North Vietnam, no fewer than 1,365 out of 1,855 senior positions in the organization were held by intellectuals or other members of bourgeois background, a total of 74 percent, while peasant families accounted for only 351, or 19 percent, and worker families for 139, or 7 percent. This in a country where 90 percent of the population was employed in agriculture, and less than 1 percent could be classified as "intellectuals," that is, people in one of the learned professions. More than a decade later

Truong Chinh, a leading member of the politburo, was forced to concede that "our Party was born and has grown up in an agricultural country with a small working class. The overwhelming majority of our cadres and Party members come from the petty-bourgeoisie."

Less is known about the leaders of the revolutionary movement in South Vietnam. Having to operate underground, they tried to keep their identities secret or at least obscure. Nevertheless, a study concluded in the 1960s of the social background of the National Liberation Front, a coalition of various opposition groups in which Communists played a major role, was able to obtain data on the class origin of 8 of the 38 members of the organization's high command. Three came from mandarin families, 1 was the son of a rubber plantation manager, and another the son of a civil servant. There were also 2 women among them, daughters respectively of a businessman and a prominent nationalist politician. Only 1 of the 8 had working-class parents.

Information on the occupational history of the group is more extensive, covering over half of the members. They belonged almost without exception to the familiar category of middle-class pursuits. Seven had been teachers, while the rest were scattered across a variety of other employments requiring higher learning: doctor, pharmacist, architect, engineer, lawyer, writer, journalist, labor organizer, French militiaman, Buddhist monk, and colonel in the military organization of one of the Vietnamese sects. The lower levels of leadership in the National Liberation Front did include some men of peasant background; but their relative number was inversely proportional to the importance of the echelon to which they belonged. The higher the position in the organization's hierarchy, the more likely it was to be held by someone of upper-class or middle-class origin.

As for the size of the revolutionary movement, the same distinction between activist cadre and mass following prevailed in Vietnam as in Russia, China, and Cuba. That is, although the leadership sought to enlist the lower classes in the struggle against the old order, positions of importance were reserved for an elite of dedicated militants. According to figures published by the Cominform, the membership of the Communist party of Vietnam was 20,000 in

1946, the year it was ostensibly disbanded, 50,000 in 1947, and 168,000 in 1948. Of the latter number, 102,000 came from the north, 43,000 from the central region, and 23,000 from the south. For 1950, four years after the official dissolution of the Communist party and one year before the founding of its successor, the Workers party, the membership was reported to be about 500,000.

These figures may not be entirely reliable, since information later provided by sources in Hanoi estimated the number for 1946 at 5,000 and for 1948 at 180,000. Yet despite discrepancies in the data, it is clear, first of all, that the size of the revolutionary organization increased with the likelihood of its success and, secondly, that it remained small even by the calculations of the Cominform. A membership of half a million in a population of over forty million represented not much more than 1 percent, roughly the same proportion as in other countries experiencing a major social upheaval.[7]

The Defection
of the Educated Classes

A comparative examination of the process of disintegration of the *ancien régime* thus helps establish a typology of the radical elite. Its chief characteristics seem to be exclusivity, youthfulness, and high social status. The success of the political opposition in winning converts among the well-to-do, especially among young people of talent and education, is the clearest sign of the impending collapse of the old order. During the 1930s the historian Crane Brinton called this shift in allegiance "the desertion of the intellectuals." He saw in it a common indication of the abandonment of established authority by those groups in the community that have most to lose from its overthrow. It was a symptom of civic disorder and social morbidity. "We may say," he argued, "that in a society markedly unstable there seem to be absolutely more intellectuals, at any rate comparatively more intellectuals, bitterly attacking existing institutions and desirous of a considerable alteration in society, business, and government. Purely metaphorically, we may compare intellectuals of this sort to the white corpuscles, guardians of the bloodstream; but there can be an excess of white corpuscles, and where this happens you have a diseased condition." The spread of class disloyalty seemed to him a portent of the imminent fall of the *ancien régime*.[8]

But what accounts for this reversal of civic allegiance? Why should significant numbers of people who have benefited from the existing system turn against a form of authority that has assiduously protected their interests? This is the most puzzling aspect of the decline of the old order. Some writers have argued that there is in fact a perfectly logical explanation for the spread of disaffection among the educated and affluent. Those most likely to turn against the *ancien régime* are people who feel that, despite their achievements, they are being victimized by the bigotry of the status quo. In Russia hostility toward czarism was especially strong among some of the minority nationalities—Jews, Georgians, and Latvians, for example —which were regarded by state authorities as alien and not entirely trustworthy. In Vietnam a considerable number of underemployed graduates of institutions of higher learning constituted a native intellectual proletariat, unable to find work commensurate with their education, condemned to a subordinate position in the country's government, and resentful of a regime that deprived them of what they considered their birthright. Here, so the argument goes, is the basic cause of "the desertion of the intellectuals."

Yet there are obvious weaknesses in this line of reasoning. While it is true that victims of religious or ethnic discrimination are disproportionately represented among opponents of the old order, most members of the revolutionary elite come from families occupying a favored position in the social system. Their conversion to the cause of revolution is not a result of private humiliation or personal grudge. Indeed, they can expect to be generously rewarded for loyalty to the status quo. Their rejection of established authority, on the other hand, means the abandonment of important advantages. It cannot therefore be explained by a simple calculation of debits and credits. Even those who become revolutionaries because of the discriminatory policies of the system realize that they will not thereby improve their position. On the contrary, the lawyer, doctor, or businessman embittered by ethnic bigotry knows that by defying his government he will only worsen the material circumstances of his life. He will exchange a comfortable though precarious livelihood for the hunted existence of a professional radical. The abandonment

of the old order by a growing number of people of wealth and learning cannot be accounted for by any computation of self-interest.

It represents rather a triumph of idealism over practicality, of principle over expediency. It attests to the power of pure idea. And this is
precisely what makes defection from the ranks of the well-to-do so
dangerous to established authority. Those who embrace the revolutionary faith, determined to bring about a fundamental reconstruction of society, cannot be intimidated or cajoled or suppressed. They
wage their struggle with a religious fervor, whatever the odds, convinced that justice, history, and perhaps even providence are on
their side. The defenders of the old order, on the other hand, though
also persuaded of the rightness of their cause, are to some extent
motivated by considerations of private gain. They may be more numerous, at least in the early stages of the conflict, but their morale is
generally weaker. In the long run, therefore, they are no match for
the youthful rebels who have selflessly turned against the social
system that safeguards their privileged station. The strength of the
revolutionary elite lies in this imperviousness to calculations of
advantage.

The growing opposition of young people from the propertied
classes to established institutions, however, is not merely a sign of
their greater altruism or benevolence. Their disaffection comes at a
time when the underpinning of collective myths on which the old
order rests has begun to erode. The crisis of the *ancien régime*, initiated by economic modernization and aggravated by military defeat
or political ineffectualness, has aroused doubts about the legitimacy
of its claim to power. An increasing number of men and women—
most of them youthful, educated, and affluent—become convinced
that the ills of society, previously accepted as inherent in the human
condition, are actually the result of oppression and exploitation.
They are not beyond the scope of governmental power; they can and
must be dealt with by collective action. But the old order appears incapable of undertaking the task of reconstruction. It is too weak and
corrupt. Only a new political system based on the principles of freedom and justice can rebuild society.

This is the reason for the gradual alienation of the well-to-do from
the status quo. Their rebelliousness grows, not despite, but because
of their economic and social advantages. They are troubled by a

sense of guilt about their wealth amid the abject poverty of the lower classes. Their education has familiarized them with the writings of radical political theorists. They are therefore able to undertake a broad critical analysis of the existing system. They have time to reflect on the problems of civic reform, more time than the masses toiling endlessly in shops and fields. They are in a position to conceive of a political order fundamentally different from the one into which they were born. Their radicalization is in a sense a function of their status.

Yet the spread of disaffection among the upper strata of society is by no means a uniform process. It is to a large extent a correlate of age. The older generation, whose formative experiences were shaped by the traditions of the *ancien régime*, generally remains loyal during the crisis of the established system. Its members are just as kindhearted and well-intentioned as those of the younger generation. Nor are they blind to the oppressiveness, bigotry, corruption, and exploitation of the existing system. But they believe that these are the failings of all human institutions; they are ineradicable. They may be mitigated, but they can never be completely eliminated. Any attempt to achieve an impossible perfection in state and society will only lead to greater injustice. Those who seek to improve the condition of the less fortunate should work within the established order, so that it may become more efficient, benevolent, honest, and responsive. Sedition will just make matters worse.

The emergence of a revolutionary situation thus engenders a generational conflict within the propertied classes. Truong Nhu Tang, who was minister of justice in the Provisional Revolutionary Government of South Vietnam, recalled that in the late 1940s, after he had become a follower of Ho Chi Minh while attending the university, his father, a businessman, landowner, and professor at a *lycée* in Saigon, hoped that the responsibilities of marriage and a lucrative profession would cure him of his wild political ideas. But it was too late for that. The son had set out on a course from which paternal disapproval could no longer deter him:

To my father's way of thinking, of course, the peace and sweetness of conjugal life and obvious prospects for a family and established career could hardly fail to snap his son out of the spell that had strangely trans-

formed him into a political sorcerer's apprentice. But nothing in my father's experience or training had prepared him for the earthquake that
was now swallowing up the old familial and colonial order of things. As
for me, my heart had embraced the patriotic fire, and my soul was wing-
ing its way toward the empyrean of national liberation. I was already
well on the far bank of my personal Rubicon.

The estrangement between father and son only deepened with the
passage of time. Their last meeting took place twenty years later, in
1967. By then the latter was a political prisoner in Saigon, condemned by the authorities as a traitor to his country. The elder
Truong came to visit his unfortunate, misguided child:

> Emaciated and half-blind, I had tottered unsteadily from my "coffin"
> to the visiting room, where he was waiting. His expression as we em-
> braced was one of bottomless grief. His words had burned themselves
> into my memory. "My son," he had said, "I simply cannot understand
> you. You have abandoned everything. A good family, happiness,
> wealth—to follow the Communists. They will never return to you a par-
> ticle of the things you have left. You will see. They will betray you, and
> you will suffer your entire life." I had answered him then, "My dearest
> father, you have six sons. You should be content to sacrifice one of them
> for the sake of the country's independence and liberty." Now . . . the sor-
> row of that last parting could never be erased.

A decade later the revolutionary idealist Truong Nhu Tang was a political refugee, escaping from the new Vietnam in the exodus of the
"boat people."[9]

To many of those who grew up before the crisis of the old order, established authority always retains a measure of political legitimacy, a
residue of historical or providential sanctification. Despite all failings,
it continues to be regarded as still capable of reformation. To their
children, on the other hand, the existing system often appears corrupt
beyond redemption. Its weaknesses are so glaring, its injustices so ingrained, that only a revolution can end them. It must be destroyed
root and branch. Hostility toward those in power is only intensified
by their efforts to defend themselves. The restrictions imposed on opponents are denounced as proof of tyranny. The reforms designed to

propitiate critics are derided as ineffectual. There is something ineluctable in the growing alienation of the well-to-do.

Alexis de Tocqueville, writing about the decline of the *ancien régime* in France despite its attempts to mollify the third estate, analyzed this process of class defection: "The most dangerous moment for a bad government is, generally speaking, when it begins to mend its ways. Only a great genius is able to save a prince who, after a long period of oppression, tries to conciliate his subjects." For a grievance that people had patiently endured as something inevitable begins to appear unendurable as soon as they conceive of the possibility of redressing it. "All the abuses which are then corrected seem only to reveal more clearly those which remain. The grievance has been diminished, to be sure, but the sense of grievance is keener." Once that happens, nothing the old order does can arrest its disintegration.[10]

The pattern appears to be roughly the same in all revolutionary situations. The portents of class defection that Tocqueville perceived in France before the overthrow of Louis XVI are also discernible in China before the fall of Chiang Kai-shek. In the spring of 1947 the liberal Shanghai weekly *Kuan-ch'a* examined the growing opposition to the Kuomintang regime. The young people, who were generally "pure," had at first no fixed ideas about public affairs. As long as "everything is on the right track," as long as politics were not corrupt, as long as society was secure and the nation had a future, they would support the government. Recent activities of the authorities, however, had caused them to give up hope. As for the older generation, the basis of support for the existing system had previously been the urban population, especially civil servants, teachers, and intellectuals as well as "business and industrial circles." Yet now "no one among these people has any positive feelings toward the Nanking regime." The Kuomintang's "tyrannical style of behavior" was arousing "deep hatred" among liberals. Because the salaries of civil servants and teachers, moreover, had remained low since the end of the war with Japan, they were now losing confidence in the system. Government officials, "by indulging in corrupt practices and creating every kind of obstruction," had aroused dissatisfaction in the business and industrial community. And finally, the sharp increase in prices resulting from "erroneous financial and monetary policies" as well as the continuation of civil conflict were provoking expressions of resentment that could be heard everywhere among the urban population. The situation seemed desperate.

A few months later the American correspondent A. Doak Barnett described a discussion with some of the leaders of the Democratic League, an organization representing the liberal, noncommunist opposition to the Kuomintang. All felt that the Nationalist government had become completely discredited. Its removal was the first requisite of a political or economic revival. "The present regime is so utterly corrupt that it is beyond redemption," one of them maintained. "It is beyond the possibility of any help. It is not worthy of any help." Another argued that "the present regime must go. Something will come next. It couldn't be as bad as the present regime. Even if it has faults, the people will be able to cope with the situation."

Hostility toward the established system ran so deep that a Communist form of government actually seemed to represent an improvement. "Ideally, our middle group would like to see a third party or group of parties in power," said one of those present. "Unfortunately, there is no hope for that under the present regime. You would say that there probably wouldn't be any more chance for it under the Communists. We don't believe that is so, because the Communists are at least going in the right direction. We believe we would fare better under the Communists." Another participant agreed: "We may have reason to have some fear of the Communists, but at least they are going in the right direction. They are for the people and are going in the direction of justice and democracy." Disillusionment was pushing the middle-of-the-roaders farther and farther to the left.

A year later another American observer, the sinologist Derk Bodde, described in his diary similar views expressed by a liberal professor at Tsinghua University outside Peking: "At first, most of us supported the government, recognizing its many faults, but hoping it would reform. Then we became increasingly discouraged with reform prospects, but saw no feasible alternative. Though the present government, we felt, was bad, what might take its place would be even worse." During this phase most intellectuals felt confused, unsure, wondering what they should do. But "then came the present, third phase. We have become so completely convinced of the hope-

lessness of the existing government that we feel the sooner it is removed the better. Since the Chinese Communists are obviously the
only force capable of making this change, we are now willing to support them as the lesser of two evils. We ourselves would prefer a
middle course, but this is no longer possible." Any political system
would be better than the existing one.[11]

Mass defection is thus an unmistakable symptom of the decline of
the old order. The lower classes, their traditional way of life dis-
rupted by economic modernization, are increasingly skeptical toward established authority. The hardships they had endured in the
past as inescapable begin to seem unbearable. Their incoherent dis-
contents, moreover, are now being articulated and organized by a
revolutionary elite, largely of middle-class origin, which has turned
against the existing social system. The idealism and dedication that
this elite brings to the struggle against the *ancien régime* are of central importance. Finally, there is a large, influential group of people
of wealth and learning who, though moderate in their political outlook, have become so disillusioned with the status quo that they are
prepared to collaborate with the hard-core radicals. The revolutionary movement, in other words, comprises a variety of political ideas
and economic interests, all of them distinct, some of them incompatible, joined only by a common rejection of established authority.
Their underlying differences, however, are for the time being subordinated to their shared objectives. As the crucial test of strength approaches, they stand united in their opposition to the old order.

The Redemptive Power
of Rebellion

The revolution, however, is inspired by more than hostility to the *ancien régime*. It reflects something even deeper, even more compelling
than anger at the injustices for which the existing system is held responsible. Many of those who dedicate themselves to the overthrow
of established authority feel that they are fighting to liberate all
mankind. Society seems to be witnessing the dawn of a golden age,
an age of wondrous, exciting opportunities. They may still not be
fully discernible, but they are there, just beyond the horizon.

Human nature itself is about to be transformed. A new order is emerging, more idealistic, more noble than the old. Anything is now possible. And because people begin to believe that anything is now possible, important changes actually take place that otherwise would have been impossible. They attest to the might of the revolutionary idea. The restraints on human expectations imposed by daily experience appear to dissolve; men and women who had been leading drab, drudging lives suddenly find the strength to perform deeds of heroism. The imminent fall of the old order engenders a mood of exaltation that helps liberate unsuspected popular energies. For a brief period of time society becomes capable of achievements that under ordinary circumstances would have remained unattainable.

Brinton aptly described this sense of sudden liberation that an insurrectionary movement engenders, this feeling of intense excitement produced by the vision of fundamental social change: "To what do these revolutionary intellectuals desert? To another and better world than that of the corrupt and inefficient old regimes. From a thousand pens and voices there are built up in the years before the revolution actually breaks out what one must now fashionably call the foundations of the revolutionary myth—or folklore, or symbols, or ideology." Many ethical and religious systems, especially Christianity, have contrasted some such better world of the ideal with the immediate and imperfect world of everyday reality. But "what differentiates this ideal world of the revolutionaries from the better world as conceived by more pedestrian persons is a flaming sense of the immediacy of the ideal, a feeling that there is something in all men better than their present fate, a conviction that what is, not only ought not, but need not, be." The strength of the revolutionary idea derives from the sense of an imminent rebirth of human society.[12]

Brinton was writing mostly about the revolutions of the seventeenth and eighteenth century in Europe and North America. But the same feeling of discovery, the same mood of excitement is manifest in the revolutions of the twentieth century in Asia and the Caribbean. Shortly before the overthrow of the Manchus, Li Po-yuan prophesied in the preface to a novel dealing with "modern times" that China was about to enter a new age. "What period have we reached in our world today?" he asked. "One person will say: 'An ancient empire cannot be rejuvenated.' Another will say: 'There is nothing difficult about growing from childhood to adulthood.'" In his own view, "our present circumstances are not those of childhood, and it is most probable that the time for the sun to rise and the rain to fall is not far distant." This conclusion was based on the exciting developments of recent years. "There have been new measures and policies in government and education, repercussions of which have filled the heavens with their din. Some things have been done well and some badly; some changes have been carried through with sufficient knowledge and some with insufficient." But what mattered was that "whether good or bad, there have been those who have been willing to make the changes, and whether there has been sufficient knowledge or not, there have been those who have been willing to learn."

Yet he felt that something was in the air that was even more important than the willingness of those in authority to initiate change. "When one adds to this the fact that people's minds have been stimulated and that all levels of society have been raised to action, are these not indications, like the sea and the wind, that the sun is about to rise and the rain to fall?" Those responsible for the introduction of reform deserved praise. "Irrespective of whether these people have succeeded or failed, been cast aside or are flourishing, been public-spirited or selfish, proved genuine or false, they will eventually be regarded as men of merit in a civilized world." That was the reason, he concluded, that he had written a book publicizing their achievements. "Far be it from me to deny the pains they have taken on the lonely path of progress." As with other great men, their achievements had never been fully recognized. But in the future, history would bestow on them the fame they richly deserved. In the meantime, he greeted in verse the dawning age of enlightenment:

Ssu-ma was disparaged from earliest times because of his outspokenness,
And some today scorn Tung Hu for his honesty.
But change determines what is rotten and what is marvellous,
And with these words I felicitate the future.

This feeling that society was about to be regenerated began to spread, as it became apparent that the collapse of the Ch'ing dynasty was near. The historian Ku Chieh-kang recalled in his autobiography how, though still in his teens, he succumbed to it as well. "Public opinion leaned more and more toward revolution, and I, too, was one of the multitude to be swept away by this tendency. The calm and willing self-sacrifice of men . . . who lost their lives in the Revolution impressed me as something worth lamenting with tears or extolling in song." His zeal for the radical cause only increased with the success of the insurrection of 1911. "I fancied that there is nothing under the sun too difficult for men to accomplish; that the good, the true, and the beautiful need only to be advocated, and they will become actualities." But a "race-revolution," an uprising of the Oriental masses against Occidental domination, was only a small part of the program that the overthrow of the old order seemed to make possible. "We would not consider our revolutionary task accomplished until we had abolished government, had discarded the family system, and had made currency unnecessary!"

Such were the convictions that led to Ku's conversion to socialism despite the disapproval of his scholarly, well-to-do family. "Intoxicated as I was with such far-reaching ideals, I was quite prepared, when the opportunity came, to cast in my lot with the Socialist Party of which . . . I was one of the most devoted members, often not getting to sleep until far into the night in order to perform some public service." To many friends and relatives his political beliefs seemed incomprehensible. "Why do you associate with those vagabonds and ne'er-do-wells?" they would ask. "Their business should be no concern of yours." But criticism of this sort, "so evidently motivated by prejudice," made little impression. "I had already come to the conclusion that the gentry, as well as vagabonds, are the products of an evil social order. I felt that the former, especially, were the means of blocking a program of reform, and I could not be content until this class was eliminated." The spell of the revolutionary idea had made him deaf to the pleas of his family.

Not only young students or cloistered intellectuals felt the thrill of participating in the liberation of mankind. Even veteran revolutionaries, men hardened in the struggle against established authority, found it irresistible. In 1897 Sun Yat-sen, driven into exile after an abortive uprising against the old order, described his dream of social regeneration to Miyazaki Torazō, a former samurai who had embraced the idea of a revival of the peoples of East Asia under the leadership of Japan. With help from Tokyo, he explained, his party would be able to organize a successful revolution against the Manchus. Thereby it would "save China's four hundred million people [and] wipe away the humiliation of Asia's yellow race." More than that, it would "restore the universal way of humanity." The creation of a new order for the Chinese nation was to be part of a great transfiguration of mankind. Once the revolutionary movement had triumphed, society would enter an era of peace and justice. "All other problems will be solved as easily as splitting bamboo." Behind Sun's plots and conspiracies against the *ancien régime* was the messianic vision of a golden age on earth.

The same feeling that the struggle against established authority was essentially a crusade for the rebirth of humanity inspired the tribute to the Bolshevik revolution that Li Ta-chao, founder and theoretician of the Chinese Communist Party, published early in 1919, greeting the coming year as the dawn of a new age for all peoples of the world. The Soviet regime, he declared, had made it clear that "productive systems can be reformed, national boundaries can be as if struck down, and human kind can all enjoy opportunities for work." Not only hunger and exploitation but pain and grief would soon be banished. "All kinds of sorrow, hardship, anxiety, strife, can all naturally vanish." What the Russians had achieved was encouraging the growth of a mighty international revolutionary movement. "The united working class and their comrades all over the world will make rational production unions, break down national barriers, and overthrow the world capitalist class." To Li these were "the glories of our new era!" All the abuses of the old order were about to be rectified and expiated. "Like ice exposed to spring sun, in the light of these glories the evils of the past will gradually melt away, the residues of history will as leaves blown by autumn wind fall to the ground." The ultimate goal of the revolution was the redemption of man.[13]

A mood of millenarian fervor, of prophetic exaltation, seems to affect every society on the eve of a revolution. William Wordsworth, watching the disintegration of the *ancien régime* in France in the 1790s, felt this excitement at the coming redemption of mankind. "Bliss was it in that dawn to be alive, / But to be young was very

Heaven!" He remembered years later how, seeing a "hunger-bitten" young girl during a walk along the Loire, he was suddenly seized by the burning conviction

> *That a benignant spirit was abroad*
> *Which might not be withstood, that poverty*
> *Abject as this would in a little time*
> *Be found no more, that we should see the earth*
> *Unthwarted in her wish to recompense*
> *The meek, the lowly, patient child of toil,*
> *All institutes for ever blotted out*
> *That legalised exclusion, empty pomp*
> *Abolished, sensual state and cruel power*
> *Whether by edict of the one or few;*
> *And finally, as sum and crown of all,*
> *Should see the people having a strong hand*
> *In framing their own laws; whence better days*
> *To all mankind.*

The experience of witnessing a fundamental reconstruction of the state, Wordsworth recalled, aroused everywhere a sense of intense elation. "But Europe at that time was thrilled with joy, / France standing on the top of golden hours, / And human nature seeming born again."[14]

This vision of a world redeemed inspires all revolutionary movements, in China as well as in Russia, in Cuba no less than in Vietnam. It has the effect, for a short period of time, of transforming ordinary men and women into warriors and heroes; it reveals hidden popular talents and energies enlisted in the struggle for a better society. The decalogue of pieties justifying the old order suddenly gives way to a new complex of convictions and ideals. Belief in the redemptive promise of revolution replaces faith in the protective power of tradition. Thus the established system is divested of its political power; it loses its moral authority. Only one sharp blow is now needed to bring about its downfall.

CHAPTER 3

The Struggle
for Public Opinion

The armed conflict culminating in the victory of the revolution is accompanied by a war of words in which the antagonists seek to gain popular support by appealing to emotions as well as ideas. This war generally assumes the form of a clash between opposing theories or principles. Each side presents a more or less coherent structure of political and economic doctrines designed to prove that its cause is right and the opposing cause wrong. But there is also the arousal of fears and passions. The defenders of the *ancien régime* argue that their adversaries are atheists and materialists. They have no respect for the inherited traditions of the nation. They seek to weaken the sense of common purpose in society, pitting class against class, inciting the poor against the rich, spreading envy and resentment among the masses. Once in power, they will destroy the religious and moral basis of the community. Churches and temples will be desecrated, women dishonored, elders humiliated, and opponents tortured and killed. The social system will be torn apart by violence and pillage, by a war of all against all. For whenever the legitimate, historic foundations of national life are undermined, the result is bound to be anarchy followed by tyranny.

The revolutionary movement is equally adept at preaching and dogmatizing. It maintains that the loyalties and values espoused by the old order are only a clever disguise for greed and selfishness. Behind all the pious rhetoric about the moral foundations of society are the harsh realities of exploitation, despotism, avarice, and corruption. Established authority is only the means by which the strong rule the weak, the haves batten on the have-nots. Just look around you to see how the rich prosper amid the poor, how the mighty oppress the defenseless. Only the overthrow of the existing system will lead to true social justice. As soon as those who labor can enjoy the fruits of their labor, as soon as those who maintain the state can control the state, the inhumanity of man to man and of class to class will cease. True civic morality will never be found on the side of the *ancien régime;* it always resides in the camp of the revolution.

Charges of Mass Brutality

The war of words between the defenders and opponents of the old order goes beyond statements of doctrine, however. It has a psychological dimension which becomes increasingly important as the armed struggle approaches its climax. Here the confrontation of basic principles is overshadowed by something more concrete, more emotional or visceral. Each side begins to emphasize the cruelties and barbarities allegedly committed by the other: the execution of innocent civilians, the rape of defenseless women, the torture of political opponents, the plunder of private possessions. This exchange of accusations has to be distinguished from the conflict of political ideologies or social theories. Atrocity stories are not designed to demonstrate the falseness of the fundamental beliefs advocated by the enemy. They serve rather to arouse hostility toward him as an individual, as someone savage and brutal quite apart from the cause he espouses. Resentment or outrage can be as useful as logic or idealism in the struggle for power. The battle between the old and the new order is therefore waged amid a barrage of charges by which each of the antagonists tries to demonstrate that the other is guilty of acts of cruelty.

In this contest the opponents of the *ancien régime* are invariably victorious. Though both sides employ violence against unarmed adversaries, the forces of established authority are perceived to be more ruthless and oppressive. This is partly because in fact they rely more heavily on tactics of intimidation, but partly also because their use of coercion is more random and haphazard. Indeed, the greater incidence of the brutalities they commit is a direct result of this randomness. The forces defending the government, unsure of what they are fighting for, sometimes frightened and demoralized, often without confidence in their commanders, engage in atrocities out of boredom, frustration, anger, or concupiscence. Their officers are frequently unable or unwilling to enforce discipline. Occasionally they themselves are guilty of cruelty and corruption. The longer the struggle drags on, the more common the incidents of brutality. By the time the conflict enters its final phase, the authorities, blinded by panic, seeing hidden enemies on all sides, are lashing out wildly at anyone suspected of sympathy with the enemy. And as their deeds of arbitrary cruelty multiply, public opinion begins to turn against them.

The revolutionaries, to be sure, are by no means guiltless. They too engage in acts of violence against unarmed opponents. They bomb government offices, blow up power stations, destroy bridges and dams, and assassinate political adversaries. They can be as ruthless as the defenders of the old order. But for them intimidation and repression are rational, calculated means of waging the struggle. They avoid arbitrary or capricious acts of cruelty. Disciplined by an ideology that emphasizes the need to gain the confidence of the lower classes, they try to demonstrate their solicitude for the poor and oppressed. Their brutality is better organized, more purposeful. It serves a political function. Revolutionary troops are therefore as a rule more successful in winning the support of the civilian population. As the downfall of the *ancien régime* approaches, public opinion shifts more and more to the side of its opponents.

Those who support the old order cannot understand why the atrocities committed in its defense are so widely publicized, while those of which the other side is guilty are largely ignored. Soon after his overthrow, Batista wrote bitterly about the "nuclei of action" that were organized by "the terrorists in various countries" to protest and demonstrate against any measures taken by his government to ensure its security. "They saw to it that the news agencies reported any incident—a building damaged by a bomb, a worker assassinated because he refused to strike, a child destroyed by a shell burst, a young woman mutilated by an infernal machine; a citizen blown to bits, or a woman and her three children shot to death in their automobile on a highway blocked by the rebels." Such atrocities, though committed by the enemies of legitimate authority, were cited as evidence that a "dictatorial and bloody regime" ruled Cuba. Those captured or killed by the "forces of order" for criminal acts were portrayed as "victims of an implacable 'tyranny.'" Those risking their lives in defense of the law, on the other hand, were depicted as bullies and villains. "The person involved would not be the policeman or soldier who, in enforcing the laws, was acting to preserve order, to protect the rights of an individual and the security of the family, to guarantee life and property, to defend society or to protect himself; he would be made to appear as a man who used delegated authority to commit a crime."

And what about the atrocities perpetrated by the revolutionary forces? Government troops, "provoked, sometimes to the limits of human endurance, by the carefully contrived campaign of hatred, violence and murder," may have been guilty of the occasional use of excessive force, Batista conceded. But "was it meritorious to murder a soldier or policeman while he was performing his duty to defend his country or to enforce the laws? Should terrorists be praised when they throw bombs into crowded places, tearing apart the bodies of workers, teachers, government employees, women and, for that matter, children, splattering blood, tissue and human organs in all directions?" The worst crimes were committed not by the defenders but the opponents of the legal government.

According to its apologists, moreover, the old order in Cuba treated political adversaries fairly, with perhaps a few minor exceptions. "We respected the rights of all. We even commuted Castro's prison sentence so he could seek political power via the polls rather than through violence and terror. . . . We never deprived anyone of his property or his rights." To Batista the most convincing evidence of the humaneness of the *ancien régime* was the treatment accorded to his enemies when he had them in his power. "Every important leader of the Castro movement, with the single exception of Ernesto (Che) Guevara had at one time or another been in the hands of the Cuban Police. These former prisoners of Batista were living refutations of the Castro propaganda, imputing atrocities and bestial tortures to my regime. The plain and self-evident fact was that all of these former prisoners were alive, healthy, unmutilated and untortured." Does this not disprove the "black legend" of the old order's cruelty?[1]

Yet there is clear evidence that in fact the Batista regime did commit unprovoked acts of brutality during the struggle against Castro, that it employed arbitrary violence as a means of enforcing obedience, and that it tolerated widespread atrocities against unarmed civilians. So many accounts exist of random, capricious cruelty, some of them from highly reliable sources, that they cannot be dismissed as wartime propaganda. Pedro A. Barrera Pérez, a former colonel in the Cuban army, described how after Castro's abortive attack on the Moncada barracks in Santiago on July 26, 1953, the military commander of the city "made torrents of blood flow in Oriente Province, which underwent a reign of terror without precedent up to that time. Those killed during the barbaric repression ordered by the commanding officer of the Maceo Regiment numbered in the hundreds."

A few years later, according to Barrera, soon after Castro landed in Cuba to start a more successful uprising, some of the army officers leading the campaign against the invaders in the Sierra Maestra reached an agreement with local property owners to force peasant squatters from lands they had occupied on the charge that they were assisting the rebel forces. "One of the officers stationed in the region irresponsibly organized a raid into a district called 'Palma Mocha,' in which there were about 40 squatter families. He proceeded to burn their houses and to kill the heads of families he managed to capture on the pretext that they were cooperating with those who had come in [Castro's] expedition. The survivors of this massacre, for the most part women and children, took refuge in two dilapidated ranches on the edge of 'Chirivico' beach."

At about the same time, early in 1957, an official report on allegations of army brutality described "the capture of some thirty-odd other squatters, who were carried by ship during the night from naval headquarters to a spot far from the shore, thrown into the sea, and shot at with machine guns. To give the report greater credibility, Major Casillas presented to [Barrera] someone who, as I remember, was called Margarito, and was the only survivor of that criminal action."[2]

It is clear that the atrocities of which the old order is accused are not always distortions or fabrications. The brutalities are not always committed in self-defense, in response to attack or provocation. There is a great deal of arbitrary violence, some of it the result of fear and anger, some perpetrated with purpose and calculation. This violence, moreover, is directed primarily against members of the lower classes, against those who have been traditionally looked down upon with disdain. The apprehension that the common rabble could be conspiring against established authority is infuriating to those responsible for law and order. They may display restraint in dealing with a Lenin or a Castro, men whose social origin is generally similar to their own. But the thought that the ignorant masses are plotting against their betters appears intolerable. This helps account for the cruelty that government forces so often display toward workers or peasants suspected of sedition. The revolutionaries may be equally ruthless, but their violence is aimed at landowners, businessmen, government officials, and military leaders. It seems better organized and disciplined, more rational. Therefore, as the struggle goes on, public opinion turns increasingly against the old order. In the end the established system stands convicted of chronic, pervasive brutality.

Yet while the *ancien régime* is no doubt guilty of atrocities, their scope and frequency are as a rule exaggerated. Each side makes allegations against the other that are based partly on objective evidence, but that also contain distortions, embellishments, and outright fabrications. In a revolutionary struggle factual accuracy ceases to be a virtue. The accusations flying back and forth should not therefore be taken at face value. A few days after seizing power, Castro charged that the Batista regime was responsible for the death of twenty thousand Cubans. Yet when the Havana weekly magazine *Bohemia*, which had long been critical of the old order, published at about the same time a list of the victims of official brutality, it could come up with no more than one thousand names. Batista himself maintained that these were primarily "saboteurs and terrorists who were killed in gun battles with the authorities or else in immediate and passionate reprisal by soldiers and policemen who were understandably emotional about seeing their friends and comrades blown to bits." In addition, he asserted, there was the large category of "innocent bystanders who got killed in these bombings and gun battles." This claim may not be entirely accurate either. But it is apparent that while the old order may indeed be responsible for numerous atrocities, their incidence and extent are invariably inflated in order to shock public opinion into revulsion.[3]

Allegations
of Moral Corruption

The revolutionary forces level another charge against the *ancien régime*. Not only is it cruel but it is immoral. There is something faintly ironic in this accusation, to be sure. Ordinarily it is the old order that portrays its opponents as hedonists and materialists, agnostics and libertines. They are denounced for scorning the values of marriage and the family. They believe in free love, casual cohabitation, or even the "communal ownership of women." Yet as the struggle for public opinion intensifies, it is the established system that comes to be perceived as the protector of commercialized vice and sexual license. Despite its professions of lofty moral standards, it is accused of tolerating the exploitation of lower-class womanhood for indecent purposes. Even while the rich and powerful pay lip service to conventional morality, they allegedly seduce the daughters of the poor and oppressed to gratify their obscene lust. The charge arouses a profound feeling of resentment; it offends an elemental collective sense of self-respect. It is designed to incite among the masses an instinctive rage against the established system.

The accusation carries all the more weight because of a strong element of puritanism in the revolutionary ideology. Those who advocate the overthrow of the old order adopt a standard of sexual conduct that is in keeping with their commitment to self-sacrifice. They may not always observe the conventions of traditional marriage, but they discourage licentiousness and vice. The relationship between men and women, they preach, should be based on mutual respect and free consent, not on considerations of gain or advantage. The soldiers fighting against the established system are taught to shun low forms of amusement, to avoid taverns and brothels. Their behavior is usually in sharp contrast to the conduct of the government forces. The self-discipline they display is not only ideologically consistent but politically advantageous. It helps underscore the dissoluteness of the *ancien régime* as opposed to the principled purity of those seeking a new order. It becomes an important weapon in the struggle for public opinion.

This puritanical tone of the rhetoric of revolution is clearly discernible in the instructions given by Ho Chi Minh to his troops in October 1954, as the Vietnam People's Army was about to enter Hanoi in accordance with the Geneva Agreements concluded with the French, a few months earlier:

> Urban life is complicated, many temptations can lead people to stupidity, debauchery and degradation. To avoid these dangerous traps and fulfill the lofty task of the people's army, all our officers and men must bear in mind and correctly carry out the following advice:
> Avoid conceit and self-complacency.
> Abstain from drinking alcohol, gambling, sexual pleasures and opium smoking.
> Let no secrets leak out.
> Abstain from luxury, waste and corruption.
> Respect the people, help them and unite with them.
> Be modest and correct.
> Maintain the purity and simplicity of revolutionary fighters.
> Practice industry, economy, integrity and justice.
> Correctly apply the ten points of discipline.
> Be always vigilant, and conduct self-criticism and criticism to
> make continuous progresses.

There is something ascetic, something almost religious in this emphasis on the moral dimension of the soldier's calling. Gustavus Adolphus and Oliver Cromwell must have addressed their troops in such a tone after a victorious battle won in the name of the one true God.

Judged by this high moral standard, the behavior of the old order seems corrupt and licentious. Not only do the authorities wink at dissoluteness in high places, but they tolerate the debauchery of native women by lewd foreigners. It is this thought, this image of aliens, men of a different nation, culture, and race, gratifying their lust at the expense of the country's womanhood, that is most abhorrent to the popular imagination. It festers and rankles, inflaming public opinion against a system of authority that appears indifferent to such profound social humiliation. And that is why insurrectionary discourse dwells so persistently on the moral degradation of the old order.

In the writings of Ho Chi Minh, the most puritanical of the revolutionary leaders of the twentieth century, the corrupting effect of foreign domination is a constant theme. As early as the 1920s, while he was still an exile in Europe, hoping to enlist the international communist movement in the struggle for his country's liberation, he condemned French rule in Southeast Asia for debauching the native population. "In Cochin-China (French for more than half a century): 51,000 pupils out of a population of 3,500,000 souls. Fortunately, though we lack schools, France lavishes upon us brothels, opium-dens and bars." French imperialism in North Africa was equally degrading. Marshal Lyautey, the proconsul dispatched by the government in Paris to safeguard its interests in Morocco, seemed to believe, according to Ho, that "alcohol, narcotics and prostitutes (public houses [in the protectorate] and brothels grow in number 280 percent every five years) have a greater 'civilizing' value and are more useful in colonization than the platonic Declaration of the Rights of Man and the Citizen." So much for the *mission civilisatrice* of France in the colonial world.

But the most fiery denunciation of the immorality of alien rule appeared in Ho's *French Colonization on Trial*, especially the chapter dealing with "The Martyrdom of Native Women." Here he described in sensational detail how the Vietnamese woman was "protected" from abuse by "our civilizers." She was in fact never safe from the brutality of the foreign oppressor. "In town, in her house, at the market or in the countryside, everywhere she is exposed to ill-treatment from the administrator, the officer, the policeman, the customs officer, the station employee." She had to endure in silence the taunts and insults of those in power. "It isn't rare to hear a European call an Annamese woman *con di* (prostitute) or *bouzou* (monkey). Even in the Central Market in Saigon, a French town so they say, European guards do not hesitate to strike native women with bull's pizzles or truncheons—to make them circulate!"

Still more lurid was his account of the sexual abuse of Vietnamese womanhood by dissolute French colonial administrators: "Customs officers go into native dwellings, *oblige women and young girls to undress completely in front of them and, when they are in the garb of Eve, carry their lewd whims as far as affixing the customs stamp on the body.*" Here was the most shocking insult to patriotic pride, the ultimate proof of national impotence. Ho denounced the system of government that made such indignities possible. "It was said: 'Colonization is theft.' We add: rape and assassinations." To him the struggle against the old order was in essence a struggle for the redemption of his country's honor.[4]

Allegations of American misconduct served the same function in China as allegations of French misconduct in Vietnam. That is, once hostilities against Japan came to an end and the United States became the chief ally of the Kuomintang in the civil war, stories about improper or illegal behavior by American troops began to circulate. Not only newspapers on the left but even those favorable to the government reported numerous instances of reckless driving, robbery, drunkenness, rape, and murder. The United States military authorities, to give them their due, were not deaf to these complaints. They listened, they conducted investigations, and sometimes they even imposed appropriate punishment. Yet incidents of lawlessness seemed to continue and grow.

The climax came with the assault by two American marines on a Chinese girl in Peking on Christmas Eve, 1946. The victim, a student at the university, charged that she had been raped. What made the situation worse was that she did not come from the social class to which most women consorting with foreign soldiers belonged. Her grandfather had been a provincial viceroy and her father was an official in the Communications Ministry. The American consular report on the crime did point out that it was unusual for Chinese girls "of good breeding" to go unaccompanied to "late evening moving pictures." The local authorities, moreover, seeking to allay growing popular outrage, began circulating rumors that she was actually a Communist agent, a member of the Eighth Route Army, who had deliberately set out to create an incident. There were other stories that she was a common streetwalker, that she had known the marines, and that she had been with them for at least three hours before the alleged attack occurred. But the facts of the case could not be suppressed. It became apparent to most Chinese that a young woman from a well-to-do family had been assaulted by debauched foreigners who seemed to assume that all native girls were fair game. To make matters worse, although one of the marines was court-martialed, convicted, and sentenced to ten years' imprisonment, the naval authorities in Washington overturned the verdict a few months later on the grounds that it was difficult to verify the charge of rape and that the political atmosphere had made it impossible for the accused to receive a fair trial.

The effect on public opinion in China was profound. Thousands of university students in more than twenty cities protested against the behavior of American troops, petitioning, demonstrating, and boycotting classes. Many faculty members supported them. The prominent economist Ma Ying-ch'u declared in Shanghai that "the Americans regard China as their colony and the young men . . . should be more outspoken in demanding evacuation of American forces from China." The Communists could scarcely conceal their satisfaction. At a mass meeting in their capital at Yenan, held in support of student strikes in nationalist territory, "Professor Ch'en (Ching-k'un) . . . charged that Chiang Kai-shek, as obsequious invitor of American troops to remain in China, is a legal accessory to the American Marines' criminal assault." Similarly, "Ten Ying-chao (Mme. Chou En-lai) . . . denounced the [Peking] atrocity as a violation not only of a Chinese university student, but also of the national dignity of the Chinese people." She maintained that "this is but one of thousands of atrocities committed by American troops in Kuomintang-held areas."

Even the Nationalist press could not swallow its indignation. An article in the Kuomintang newspaper *Peiping Hsin Pao* acknowledged that "public sentiment was aroused to a fury. At the time we were instructed repeatedly by local authorities to be discreet in publicizing the news." But now silence was no longer possible. "Severe punishment should be meted out to the criminals involved." As a result of the incident, Sino-American friendship would be impaired. "The problem whether American troops should be withdrawn from China will affect major policies of both the Chinese and American governments."

An editorial in the *Peiping Jih Pao*, another Nationalist newspaper, described sympathetically the public outrage provoked by the incident. "This infamous deed has aroused the anger of every Chinese." Young students were demanding that the "criminal perpetrator" of the atrocity receive proper punishment. "Since China is an ally, American soldiers should fully show the spirit of friendship and love. To represent America they should manifest the manners of citizens of a civilized nation." There was a widespread suspicion, moreover, that the United States authorities, "with a view to concealing the infamous deeds of the American soldier," might declare him not guilty. But that would be highly inadvisable. "The eyes of the Chinese people all over the country are watching the trial intently."

Even more surprising was the critical tone of the official *Kuo Min Hsin Pao*, published by the Nationalist Military Council. There was no attempt to conceal its concern that the culprit might succeed in wriggling out of just punishment. "We are afraid that the American Naval Court will only charge 'conduct prejudicial to good conduct and discipline.'" Yet that would never do. "What we are expecting is a solemn and justified declaration of guilty, according to testimony in the American Naval Court." The important thing was not the harshness of the verdict. "It is whether the spirit of government by law which prevails in America will be displayed unreservedly in foreign countries as well." China's pride and dignity were at stake.

Still, by the time the court-martial came to a decision, it had really ceased to matter. The issue was no longer whether an American marine would be punished for assaulting a Chinese woman. Rather, the incident released a flood of resentment at the misconduct of dissolute foreigners and at a national government that tolerated it. Moral outrage combined with popular xenophobia to give the revolutionary forces in China the advantage in the struggle for public opinion. The Communists had won an important propagandistic victory.[5]

Nowhere was the belief that the authorities protected and promoted immorality more widespread than in Cuba. For here commercialized vice had become a major national industry. In Havana alone there were about 2,000 houses of prostitution, some catering to a lower-class clientele, others pandering to the rich and powerful. The police not only winked at this traffic but exploited it. Each *casa* paid graft calculated by local patrolmen from the number of patrons and the level of prices. Thus the humble establishments were expected to pay between 50 and 70 dollars a night, while the richest of all, the Casa Marina, might go as high as 3,000 to 5,000 dollars. No attempt was made to disguise these transactions; they were conducted quite openly in the presence of clients and employees. Indeed, some of the police officers were themselves procurers or drug dealers. As for recruits into the trade, they were frequently *guajiritas,* young peasant girls transported from the countryside, distributed among the establishments of Havana, and initiated into *la vida,* the prostitute's way of life. The price paid for them by the proprietors of bordellos was often considerable, usually depending on their age. A *guajirita* twelve to fifteen years old might bring as much as 1,000 dollars from a wealthy customer. And the chronic poverty of the rural population kept the *casas* in the large cities well-supplied with newcomers.

To many Cubans this commerce in vice seemed simply one of the harsher realities of life, an inescapable condition of the struggle for survival. They accepted it with the same resignation with which they faced hunger, disease, or privation. But there were others who regarded it as a shocking indictment of the existing economic system. Especially among young people of education and means, the social group in which revolutionary movements generally find their most devoted followers, the view prevailed that the sexual exploitation of lower-class womanhood was essentially a result of the corrupt system of authority by which the country was governed. What made the prevalence of prostitution particularly demeaning in their eyes was that it pandered to the appetites of dissolute foreigners. To many of them the underlying cause of the traffic in immorality was not only economic oppression but alien domination or, rather, one was the consequence of the other. They complained that their nation had become "the playground of the United States" or, less euphemistically, "a brothel for the Americans." Xenophobia thus fed resentment of the *ancien régime* in Cuba even more than in China.

Still, here too the political opposition exaggerated the extent to which alien licentiousness contributed to the country's moral degradation. The commerce in vice depended more on native customers than on foreign visitors. Some of the most prodigal patrons came from abroad, to be sure. American tourists in particular frequented the fancier bars, bordellos, and gambling dens. There was rejoicing in the red-light district of Havana, moreover, and a feverish search for new recruits for the *casas* whenever a large warship of the United States Navy arrived in port. Nevertheless, Cubans from various classes of society, but especially the well-to-do, contributed far more to the support of prostitution than all the visitors from Europe or North America. Many of those who opposed the Batista regime recognized that class differences and economic disparities were the true source of institutionalized immorality. Indeed, their ideology said as much. And yet in their rhetorical war against the established system they could not resist the temptation to exploit the xenophobia of the masses. For to the popular mind, the sexual degradation of women from the poorer classes was especially reprehensible for gratifying foreigners rather than natives. The idea that Cuban girls were selling themselves to licentious Americans seemed more abhorrent than the thought of their consorting with their own lusty, fun-seeking countrymen. In Cuba, as in other countries on the eve of a social revolution, the opponents of the old order succeeded in persuading public opinion that the government had betrayed the nation's honor by its blatant immorality.[6]

The Effect
of Economic Xenophobia

Yet of all the offenses for which the opposition indicts the *ancien régime*, the most common is economic exploitation, especially by foreign interests. The atrocities of which the established system stands accused affect, after all, relatively few people, mostly those suspected of sympathy with the enemies of the existing system. Even commercialized vice, though repugnant to national pride and moral decency, has a direct effect on a proportionately small number of women. It leaves the bulk of the population untouched. But poverty is pervasive in all prerevolutionary societies. Many inhabitants have to live from hand to mouth; for them hardship and privation are a daily experience. Hence the argument that their suffering is the result of the greed of those in power sounds reasonable and persuasive. They hear from the opponents of the old order that the rich are battening on the poor, the strong are thriving at the expense of the weak. That seems to them to account for the vast disparities of income and status in existing society. And so the belief begins to spread among the masses that they are the victims of a cruel, unjust economic system.

The denunciation of the rapacity of the *ancien régime* is generally reinforced by an appeal to the xenophobic fears of the lower classes. That is, the authorities are accused of betraying the interests of the workers and peasants to foreign states or, rather, to the bankers and financiers of foreign states. In return for loans, grants, gifts, and bribes, the government allegedly allows aliens to gain a dominant influence over the political and economic policies of the nation. The needs of the people are ignored in order to meet the demands of alien moneylenders, the real masters of the established order. The masses toil to enrich greedy foreigners; the taxes they pay end up in the pockets of international bankers; the laws governing them are dictated from abroad. Only the overthrow of the established system can free them from the stranglehold of financial imperialism.

This indictment is not entirely without foundation, to be sure. The old order, economically weak and backward, eager to modernize and industrialize, is a heavy borrower of capital from more developed countries. And this financial dependence often leads to political dependence as well. Sometimes even the supporters of the *ancien régime* concede privately that their country has become an economic sphere of influence of its creditors. In a confidential report submitted to the czar in 1899, the Russian Minister of Finance S. Y. Witte admitted that in its financial dealings with the West, the empire was in a position similar to that of some overseas colony:

> The economic relations of Russia with western Europe are fully comparable to the relations of colonial countries with their metropolises. The latter consider their colonies as advantageous markets in which they can freely sell the products of their labor and of their industry and from which they can draw with a powerful hand the raw materials necessary for them. This is the basis of the economic power of the governments of western Europe, and chiefly for that end do they guard their existing colonies or acquire new ones. Russia was, and to a considerable extent still is, such a hospitable colony for all industrially developed states, generously providing them with the cheap products of her soil and buying dearly the products of their labor.

What the defenders of the old order acknowledge in private, its critics proclaim in public. The charge that czarism had allowed the economy of Russia to fall under the control of foreign capitalists appeared over and over again in the rhetoric of the Bolsheviks, after the revolution as well as before. As early as 1902 Lenin, commenting on a report concerning the national budget, condemned the government for selling out to French and German bankers. "No one doubts that the Russian people have plenty of 'assets,'" he wrote; "but the greater these assets, the greater the guilt of those who, despite the abundance, conduct the economy by increasing loans and taxation." The regime had demonstrated to the masses that "they should get rid of those who squander their assets, and do so as quickly as possible. . . . The economy of the 'great Russian state' administered by representatives of Rothschild and of Bleichröder—what glittering prospects you open up before us, Mr. Witte!"

Was it coincidence that Lenin used the names of the two best-known Jewish financiers to symbolize the sinister forces of international capitalism? He could just as easily have mentioned some of the big, impersonal banking houses—the Banque de Paris et des Pays-Bas, for instance, or the Berliner Handelsgesellschaft— which were also providing credit to Russia. Or was he, perhaps without fully realizing it, playing on the popular fear of cunning Semitic moneylenders? In any case, when during the First World War he returned to the subject of czarism's economic subservience to the West, there was no longer any suggestion of the exploitative role of Jewish bankers. He did repeat, however, even more forcefully, the charge that alien financial interests were dominating the Russian economy. "Of the approximately 4,000 million rubles making up the 'working' capital of the big banks [of the empire], *more than three-fourths*, more than 3,000 million, belonged to banks which in reality were only 'daughter companies' of foreign banks, of Paris banks . . . and of Berlin banks." Two of the largest financial institutions in the country, the Russian Bank for Foreign Trade and the Saint Petersburg International Commercial Bank, were actually controlled by German capital, the former by the Deutsche Bank and the latter by the Disconto-Gesellschaft. "Naturally, the country which exports capital skims

the cream." For example, "the Berlin Deutsche Bank, before plac-
ing the shares of the Siberian Commercial Bank on the Berlin market, kept them in its portfolio for a whole year, and then sold them
at the rate of 193 for 100, that is, at nearly twice their nominal
value, 'earning' a profit of nearly six million rubles." Those who
had to pay for that profit, however, were the exploited, overtaxed
masses of Russia.

Before the Bolsheviks came to power, economic xenophobia
helped turn public opinion against the old order. Afterward it served
to underscore how much better the new one was. In a series of lectures delivered in 1924, Stalin maintained that "czarist Russia was a
major reserve of Western imperialism, not only in the sense that it
gave free entry to foreign capital, which controlled such basic
branches of Russia's national economy as the fuel and metallurgical
industries, but also in the sense that it could supply the Western imperialists with millions of soldiers." He reminded his listeners of "the
Russian army, fourteen million strong, which shed its blood on the
imperialist fronts to safeguard the staggering profits of the British
and French capitalists."

But czarism was not only "the watchdog of imperialism" in Eastern Europe. It was also "the agent of Western imperialism for
squeezing out of the [Russian] population hundreds of millions by
way of interest and loans obtained in Paris and London, Berlin and
Brussels." The *ancien régime*, moreover, was a loyal ally of "Western
imperialism" in the partition of Turkey, Persia, and China. "Who
does not know that the imperialist war was waged by czarism in alliance with the imperialists of the Entente, and that Russia was an
essential element in that war? That is why the interests of czarism
and of Western imperialism were interwoven and ultimately became merged in a single skein of imperialist interests." The dependence of the old order on loans and investments from Western
Europe had made Russia an economic colony of foreign finance
capitalism.

Although Trotsky was in disagreement with Stalin on most political
questions, on the issue of the czarist government's subservience to
alien moneylenders there was no difference between them. Writing in
exile in the early 1930s, he expressed views indistinguishable from
those of his archrival. "The subjection of [Russian] industries to the

banks," he maintained, "meant . . . their subjection to the western European money market. Heavy industry (metal, coal, oil) was almost wholly under the control of foreign finance capital, which had created for itself an auxiliary and intermediate system of banks in Russia." The situation of light industry was not much better. All in all, foreigners owned about 40 percent of the stock capital in Russia, and in the most important branches of manufacture the proportion was even greater. "We can say without exaggeration that the controlling shares of stock in the Russian banks, plants and factories were to be found abroad." Ownership of the leading industrial and financial enterprises of the nation was thus in the hands of alien capitalists, "who realized on their investment not only the profits drawn from Russia, but also a political influence in foreign parliaments, and so not only did not forward the struggle for Russian parliamentarism, but often opposed it."

This economic subordination, according to Trotsky, explained the decision of the czarist regime to enter the First World War. "The participation of Russia falls somewhere halfway between the participation of France and that of China. Russia paid in this way for her right to be an ally of advanced countries, to import capital and pay interest on it—that is, essentially, for her right to be a privileged colony of her allies." Yet at the same time, by acquiescing in its financial subservience, the imperial government gained the right "to oppress and rob" countries even more backward than its own, countries like Turkey and Persia. Hence "the twofold imperialism of the Russian bourgeoisie had basically the character of an agency for other mightier world powers." Although Russia occupied a position in the hierarchy of states above that of China, "the Russian autocracy on the one hand [and] the Russian bourgeoisie on the other contained features of compradorism, ever more and more clearly expressed." That is, "they lived and nourished themselves upon their connections with foreign imperialism, served it, and without its support could not have survived. . . . The semi-comprador Russian bourgeoisie had world-imperialistic interests in the same sense in which an agent working on percentages lives by the interests of his employer." Only the overthrow of czarism could have freed the nation from its economic bondage.[7]

Myths and Realities
of Foreign Investment

How much truth is there in the contention that before the revolution Russia was a captive of international finance capitalism? A fair
amount, no doubt, though not nearly as much as critics of the old
order claim. While the government and the economy were indeed
dependent on foreign loans and investments, the degree of that de-
pendency has often been overstated. Defending his policy of rapid
industrialization, Witte pointed out around the turn of the century
that "the extent of the influx of foreign capital into Russia is usually
much exaggerated." The number of foreign corporations founded
in 1896 was 22 with a basic capital of 80,000,000 rubles, while in
1897 the number was 15 with 55,000,000 rubles in basic capital.
"Even if one adds foreign capital invested in Russian corporations
(12,000,000 rubles in 1896 and 22,000,000 in 1897) one finds that, all
together, foreign capital does not amount to more than one-third of
the capital of all joint-stock companies formed annually."

As Witte pointed out, moreover, "the corporation is still something
very strange and unpopular with Russian entrepreneurs." The form
of business organization they preferred was the personal enterprise
or, to a lesser extent, the family partnership. "A considerable part of
Russian capital is invested in such enterprises; the number of these
formed every year equals that of the joint-stock companies." It would
thus appear, he argued, that of the total capital invested annually in
the development of Russian industry, foreign sources accounted for
hardly more than one-fifth or perhaps even one-sixth. "Ninety-two
million rubles in 1897; 77,000,000 rubles in 1897; 376,000,000 rubles
all together since 1887—do these statistics prove that there is a danger for our vast Russian economy? Can our productive forces be sold
at such a figure?" Investments from abroad were no more than a
"leaven," whose importance derived not from their volume but
from the energy they galvanized in "our sluggish industrial community." Their conspicuousness was far out of proportion to their size.
"Foreign capital, five times smaller than Russian, is nonetheless
more visible; it arouses attention because it carries with it better

knowledge, more experience, and more initiative." But to assert that it controlled the economy of the empire was absurd.

Almost a hundred years later, this assessment of the role of international finance in the economic development of Russia still holds up. Although there was a great deal of foreign investment, most of it was concentrated in the highly visible growth sectors: mining, metallurgy, engineering, municipal development comprising mostly public utilities and urban transportation, and credit institutions such as banks and insurance companies. Textiles, on the other hand, the most important traditional sector of industrial production, attracted less than 9 percent of total capital imports.

Even according to the calculations of Soviet scholars, the percentage of the entire common stock in banks and corporations operating in Russia that was owned by foreigners rose from 25 in 1890 to 26 in 1895 and 37 in 1900, before dropping to 35 in 1905 and then rising again to 38 in 1910 and 41 in 1913. The share of foreign capital in industry was somewhat greater than in finance, but even there most investments came from domestic sources. Foreigners owned 26 percent of total common-stock capital in Russian industrial enterprises in 1890, 27 percent in 1893, 45 percent in 1900, 47 percent in 1906, 46 percent in 1909, and 38 percent in 1916. It becomes apparent that the most rapid growth of investments from abroad occurred during the 1890s, and that by the time of the First World War the proportion of foreign capital in Russian industry and finance had leveled off at less than half.

International financiers, moreover, were attracted primarily to a few highly visible branches of heavy industry, ignoring to a large extent older, less mechanized and concentrated enterprises. Thus foreign capital accounted for 65 percent of the total invested in Russian mining and metallurgy in 1890, 61 percent in 1893, and 72 percent in 1900. In engineering and machinery the percentage rose from 50 in 1890 and 1893 to 71 in 1900. But in paper manufacture investments from abroad played a relatively minor role: 9 percent of the total in 1890, 7 percent in 1893, 20 percent in 1900, and 20 percent in 1915. In the manufacture of textiles the share of foreign capital rose rapidly at first from 13 percent in 1890 to 26 in 1893, but then fell to 20 percent in 1900 and 21 in 1915. And in a traditional, plodding branch of production like food processing, investors abroad showed almost no interest: 8 percent of total capital in 1890, 8 in 1893, 7 in 1900, and 8 in 1915. In short, while foreign finance had a controlling share in the ownership of a few important Russian industries, in others its influence was negligible or nonexistent.

A balance sheet of the penetration of the Russian economy by international capitalism which was published in the Soviet Union just before the Second World War offered little support for the extravagant claims of many opponents of czarism. It showed that while investments from abroad predominated in some branches of industry on the eve of the Bolshevik revolution—in mining, for example, with 90 percent of total capital, and in chemicals with 50 percent—there were other branches, like metal smelting, with 42 percent, wood processing, with 37 percent, and textiles, with 28 percent, in which foreign financiers played a subordinate part. All in all, the international capital invested in industrial enterprises in Russia in 1916–17 was 1,749,000,000 rubles out of a total of close to 5,000,000,000 rubles, accounting for approximately 34 percent. This seems to be the best general estimate of the degree of control over the economy of czarist Russia exercised by international finance capitalism.[8]

Does it justify the charge that the wealth of the nation had fallen under the domination of alien bankers? And what about the claim that the entry of Russia into the First World War was a result of the sinister influence of French and British moneylenders? Little factual basis exists for such assertions. To be sure, investors abroad provided much of the capital in Russian industry and finance, enough to lend credibility to the denunciation of the *ancien régime* for selling out to international financiers. But the actual extent of foreign economic control was vastly inflated by half-truths, rumors, myths, and fabrications. There is even less foundation for the charge made by the Bolsheviks that Russia had been dragged into the First World War by the machinations of her allies and creditors in the West. In fact, the diplomatic crisis of the summer of 1914 was far more a result of czarist expansionist policy in the Balkans than of financial aggression by France and England. But in the struggle for public opinion that preceded the overthrow of the old order, the accusation that the government was enriching alien capitalists at the expense of the Russian masses helped prepare the way for a revolution.

The theme of the established system's betrayal of the national interest to foreign financiers appears repeatedly in insurrectionary rhetoric, and in roughly the same proportions of fact and fiction. In China, for example, it was used with great effectiveness not only against the old imperial regime but against the new republican one as well. That is, the authority of both the Manchus around the turn of the century and the Kuomintang forty years later was undermined by the persistent charge that the impoverishment of the lower classes was a result of the control that alien capitalism had gained over the country's economy. And yet, although foreign investors did provide much of the capital for Chinese industry and finance, its relative importance was even less than in Russia. In 1933 enterprises owned by natives accounted for 78 percent of the gross value of factory output in China proper, excluding Manchuria, while the proportion of all workers employed in those enterprises was greater still, 83 percent. This preponderance of indigenous industrial production is all the more remarkable because the share of the total capitalization of manufacturing establishments in China owned by native investors was only 37 percent. And that raises the question whether excessive attention to capitalization does not tend to exaggerate the extent of foreign ownership of industry by underrating the importance of light manufacture, primarily owned by natives, in which the volume of investment is small and labor can to a considerable degree be substituted for capital.

Even in large-scale industry the role of international finance was diminishing during the period of the republic. Whereas in 1913 coal mines owned by Chinese accounted for only 7 percent of total output, by 1936 their share had risen to 34 percent. Native factories manufactured 57 percent of all cotton yarn in 1919 and 71 percent in 1933. Between 1923 and 1936 the percentage of the country's electric power produced by Chinese companies almost doubled from 23 to 45. Only in the manufacture of cotton cloth did foreign mills enlarge their share of total output somewhat from 59 percent in 1919 to 64 percent in 1936.

International investment in Chinese industry, moreover, was

largely concentrated in four areas: coal mining, cotton yarn and cloth, electric power, and the manufacture of cigarettes, hardly one of the major components of an industrializing economy. Besides, the volume of capital imports was relatively low, since most forms of production were beyond the reach of foreign finance. Investments from abroad totaled about 733,000,000 dollars in 1902, 1,610,000,000 dollars in 1914, 3,243,000,000 in 1931, and 3,483, 000,000 in 1936. On a per capita basis, estimating the population of the country at 430,000,000 in 1914 and 500,000,000 in 1936, the figures for those two years were 3.75 dollars and 6.97 dollars respectively. Such modest amounts were well below the per capita foreign investment in other "underdeveloped" regions. For India, for example, the figure in 1938 was 20 dollars, for Africa, excluding the Union of South Africa, it was 23 dollars, and for Latin America 86 dollars. By a rough calculation, the net inflow of private capital from abroad accounted in the early 1930s for not quite 1 percent of the gross national product of China and for perhaps 20 percent of total investment.

In short, the very backwardness of the country's system of manufacture, its continuing dependence on small family shops and artisan establishments, insulated it to a large extent against outside control. Although the alien presence was highly visible, especially in the modern sector of production, that sector was only a small part of the entire economy. Despite the steady growth of both native and foreign large-scale enterprise, neither was of major importance under the imperial or even the republican regime. If all the business ventures owned, controlled, operated, or influenced by foreigners had been nationalized in 1915, and if all the public and private debts owed to international creditors had been cancelled, the resultant surplus available for economic and social development would have been minuscule. Indeed, as late as the 1930s, close to two-thirds of gross domestic product still originated in agriculture, which was almost entirely free of financial control from abroad.

Foreign manufacturing companies in China undoubtedly benefited from their extraterritorial status, their exemption from some direct taxation, their freedom from the heavy-handed supervision of the native bureaucracy, their access to the international capital market, and sometimes their better management and superior technology. But their privileged position, their superiority and conspicuousness, also generated a nationalist backlash expressed in campaigns to "buy Chinese" and in boycotts against goods imported from abroad or produced by foreign plants in China. Anti-imperialist popular sentiment also accounted in all probability for a higher incidence of labor disputes in factories owned by foreigners than natives. Yet to the extent that such traditional sectors of the economy as the handicraft trades were undermined by industrialization, companies owned by Chinese, which served chiefly the rural market, were far more responsible than foreign mills, which catered above all to relatively well-to-do urban customers.

The statistical evidence suggests, moreover, that not only were manufacturing enterprises that belonged to natives growing at least as rapidly as those owned by foreigners, but that a gradual increase occurred in the Chinese share of capitalization and output in commerce and finance as well as industry. The most important long-term consequence of international investment in China was probably the spread of modern industrial technology in the form of superior machinery, organization, and technical skill. The "demonstration effect" of economic imperialism was responsible, in part at least, for the growth of native banking houses and insurance companies, not to mention native industrial plants and commercial ventures. The final verdict regarding the effect of Western finance capitalism on the economy of China is by no means clear-cut.[9]

Its role in Cuba was even more ambiguous. On the face of it, there appears to be little doubt that prior to the Castro regime the island's economic development, especially in agriculture, was controlled by foreign capital, most of it American. At the beginning of 1960 the total amount of North American investment in the Cuban economy was estimated at 1,000,000,000 dollars. It had increased considerably during the preceding decade, moreover, and become the second largest in Latin America, exceeded only by the capital exported from the United States to Venezuela. International finance was particularly important in the growing and refining of sugar. Mills owned by Americans accounted for about half of total production after the First World War; by the time of the Second World War their share was 56 percent. Of the 174 sugar refineries in the country in 1940, 67 were the property of citizens of the United States, 55 of Cuba, 33 of Spain, and 10 of Canada. Here at first glance, seemed to be a classic case of a semicolonial region subject to alien financial control.

The reality of the economic situation in Cuba, however, was more complex than its appearance. First of all, although direct United States investment in the island increased substantially in some sectors between 1929 and 1958—from 9,000,000 to 270,000,000 dollars in petroleum and mining, from 45,000,000 to 80,000,000 dollars in manufacturing, and from 290,000,000 to 386,000,000 dollars in services—in what had been the most important sector of all, agriculture, there was a precipitous drop from 575,000,000 to 265,000,000 dollars. The proportion of American capital in Cuba devoted to agricultural production declined from 62 percent in the late 1920s to 41 percent in 1950 and 32 percent in 1957. The percentage devoted to industrial output during the same period rose, to be sure, from 5 to 8 and then 12 percent. Yet the total amount of direct United States investment grew slowly, more slowly than the economy as a whole, from 919,000,000 dollars in 1929 to 1,001,000,000 dollars in 1958. The tendency of the island's financial development was clearly toward "Cubanization."

Nor was the overall effect of foreign capital in Cuba simply to drain away the island's wealth for the enrichment of alien investors. American companies spent about 730,000,000 dollars in the country in 1957. Of this amount, 70,000,000 went for taxes, accounting for nearly 20 percent of the national budget, 170,000,000 was spent on salaries and wages, and 490,000,000 covered the purchase of local goods and services. At the same time Cuba received a total of 361,000,000 dollars in foreign exchange as a result of American investment: 273,000,000 in payment for exports and 88,000,000 from the inflow of capital from the United States. Against this there was an outflow of 156,000,000 dollars: 56,000,000 for interest and profits, and 100,000,000 for imports of machinery and raw materials. About 85 percent of the entire output of American industry on the island, moreover, was sold on the Cuban market.

As for the effect of international finance on native labor, in the last years of the Batista dictatorship companies owned by citizens of the United States employed about 160,000 people, 90 percent of them Cubans, in a work force totaling roughly 2,000,000. Furthermore, these companies, the most modern and efficient in the country, paid substantially higher wages than those offered by native entrepreneurs. The agreements they concluded with local trade unions were acknowledged by the Cuban labor movement to be among the most favorable. Thus here too there was a kind of "demonstration effect" by which foreign capital helped improve the skill and productivity of domestic industry, commerce, and banking.

Finally, the dependence of the economy of Cuba on American financing was to a large extent a result not of the insufficiency of native capital but its distribution. That is, investment from the United States has been estimated at no more than approximately 5 percent of the total Cuban valuation before the Castro revolution. Hence the bulk of that investment could have been easily paid back with native assets outside the country. The trouble was that many wealthy Cubans preferred to send their money abroad, to North America or Western Europe, where they felt more secure against political and social upheaval. From the point of view of the nation's economic development, to be sure, it made little difference whether the central role of international finance was a result of the usurpation or maldistribution of domestic resources. In either case, the country had undoubtedly become dependent on the influx of capital from the United States. Still, the argument that the impoverishment of important groups in Cuban society resulted from the greed of alien moneylenders was largely unfounded.[10]

Insurrectionary rhetoric, however, feeds on pathos and hyperbole, not hard, sober reality. In the war of words preceding the outbreak of a revolution, the old order ends up convicted of cruelty, corruption, and rapacity. Its condemnation results in part, no doubt, from its misdeeds. For the established system is in fact guilty of conniving at police brutality and the commercialization of vice. It tolerates or protects the grip of international finance on the country's economy. But its shortcomings are magnified, its offenses sensationalized. Public opinion turns against the *ancien régime* not only because it has transgressed, but because it has declined. It has lost its moral authority, its sacred legitimation. Once the masses begin to desert the old order, no charge seems too outrageous, no rumor too shocking to be believed. They grow increasingly convinced of the inherent wickedness of the established system because they want to be convinced. After all, the greater its depravity, the more justifiable their defection. Their revulsion against the *ancien régime* becomes in time as profound as their faith had once been.

The Revolutionary Promise
of Democracy

Those who advocate revolution, however, are not content to rest their case on the iniquity of the old order. They proclaim that a new era of justice and freedom is dawning, that society is about to experience a glorious rebirth. The oppression of the weak by the strong, the exploitation of the poor by the rich, will finally cease. The mighty will be humbled and the evildoers punished. Those who toil will be rewarded, those who hunger fed, those who suffer comforted. The tyrannies and indignities that had been the daily lot of the lower classes will come to an end. And all of this will be achieved in accordance with the will of the people. Coercion and intimidation are the chosen weapons of the *ancien régime*. The new order will base its authority on democratic principles guaranteeing political freedom to all.

Hence every insurrectionary movement, during the period of its struggle against the established system, declares that once it is in power, government policies will be determined by the wishes of the majority expressed in free elections. This assurance echoes and reechoes in the rhetoric of revolution. In Russia it took the form of a demand for a democratically chosen constituent assembly. The second congress of the Social Democratic Workers Party, meeting in Brussels and London in the summer of 1903, offered support to "any opposition or revolutionary movement directed against the existing social and political order in Russia," urging as a first step "*the overthrow of the autocracy and the calling of a constituent assembly freely elected by the whole people.*" Although this program was debated at considerable length and amended in some detail, in the end only one member opposed its adoption.

The call for a democratically elected constituent assembly remained part of the party platform until the Bolshevik seizure of power. Even the fall of czarism did not seem to weaken the party's

commitment to political democracy. In March 1917 a manifesto published by the Russian Bureau of the Bolshevik Central Committee
urged the formation of a "provisional revolutionary government"
that would establish a republic, introduce the eight-hour day, order
the confiscation of large estates, and convoke a constituent assembly
elected by universal suffrage and secret ballot. At the same time the
party newspaper *Pravda*, which had just resumed publication after
being suppressed at the outbreak of the war, denounced the newly
formed provisional government as "a government of capitalists and
landowners," proposing instead that the Petrograd Society convene
a constituent assembly to establish a "democratic republic."

Lenin himself, on his return to Russia a month later, still believed apparently that a constituent assembly remained an essential part of the
bourgeois revolution that had not yet run its course. The Bolshevik
conference in Petrograd at the end of April declared that both the soviets and the constituent assembly were possible sources of political
power, without choosing between them. Indeed, until November the
Bolsheviks, like all other radical groups, continued to demand a constituent assembly and to criticize the provisional government for delaying
its convocation, seeing no inconsistency between this demand and the
simultaneous call for "all power to the soviets."[11]

In China the opponents of the established system expressed their
commitment to democratic principles even more clearly, advocating
civil rights as well as free elections. In its first manifesto of June 10,
1922, the recently founded Communist party included among "our
most immediate aims" the introduction of "general suffrage" and the
"freedom of assembly, speech and press; annulment of laws for safeguarding of 'public order' by police; [and] freedom to strike." There
were even demands for "revision of the entire Law Code with immediate abolition of the death penalty and physical torture," as well as
for recognition of the "equality of the rights of men and women." A
month later the second congress of the party repeated the pledge to
work for "the achievement of a genuine democratic republic" and
the establishment of "absolute freedom of speech, assembly, publication, association, and strike."

As the conflict between the Kuomintang and the Communists intensified, the latter avowed their faith in the democratic process
more emphatically. In 1936 Mao Tse-tung declared in an interview

with Edgar Snow that "we will therefore support a parliamentary form of representative Government, an anti-Japanese salvation Government, a Government which protects and supports all popular patriotic groups." If such a free republican regime were formed, "the Chinese Soviets will become a part of it." In the meantime, they would introduce in the areas under their control "measures for a democratic parliamentary form of Government."

In 1940 Mao again insisted that "as far as political power is concerned, . . . we do not favor one-party dictatorship either by the Communist Party or by any other party. . . . Anybody may take part in the work of the government. . . . Every political party or groups shall have the right to exist and carry on its activities under the anti-Japanese political power."

Finally, in 1945, only a few months before the Japanese surrender, he tried once more to dispel any remaining doubts about his adherence to a democratic form of government. "Some people are suspicious and think that once in power, the Communist Party will follow Russia's example and establish the dictatorship of the proletariat and a one-party system. Our answer is that a new-democratic state based on an alliance of the democratic classes is different in principle from a socialist state under the dictatorship of the proletariat." During the stage of "New Democracy," China could not in any case establish a one-class dictatorship and a one-party government, so that the Communists would be shortsighted even to try. "We have no reason for refusing to co-operate with all political parties, social groups and individuals." In brief, "the Chinese system for the present stage is being shaped by the present stage of Chinese history, and for a long time to come there will exist a special form of state and political power, a form that is distinguished from the Russian system but is perfectly necessary and reasonable for us, namely, the new democratic form of state and political power based on the alliance of the democratic classes." As the Communists approached their showdown with the Kuomintang, their protestations of loyalty to democracy grew louder and louder.[12]

In Southeast Asia the opponents of the old order also insisted that their goals would be achieved under a system of government committed to civil rights and free elections. The constitution of the Democratic Republic of Vietnam, which a national assembly convened by Ho Chi Minh adopted in November 1946 in Hanoi, included in the section on "The Duties and Rights of Citizens" a solemn declaration that "Vietnamese citizens enjoy: freedom of speech, freedom of the press, freedom of assembly and meeting, freedom of religion, [and] freedom to reside and travel in the country or to go abroad." It contained assurances, moreover, that "Vietnamese citizens may not be arrested and detained except under the law, and their residence and correspondence are inviolable," and even the pledge that "the rights of property and possession of Vietnamese citizens are guaranteed." Similarly, the program of the Lien Viet, which combined with the Viet Minh in 1951 to form the United National Front of Vietnam, granted to all citizens "political and social-economic rights," including "the rights of man, such as freedom of political beliefs and religious liberty, freedom of choice of residence and of movement; political rights, such as the right to elect and be elected, to take part in the government of the nation, and other democratic freedoms, such as freedom of speech, press, organization, assembly, etc.," not to mention "economic rights, such as private enterprise, personal property and inheritance."

After the defeat of the French in northern Vietnam, the call for the introduction of democratic reforms also began to be heard in the political discourse of the revolutionary movement in the south. The "Manifesto and Program" of the National Liberation Front of South Vietnam adopted in 1960 proclaimed its resolve to create "a broad and progressive democracy." Four major steps were to be taken toward the achievement of that goal:

1. To abolish the current constitution of the Ngo Dinh Diem dictatorial administration—lackey of the United States. To elect a new National Assembly through universal suffrage.
2. To promulgate all democratic freedoms: freedom of expression, of the press, of assembly, of association, of movement, etc. To guarantee freedom of belief; to do away with discrimination against any religion on the part of the State. To grant freedom of action to the patriotic political parties and mass organizations, irrespective of their political tendencies.
3. To grant general amnesty to all political detainees, dissolve all concentration camps under any form whatsoever. To abolish fascist [and]

antidemocratic laws. To permit the return of all these who had to flee abroad due to the U.S.-Diem regime.

4. To strictly ban all illegal arrests and imprisonments, tortures and corporal punishment.

There was nothing ambiguous about this declaration of loyalty to democracy.

The program adopted in 1968 by the Vietnamese Alliance of National, Democratic, and Peace Forces, an organization sympathetic to the National Liberation Front of South Vietnam, sounded equally forthright. It promised "to establish a truly democratic and free republican regime; and to organize general elections in accordance with the principles of equality, universal, direct suffrage, and a secret ballot in order to elect a constituent National Assembly that truly represents the people." The purpose of such an assembly would be to frame "a democratic Constitution" defining the conditions for establishing and organizing "a healthy and truly democratic state structure" resting on a "broad national coalition." Thereafter "all citizens will enjoy equality in all respects." In addition, "the people will enjoy all truly democratic freedoms: freedom of speech, freedom of the press, freedom of religious belief, freedom of movement, freedom of assembly, freedom of association, freedom to travel abroad and so forth." Everyone, regardless of class or party, would be secure against the arbitrary exercise of government power. "There will be no discriminatory treatment of any citizen. Inviolability of the human person, freedom of residence and secrecy of correspondence will be respected for all citizens." The promise of civic liberty was a direct challenge to the established dictatorial system in South Vietnam.[13]

Still, no revolutionary movement could match the Cuban in solemn pledges of democratization. During the period of guerrilla warfare, Castro never seemed to tire of assurances that dictatorial power was the farthest thing from his mind. In a manifesto published in the summer of 1957, he declared that once victory had been achieved, "the provisional government will hold general elections for all offices of the state, the provinces, and the municipalities at the end of a year, [and] power will be given immediately to the elected candidates." The triumph of the revolution, moreover, would lead to other democratic reforms:

a. Immediate freedom for all political, civil, and military prisoners. b. Absolute guarantee of freedom of information, of the spoken and written press, and of all the individual and political rights guaranteed by the Constitution. c. Designation of provisional mayors in all the municipalities after consultation with the civic institutions of the locality. d. Suppression of embezzlement in all its forms and adoption of measures that tend to increase the efficiency of all state agencies. e. Establishment of the civil service on a career basis. f. Democratization of labor politics, promoting free elections in all unions and industrial federations.

Were not these proposals fair and reasonable? Early in 1958, in an article published in *Coronet* magazine under the title "Why We Fight," Castro complained of widespread "misconceptions about my ambitions and those of our movement." He was disappointed that "we have been often accused of plotting to replace military dictatorship with revolutionary dictatorship." Indeed, "nothing has been so frequently misunderstood as our [political and] economic program." All he wanted was to bring freedom to Cuba.

In the summer of 1958, less than six months before the overthrow of the old order, Castro reiterated, this time more laconically, his commitment to political liberty. It was important, to start with, that those opposed to the Batista regime adopt "a common strategy to defeat the dictatorship by means of armed insurrection" supported by "a great general strike on the civilian front." Once that had been accomplished, the process of civic reconstruction could begin. First of all, "guiding our nation, after the tyrant's fall, to a normal state of affairs, a brief provisional government will be formed to establish full constitutional and democratic rights." And then, "a minimum governmental program will be formed to guarantee the punishment of those who are guilty of crimes, workers' rights, fulfillment of international agreements, public order, peace, freedom, as well as the economic and political progress of the Cuban people." Although this declaration was not quite as detailed as some of the earlier ones, its pledge of democracy seemed quite clear.[14]

How sincere are all such promises? Do they spring out of inner conviction or political expediency? In the light of what happens after the victory of the revolution, it is tempting to dismiss them as little more than propaganda, a stratagem in the struggle for public opinion. Yet in this case too much skepticism may be almost as misleading as blind faith. For it is apparent that those who lead the opposition against the established system by and large believe what they are saying, if not entirely, then at least in part. Their experience teaches them that intimidation and oppression are essentially the political means by which the old order maintains itself in power. They have seen their followers hounded, imprisoned, and executed by the authority of the state. They themselves have often been forced into exile because of their denunciation of political and social injustice. Hence it is logical for them to assume that once the *ancien régime* has been defeated, the need for government coercion will cease. The masses, having been liberated by the revolutionary movement, will naturally tend to support the new order. There will therefore no longer be any reason for despotic rule. The establishment of political freedom can only facilitate the reconstruction of society initiated by the overthrow of the *ancien régime.*

And yet, despite the avowed belief that democracy will help the revolutionary movement, a few lingering doubts always seem to remain. What would happen if the masses, stupefied by centuries of ignorance and superstition, failed to see the benefits of the political program of the new order? What if they were misled by reactionary demagogues or religious fanatics into rejecting measures that are in their own best interest? Is the establishment of a just social system to be made dependent on the vagaries of public opinion? Is the victory of the revolution, won with so much blood and sacrifice, to be jeopardized by shifting party politics and ephemeral parliamentary majorities? Such are the questions that trouble the opponents of the established system, and that is why, despite their public commitment to democracy, they generally leave room in their pronouncements for unexpected circumstances, for special contingencies.

Thus in 1905, only a few months after the third congress of the Russian Social Democratic Workers Party had called for the convening by secret ballot of a constituent assembly on the basis of universal, equal, and direct suffrage, Lenin derided those who thought that "a constituent assembly can be generated spontaneously." It was naive to imagine that such an assembly "will be immaculately brought forth by the people themselves, who will not defile themselves with any 'intermediary' by way of a government, even a provisional, even a revolutionary one." Only visionaries would assume that "this will be birth 'without original sin,' by the pure method of general elections with no 'Jacobin' struggle for power, with no defilement of the holy cause through betrayal by bourgeois representative assemblies, and even without any coarse midwives, who hitherto in this profane, sinful, and unclean world had punctually appeared on the scene every time the old society was pregnant with a new one." The idea was "insane," for "without an armed uprising a constituent assembly is a phantasm, a phrase, a lie, a . . . talking shop." To Lenin the constituent assembly could not be convoked until a popular uprising had first overthrown the *ancien régime* and an insurrectionary provisional government had been established. Its function, in other words, would not be to create a new political order in place of the old, but to ratify the reorganization of state and society that the revolution had already inaugurated.

Mao Tse-tung was also convinced that the "New Democracy" he preached did not include the right to oppose the fundamental reforms that the revolutionary movement was fighting to introduce in China. Early in the Second World War, commemorating the anniversary of the founding of the Communist party, he declared that "we stand for united front organs of political power," for the participation in public life of "all political parties and groups, [of] people in all walks of life and all armed forces." This meant that "anybody may take part in the work of the government so long as he is not in favor of capitulation or is not an anti-Communist." Shortly before the surrender of Japan, he again disavowed any intention of establishing a "one-party system." And yet, "beyond all doubt, our system of New Democracy will be built under the leadership of the proletariat and of the Communist Party." Clearly, the freedom he advocated could never tolerate efforts by supporters of the old order to retain power.

Here and there some leader of the revolution will even admit, though always afterward, that his acceptance of democracy had been only a subterfuge to win support, a device to be cast aside after serving its purpose. Che Guevara wrote, following the fall of the Batista regime, that the "Sierra Maestra Manifesto" of July 12, 1957, with its pledge of political freedom, to which Castro had assented, was just an expedient. "We were not satisfied with the commitment, but it was necessary; at the time, it was progressive. It could never last beyond any moment that would represent an obstacle for the development of the revolutionary movement. In this matter, the enemy helped us to break the uncomfortable bonds and gave us the opportunity to show the people what their real intentions were." The goal of the revolution simply could not be made hostage to declarations and manifestos. "We were aware that this was a minimal program, limiting our own efforts, but we had to recognize that it was impossible to impose our will from the Sierra Maestra; for a long period of time we would have to depend upon a whole series of 'friends' who were trying to use our military strength and the people's great trust in Fidel for the Machiavellian maneuvers, and above all, to maintain imperialist domination of Cuba, through the importing bourgeoisie, closely linked with the United States owners." Hence "to us, the declaration was simply a short rest period on our march forward." The creation of a new social system was too important to be shackled by documents or speeches.[15]

Yet whether sincere or disingenuous, the promise of democracy that the revolutionary movement makes prior to its seizure of power helps win popular support. The old order, divested of its moral legitimation, discredited by its military weakness, is increasingly perceived as cruel, immoral, venal, and oppressive. Those who oppose it, on the other hand, seem committed to liberty and justice, they appear to stand for compassion, decency, economic independence, and civic freedom. By the time the two sides confront one another in their decisive encounter, a drastic shift in mass loyalties has taken place. Obedience to traditional authority has been replaced by faith in a new social order. The *ancien régime*, isolated, demoralized, has ceased to be capable of self-defense. Victory in the struggle for public opinion thus not only precedes but predetermines victory in the struggle for political power.

CHAPTER 4

The Overthrow
of the Old Order

The Strategy
of Collective Dissidence

The fall of the *ancien régime* is brought about by a revolutionary coalition that has been steadily gaining strength at the expense of the established system. This coalition is sometimes a formal alliance of several political parties and programs, sometimes a tacit agreement among diverse opposition groups and ideologies. It includes moderates as well as radicals, occasionally even a few disgruntled or opportunistic conservatives. The ultimate objective of each of the participants remains as a rule deliberately vague or ambiguous. For the goals of some are essentially incompatible with those of others. What holds the coalition together is only a common hostility to the established system. Each member organization has its own grievances against the status quo; each hopes that once the existing government has been overthrown, its own aims will be achieved. There are thus important underlying contradictions within the opposition to the *ancien régime*. But for the time being they are subordinated to a collective purpose: the overthrow of a corrupt, tyrannical old order and the creation by democratic means of a better one.

The coalition that effects the downfall of the established system rests sometimes on a formal compact, an explicit program defining the objectives to which each of the participants subscribes, at least as the first step toward the realization of an ultimate objective. At other times there is only an implicit understanding that the various groups opposed to the *ancien régime* will play down their incompatible demands. In either case, little agreement exists among them regarding what will happen once the revolution succeeds in toppling the old order. There is only the faith that some better, freer, more compassionate form of government will replace the discredited established system. The participants in the coalition are forced by the circumstances of their struggle to emphasize objectives on which there is general concurrence: the establishment of political democracy, the elimination of bureaucratic corruption, the introduction of economic reform, and the improvement of social welfare. This appearance of a common cause is maintained until the *ancien régime* finally falls. Only after the revolution has been victorious do the underlying differences and incompatibilities rise to the surface.

This pattern is not as apparent in Russia as in most other countries going through a revolution, because there the radicals declared openly that their program was fundamentally opposed to that of the moderates. The Bolsheviks in particular emphasized the theoretical distinction between their objectives and those of democratic bourgeois parties as well as rival proletarian movements. Weak and isolated, they were afraid of being overshadowed by the larger, more influential participants in the opposition to czarism. Their boldness was a result not of confidence but insecurity. They sought to disguise their doubts by a show of self-assurance; they hoped to compensate for their lack of strength by a display of defiance. Their refusal to join formally any political coalition against the *ancien régime* was a way of maintaining their identity, a form of self-preservation. It became a condition of their survival as an independent organization.

Yet the radicals were prepared, not only in practice but even in theory, to collaborate with the moderates in resisting the old order. The rhetoric of the Bolsheviks was always more uncompromising than their policy. Thus the second congress of the Russian Social Democratic Labor Party declared in 1903 that "social democracy must support the bourgeoisie in so far as it is revolutionary or even oppositional in its struggle with czarism." Although the party was obliged "to unmask before the proletariat the limited and inadequate nature of the bourgeois movement for liberation whenever these limitations and inadequacies are evident," it should also welcome

"the awakening of political consciousness in the Russian bourgeoisie." Hence, "in striving to achieve its immediate goals," the RSDLP
would support any resistance movement directed against "the existing social and political order in Russia," while rejecting "all reformist
projects involving any broadening or strengthening of police or bureaucratic tutelage over the toiling classes." The party remained convinced that "the complete, consistent, and lasting realization of [the]
political and social changes" it advocated could only be achieved by
overthrowing the autocracy and convoking a freely elected constituent assembly.

This meant in practice that the socialists were willing to enter into
a temporary alliance with the democrats in election campaigns
where otherwise conservative candidates were likely to prevail. In
1906 an "All-Russian Conference" of the RSDLP meeting in
Tammerfors in Finland declared that in voting for the Second Duma,
"the Social Democratic Party everywhere stands on an independent
party platform." And yet, "if during the course of the election campaign there appears to be a danger that the lists of the right-wing
parties will win, local agreements are permitted with revolutionary
and democratic opposition parties in accordance with local conditions and under the general supervision of the central [party] institutions." The statement concluded, almost as an afterthought, with the
ritual reminder that "party candidates and organizations are absolutely forbidden to commit themselves to any concessions of principle with respect to the other parties entering into the agreement."

The readiness of the conference of 1906 to collaborate with moderates might be ascribed to the fact that the Mensheviks had a majority at Tammerfors. But the conference of 1912 which met in
Prague, though firmly under the control of the Bolsheviks, adopted
a similar strategy for the forthcoming elections to the Fourth Duma.
"In cases of a [runoff] ballot," it declared, "agreements may be concluded with the bourgeois democratic parties against the liberals,
and then with the liberals against all the governmental parties."
Such agreements could take the form of "the compilation of common lists of electors for one or several cities proportional to the number of votes cast in the first stage of the elections." Only in the case of
five major cities with a large working-class population—Saint
Petersburg, Moscow, Riga, Odessa, and Kiev—did the conference

insist that "because of the clear absence of any [reactionary] Black Hundred threat," interparty agreements, even in the event of a runoff, "are allowable only with democratic groups against liberals."

Until the outbreak of the revolution in 1917, there was thus a loose, informal coalition of moderates and radicals in Russia directed toward the overthrow of the old order. Each of the participating political groups believed that the end of czarism was essential for the realization of its goals. To the moderates the fall of the *ancien régime* meant an end to the revolutionary movement with the inauguration of a new, enlightened system of authority based on individual liberty and parliamentary government. To the radicals it meant the beginning of a relentless class struggle to achieve a socialist form of polity and economy for which bourgeois democracy would prepare the way. To the former the downfall of autocracy was an end in itself; to the latter it was a means of attaining more important objectives. Although they were both willing to join forces in opposition to the status quo, their underlying reasons were not only different but incompatible.

Lenin defined the political strategy of the Bolsheviks in his *Two Tactics of Social-Democracy in the Democratic Revolution*, written during the summer of 1905. "It is quite absurd to think that a bourgeois revolution does not at all express proletarian interests," he argued. "Marxism teaches us that at a certain stage of its development a society which is based on commodity production and has commercial intercourse with civilized capitalist nations must inevitably take the road of capitalism." It followed that "the idea of seeking salvation for the working class in anything save the further development of capitalism is *reactionary*." In a backward country like Russia, "the working class suffers not so much from capitalism as from the insufficient development of capitalism." The proletariat should therefore encourage "the broadest, freest, and most rapid development of capitalism," since "the removal of all the remnants of the old order which hamper the broad, free, and rapid development of capitalism is of absolute *advantage* to the working class."

Lenin's conclusion was that "the bourgeois revolution is precisely an upheaval that most resolutely sweeps away survivals of the past, . . . and most fully guarantees the broadest, freest, and most rapid development of capitalism." Hence a bourgeois revolution would prove *"in the highest degree advantageous to the proletariat"*; it was *"absolutely necessary in the interests of the proletariat."* On this point there could be no doubt. "The more complete, determined, and consistent the bourgeois revolution, the more assured will the proletariat's struggle be against the bourgeoisie and for socialism."

Even after the outbreak of the First World War, the Bolsheviks continued to maintain that the establishment of a democratic government and the development of a capitalistic economy were essential preconditions for the victory of socialism. For the time being, therefore, they must not divide the opposition to czarism by making radical demands. In an article on "The War and Russian Social-Democracy," which was published by the Central Committee of the RSDLP in November 1914, Lenin argued that the military conflict had indeed created in the industrialized nations of Western Europe the opportunity for a successful proletarian uprising. "In all the advanced countries the war has placed on the order of the day the slogan of socialist revolution," he wrote, "a slogan that is the more urgent, the more heavily the burden of war presses upon the shoulders of the proletariat, and the more active its future role must become in the re-creation of Europe, after the horrors of the present 'patriotic' barbarism in conditions of the tremendous technological progress of large-scale capitalism."

In Eastern Europe, however, the situation was different. Here the radicals could not as yet end their tacit alliance with anti-czarist moderates. "Since Russia is most backward and has not yet completed its bourgeois revolution," according to Lenin, "it still remains the task of Social-Democrats in that country to achieve the three fundamental conditions for consistent democratic reform, viz., a democratic republic (with complete equality and self-determination for all nations), confiscation of the landed estates, and an eight-hour working day." Not even the more cautious members of the political opposition were likely to be alarmed by demands of such modest scope. The united front against the *ancien régime*, informal yet effective, did not disintegrate until after the downfall of the autocracy early in 1917.[1]

In China the coalition opposing the established system was at first even more amorphous than in Russia. Indeed, it might be best not to speak of a coalition at all. There were rather several diverse, disaffected groups or factions—small, obscure, undisciplined, and uncoordinated—with little in common except the conviction that there must be an end to Manchu rule. Some favored a democratic republic, others wanted to establish a constitutional monarchy, and still others hoped to preserve the old order in a new guise, to maintain the status quo by a change in dynasty. The outbreak of the revolution in 1911 caught all of them by surprise; none was able to gain power in the chaos which followed the collapse of the *ancien régime*. The result was a long, confused period of political instability and civil war. Not until the late 1920s did the right wing of the Kuomintang under Chiang Kai-shek emerge victorious, establishing a functioning central government in China for the first time since the abdication of the Ch'ing emperor.

In the course of the next two decades, however, the new republican regime began to display the same symptoms of decay that had characterized the old imperial one. It became increasingly oppressive, inefficient, and corrupt. And this in turn led to the emergence of a second antigovernment coalition, better organized and more disciplined than the first, again embracing a variety of organizations and ideologies, but with the Chinese Communist Party now playing the dominant role. The radicals in China, however, were as careful as those in Russia had been to avoid policies that might weaken the united front against the Kuomintang. Accordingly, they adopted a program of economic and social reform to which even most bourgeois democrats could readily subscribe.

The manifesto issued by the second congress of the CCP in the summer of 1922, for example, asked for no more than what many middle-of-the-road reformers had long been advocating:

(a) Better treatment of workers. Abolition of the contracting system. The eight-hour working day. Provision of employees' clinics and sanitary installations in factories. Factory insurance. Protection for female and child labor. Protection for the unemployed.

(b) Abolition of heavy poll and transport taxes. Establishment of a national—municipal and village—land-tax.

(c) Abolition of [internal tariffs] and all extraordinary taxes. Establishment of a progressive income tax.

(d) Passing of legislation limiting land-rents.

(e) Abolition of all legislation restricting women.

(f) Improvement of the educational system.

Only a hidebound conservative could quarrel with such modest proposals.

As the Chinese Communist Party gained strength and influence, its program became more ambitious, more assertive. But it continued to reiterate that, in order to maintain the united front against the Chiang Kai-shek regime, it was willing to negotiate and compromise. That meant first of all a readiness to share power with the moderates. In the summer of 1940, commemorating the third anniversary of the outbreak of the war with Japan and the nineteenth anniversary of the founding of the CCP, Mao Tse-tung rejected the concept of one-party rule. "We stand for the joint dictatorship of all political parties and groups," he declared, "that is, for united front political power." The practical consequence of this position was that "whenever we establish organs of anti-Japanese political power in the enemy rear after destroying the enemy and the puppet regimes there, we should adopt the 'three thirds system' as decided upon by the Central Committee of our Party, so that Communists take only one-third of the places in all government or people's representative bodies, while the remaining two-thirds are taken by people who stand for resistance and democracy whether or not they are members of other parties or groups."

Even the rights of private property would not be threatened by a victory of the revolutionary coalition. Late in 1935, two months after the completion of the "Long March," Mao sought to reassure middle-class opponents of the Kuomintang on this point. "If the national bourgeoisie joins the anti-imperialist united front, the working class and the national bourgeoisie will have interests in common." This in turn would insure that "in the period of the bourgeois-democratic revolution, the people's republic will not expropriate private property other than imperialist and feudal private property, and so far from confiscating the material bourgeoisie's industrial and commercial enterprises, it will encourage their development." The labor laws of the people's republic, while protecting the interests of the workers, "will not prevent the national bourgeoisie from making profits or developing their industrial and commercial enterprises, because such development is bad for imperialism and good for the Chinese people." Individual entrepreneurship would be free to grow and develop alongside collective forms of ownership, for "in the stage of democratic revolution there are limits to the struggle between labor and capital."

Ten years later, as the war against Japan was drawing to a close, Mao repeated, in a report "On Coalition Government" presented to the seventh congress of the CCP, that the party was not opposed to the maintenance of the capitalistic system in China. Indeed, it was eager to liberate the forces of free enterprise:

> It is foreign oppression and feudal oppression that cruelly fetter the development of the individual initiative of the Chinese people, hamper the growth of private capital and destroy the property of the people. It is the very task of the New Democracy we advocate to remove these fetters and stop this destruction, to guarantee that the people can freely develop their individuality within the framework of society and freely develop such private capitalist economy as will benefit and not [in Sun Yat-sen's words] "dominate the livelihood of the people," and to protect all appropriate forms of private property.

Mao was quite explicit on this point. "In accordance with Dr. Sun's principles and the experience of the Chinese revolution, China's national economy at the present stage should be composed of the state sector, the private sector and the co-operative sector." Seemingly, no patriotic, democratic capitalist, however prominent or wealthy, had anything to fear from the revolutionary coalition.[2]

This appeared to be even more clearly the case in Cuba. Lenin and Mao were, after all, professed Marxists; they had the delicate task of reconciling a radical ideology with a moderate program. But Castro was something of a political enigma. He had no left-wing reputation to live down, no inflammatory rhetoric to explain away. He seemed militant only in his opposition to the Batista dictatorship. Otherwise he sounded uncommitted, perhaps even indecisive, in all probability a bourgeois democrat favoring a parliamentary form of government and an enlightened, progressive welfare capitalism. Indeed, throughout the period of struggle in the Sierra Maestra, Castro diligently sought to reinforce this image of the political and social moderate.

He promised, to begin with, that the victory of the revolution would lead swiftly and directly to the democratization of civic authority. To guide Cuba "after the tyrant's fall," a "brief" provisional government would be established to introduce a system of constitutional freedom. "The civic-revolutionary front, by republican and independent tradition, will not allow any type of . . . military junta to rule the Republic." Instead, there would be a general election for all state offices within a year, and those who prevailed at the polls would receive power without delay. The transition to a permanent form of parliamentary democracy would be prompt as well as complete.

Although the revolution would also introduce social and economic reforms, their scope would rarely go beyond what was the norm in most democratic countries. Castro spoke of the "immediate initiation of an intensive campaign against illiteracy, and civic education emphasizing the duties and rights of each citizen to his society and fatherland." There may have been disturbing overtones in his proposal "to distribute barren lands and convert into owners all the tenant farmers, sharecroppers, squatters, and lessee planters who have small parcels of land, be it property of the state or of private persons, with prior indemnification to the owners of the land." But who could oppose the "adoption of a healthy financial policy that safeguards the stability of our currency and tends to use the credit of the nation in productive works," or argue against the "acceleration of the process of industrialization and the creation of new jobs"? These had, after all, been the common demands of Cuban reformers for a long time.

Castro was especially eager to convince the business community, abroad as well as at home, that he had no intention of interfering with freedom of enterprise. On the contrary, capitalism would find the new order more favorable to its development than the Batista regime had been. In an interview in *Look* magazine, he assured the American public that "our 26th of July Movement has never called for nationalizing foreign investments, though in my twenties I *personally* advocated public ownership of Cuba's public utilities." That had been a youthful folly. "Nationalization can never be as rewarding as the right kind of private investment, domestic and foreign, aimed at diversifying our economy." He acknowledged that the word "revolution" sounded like "bitter medicine" to many business-men. "But after the first shock, they will find it a boon—no more thieving tax collectors, no plundering army chieftains or bribe-hungry officials to bleed them white." The climate for foreign investment in Cuba would actually improve, for "our revolution is as much a moral as a political one."

This argument was repeated still more emphatically in Castro's article in *Coronet*. He complained that his economic views had been misunderstood or distorted by the American press. "Various influential U.S. publications have identified me as a tool of big business, as a dangerous radical, and as a narrow reactionary manipulated by the clergy. U.S. companies with business interests in Cuba have been repeatedly warned that I have secret plans in my pocket for seizing all foreign holdings." But those were all wild rumors. "Let me say for the record that we have no plans for the expropriation or nationalization of foreign investments here. True, the extension of government ownership to certain public utilities—some of them, such as the power companies, U.S.-owned—was a point of our earlier programs; but we have currently suspended all planning on this matter."

Free entrepreneurship was in fact essential for the attainment of the goals of the revolution. "I personally have come to feel that nationalization is, at best, a cumbersome instrument. It does not seem to me to make the state any stronger, yet it enfeebles private enterprise. Even more importantly, any attempt at wholesale nationalization would obviously hamper the principal point of our economic platform—industrialization at the fastest possible rate. For this purpose, foreign investments will always be welcome and secure here." Indeed, capitalism would flourish in the new Cuba as never before, because "industrialization is at the heart of our economic progress." To discourage foreign investments, on the other hand, would make the task of the revolutionary coalition more difficult. Only civic democracy and economic freedom could provide a sound basis for a program of national regeneration.[3]

The united front against the *ancient régime* in Vietnam employed the same rhetoric of cautious reformism during its struggle for power. While the Japanese were still occupying the country, the Viet Minh—comprising such diverse political organizations as the New Annam Party, the Association of Young Revolutionists, the Indochinese Communist Party, the Indochinese Section of the International Anti-Invasion Association, and some groups from the Annamite Nationalist Party—issued a declaration to which moderates and radicals alike could adhere. First came the familiar demand for the democratization of authority through the "election of a representative Assembly from all classes of the population whose task it would be to make a Constitution for the Indo-Chinese State with a form of government based on democratic principles." This was followed by the usual list of "democratic rights and privileges for the individual," including the "right to own property, freedom to organize, freedom of the press, right to assemble, freedom of thought and belief, right to strike, right to travel, etc." Finally, the declaration called for the organization of a national army, the confiscation of property belonging to the "Japanese, French and Indo-Chinese fascists," a general amnesty for all prisoners, "equal rights for women," and respect for the "rights of national minorities."

The proposals for reforming the economy were equally modest. There was a demand for the "abolition of the poll tax and all other taxes promulgated under foreign domination." New taxes were to be levied only "under the most democratic principles." All banks owned by the "Japanese and French fascists" were to be nationalized, and in their place a "National Indo-China Bank" should be established. The section of the declaration devoted to the "economic sphere" concluded with a list of irreproachable suggestions for "building a national economy by the development of industry, commerce and agriculture," the "development of irrigation projects [and] clearing of uncultivated land," the "granting of necessary aid to agriculture," and the "construction of new roads."

Next appeared a series of demands for educational and social reform, all of them moderate and reasonable but a little vague. They included an appeal for the "development of national education and the intellectual life of the people," followed by "all possible help for intellectual and scientific study and research," "the formation of specialized societies, institutes and laboratories," and the "opening [of] primary, grammar and high schools, universities and technical schools." The proposals for improving social conditions in Vietnam were modest as well; some might have considered them timid. The declaration urged the "promulgation of social laws, the 8-hour day, social insurance, [and] the fixing of a minimum wage." In addition, there ought to be "aid to large families," the building of "general hospitals, lying-in hospitals and orphanages," and the construction of "municipal theaters, movie houses and clubs." The section concluded with an exhortation to "fight against the social evil," without further specifying its source or nature.

The Viet-Minh program seemed so fair, so restrained, as to disarm opposition. Indeed, the united front against the old order succeeded in gaining the support of many moderates, abroad as well as at home. To the American scholar Ellen Hammer, for instance, it appeared that the demands of the revolutionary movement were in one sense "a commentary upon eighty years of French rule in Indochina"; they were a "protest against decades of arbitrary police methods, political arrests, few personal liberties, and little freedom of press or assembly." The aim of the Viet-Minh was simply "a national economy, with industry developed and agriculture modernized and improved." The social legislation that it advocated was "not unlike that which the Popular Front had brought to France, but revolutionary for Indochina." Here was a program on which liberal reformers and radical revolutionaries could unite in resisting political oppression and economic exploitation.[4]

A close similarity can thus be found in the political discourse of all revolutionary coalitions; the same ideas, the same themes appear and reappear. First comes a fiery denunciation of the old order. It is cruel and oppressive, corrupt and immoral. Since its faults are inherent, since they are beyond correction, the established system must be destroyed. This is followed by a description of the democratic rights and civil liberties that the victory of the revolution will establish. Everyone will be free to express his opinions, publish his views, assemble and organize, hold public office, pursue an occupation, acquire property, and seek wealth. As for the form of political authority, that will be determined through a system of popular elections, with all parties and ideologies invited to participate, leading to the creation of a government responsible to the will of the majority.

Even the economic reforms that the revolutionary coalition proposes appear to present no serious threat to existing property relationships. The manufacturer will still be able to produce goods; the financier will go on making loans; the merchant will continue to sell his wares. The abuses and excesses of free enterprise will be curbed, to be sure, but no more so than in the industrialized, democratic nations of the West. Only occasionally does some bit of evidence suggest that in fact there are significant differences within the united front regarding the democratization of state and society. The constitution of the Chinese Soviet Republic, which was briefly established in Kiangsi province in the early 1930s, declared, for example, that "militarists, bureaucrats, landlords, the gentry, *t'u hao* [village bosses], monks—all exploiting and counter-revolutionary elements —shall be deprived of the right to elect deputies to participate in the government and to enjoy political freedom." But undisguised expressions of class hostility during the period of struggle against the *ancien régime* are infrequent. The rhetoric of the revolutionary coalition is designed rather to attract support among various and disparate strata of society for the resistance against the old order.[5]

The Language
of Nonpartisan Opposition

The conciliatory tone of the opposition's program is usually reinforced by direct appeals to all classes to join in the war against the established system. Even the most radical elements in the revolutionary coalition are in general prepared, for the time being, to tone down their doctrines of class struggle and proletarian dictatorship. Mao himself declared in 1939: "The Chinese revolution at the present stage must strive to create a democratic republic in which the workers, the peasants and the other sections of the petty bourgeoisie all occupy a definite position and play a definite role. In other words, it must be a democratic republic based on a revolutionary alliance of the workers, peasants, urban petty bourgeoisie and all others who are against imperialism and feudalism." And in 1947, during the final stage of the struggle against the Kuomintang, he repeated this view in the "Manifesto of the Chinese People's Liberation Army." The goal of the Communist party should be to "unite workers, peasants, soldiers, intellectuals and businessmen, all oppressed classes, all people's organizations, democratic parties, minority nationalities, overseas Chinese and other patriots; form a national united front; overthrow the dictatorial Chiang Kai-shek government; and establish a democratic coalition government." Not until the collapse of the old order two years later did the importance of economic reorganization and social reconstruction begin to outweigh the need to preserve a united front.

In Cuba there were similar appeals to all groups in society to join the revolutionary coalition against the Batista dictatorship. In the "Unity Manifesto of the Sierra Maestra," broadcast by the rebel radio on July 20, 1958, the leaders of several resistance organizations, including Castro, spoke of the need to arm "the thousands of Cubans willing to fight for freedom," urging "the popular mobilization of all labor, civic, professional and economic forces." They even exhorted the army to join in the people's struggle against the despot. "To our soldiers, we say that the moment has arrived to deny their support to the tyranny. We trust them because we know that there are decent men in the armed forces. . . . This is not a war against the armed forces of the Republic but against Batista, the only obstacle to the peace desired and needed by all Cubans, both civilian and military."

More important, however, was support for the revolution by freedom-loving men and women from all walks of life, from all classes in society. "We urge workers, students, professionals, businessmen, sugar plantation owners, farmers, and Cubans of all religions, ideologies, and races to join this liberation movement which will overthrow the infamous tyranny that has soaked our soil with blood, decimated our best human resources, ruined our economy, destroyed our republican institutions, and interrupted the constitutional and democratic evolution of our country, thus bringing about a bloody civil war which will come to a triumphant end only with a revolution backed by all the people." No mention was made of economic inequalities or social differences, material interests or class antagonisms. The manifesto portrayed the revolutionary coalition as an organization dedicated solely to the achievement of political liberty.

The same resolve to avoid touchy questions regarding the distribution of wealth and power characterized the "Declaration of Former Resistance Fighters on the Present Situation in South Vietnam,"
which appeared in the spring of 1960. Urging the initiation of an
armed struggle against the Saigon regime, it claimed widespread
popular backing for a program of national independence and democratic reform. Among its supporters, according to the preamble,
were first of all *"Former Resistance Fighters*, leaders and members of
the Vietminh-Lien Viet Front, of organizations of the Resistance:
Workers, peasants, youths, women, old people, high school and university students, Mothers of Resistance Fighters, Pioneers." Then
there were "Members of *Religious Organizations*: Cao Dai, Hoa Hao,
Buddhists, Catholics." They were followed in turn by professional
and ethnic organizations: *"Associations of Journalist Resistance Fighters, Artist Resistance Fighters, Chinese Nationals for Liberation."* Next
came political groups like the "Communist or Workers' Party [and
the] Vietnamese Democrat or Vietnamese Socialist [Party]." And finally there were *"Cadres* and *Members of State Organisms* during the
Resistance" as well as *"Individuals Not Adhering to Any Party."* The
declaration claimed that "we [comprise], therefore, the vast majority
of the Vietnamese people."

But apparently that was not enough. The "Former Resistance
Fighters" also announced that "in the present circumstances, we
launch an urgent appeal to all classes, all social strata, all milieus to
struggle even more courageously, even more resolutely, to oblige the
South Vietnamese authorities to ... change their policies." This
meant primarily that the latter should "liberate themselves from
submission to America, eliminate all U.S. bases in South Vietnam,
expel the American military advisors and not accept any form of
American interference in South Vietnam." There were also irreproachable but ambiguous demands for the democratization of the
country's legal and political institutions, demands to "liberate those
in prison without valid cause" and to "dissolve the concentration
camps." The government was urged to "eliminate all coercive measures against intellectuals, journalists, writers, and members of liberal professions," and to "end the policy of repression of religious
sects, ethnic minorities and progressive foreign nationals." The authorities ought to "respect the desires of civil servants, soldiers, city

officials and refugees." They must learn, moreover, to "respect and apply democratic liberties," yet at the same time "outlaw all depraved 'culture' of American origin." Indeed, in order to "revitalize and develop national culture," the government would have to "build new schools, institute new scholarships, reform the teaching curriculum, [and,] respecting national feelings and democratic spirit, use the mother tongue in all classes." Only such a program could achieve "national independence, peace, democracy and a free Vietnam."

The declaration avoided economic or social questions that might disturb the comfortable and well-to-do. The three or four sentences dealing with the reform of the Vietnamese economy were so moderate, so vague, as to sound entirely innocuous. They did not go beyond the need to "reduce taxes, abolish unjustified taxes, eliminate the fines and other methods designed to exact money from the people, [eliminate] forced labor; find solutions to unemployment, stop dismissals, introduce social security, be concerned with labor conditions, and female civil servants, [and] improve the situation of artists." Nothing here would frighten even the most timid of bourgeois liberals.

The conciliatory tone of the declaration was clearly intentional. Those who composed it hoped to organize a broad united front against the government of Ngo Dinh Diem. They urged all Vietnamese, regardless of class or wealth or status, to join in a great revolutionary coalition for national freedom and independence. "The present struggle in South Vietnam is that of all the people and includes all political opinions, from the communists to individuals who merely desire reform, in other words the great majority of patriots. The force of our union, with the active support of our northern compatriots and the progressive peoples of the world, will prevail." For the time being, the need to gain broad popular support transcended differences in class interest or political ideology. To debate the ultimate purposes of the revolution now would only play into the hands of the established system.

When in the fall of 1960 the government of North Vietnam decided to back openly the incipient insurrection in the south, it too was careful not to raise issues that might alarm middle-of-the-road opponents of the Ngo Dinh Diem regime. The resolution adopted by the third national congress of the Vietnam Workers Party in Hanoi regarding the "tasks and line of the Party in the new stage" said nothing about a collectivized economy or a proletarian dictatorship, the class struggle or the overthrow of capitalism. The goal of the revolutionary coalition was simply to "expose the perfidious schemes and acts of the U.S. imperialists and their henchmen, in order to divide and isolate them as much as possible." That in turn would make it possible "to maintain and develop the revolutionary forces in the South and create favorable conditions for peaceful national reunification."

The achievement of this objective would require the collective effort of all Vietnamese, north and south, rich and poor, moderate and radical. A patriotic, democratic front should therefore be formed capable of attracting support among diverse classes of society. "We must pay special attention to the work of organizing and educating the people, first and foremost the workers, peasants, and intellectuals, promoting to the highest degree the patriotism of the various strata of our people." This meant specifically that "our people [in the south] must strive to establish a united bloc of workers, peasants and soldiers, and to bring into being a broad National United Front directed against the U.S. and Diem and based on the worker-peasant alliance." The revolutionary coalition, however, should not be restricted to the urban and rural proletariat. That would be a serious mistake. "This Front must rally all the patriotic classes and sections of the people, the majority and minority nationalities, all patriotic parties and religious groupings, together with all individuals inclined to oppose the U.S. and Diem."

Indeed, the program of the united front should appeal to the love of country and devotion to freedom shared by all Vietnamese, regardless of party or ideology. "The aims of its struggle are peace, national independence, democratic freedoms, improvement of the people's living conditions and peaceful national reunification." The just purpose of the revolution would reconcile opposing political objectives and economic interests. "The Front must rally all forces that can be rallied, win over all forces that can be won over, neutralize all forces that should be neutralized and draw the broad masses into the general struggle against the U.S. and Diem for the liberation of the South and the peaceful reunification of the Fatherland." Whatever theoretical differences separated the members of the united front should be subordinated to the task of defeating the established system.[6]

It is clear that during the period of struggle against the *ancien régime,* the revolutionary coalition maintains the appearance of harmony by carefully avoiding issues on which there is disagreement. While dwelling on the faults and weaknesses of the old order, it remains purposely vague regarding the future reconstruction of state and society. There are only promises that once the established system has fallen, political oppression and economic exploitation will come to an end. Liberty and equality, prosperity and justice will be enjoyed by all. Everyone will have the right to voice an opinion, join a party, obtain an education, practice an occupation, and achieve affluence. Free elections will be held, moreover, to determine the form of government. Political authority will no longer rest on the arbitrary exercise of power, but on the give-and-take of ideas and arguments.

Hoping to attract public support, the united front carefully avoids divisive questions of economic disparity and social inequality. No established group, class, or interest seems to be threatened by its rhetoric. It appears to seek change only in the political system, in the structure of authority, not in the distribution of wealth or status. Its strategy is to focus popular resentment on the small native ruling elite or to externalize it against foreigners who, directly or indirectly, dominate the country: the Japanese in China, the Americans in Cuba, or first the French and then the Americans in Vietnam. As long as it is still striving for power, the revolutionary coalition always assumes the role of champion of democracy and nationalism.

Internal Support
for the United Front

This strategy is by and large successful, especially in the later stages of the war against the old order. As the conflict intensifies, a significant shift in popular loyalty begins to take place from the established system to the political opposition. Although this process of defection affects all groups in society, it is more pronounced among the upper and middle strata than among the lower classes. The masses become increasingly disaffected as well, but their alienation does not as a rule lead to open rebellion. It is manifested rather in a growing passivity or detachment from established authority, in a wait-and-see attitude that may lead to sporadic violence in response to some local grievance, but that rarely becomes transformed into a sustained insurrectionary movement.

The defection of the propertied and educated, on the other hand, is overt and obvious. Repelled by the weaknesses, corruptions, and excesses of the established system, which the struggle for survival usually aggravates, the bourgeoisie in particular turns against the *ancien régime*. Some of this is pure opportunism, no doubt. Sensing that the government is losing ground, many of its traditional supporters decide to ingratiate themselves with the prospective victors by changing sides. But most middle-class converts to the revolution act out of conviction rather than expediency. They too are tired of dictatorial rule, venal administration, arbitrary authority, and foreign domination. Besides, has not the united front given solemn assurances that it is nonpartisan, that it does not favor one class over another, one party over another, one interest over another? Has it not promised repeatedly that no sincere democrat, no true patriot has anything to fear from the new order? Ideals and advantages, principles and calculations thus intermingle to encourage the defection of the bourgeoisie from the established system. A study by the French of Viet Minh prisoners of war revealed that 46 percent of them were peasants or workers, with the latter outnumbering the former, although the national economy was largely agricultural; 48 percent were minor officials; and the remaining 6 percent came from miscellaneous occupations and professions. These figures provide a rough gauge of the intensity of political discontent among the different classes of Vietnamese society.

The revolutionary coalition is especially successful in winning support among the intelligentsia. Here is an occupational group highly sensitive to the indignities of corruption in high places and foreign influence over national policy. Writers, musicians, artists, professionals, academics, and students, versed in the writings of political democracy, familiar with the literature of social protest, are usually among the severest critics of the *ancien régime*. Though they generally come from a background of status and affluence, neither their source of livelihood nor their position in society depends on the maintenance of the established system. Not only do they therefore enjoy greater freedom of action than most other occupational groups, but the central role they play in the cultural life of the community gives them a major influence in the shaping of public opinion.

The intelligentsia is numerically small, to be sure. In the early 1930s there were fewer than 45,000 college students in all of China. The number of secondary-school students was substantially greater, but the two groups together came to little more than 500,000 in a population exceeding 400,000,000. Most of them, moreover, remained politically inactive, except at times of extraordinary national crisis or in the face of some particularly outrageous imperialist affront. Probably fewer than 50,000 were consistently involved in civic affairs, and no more than about 5,000 exercised control over the various municipal, provincial, or national student organizations, often as cadres of the Kuomintang or the Communist party. But the social status, cultural prominence, and political sophistication of the Chinese students, and of Chinese intellectuals in general, gave them an importance in public life far out of proportion to their numbers.[7]

Many of those who backed the revolutionary coalition felt slightly uneasy about joining forces with militant radicals. They were not entirely convinced by the conciliatory rhetoric of the far left; some doubts about its ultimate purposes and goals seemed to persist. And yet they felt that the hopeless corruption of the established system left them little choice. "We are against the Kuomintang, but not all of us will go all the way with the Communists," a leading Chinese liberal told A. Doak Barnett in 1947. "Lo Lung-chi [spokesman for the Democratic League], for example, says he goes 70 percent of the way with the Communist program, and that's probably about right." Even that may have been farther than some opponents of the Chiang Kai-shek regime were prepared to go. American Ambassador Leighton Stuart reported that a friend of his in Peking estimated that "90 to 95 percent of the students are opposed to Communism in China, and 90 percent are opposed to the present government."

It is apparent that those intellectuals who turned against the established system did not in most cases favor a radical program of civic and economic reconstruction. They would have preferred a policy of gradual political democratization and greater national assertiveness. But since the Kuomintang was so utterly inept, they felt compelled to enter into an alliance with the left as a *pis aller*. A student at Peking National University told Barnett that "there are very few actual Communists [in the school], but I would say that at least 50 percent are sympathetic to Communism—or at least the Chinese Communists. At least 50 percent!" When asked what "sympathetic" meant, he explained: "Well, it means that they think the Chinese Communists are a better group than the present government." To them the overthrow of the established system was an essential precondition for the reform of polity and society. "The first thing we want and need," according to one of the students in Peking, "is peace and effective constitutional government: the protection of civil rights under a rule of law. When that is achieved, we can bring about the necessary economic revolution, and attack the problems of agrarian reform and industrialization on the basis of a sort of socialist economy." Many of those who supported the revolutionary coalition in China, perhaps most of them, wanted essentially some form of Fabian socialism rather than a soviet system on the Russian model.

Their willingness to enter into an alliance with the radicals was based partly on the obvious incorrigibility of the Chiang Kai-shek regime, partly on the conciliatory pledges of the far left, and partly on hopes and intuitions, on wishful thinking. A widespread belief existed, and not only among students, that the Communists were really moderate reformers, that whatever their ultimate goal, for the time being they would not go beyond greater efficiency in the functioning of government, more independence in dealing with foreign powers, and increased concern for the well-being of the poor and oppressed.

The socialist intellectual Shih Fu-liang, for example, maintained in 1947 that the Communist party was unlikely to try to put into effect the principles of Communism or even socialism, since material conditions in China were not ripe for a basic reorganization of society. At most it would seek to establish a "new-democratic" state. As for the call by the radicals for the formation of a coalition government, Shih was not sure, but he hoped that it was sincere. "Some say this is just a stratagem and that when the time is right, the CCP will carry out a Soviet system and a proletarian dictatorship. I do not dare to say they will not and that this is not a possibility. But 'when the time is right' is an objective question." Why assume the worst? "Perhaps China can go its own road and we will be able to move peacefully to socialism from the new capitalism and the new democracy." In any case, he concluded, under today's conditions, no democratic citizen, no democratic party needs to fear the danger of communism.

The revolutionary coalition against the *ancien régime* is thus held together by hopes and illusions, yet its unity is also threatened by doubts and suspicions. The moderates cannot entirely suppress their distrust of the soothing rhetoric of the radicals. They have the uneasy feeling that once the old order has been overthrown, the far left may try to establish a dictatorial regime in which no room will exist for opposition or dissent. The radicals, on the other hand, question the trustworthiness of the moderates, especially of the intellectuals among them. They suspect that what attracts the intelligentsia to the revolution is not the resolve to replace an exploitive with a benevolent form of authority, but hostility to authority as such.

In other words, the radicals suspect that the writers, artists, professionals, and academics who oppose the established system of today will also oppose the established system of tomorrow. At heart they are neither democrats nor socialists but anarchists. What they really want is rampant individualism, the right of everyone to follow his own private conscience wherever it may lead. They reject all direction, all discipline. They may be useful during the struggle against the *ancien régime,* but once the work of building a new political and social system has begun, they will prove a nuisance or even a threat. Although they should therefore be invited to join the united front in resisting the old order, their role must always be restricted and subordinated.

Sometimes the radicals express this distrust quite openly. In 1904 Lenin, lashing out against his Menshevik critics in *One Step Forward, Two Steps Back,* denounced "the mentality of the bourgeois intellectual, who counts himself among the 'elect minds' standing above mass organization and mass discipline." He insisted that "to the individualism of the intellectual, [with] its tendency to opportunist argument and anarchistic phrase-mongering, *all* proletarian organization and discipline seems to be *serfdom.*" The only true defenders of the revolution are the workers. "Let me tell you . . . that the proletariat is not afraid of organization and discipline! The proletariat will do nothing to have the worthy professors and high-school students who do not want to join an organization recognized as Party members merely because they work under the control of an organization. The proletariat is trained for organization by its whole life, far more radically than many an intellectual prig."

The factory unites and disciplines the working class, Lenin explained, teaching it to organize in defense of its economic interests. Hence "the discipline and organization which come so hard to the bourgeois intellectual are very easily acquired by the proletariat just because of this 'factory' schooling." But while the working class provides the disciplined strength of the revolutionary movement, the petty-bourgeois intelligentsia sows dissension and factionalism. "With large numbers of radical intellectuals in the ranks of our Marxists and our Social-Democrats, the opportunism which their mentality produces has been, and is, bound to exist in the most varied spheres and in the most varied forms." They are at best a useful but unreliable weapon in the war against the established system.

Mao was less vehement in his criticism of the intelligentsia, but he too had serious doubts regarding its role in the revolutionary movement. Writing in 1939 about "The Different Sections of the Petty Bourgeoisie Other than the Peasantry," he argued that "the intellectuals and student youth . . . do not constitute a separate class or stratum." In view of their family origin, living conditions, and political outlook, they could by and large be placed in the "petty-bourgeois category." Although some had become allies of "the imperialists and the big bourgeoisie," most of them "are oppressed by imperialism, feudalism and the big bourgeoisie, and live in fear of unemployment or of having to discontinue their studies." They thus tend to be revolutionary, often playing "a vanguard role" or serving as "a link with the masses" in the present stage of the class struggle. "The movement of the Chinese students abroad before the Revolution of 1911, the May 4th Movement of 1919, the May 30th Movement of 1925 and the December 9th Movement of 1935 are striking proofs of this." Large numbers of "more or less impoverished intellectuals" can therefore join hands with the workers and peasants in China in supporting the revolution. Indeed, "the revolutionary forces cannot be successfully organized and revolutionary work cannot be successfully conducted without the participation of revolutionary intellectuals."

Still, it would be risky to allow them to acquire too much influence:

> The intellectuals often tend to be subjective and individualistic, impractical in their thinking and irresolute in action until they have thrown themselves heart and soul into mass revolutionary struggles, or made up their minds to serve the interests of the masses and become one with them. Hence although the mass of revolutionary intellectuals in China can play a vanguard role or serve as a link with the masses, not all of them will remain revolutionaries to the end. Some will drop out of the revolutionary ranks at critical moments and become passive, while a few may even become enemies of the revolution. The intellectuals can overcome their shortcomings only in mass struggles over a long period.

To Mao, as to Lenin, the intelligentsia was useful but unpredictable and unreliable. Its activities in the revolutionary coalition had to be carefully supervised.[8]

The undercurrents of doubt and suspicion within the united front are generally disguised, however, by the outward appearance of agreement and harmony. The program of the opposition to the *ancien régime* seems broad enough to accommodate the most diverse policies and ideologies. Who can object to demands for more freedom in domestic affairs or greater independence in international relations? The revolutionary coalition is all things to all men. Some support it because it will change only the surface of politics and economics; it will preserve old institutions in new forms. It may alter the shape of government, the structure of authority. But behind the parliamentary facade, traditional property rights and class distinctions will remain, perhaps even more secure against popular discontent than before. Others have different expectations. To them the fall of the *ancien régime* will be the prelude to a fundamental reorganization of state and society, a basic alteration in the relationship of the haves to the have-nots. Yet for the time being these differences are submerged in a collective resistance against the established system.

External Support
for the United Front

The revolutionary coalition is also successful in winning considerable sympathy abroad. An obvious similarity exists in fact between its native and its foreign supporters. Both come from a social background that is generally middle-class; both espouse an ideology lying somewhere left of center; both are disproportionately numerous among the intelligentsia. But while the former are largely motivated by a sense of collective humiliation, the latter are haunted by a feeling of collective guilt. They believe that their society has battened on the exploitation and impoverishment of weaker nations, that the high standard of living they enjoy has been achieved at the expense of oppressed peoples and races. It is their solemn obligation to atone for the sins committed by their country. They must reject imperialism; they must proclaim the essential oneness of all mankind, regardless of color, culture, or creed. By supporting the resistance against the older order throughout the world, they are performing a sacred moral duty.

More than that, their sympathy for a revolution in some distant part of the world expresses vicariously their opposition to the political institutions and social values of their own nation. To many intellectuals of the twentieth century, the heroic rebel is what the noble savage was to those of the eighteenth century. He symbolizes a rejection of the corruption and materialism of the West. He represents a commitment to freedom, justice, equality, and altruism. By supporting the revolutionary coalition abroad, whether in Asia, Latin America, or Eastern Europe, political dissenters are voicing their opposition to the government at home. By criticizing the established system in China or Cuba, they are opposing it in England or the United States. And thereby they are in effect assisting the revolution, making it more difficult for their government to protect its diplomatic or economic interests by intervening in defense of the *ancien régime*. Their opposition to a policy of support for the old order renders that policy more risky, more likely to fail. In this sense, foreign sympathizers of the revolutionary coalition make an important contribution to its victory.

During the First World War the defeats suffered by the czarist armies were clearly weakening the resolve of Russia to continue the struggle against the Central Powers. Yet to many intellectuals in Western Europe and America the prospect of a collapse of the *ancien régime* was not unwelcome. A successful revolution was bound to replace the discredited autocracy with a democratic government. The British socialist Henry Noel Brailsford, member of the Independent Labor Party, wrote in 1915 that the situation in the east resembled that of ten years before, in the period following the Russo-Japanese War. "Then as now reverses in war had shaken the supreme bureaucracy, and then as now the Russian people discovered in defeat a will and an insight which it has rarely shown in prosperity."

Important differences were apparent, however. "It might seem at first glance that . . . conditions [now] were less favorable to reform than those of a decade ago." But that would miss the main point of the present movement. "In 1905 the leadership had fallen to groups which stood dangerously in advance of average national sentiment. They were critics, theorists, 'intellectuals,' internationalists, and they had watched the disasters in Manchuria without an affectation of regret." Now, on the other hand, the chief object of the reformers was victory. "They are a middle and upper-class coalition. They profess and feel an intense Russian patriotism. . . . Theirs are neither eccentric nor exceptionally advanced opinions." They were demanding change, "even in this hour of danger," because they distrusted the ability of the bureaucracy in general and the ministry in particular to lead the nation to victory.

There was no risk, moreover, of repeating the mistakes of 1905. "War narrows the field of possible change. . . . You cannot amid war sit down to frame an elaborate and permanent constitution, and still less can you undertake a big program of agrarian reform." Here was the crucial difference. "Just because the scope of any changes which are possible today is limited, the outlook for the present reform movement is incomparably more hopeful than ever was the prospect ten years ago. The changes must be confined to the indispensable minimum, and over that minimum there is a chance that all the moderate parties of the Duma may remain in agreement."

The danger that the radicals would seize power was minimal, Brailsford felt sure. "If the great change comes, it will not be, as that of 1905 so nearly was, a Slav version of the French Revolution, for it will involve neither social upheaval nor economic reconstruction. But it may be a Whig revolution, a 1688 rather than a 1789." Since three-fourths of the Russian population was still illiterate, since the empire itself was only "a half-welded mass composed of peoples in a dozen divers stages of civilization," it would be remarkable enough "if the bare elements of civic freedom can be won." Hence the fall of czarism would prepare the way for a democratic, reformist regime in Russia; it would lead to an East European equivalent of the United Kingdom or the Third Republic.[9]

Two decades later equally optimistic predictions appeared regarding the outcome of the revolution in China. In 1936 the young American newspaperman Edgar Snow spent four months studying conditions in the Communist stronghold in Shensi province. He emerged convinced that the hostile attitude toward the radicals common in official circles in Nanking and Washington was unfounded. The Communists were not ideologues or doctrinaires; they were essentially agrarian reformers. "Whatever it may have been in the South [before the "Long March"], Chinese Communism as I found it in the North-west might more accurately be called rural equalitarianism than anything Marx would have found agreeable as a model child of his own. This was manifestly true economically, and although in the social, political, and cultural life of the organized Soviets there was a crude Marxist guidance, limitations of material conditions were everywhere obvious."

Nor was it accurate that the Communists sought the outright abolition of private property. They were too realistic to confuse theory with practice; they were ready to subordinate ideal objectives to attainable goals. "A popular and never-dying notion of the Communist movement in China is that it is anti-capitalist in the sense that it does not see the necessity for a period of bourgeois or capitalist economy, but wants right away to proclaim Socialism. This is rubbish." All the pronouncements made by the Communists had clearly shown that they accepted the "bourgeois character" of the revolutionary movement. The struggle against the Kuomintang was therefore not over the nature of the revolution but over the nature of its leadership. "The Communists recognize that the duties of that leadership are to realize, as quickly as possible, two primary historic tasks: first, to overthrow foreign imperialism and establish national independence (that is, liberate China from its semi-colonial status); second, to overthrow the power of the landlords and gentry, and establish democracy (that is, liberate the masses from 'semi-feudalism')." The radicals believed that only after those tasks had been accomplished would it be possible to move toward socialism.

Snow concluded with an impassioned prophecy. The revolutionary ideal was invincible; it was the wave of the future. Its victory was assured by the very course of history:

> And another thing is . . . certain. Neither can the democratic Socialist ideas for which tens of thousands of youths have already died in China, nor the energies behind them, be destroyed. The movement for social revolution in China may suffer defeats, may temporarily retreat, may for a time seem to languish, may make wide changes in tactics to fit immediate necessities and aims, may even for a period be submerged, be forced underground, but it will not only continue to mature; in one mutation or another it will eventually win, simply because . . . the basic conditions which have given it birth carry within themselves the dynamic necessity for its triumph. And that triumph when it comes will be so mighty, so irresistible in its discharge of katabolic energy, that it will consign to oblivion the last barbarities of imperialism which now enthral the Eastern world.

Those witnessing this historic conflict could choose either to support the forces of liberation, thereby hastening their victory, or oppose them and go down to inevitable defeat.[10]

About ten years later another young American journalist professed his faith in the cause of the revolution, this time in Southeast Asia. Harold R. Isaacs, who had been a correspondent in the Far East for *Newsweek* during the Second World War, maintained that the united front against the *ancien régime* in Vietnam expressed a deep popular yearning for freedom and democracy. Even its radical members were committed to a policy of moderation. "The Viet Minh was . . . formed . . . as a coalition of various groups, democrats, socialists, communists, and other less well defined sections of the independence movement," he wrote in 1947. "They are agreed primarily on a program of common struggle for independence and a social pro-

gram based on the idea of a democratic republic." This program had
won the approval of the overwhelming majority of the native population, for under colonial rule "all the people shared the bond of
subjection."

Support for the old order, on the other hand, came primarily from
"the real ruling class of the country [consisting] of the 45,000
Frenchmen who lived in it as the administrators and representatives
and defenders of French capital." Allied with them were the native
lackeys of the old order, "the only group [of Vietnamese] with any
share in the exploitation of the country . . . , roughly estimated to
number no more than 10,000." They included "landlords, with relatively small holdings, a few minor industrialists, [and] a larger group
of agents and functionaries of the French regime and of French business." But they were a threat to Vietnamese nationalism only as long
as the colonial authorities offered them armed protection. "Cut
adrift and left to their own resources, these Annamites were weak,
their grasp on wealth too feeble, their impact on the nation too
light." They could not in the long run resist the will of the people.

Opposed to them was the great bulk of the Vietnamese population. The various states of Indochina—Cambodia, Cochin China,
Laos, Annam, and Tonkin—"had known historic rivalries but had
always managed somehow to federate their common interests."
Once the divisive influence of the French had been removed, there
would be no obstacle to their union. There remained the problem of
the Chinese, to be sure, "the merchants and traders of the country,"
who were basically "a conservative factor as well as a disturbing
one." But this "important minority" had to face severe restrictions
under colonial rule; it too stood to gain from national independence.
Some of its members had even given shelter to Vietnamese insurgents, suffering the destruction of their shops and homes in acts of
reprisal by the authorities. "Officially we're neutral," a leader of the
Chinese community had told Isaacs. "In fact, we sympathize fully
with the Annamites." As for the broad masses, "peasants and fisher-
men, tenant workers of the land and seasonal workers on the plantations, . . . it was among these people, with the least to lose, that the
Viet Minh found its greatest support."

The popularity of the revolutionaries was quite understandable,
for their program seemed "mild, limited to land reforms and guaran-

tees of living wages and working conditions." As long as the people believed that it would live up to its promises of greater security, the united front had little to fear from the well-to-do classes in Vietnam. The "inevitable process of differentiation" would come only after colonialism had been defeated and the interplay of indigenous class interests had begun to assert itself. For the time being, however, the few wealthy Vietnamese who toadied to the French were no threat. And as for the rest, as for those who "prayed that some other power or powers would rescue them from the anarchy of the mass," they too would prove weak and helpless. Isaacs felt confident that "the Viet Nam Republic was secure enough," because it represented the forces of liberty and justice.[11]

But no foreign sympathizer did more for the cause of the revolution than Herbert L. Matthews of *The New York Times*. A widely known, highly regarded newspaperman, he had witnessed the victory of fascism in the Spanish Civil War and the tyranny of the Axis in the Second World War. These experiences had helped convince him that the age in which he lived was a vast battleground of the opposing armies of good and evil, freedom and oppression. He saw in the Cuban uprising another manifestation of that cosmic Manichaean conflict. To the revolutionaries on the island his decision early in 1957 to have a secret interview with Castro came as a godsend. The Expedition of the *Granma* three months earlier had resulted in a succession of reverses and disappointments. The small band of invaders had been badly defeated by the Batista forces; only twenty or so had managed to find a precarious refuge in the Sierra Maestra. There were even rumors and speculations that Castro himself had been killed in the fighting. Hence the series of articles by Matthews that appeared in this dark hour was of major importance in reviving the morale of the faltering insurrection. On this point, both supporters and opponents of the 26th of July Movement have been in basic agreement.

He began with a dramatic announcement on the front page of the Sunday *Times*. "Fidel Castro, the rebel leader of Cuba's youth, is alive and fighting hard and successfully in the rugged, almost impenetrable fastnesses of the Sierra Maestra. . . . This is the first sure news that Fidel Castro is still alive and still in Cuba." But Castro was not only alive; he was heroic, he was charismatic. "The personality of the man is overpowering. It was easy to see that his men adored him and also to see why he has caught the imagination of the youth of Cuba all over the island. Here was an educated, dedicated fanatic, a man of ideals, of courage and of remarkable qualities of leadership."

Standing behind him were patriotic, idealistic Cubans from every walk of life. "The old, corrupt order . . . is being threatened for the first time since the Cuban Republic was proclaimed early in the century. An internal struggle is now taking place that is more than an effort by the outs to get in and enjoy the enormous spoils of office that have been the reward of political victory." The revolution was seeking rather to purify, to ennoble the fundamental political values of the nation. "At last one gets the feeling that the best elements in Cuban life—the unspoiled youth, the honest business man, the politician of integrity, the patriotic Army officer—are getting together to assume power. They have always made up the vast majority of Cubans, but Cuba has never had majority rule." That was about to change.

The program of the insurrection was admittedly vague on some points, maybe even a little naive, but there could be no question about its commitment to democracy. "Señor Castro's men, the student leaders who are on the run from the police, the people who are bombing and sabotaging every day, are fighting blindly, rashly, perhaps foolishly. But they are giving their lives for an ideal and for their hopes of a clean, democratic Cuba." The revolutionary movement, Matthews reported, called itself "socialistic." It was also "nationalistic," which "generally in Latin America means anti-Yankee." Yet Castro had also assured him that "we have no animosity toward the United States and the American people." The rebel leader had "strong ideas" about economics, although "an economist would consider them weak." He had "strong ideas," moreover, about "liberty, democracy, social justice, the need to restore the Constitution, [and] to hold elections." While his program might seem "vague and couched in generalities," it amounted to a new deal for Cuba, "radical, democratic, and therefore anti-Communist." The real source of its strength was "that it is fighting against the military dictatorship of President Batista." In short, here was a typical Latin revolution, romantic perhaps, slightly visionary, yet idealistic in motive and noble in purpose. It deserved the support of right-thinking people throughout the world.[12]

The arguments employed by foreign sympathizers of the revolution, whether in Russia, China, Vietnam, or Cuba, are so similar as to be almost interchangeable. The same beliefs and assumptions appear over and over again. Yet it is clear that what these external supporters of the resistance movement generally favor is not radicalism but moderation, not conflict but reconciliation. For them the overthrow of the old order means individual liberty rather than class dictatorship. They are essentially middle-of-the-road reformers, outraged by the corruptions and cruelties of the existing system, who expect its fall to lead to representative democracy. Some of them will become disillusioned after the victory of the new order; a few will turn violently against it. But during the period of struggle against the *ancien régime*, they make an important contribution to the success of the opposition. They turn public opinion abroad against the established system, discrediting and isolating it, and thereby impeding economic, diplomatic, and military assistance from foreign states that fear the consequences of its downfall. Like the native moderates, they help ensure a revolutionary victory whose result they do not foresee and whose outcome they do not approve.

The Triumph of the Revolution

It should come as no surprise, though it usually does, that the final victory of the new order is almost always swift and easy. The *ancien régime* is not really overthrown; it topples. Before the issue is actually decided, a widespread assumption exists that the struggle will be long and bitter. There will be violence, destruction, suffering, and bloodshed. The fighting will spread and intensify until one side or the other prevails through greater determination and steadfastness. But in fact the established system falls largely of its own weight. It manages until the very end to maintain the outward appearance of strength and resolve; it seems to cope effectively with the conspiracies, mutinies, coups, and revolts that proliferate in the last years of its existence. But inwardly it has become insecure and demoralized. It senses the defection of those who have in the past accepted its authority. It knows that the masses have grown indifferent to its fate, that the propertied and educated classes are openly critical. The moral traditions and ethical precepts on which its claim to allegiance rested have become eroded. Now that the creative role of the old order in the political process has been played out, there is no longer any justification for its exercise of power. It has performed its historic function; it can go. One good push is all that is needed to bring about its collapse.

To illustrate this point, the fall of the imperial government in China came about almost through inadvertence, almost by chance. In Wuhan, a collective name for the three adjacent cities of Wuchang, Hankow, and Hanyang, a local military conspiracy, one of many organized during the final decade of Manchu rule, was forced into open rebellion late in 1911 by an explosion at one of its secret ammunition dumps. In Hong Kong and Shanghai leaders of the revolutionary movement had been warning against half-baked *putsches*, and the Wuhan conspirators had in fact been inclined to move with caution. But now that their plans were uncovered as a result of the accident, the choice before them was either to launch an immediate uprising or wait to be picked off by the police one by one.

On October 10 a handful of mutinous enlisted men in Wuchang killed their officers, headed for the nearby arsenal, and persuaded the company on guard there to join them, so that now the insurgents numbered around 300. A junior officer with republican sympathies agreed to take charge, and under his leadership the rebels, whose ranks soon increased to 4,000, attacked the headquarters of the governor general. By the following morning Ch'ing authority in Wuchang had been overthrown, and the rebels proceeded to proclaim a republic. Their losses had been less than 100, although the casualties suffered by the government troops were much heavier. Most soldiers of the garrison had simply refused to take part in the fighting on either side.

Rebel soldiers in Hanyang captured the city on October 12 with even greater ease, the only casualty being one of the platoon commanders. In Hankow there was still less fighting but much more looting, until troops from Wuchang arrived to help restore order. Stability soon returned, so that the shops could reopen on October 14. From Wuhan the revolutionary movement spread rapidly to other parts of China, and in the course of the next four months an imperial regime that had endured for more than three millennia came to an end. No precise figures exist on the loss of life during the revolution, but it is unlikely to have been more than 2,000, and it may well not have exceeded even half that number.

The revolution, moreover, was largely free of the looting, arson, rape, and murder in which troops of the old order had frequently engaged during periods of disorder. On October 16 the British minister in Peking reported to Sir Edward Grey in the Foreign Office that "the prospect which faces the Manchu dynasty is a gloomy one," for "it is largely discredited amongst its own people." On the other hand, "the orderly manner in which the [revolutionary] movement is being conducted and the marked consideration shown for foreign interests distinguish it from all previous risings of this kind and has enlisted for it a measure of sympathy amongst the Chinese which the Manchu dynasty can no longer claim to command." The new revolutionary soldier displayed a sense of purpose and mission; he accepted discipline and order. He was not a mercenary but a fighter for a cause. Indeed, the prospect of creating a better political system seemed to engender throughout China a mood of euphoric, exhilarating idealism.[13]

The revolution in Russia followed roughly the same pattern. The available statistical information, much more detailed than in China, suggests that the czarist authorities had taken measures to protect the government that on paper seem impressive. At the beginning of 1917 there was a huge garrison of about 160,000 men in Petrograd, although most of the crack regiments had been sent to the front. The troops left in the capital were to a large extent new recruits, poorly trained, housed, and fed. But the government did not rely primarily on the regular army to deal with a possible uprising. In January a detailed plan for the suppression of insurrectionary activity in the city had been presented to the czar, and a combined force of 12,000 soldiers, gendarmes, and policemen had been formed to help maintain law and order. The revolution did not catch the established system unawares.

Yet all these careful preparations proved useless when a popular insurrection began early in March. Neither the soldiers nor the gendarmes nor the policemen were prepared to die for a regime that was now widely perceived as corrupt and inept. The Romanovs fell even more swiftly than the Manchus. There was a week of fighting, confined largely to Petrograd, and then it was all over. The number of those killed, wounded, and injured in the city totaled 1,315, including 53 officers, 602 soldiers, 73 policemen, and 587 civilians, women as well as men. Elsewhere in Russia the revolution can almost be said to have triumphed via the telegraph. Serious excesses occurred only in naval centers such as Kronstadt and Helsingfors, where the hatred of the sailors for those in authority led to a number of killings. Several officers, including two admirals, were put to death, while others were jailed in the local prisons. Additional incidents of violence were reported here and there. A brigadier general died in Penza during a demonstration by soldiers; a provincial governor was killed in Tver, where there was much rioting and looting. But such cases were rare. The fall of the *ancien régime* was accepted nearly everywhere without much bloodshed.[14]

The loss of life in Cuba in two years of revolutionary struggle, from the end of 1956 to the beginning of 1959, was probably less than in Petrograd during that one week in March 1917. At first glance, the disparity in strength between defenders and opponents of the old order seems enormous. On one side was the regular army, which during the period of the Batista dictatorship numbered about 45,000 men. On the other stood a small band of rebels, more than the twenty who had survived the early disaster at Algería de Pío, but still only a few hundred inadequately trained, poorly equipped guerrillas. In September 1958, barely four months before the triumph of the revolution, Castro had a force of no more than about 300 in the Sierra Maestra, while further west in the Escambray Mountains there was another group of approximately 800, with 150 recruits in training and 50 messengers enlisted from among the young men of the district. Even when the rebel troops finally reached Havana in January 1959, after the waverers and doubters had decided that it was now safe to join the guerrillas, they numbered only a little over 1,500. Thus the estimate that the total loss of life on both sides resulting from military operations did not exceed 1,000 appears reasonable. The victory of the revolutionary cause was won by a test of will in which morale and commitment proved more important than armed force.[15]

Yet nowhere was the fall of the old order more humiliating or ignominious than in Southeast Asia. The defeat of France in June 1940 emboldened the Japanese to present to the colonial authorities in Indochina an ultimatum demanding the admittance of a military mission to supervise the cessation of all aid to China. Governor General Georges Catroux, though no defeatist, had little choice but to accept. Still, the Pétain government, which was about to surrender to Hitler, decided that its proconsul in Vietnam had failed to display sufficient heroism. Catroux was therefore replaced by Vice-Admiral Jean Decoux, who soon had to face additional demands from Tokyo for "certain military facilities in Tonkin for the liquidation of the China incident." In return the Japanese offered as a "concession" the recognition of French sovereignty over Indochina, whose destruction was in fact one of the main objectives of their policy.

Decoux knew that resistance was hopeless, but he hoped to shift the onus of capitulation to the authorities in Vichy. With an eye to posterity, he declared that "if we must run the risk of losing Indochina, it is better to lose it in defending it than by betraying it." Still, when Pétain urged him "to set an example of discipline to all Frenchmen" by negotiating with the Japanese, he readily acquiesced. His agreement with General Issaka Nishihara concluded in Hanoi early in the fall gave Tokyo the right to station 6,000 men north of the Red River and up to 25,000 men throughout Vietnam. Yet the Japanese government, though it had gotten everything it wanted, decided to teach the French a lesson so as to prepare the way for future extortions. On September 22, the same day the agreement with Decoux was signed, its troops in southern China, allegedly unaware of what was happening in Hanoi, crossed into Tonkin and attacked the cities of Dong Dang and Langson. Although at first there was stiff resistance—the defenders lost some 800 men—the French forces decided within forty-eight hours to give up. The old colonial order in Indochina had now come to an end.

To the Vietnamese these events meant simply the exchange of one master for another. They had been subject to the domination of France; now they would be subject to that of Japan. It seemed to make little difference which foreign conqueror ruled the country. As for the French colonial authorities, which were permitted by Tokyo to go on exercising nominal sovereignty, they continued to hope that once the war ended in the defeat of the Axis, they would be able to regain their former predominance in Southeast Asia. They could not see that whatever the outcome of the world conflict, their role in Vietnam was finished. It was no longer possible to return to the *status quo ante*. After the defeat of Japan in 1945, the French came back to Southeast Asia in greater strength than before, with a larger army and a more conciliatory policy. But their material superiority could not prevail against a growing popular conviction in the region that alien domination, in whatever form or guise, should no longer be endured. Neither soldiers nor politicians, neither threats nor concessions were able to save the *ancien régime*.[16]

The fall of the old order is thus never the result of inferiority in military forces or financial resources. On the contrary, by any conventional assessment of the odds, the established system should be able to defeat its opponents quite easily. What ultimately accounts for the success of the opposition is stronger conviction and greater determination. The outcome of the revolution represents a victory of new faith over outworn orthodoxy, of dissenting ideas over established institutions. Weapons are no better than the men who use them; supplies are no substitute for boldness and dedication. In the struggle between the old order and the new, imponderable moral and ideological factors prove more important than palpable material advantages. The *ancien régime* falls because it has ceased to express the underlying beliefs and aspirations of the community, because it no longer conforms to the popular conception of what government should be. It therefore disintegrates; it succumbs to internal weakness rather than external assault. Its end is greeted with a universal sigh of relief, not only among adversaries but even supporters. There has been a widespread, growing feeling that the established system cannot endure, that sooner or later it must give way to something different, something better. And now that it has fallen, a heavy burden seems to have been lifted from society. The work of creating a new political and economic order can finally begin.

CHAPTER 5

From United Front to Radical Dictatorship

The collapse of the *ancien régime* leads directly to the disintegration of the revolutionary coalition. Victory deprives it of cohesiveness by fulfilling its common purpose, the overthrow of a corrupt and repressive system of authority. To the moderates the goal of the revolution has been reached. Now that the defeat of the old order has made possible the establishment of a democratic form of government, the process of gradual reform can begin. The use of force, which may have been justifiable while the war against political oppression was going on, will hereafter only violate the principles for which it had been fought. Hence it is best to let the give-and-take of free, reasoned debate decide the future of the nation.

To the radicals, however, this reasoning seems specious. They find it shortsighted and timid. The disintegration of traditional authority has made possible a fundamental transformation of the community; it has provided an opportunity to reconstruct political institutions and economic relationships. Should this great chance be jeopardized for the sake of some textbook concept of democracy? Should it be made dependent on the whims of an electorate blinded by years of fear and ignorance? The radicals see in the fall of the *ancien régime* the first step in a process of political, economic, and social reorganization leading to the creation of a classless society.

The Revolution Moves to the Left

The result is that the overthrow of the old order is always followed by a struggle, political and ideological rather than military in nature, between the members of the revolutionary coalition. What had started out as a united front among a diversity of parties and ideologies ends up as a dictatorial regime of the far left. The transformation is swift, as a rule. It rarely exceeds two or three years; sometimes it takes only a few months. But it is the outcome of unforeseen circumstances, of changed conditions, rather than of premeditation. The defeat of the *ancien régime* releases a torrent of popular hopes, expectations, demands, and passions that neither the radicals nor the moderates had anticipated. The collapse of the traditional restraints maintained by established authority arouses among the masses a violent clamor for economic and social change that goes far beyond the announced objectives of the revolutionary coalition. Now that the old order has been overthrown, anything seems possible. No party, no government can satisfy all the new expectations. But the radicals are able to capitalize on the millennial mood of the lower classes more successfully than the moderates. Their militant ideology and impassioned rhetoric, their sweeping promises of fundamental reform, accord more closely with the spirit of the masses than appeals by the middle-of-the-roaders for reason and restraint. In essence, they prevail because they are able to respond more effectively to the material and emotional needs of the hour.

The moderates, on the other hand, soon find themselves abandoned by the revolution they helped make. What they had expected to be an orderly transition to political democracy turns into a violent, chaotic quest for the New Jerusalem. They cannot understand what went wrong. They are bewildered by the indifference of the lower classes to their generous intentions, to their pledges of enlightened reform. Yet the rejection that the moderates experience after the revolution was prophetically described as early as 1885 by Friedrich Engels in a letter to the Russian socialist Vera Zasulich. "Once the spark has been put to the powder, once the forces have been released and national energy has been transformed from potential into kinetic energy, . . . the people who laid the spark to the mine will be swept away by the explosion, which will be a thousand times as strong as themselves and which will seek its vent where it can, according as the economic forces and resistances determine."

In fact, the mistakes of the moderates only assist the process of revolutionary change, according to Engels. "Supposing these people imagine they can seize power, what does it matter?" he asked. "Provided they make the hole which will shatter the dyke, the flood itself will soon rob them of their illusions. But if by chance these illusions resulted in giving them a superior force of will, why complain of that? People who boasted that they had *made* a revolution have always seen the next day that they had no idea what they were doing, that the revolution *made* did not in the least resemble the one they would have liked to make. This is what Hegel calls the irony of history." Here was an incisive analysis of what happens to the moderates following the fall of the old order.[1]

The radicals, however, are almost equally surprised by the course of events after the revolution. To be sure, they are better prepared to cope with the altered situation. The tide of popular militancy that overwhelms the moderates sweeps the radicals along in a new and unexpected direction. They are forced to improvise, to adapt to rapidly changing circumstances. Sometimes they claim that they had foreseen what would happen; occasionally they even pretend to control the forces that are carrying them to an unknown destination. But in fact they too are confused by the outpour of mass passions and yearnings which the collapse of the *ancien régime* has released. They must begin to alter their tactics, to revise their hypotheses. They have to face a reality for which the teachings of radical orthodoxy had not prepared them.

Trotsky, reflecting in exile on the nature of the revolutionary process, spoke almost poetically about the subjective and unpredictable element in any fundamental transformation of society. "The mighty design of the Russian revolution, the consecutiveness of its stages, the inexorable pressure of the masses, the finishedness of political groupings, the succinctness of slogans, all this wonderfully promotes the understanding of revolution in general, and therewith of human society," he wrote. "For we may consider it proven by the whole course of history that society, torn as it is by inner contradictions, conclusively reveals in a revolution not only its anatomy, but also its 'soul.'" Indeed, it is during the brief interregnum between the fall of the old order and the establishment of the new that Trotsky's theory of the intervention of the masses in the revolutionary process, "spontaneously" and "on their own volition," comes closest to historical reality.[2]

This does not mean that the radicals change their ultimate objective. That always remains the same. But they are compelled to alter their basic strategy. They had assumed that a long period of coalition government by the parties of the left and center would follow the victory of the revolution. There would be a series of important but noncontroversial reforms: the election of a representative parliament, the introduction of civil rights, the elimination of corruption in government, and the adoption of social welfare legislation. Only after this initial phase of gradual democratization had been completed would it become possible to go on to the establishment of a socialist system.

The course of events after the fall of the old order, however, forces the radicals to change their plans. They perceive that if they persist in a strategy of gradualism, they will suffer the same fate as the moderates. They too will be abandoned by the masses. They are therefore compelled, partly against their will, to become more militant. Since the moderates are inherently unable to violate their commitment to peaceful change, they are destined to be overwhelmed by the revolutionary forces they had helped unleash. But the radicals are more fortunate. They too are at first surprised by the outburst of militancy that the disintegration of established authority engenders. Yet before long they learn to ride the wave of popular passions, to direct it, use it, and eventually control it.

The Process of Radicalization

It is quite apparent, for example, that the fall of czarism in the spring of 1917 caught the Bolsheviks unawares. At first they seemed to favor a continuation of the same strategy they had been pursuing under the old order. Still weak and disorganized, they went on calling, almost out of habit, for a constituent assembly that would decide the future form of government for Russia in accordance with parliamentary democracy. The transition to socialism, they continued to assume, could not take place until the bourgeois revolution had run its course. Only Lenin appears to have recognized at once that the overthrow of the *ancien régime* had completely altered the political situation, creating the possibility of an immediate reconstruction of state and society. Even before his return from exile, he became convinced that the party should capitalize on the new rebelliousness of the masses by opposing the reformism of the provisional government.

On April 17, only twenty-four hours after his arrival at the Finland Station in Petrograd, he came out for a new strategy of uncompromising radicalism. "The specific feature of the present situation in Russia," he declared at a meeting of the Bolsheviks, "is that the country is *passing* from the first stage of the revolution—which, owing to the insufficient class-consciousness and organization of the proletariat, placed power in the hands of the bourgeoisie—to its *second* stage, which must place power in the hands of the proletariat and the poorest sections of the peasants." He sensed that the growing militancy of the lower classes, especially the urban workers, was creating the opportunity for an immediate seizure of power by the left. To cling to the tactics dictated by traditional Marxist doctrine, to wait for the revolutionary process to prepare the way gradually for socialism, would condemn the Bolsheviks to impotence. They would have to compete against the middle-of-the-road parties for the support of the electorate with the same soothing promises of reform and improvement, of progress and enlightenment. Was the left likely to win out in such a contest?

By championing the rebellious urban masses, on the other hand, the Bolsheviks might gain control over a powerful new force in the struggle for political domination. Hence Lenin argued from the beginning that the collapse of the old order had created the possibility of a direct transition from a semifeudal to a socialist form of authority. He rejected the provisional government, whose program of democratic reform had only a few years earlier seemed to him the inescapable precondition for socialism, in favor of the soviets—councils representing workers, soldiers, and peasants—which reflected more accurately the growing radicalism of the lower classes in the cities. This was the strategy that the Bolsheviks adopted in 1917 under his direction.

In an article on the "Revision of the Party Program" published late in October, Lenin openly described the ultimate objective of his policy:

We are riding to battle, that is, we are fighting for the conquest of political power by our Party. This power would be the dictatorship of the proletariat and the poor peasants. In taking power, we are not at all afraid of stepping beyond the bounds of the bourgeois system; on the contrary, we declare clearly, directly, definitely, and openly that we shall step beyond those bounds, that we shall fearlessly march towards socialism, that our road shall be through a Soviet Republic, through nationalization of banks and syndicates, through workers' control, through universal labor conscription, through nationalization of the land, confiscation of the landowners' livestock and implements, etc. In this sense we drafted our program of measures for transition to socialism.

Less than three weeks later the November revolution overthrew the provisional government and brought the Bolsheviks to power. The Russian experiment in government by a united front was now over.[3]

In China the revolutionary coalition of moderates and radicals survived a little longer. Since the leftists had been the dominant partner from the beginning, they could afford to tolerate the middle-of-the-roaders for a few years after the fall of the Kuomintang. Mao himself seemed reluctant to disrupt a united front that might still prove useful during the period of transition to socialism. But he too faced pressure from some of his more zealous followers who were itching for the spoils of victory. In March 1950, six months after coming to power, he explained to the regional leaders of the Communist party that it would be best for the time being to exempt the well-to-do peasantry from the program of agricultural reorganization so as not to alarm the liberal bourgeoisie. "The tactics in question are to leave untouched not only the capitalist rich peasants but also the semi-feudal ones in the agrarian reform scheduled for this winter in the southern provinces and some regions in the Northwest and to defer the solution of the problem of the semi-feudal rich peasants for several years." He urged the local party authorities to consider whether this policy was not "more advantageous."

There were several reasons for adopting it, according to Mao. First, the agrarian reform was unprecedented in scale, and "ultra-Left deviations" were therefore likely to occur. "If we touch only the landlords and not the rich peasants, we can more effectively isolate the landlords, protect the middle peasants and guard against indiscriminate beating and killing, which would be very hard to prevent otherwise." Second, under present conditions, with the fighting against the Kuomintang "practically over," the agrarian reform "stands out in sharp relief, and the shock to society will be particularly great and the landlords' outcries particularly shrill." Hence, "if we leave the semi-feudal rich peasants untouched for the time being and deal with them a few years later, we will stand on stronger ground, that is to say, politically we will have more initiative." And third, objective conditions were still not ripe for a dissolution of the revolutionary coalition. "We have formed a united front with the national bourgeoisie politically, economically and organizationally; and since the national bourgeoisie is closely tied up with the land problem, it seems better not to touch the semi-feudal rich peasants for the time being in order to set the minds of the national bourgeoisie at rest." There could be no doubt, in Mao's opinion, that the revolutionary coalition would eventually have to be replaced by an outright radical dictatorship, but the time for that had not yet arrived.

In June 1950, at a plenary session of the Central Committee of the Chinese Communist Party, he repeated in a written report the argument that the united front with bourgeois democracy remained essential for the attainment of the goals of the revolution. "We must earnestly unite with the democratic personages in all circles," he urged, "help them solve the problem of work and study, and overcome any tendency towards either closed-doorism or excessive accommodation in united front work." They might even be permitted to help shape the new order. "We must endeavor to make a success of the [consultative] conferences of people from all circles so that people from every walk of life can unite in a common effort. All matters of importance to the people's governments should be submitted to these conferences for discussion and decision." Not only that, "representatives at these conferences must have the right to express their views fully; any attempt to hinder such expression is wrong."

In an address delivered before the plenary session of the Central Committee, Mao elaborated on his views regarding the maintenance of the coalition. "The whole Party should try earnestly and painstakingly to make a success of its united front work. We should rally the petty bourgeoisie and the national bourgeoisie under the leadership of the working class and on the basis of the worker-peasant alliance." To be sure, the national bourgeoisie would eventually cease to exist, "but at this stage we should rally them around us and not push them away." Or better still, "we should struggle against them on the one hand and unite with them on the other." The leadership of the party must make this clear to its cadres. "We should . . . show by facts that it is right and necessary to unite with the national bourgeoisie, the democratic parties, democratic personages and intellectuals. Many of them were our enemies before, but now that they have broken with the enemy camp and come over to our side, we should unite with all these people, who can be more or less united with." Since it was in the interest of the "working people" to continue the alliance with political moderates, "we need to adopt these tactics now."

As late as February 1951, in a party circular that he drafted for the Central Committee, Mao was still insisting that "it is necessary to unite intellectuals, industrialists and businessmen, leading religious figures, the democratic parties and democratic personages on the basis of the struggle against imperialism and feudalism and to carry out education among them."

But then he gradually began to change his mind. This was in part a reflection of the growing boldness of the new order, of its confidence that it no longer needed the support of squeamish sympathizers or lukewarm fellow travelers. In part, however, it was a response to the increasing demand, outside as well as inside the party, for a more radical policy. The leadership could no longer resist that demand. In June 1952 Mao conceded that "with the overthrow of the landlord class and the bureaucrat-capitalist class, the contradiction between the working class and the national bourgeoisie has become the principal contradiction in China; therefore the national bourgeoisie should no longer be defined as an intermediate class."

A few years later, in a speech to the Politburo in April 1956, he broke with the moderates once and for all, denouncing them for pretending to be in favor of the revolution while actually opposing it. "To this very day they have reservations about the suppression of counter-revolutionaries. They didn't want to have a constitution of the socialist type, for, as they said, the Common Program was just perfect, and yet when the Draft Constitution came out, their hands all went up in favor. Things often turn into their opposites, and this is also true of the attitude of the democratic parties on many questions. They are in opposition, and yet not in opposition, often proceeding from being in opposition to not being in opposition." How could such people be trusted?

While Mao did not advocate outright repression, the moderates were to be regarded with caution and suspicion. "In our country the various democratic parties, consisting primarily of the national bourgeoisie and its intellectuals, emerged during the resistance to Japan and the struggle against Chiang Kai-shek, and they continue to exist to this day." In this respect, he explained, China was different from the Soviet Union. "We have purposely let the democratic parties remain, giving them opportunities to express their views and adopting a policy of both unity and struggle towards them. We unite with all those democratic personages who offer us well-intentioned criticisms." This policy should not be abandoned. "We should go on activating the enthusiasm of . . . people from the Kuomintang army and government . . . who are patriotic. We should even provide for . . . abusive types . . . and allow them to rail at us, while refuting their nonsense and accepting what makes sense in their rebukes. This is better for the Party, for the people and for socialism."

Still, the attitude of the moderates toward the revolution was unquestionably wishy-washy. They were not exactly opponents of the new order, but neither were they ardent supporters. While they might be tolerated, they should never be trusted. "Since classes and class struggle still exist in China, there is bound to be opposition in one form or another. Although all the democratic parties and democrats without party affiliation have professed their acceptance of the Chinese Communist Party, many of them are actually in opposition in varying degrees. On such matters as 'carrying the revolution through to the end,' the movement to resist U.S. aggression and aid Korea and the agrarian reform, they were against us and yet not against us." Were they likely to prove more reliable in the future? For Mao the period of collaboration with bourgeois democracy had finally come to an end. In the space of seven years, the moderates had declined from equal partners in a united front to a small sect of political recusants.[4]

The shift to the left that always follows the victory of the revolutionary coalition appeared least likely to occur in Cuba. For there the fall of the *ancien régime* had left power in the hands not of a political party or social movement, but of a man whose only evident goal had been the overthrow of the Batista dictatorship. No one, including Castro himself, seemed to know what use he would make of the authority that had been suddenly thrust upon him. Although dark mutterings were heard on the right that he would turn out to be a tool of the Communists, most observers, in Cuba as well as abroad, continued to believe that he would eventually grope his way to some form of parliamentary democracy and welfare capitalism. Everything he had said and done during the years of struggle against the old order suggested that he was at heart just a moderate, well-intentioned bourgeois reformer.

When Herbert L. Matthews interviewed Castro shortly after his victory, he found the same dedicated but impractical idealist he had first met two years earlier in the Sierra Maestra. But now the problems facing him were even more difficult. "This is the first time he has ever had political, economic and administrative authority, and no one can yet say just what he is going to do with the power he possesses. He himself cannot know, because he is finding that some ideals . . . are not feasible. For all the searing experience of those two amazing years of conflict, Fidel Castro is still an unformed, untried, inexperienced young man, when it comes to running a country."

What he had learned fighting the old order would prove of little help in dealing with the complex issues that confronted him now. "He . . . is beginning a new struggle, but the terms this time cannot be victory or death, only success or failure or something in between for the social revolution which is his goal." During his years as a guerrilla leader, Castro had been "a confirmed, fanatical idealist." And some of those around him—his brother Raúl, for example, or Che Guevara—might still be the same hotspurs who had fought in the Sierra Maestra. But not Castro. "The responsibilities and the realities of power are forcing him to compromise, to yield, to adapt himself." The fiery revolutionary would gradually turn into a mature, responsible statesman. "To create an honest, efficient, democratic Cuba is an infinitely harder task than Fidel faced when we first talked together . . . on Feb. 17, 1957. All one can say today is that he knows it and is confident. Circumstances, not Fidel Castro, have changed."

While admitting that it was still too early to tell how Castro would exercise his authority, Matthews pooh-poohed the idea that the new government might turn to radicalism. Visiting Cuba again in the summer of 1959, he wrote that "there are no Reds in the Cabinet and none in high positions in the Government or army in the sense of being able to control either governmental or defense policies. The only power worth considering in Cuba is in the hands of Premier Castro, who is not only not Communist but decidedly anti-Communist, even though he does not consider it desirable in the present circumstances to attack or destroy the Reds—as he is in a position to do any time he wants." It was reassuring to most readers of the *New York Times* to learn that the conservative Batista dictatorship was not likely to be followed by a radical Castro dictatorship.[5]

Yet in fact Castro was already moving in the direction of a far more drastic reconstruction of polity and economy than anyone had expected. Not even he had foreseen this turn during the period of guerrilla warfare in the Sierra Maestra. Later some of his conservative critics charged that he had always been a leftist in his sympathies, waiting only for the opportune moment to cast off the mask. Some of his apologists, on the other hand, encouraged at times by Castro himself, have argued that he had been forced toward radicalism by the opposition of antirevolutionary businessmen in Cuba and anticommunist politicians in the United States. Neither of these contentions is convincing, however. No evidence exists, not even in the most private conversation or confidential letter, that Castro had plans for a radical dictatorship before 1959. And as for the claim that what drove him to the left was the hostility of foreign and domestic opponents, that was more a result than a cause of his radicalization. As long as he was still fighting in the mountains for bare survival, there was no need to wrestle with the question of what to do once he came to power. The overthrow of the Batista regime had been goal enough. But after the old order was defeated, Castro could no longer delay deciding what the new Cuba should be like. That is when his shift toward radicalism began.

He recognized that the downfall of the old order had generated throughout Cuban society, especially among the lower classes, aspirations that could not be satisfied within the framework of traditional political institutions. Once the Batista dictatorship collapsed, nothing seemed too daring to the popular mind. The extraordinary triumph of the revolution was now expected to produce an equally extraordinary result. Could Castro afford to disappoint these mass longings? Could he offer his old followers and new converts nothing more than a moderate, prudent, and honest form of representative government? Would it be enough to restore the violated constitution, reinvigorate the exhausted party system, and resume the frustrating search for parliamentary democracy? What had seemed acceptable in the remote Sierra Maestra became pathetically inadequate in jubilant postrevolutionary Havana. The conditions created by his own success forced Castro to follow a course of radical change.

He did not really have much choice. As he himself admitted in a speech on May Day 1961, the logic of the revolutionary victory had driven him far beyond the demands adopted during the struggle against the *ancien régime*. "To those who talk to us about the 1940 constitution, we say that the 1940 constitution is already too outdated and old for us. We have advanced beyond that short section of the 1940 constitution that was good for its time but which was never carried out." The revolution, which he now described as "socialist," had left that constitution far behind. "We must talk of a new constitution, yes, a new constitution, but not a bourgeois constitution, not a constitution contributing to the domination of certain classes by exploiting classes, but a constitution contributing to a new social system without the exploitation of man by man. That new social system is called Socialism, and this constitution will therefore be a socialist constitution."

Almost as soon as he came to power, months before Matthews assured the world that Castro was "decidedly anti-Communist," he started in fact to move to the left, carried by a wave of millenarian anticipation that his victory had generated. Though still denying that he was a Communist, he had nothing favorable to say about the capitalistic system either. "Our revolution is neither capitalist nor Communist!" he announced on May 21, 1959. "We want to liberate man from dogmas, and free his economy and society, without terrorizing or hindering anyone. We have been placed in a position where we must choose between capitalism which starves people, and Communism, which resolves the economic problem but suppresses the liberties so greatly cherished by man." To the new Cuba one was no better than the other. "Our revolution is not red, but olive green, the color of the rebel army that emerged from the heart of the Sierra Maestra."

Five months later, on October 26, he told a mass rally in front of the Presidential Palace in Havana that the real reason for the charge of communism directed against him by the enemies of the revolution was his effort to end alien domination of the country's economy. Without explicitly denying the accusation, he maintained that what he really sought was to give the people of Cuba greater control over their national destiny. That was why the reactionaries in the United States were so opposed to the new order:

If we plant rice we damage the foreign interests; if we produce grain we damage foreign interests; if we produce cotton we damage foreign interests; if we lower electrical tariffs we damage foreign interests; if we make a law concerning oil—which we are planning next—we damage foreign interests; if we make a Mining Law—which also will happen soon—we damage foreign interests; if we form a merchant marine we damage foreign interests; if we want to find new markets for our country, we are damaging foreign interests. If we want them to buy from us as much as we buy from them, we are damaging foreign interests. And that is the explanation for our making the Revolutionary Laws which damage national and foreign privileges; it is for that they attack us, it is for that they call us Communists, it is for that they accuse us, using every possible pretext to seize our country. Perhaps the Agrarian Reform is not Cuban? Perhaps the electric tariff was not reduced by Cubans? Perhaps the proposal to create a merchant marine was not Cuban, or the proposal to plant rice and cotton and produce grain on our own land? Perhaps it is not Cuban to construct houses for our workers, our peasants and their families?

The red scare was being fanned by the counterrevolutionaries to conceal their plots and conspiracies.

As Castro moved farther leftward, he became more open in avowing the radical goals of his government. On April 15, 1961, two days before the landing of a rebel force of Cuban exiles at the Bay of Pigs, he for the first time described the new order as a "socialist revolution carried out under the very noses of the Yankees." And on March 26, 1962, he announced on television that Cuba had become a Marxist state. "We must look forward, comrades! That is the only proper attitude to have, which all honest men should have, which all honest revolutionists, old and new, should have without reservations of any kind, without regrets of any kind, without mistrust of any kind."

Looking forward meant accepting the teachings of communism. It meant "embracing our cause, our revolution, the historic mission of this revolution, embracing Marxism-Leninism, which is the ideology of the working class, which is a science, . . . which possesses all the attractions which a true revolutionary theory, a true revolutionary science possesses." More than that, Marxism-Leninism was an "extremely rich" ideology, for "from it we can extract extraordinary lessons; in it we have an extraordinary instrument for struggle, an incomparable cause, the best cause for which to fight, the best cause for which to die, a cause which can be identified only with the spirit which is most profoundly human, most profoundly just, most profoundly generous, most profoundly good." What had started out after the fall of Batista as a nonpartisan united front ended up three years later as an out-and-out Communist regime.[6]

Still, the transition of the new order from a revolutionary coalition to a radical dictatorship is generally less a result of premeditation than of circumstance. The militants always assume, to be sure, that the united front will eventually be replaced by a government of the far left. They never deny that; sometimes they say so quite openly. But the alliance with the moderates is expected to continue for a long time, at least until it has had a chance to complete its historic task of modernization and democratization. The tide of popular passions released by the revolution, however, forces the militants to move to the left more rapidly than they had planned. They do not radicalize the masses; it is rather the masses that radicalize them, that impel them to pursue policies they had not initially favored. To do otherwise would mean risking the support of the lower classes essential for their political success. They therefore have to ride the wave of plebeian fervor until it gradually loses its momentum, until they can begin to direct it, control it, and ultimately harness it to the establishment of a dictatorial form of authority. This is the pattern that every revolution seems to follow after the defeat of the *ancien régime*, whether in Russia, China, Cuba, or Vietnam.

The Myth of Coalition Government

The radicalization of the new order, however, does not mean the immediate abandonment of the outward form of a united front. More often than not, the militants continue for a while to maintain the fiction that the government still represents a variety of political organizations and beliefs. Thereby they are able to gain the support of those moderates who are now prepared to submit to the inevitable, but who prefer to avoid the appearance of unconditional surrender. Moreover, in molding public opinion, abroad as well as at home, it is prudent to avoid the impression of a monolithic one-party dictatorship. Nevertheless, while the radical regime often retains the look and flavor of a revolutionary coalition, power remains securely in the hands of loyal militants. And in time even the semblance of a united front gradually pales and vanishes.

This process of progressive radicalization can be seen most clearly in China. Here the People's Political Consultative Conference, which served as a constituent assembly and the highest representative body from 1949 until the adoption of a new constitution in 1954, included 106 delegates from minor parties and civic organizations out of a total of 585 voting and 77 nonvoting members. In addition, there were 10 "democratic personages" not affiliated with any political group and 75 specially invited representatives. Thus almost a third of the total membership consisted of independents or delegates from 11 small parties that had existed under the old order: the Revolutionary Committee of the Kuomintang, the China Democratic League, the China Democratic National Construction Association, the Chinese Peasants' and Workers' Democratic Party, the Chinese People's National Salvation Association, the San-min chu-i Comrades' Association, the China Kuomintang Democratic Promotion League, the China Association for Promoting Democracy, the Chi-kung Tang or Freemasons, the Chiu-san Society, and the Taiwan Democratic Self-Government League.

In addition, noncommunists held important positions in the government and the bureaucracy. Three of the 6 vice-chairmen of the Chinese People's Government formed in 1949 and 2 of the 4 deputy premiers of the State Administrative Council did not belong to the Communist party. In the cabinet, 7 of the 24 ministers were leaders of various "democratic parties," 3 were "democratic personages" or "intellectuals," and there was even a former Kuomintang general among them. Their portfolios, to be sure, were not among the most important or prestigious. They included Light Industry, Post and Telegraph, Communications, Agriculture, Forestry and Land Reclamation, Water Conservation, and Culture and Education. In every case, moreover, a member of the Communist party served as vice-minister. Still, noncommunists constituted 42 percent of all the ministers and vice-ministers, while many more held lower positions in the other ministries, as well as appointments to the Supreme Court and the People's Revolutionary Military Council. On the face of it, China was being ruled by a coalition of militants and moderates.

Yet behind the facade of a united front lay the reality of one-party government. A. Doak Barnett, whose reporting on the Communists during their struggle for power had remained sober and objective, recognized almost as soon as they achieved victory that their goal had now become a dictatorship of the left:

> At present the Communist government is made up of a nominal "coalition," but it is a coalition of people who agree, rather than of people who differ, in their political points of view. The Political Consultative Conference, which assisted the Communists in creating their Central Government and which will be the only "representative" body in that government until the election of an All-China People's Congress at a future time now undetermined, is made up of Communist-picked delegates from [several] political groups and parties and representatives of various geographical regions, army units and organizations of workers, youth, women, racial minorities, religious circles and overseas Chinese. All these people have accepted the program of the Communist Party and have publicly pledged themselves to follow its leadership. There are no competing political ideas represented, and in many cases, the non-Communists seem to be trying to outdo the Communists in pushing a

Marxist program. The motivation behind the non-Communist parties' adherence to this coalition is probably mixed. Some of the support is based on the honest conviction that the Communist program holds out hope for improving the situation in China. But opportunism also seems to play a significant role. In any case none of the minor parties . . . are political parties in the real sense of the word. They fit the traditional Chinese pattern of political cliques. Their membership is small, their platforms are vague, and their power is almost nonexistent.

Apart from providing window dressing for the Communists' coalition, however, these non-Communist groups are playing a minor role in the present situation. For the Communists they offer means to sound out the attitudes of key groups, such as industrialists and intellectuals, getting their suggestions—which the Communists may heed or disregard as they wish—and attempting to obtain their support or cooperation under the new regime. The members of these groups are given an opportunity to participate in political affairs, and although they have little authority or power, the mere fact that they are put on committees and called upon for consultation makes many of them feel they are playing an important political role.

Even this sham coalition of radicals and democrats soon began to crumble. Once the Communist leadership felt secure enough to dispense with the appearance of a united front, the moderates were unceremoniously pushed aside. In 1955 Barnett, who had spent a year studying the new China from the safety of Hong Kong, observed in a report published by the American Universities Field Staff that the "People's Democratic Dictatorship" still found it useful to maintain the "facade" of a united front. "Not only do the National People's Congress and its Standing Committee contain sizeable numbers of non-Communist members, but the People's Political Consultative Conference . . . continues to exist as an advisory 'organization of the Chinese People's Democratic United Front,' even though [under the new constitution] it has been displaced as the top 'representative' body in the government by the National People's Congress." Yet in reality the "so-called 'United Front'" was little more than a charade. "It is merely a channel for participation in the government of several weak, non-Communist political groupings, and of Communist-controlled mass organizations, which serve as satellites to the Communist Party and must completely back its program." Nevertheless, Barnett found it significant that "at this stage in their revolution the Chinese Communists still feel it is desirable to make some conciliatory gestures toward non-Communist groups and individuals (including some ex-warlords)."

In the course of the next few years, however, the regime concluded that there was no longer any need to maintain even the semblance of a coalition. Early in 1958, during the "antirightist movement," the ministers representing the "small parties" were repudiated by their own supporters under pressure from the government. Before being dismissed from office, they had to undergo the humiliation of confessing their error, expressing contrition, and requesting appropriate punishment. The proportion of noncommunists in the cabinet, which had been close to half in 1949, dropped to less than a third by 1962—12 portfolios out of 39. Strictly speaking, the actual figure was even lower, no more than 10 portfolios, since 2 of the "democratic personages" serving as ministers had been granted membership in the Communist Party late in 1958 as a reward for their loyalty during the campaign against "rightists."

As a result, the percentage of Communist ministers and vice-ministers, which had been 58 in 1949, rose to 87 by 1966, and indirect evidence exists that if the statistical information were more complete, the figure might easily turn out to be higher still. Even more significant, the noncommunists in the cabinet were a senescent as well as dwindling group, their average age in 1962 being sixty-eight. By now there was no longer any need to carry on the pretense that political authority was being exercised by a coalition of moderates and militants.[7]

In Vietnam the decline of the united front followed roughly the same pattern. As long as the struggle against the French was still going on, the radicals made a strenuous effort to maintain the appearance of a revolutionary coalition. The "Government of Union and Resistance" formed in Hanoi in 1946 had only 4 known members of the Indochinese Communist Party, among them Ho Chi Minh, out of a total of 12. Yet even in those early years the moderates were shunted to positions of limited importance and influence. The socialist Hoang Ming Giam was allowed to serve as foreign minister for as long as the rebel regime had little contact with foreign states.

Once serious diplomatic negotiations began in 1954, however, he was transferred to the ministry of culture. Nguyen Manh Ha, a Catholic who enjoyed the advantage of being the son-in-law of a Communist member of the French legislature, was at first named minister of economics. Yet before long a more suitable post was found for him in Paris and Geneva, where he acted as go-between for various exile groups of Vietnamese. Even in those ministries that the moderates were permitted to retain, real power was exercised by a Communist official occupying some nominally subordinate position. Nguyen Van Huyen, the nonparty minister of education, confessed to a friend who later fled to South Vietnam that all important decisions were made by the Lao Dong Party. He himself had never been consulted.

It was not hard to see through this facade. The British novelist Graham Greene, writing from Hanoi in the spring of 1955, described perceptively the way in which political power was being exercised under the new order:

> Until the date of the elections some pretense, however slender, has to be preserved that this is a national and not a Communist Government. The Lao Dong Party, which is purely Communist, controls the government, but there is the semblance of a national front, the Lien Viet, including such minority groups as the Dan Chu which might in happier times have corresponded to the British Labour Party. A number of Ministers belong to the Dan Chu, and some of these may well be envious of colleagues who crossed the line and escaped to the South before the war was over. In theory they too could escape, but even if they reached Haiphong and Saigon the assassins would follow. The Catholics too have one so-called representative in the government. [But] non-Communist Ministers are usually assisted and controlled by a Communist Vice-Minister.

A striking resemblance exists between this report on North Vietnam and the one on China written at almost the same time by Barnett.

The political alliance between moderates and militants continued, at least on paper, long after the defeat of the *ancien régime*. As late as the 1960s there was still a small Democratic party representing, according to the official line, enlightened groups among the "bourgeoisie," and an equally small Socialist party reflecting the views of "intellectuals" and "progressive personages," both of them nominally separate and independent political organizations allied with the Communists in a united front for "socialist development" and the reunification of north and south. Denied any real power, they were nevertheless allowed to nominate candidates to the rubber-stamp parliament, who invariably received comfortable majorities of around 90 percent of the votes, though Communist candidates did much better with majorities approaching 100 percent. There were even a few noncommunists in the cabinet. The democrat Phan Anh was minister for foreign trade; another democrat, Tran Dang Khoa, was minister for irrigation; the socialist Hoang Minh Giam continued to head the ministry of culture; and the nonparty Nguyen Van Huyen held the portfolio of education. This tolerance of theoretically independent political groups was designed to demonstrate that North Vietnam was not a "single-party" state, that it was willing to share authority with "democrats" and "progressives." But no one actually believed this official myth, neither the rulers nor the ruled.[8]

In Cuba, on the other hand, the revolutionary coalition was dissolved within three years after the victory of the new order. At first Castro maintained the policy of a united front, partly because he was not quite sure what to do with the power he had acquired, but partly because it provided him with a pretext for postponing the election of a legislative assembly to decide the future of the country. Before the fall of the Batista regime he had seemed to be unequivocally committed to parliamentary democracy. In the "Sierra Maestra Manifesto" of July 12, 1957, he had declared "under formal promise" that after victory a provisional government would hold general elections at the end of a year for all offices in the state, the provinces, and the municipalities, and that power would then be transferred immediately to the victorious candidates. A year later, on July 20, 1958, he had repeated in the "Unity Manifesto of the Sierra Maestra" that "after the tyrant's fall," a "brief" provisional government would be formed to guide the nation to "a normal state of affairs" and the establishment of "full constitutional and democratic rights."

But now that the time had come to fulfill these promises, he began to have second thoughts. How wise was it to allow the achievements of the revolution to be jeopardized by reactionary demagogues who might confuse and mislead the masses? Should the creation of a new and better Cuba depend on the capriciousness of party politics and election campaigns? Would it not be better to delay a legislative assembly until the new order had the opportunity to enlighten public opinion? As Castro shifted from the pledge of parliamentary democracy to the advocacy of radical dictatorship, the facade of a united front became increasingly important for his regime. It would protect him against the charge of one-man rule, similar to that which Batista had established, or of political domination by a single party or a single ideology. Hence a revolutionary coalition composed of several groups committed to the reconstruction of state and society seemed the most effective instrument for the achievement of his objectives. Not only that, the appearance of participation in government affairs by a variety of independent civic organizations would make it that much easier to disregard the promise of general elections.

By May 1, 1960, sixteen months after coming to power, Castro felt confident enough to declare before a huge crowd gathered in the Civic Plaza in Havana that the direct involvement of the progressive forces of the nation in the process of revolutionary reconstruction had made an elected national assembly superfluous:

> Our enemies, our detractors, ask about elections. [*Prolonged shouts of "Revolution!" "Why elections?" and "We've already voted for Fidel!"*] . . . As if a true revolution like this in Cuba could come into power disregarding the will of the people! [*Shouts of "Never!"*] As if the only democratic procedure for taking power were the electoral processes so often prostituted to falsify the will and the interests of the people and so many times used to put into office the most inept and most shrewd, rather than the most competent and the most honest.
>
> As if after so many fraudulent elections, as if after so much false and treacherous politicking, as if after so much corruption the people could be made to believe that the only democratic procedure for a people to choose their leaders was the electoral procedure. And as if *this* procedure were not democratic—this procedure through which a people choose their leaders not with a pencil but with the blood and the lives of 20,000 fellow patriots, struggling without arms against a professional and well-armed army, trained and outfitted by a powerful foreign country.
>
> The people of Cuba broke their chains and by breaking the chains that enslaved them, they put an end to privileges, they put an end to injus-

tices, and they put an end forever to the practice of criminal abuse of the people.

The people of Cuba have begun a truly democratic phase of progress, of liberty, of justice. If there is any process in which the incompetent fall behind, if there is any process in which the crooked fail, that is the revolutionary process.

The decision to reject parliamentary democracy in favor of direct representation of the people's will through a revolutionary coalition accelerated Castro's drift to the left. Unwilling to risk his power on the outcome of popular elections, he was increasingly forced to rely on the support of the Communists, first as their ally, then as their sympathizer, and finally as both their leader and captive. Yet in fact they were Johnny-come-latelies in the establishment of the new order in Cuba. During his struggle for power, they had regarded him as simply a middle-class visionary, a romantic utopian. They had argued that those relying on force to overthrow the established system were led by the vain hope of "achieving the defeat of Batista through a combination of every type of minority action (counter-*coups d'état* with the aid of factions in the army, *putsch*, terrorism, etc.) with the hope of receiving the support of Washington." According to the Communists, these would-be revolutionaries, confused and divided, had produced only one result: the "sabotage of unity and popular action."

Hence the far left dismissed Castro's attack on the Moncada barracks in 1953 as just another reckless "*putsch*," another example of futile bourgeois "adventurism." It spoke with a sense of ideological superiority about the "little group of young men, well-intentioned but influenced by the *putschist* line, [who] made a frustrated assault against the military barracks in Santiago de Cuba, hoping to take possession of this important position and from there to launch an attack against . . . Havana." Even after the *Granma* expedition had landed on the island late in 1956, the Communists remained suspicious and aloof. Not until two of their emissaries visited Castro in the Sierra Maestra in the spring of 1958, barely seven months before his victory, did some of them finally begin to support the guerrillas.

Yet while their role in Castro's rise to power had been negligible, their influence on the use that he made of it was crucial. As he began to move farther and farther to the left, to the dismay and bewilderment of moderate Fidelistas, the Communists became his most reliable followers. He found in them loyal, dedicated allies in the task of political and social reconstruction.

The collaboration between them was based essentially on mutual need and advantage. K. S. Karol, a left-wing journalist sympathetic though not uncritical toward the revolution in Cuba, found during a visit to Havana in 1961 that while many of Castro's old supporters were unhappy with his growing reliance on the Communists, they blamed it mostly on "weak" comrades in their own ranks. "It was the vacillation and lack of staying power of these [weaklings] that had compelled Fidel to rely more and more on [Communist] militants; they, for one, were unlikely to flee to the United States and their loyalty to the Revolution was beyond question. Some of those to whom I spoke were all the more bitter for having relations or friends among the 'lukewarm.'" One Fidelista told Karol: "When we were all in the underground, I should never have dreamed that some of my comrades were potential traitors, and that I would have to work with the kind of men we used to despise for their lack of revolutionary imagination." Even now he held the Communists in "low esteem"; he was certain that their "dogmatic cadres" would prove incapable of running the country intelligently. "Still, he acknowledged that Fidel had no choice, that one had to work with [their organization], and possibly even under its direction." The inner logic of the policy pursued by Castro had driven him into an alliance with communism. Whether he realized it or not, he had no choice.

At first, however, it seemed best to preserve the united front, in form, at least, if not in spirit or substance. There was still some advantage in pretending that the new order in Cuba supported all democratic forces in national life without regard for class, interest, or ideology. But by the summer of 1961 those in power felt secure enough to dispense with the fiction of government by a coalition. That was when the three major political groups on the island were fused to form the Integrated Revolutionary Organizations.

The dominant element in this union was the People's Socialist Party, a Communist organization which had by now become the mainstay of the Castro regime. Then came the Revolutionary Directorate, a radical but noncommunist movement formed six years earlier on a platform demanding "the integral liberation of the nation, free from foreign interference and domestic exploitation." It advocated a national revolution that would represent an "integral change in the political, judicial, social, [and] economic system," fostering the "emergence of a new collective psychological attitude to consolidate and encourage the revolutionary program." The third partner in the new party was Castro's own 26th of July Movement, composed of moderates and militants, democrats and socialists, Marxists and anti-Marxists, previously united by their opposition to Batista, but now decomposing into cliques and factions. The Integrated Revolutionary Organizations moved rapidly leftward in policy and outlook. In May 1963 the name was changed to the less ambiguous United Party of the Socialist Revolution, and in October 1965 to the defiantly explicit Communist Party of Cuba. The country was now under the complete control of the militants.[9]

The united front thus disintegrates soon after its victory, making way for a radical dictatorship. Sometimes the process takes only a few months, sometimes a few years. Its progress is often obscured by a deliberate attempt to maintain a facade of collaborative government, of nonpartisan reformism. Yet behind the appearance of a continuing united-front policy stands the reality of growing left-wing domination. Eventually the mask is cast aside. In some cases, as in Cuba, this happens soon after the radical dictatorship has been firmly established. In others, as in North Vietnam, the sham revolutionary coalition drags on for a while, gradually fading away unnoticed and unmourned. The ultimate result, however, is always the same. The moderates, who had helped create the new order, are in the end pushed aside, silenced, exiled, or imprisoned. The militants, on the other hand, emerge victorious, gain control of the government, and proceed to reshape society in accordance with their principles and doctrines.

Why the Radicals Win Out

What accounts for this outcome of a revolution that had triumphed through the combined efforts of radicals and reformers? Why is it that militants win and moderates lose in the contest for power that follows the fall of the old order? Basically, the left is better able to sense and articulate the changing aspirations of a revolutionary society. As long as the struggle against the *ancien régime* is still going on, most of those who oppose it seek only to end its abuses and correct its mistakes. Once the old order falls, however, all that changes. The disintegration of traditional beliefs and values produces a rapid radicalization of public opinion. The demands for moderate reform that had been advanced during the struggle against established authority suddenly seem pitifully inadequate. A mood of chiliastic fervor sweeps over a community that has witnessed the overthrow of anointed and consecrated authority. In the wild, tempestuous days of revolutionary upheaval, the middle-of-the-roaders with their doctrines of sober reformism appear stodgy and dull. Committed to a program of improvement in polity and economy that, while well-intentioned, does not alter the distribution of power and wealth, they find themselves abandoned by the masses whose expectations have now risen beyond political democracy and social amelioration. The radicals, on the other hand, though also unprepared for the swift radicalization of public opinion which follows the collapse of the *ancien régime*, soon adapt to the new militant mood in society. They learn how to make use of the growing militancy of the lower classes, expressing and harnessing the inarticulate social dissatisfactions of the poor and propertyless.

This radical appeal to the popular feeling of excited expectancy, of imminent liberation, appears, for instance, in the speech by Che Guevara to Cuban militiamen in the summer of 1960. A fiery, impassioned prophet, he preached that the basic struggle in which they were engaged was not primarily in defense of their own country, but for the liberation of all mankind from injustice and oppression:

We are at the end of an era, and not only here in Cuba. No matter what is said or hoped to the contrary, the form of capitalism we have known, in which we were raised, and under which we have suffered, is being defeated all over the world. The monopolies are being overthrown; collective science is scoring new and important triumphs daily. In the Americas we have had the proud and devoted duty to be the vanguard of a movement of liberation which began a long time ago on the other subjugated continents, Africa and Asia. Such a profound social change demands [in turn] equally profound changes in the mental structure of the people.

There was something exciting and inspiring in this vision of a world being reborn.[10]

What can the moderates offer to compete with it? Only their theories of civil liberty and representative government, theories that after the fall of the *ancien régime* seem dry and pedantic. What had appeared fair and reasonable before the revolution appears dull and timid afterward. Basically, the moderates lose to the militants because their vision of the future is no longer able to arouse and inspire.

There is more to it than that, however. The radicals are victorious not only because they are more sensitive to the dominant mood of a revolutionary society, but because they are more disciplined and determined in pursuing their objective. Perhaps it would be accurate to say that their ability to maintain a sense of unity and purpose is to a large extent a reflection of their ideology. To start with, they are better organized than their opponents. The moderates soon begin to divide, to fall apart into splinters and factions, partly because of their realization that they are losing in the struggle for public opinion, but partly because of their commitment to individualism, nonconformity, and untrammeled debate. As the tide of popular support turns against them, they tend to disintegrate, forming coteries and sects. The radicals, on the other hand, are taught by the doctrines they embrace that private judgment must bow to collective judgment, that the individual will is subordinate to the general will. For them acceptance of party leadership is a virtue, compliance with party policy a duty. Their discipline becomes a vital asset in a time of revolutionary upheaval.

Raymond Robins, who was with the American Red Cross Mission in Russia in 1917, described this radical sense of organized purpose in his account of the Moscow State Conference, which met late in August, composed of former members of the Duma as well as representatives of the soviets, the trade unions, local governments, and other important civic groups and associations. He was impressed by "the demeanor of a certain set of delegates," those on the left. "They sat by themselves compactly. They behaved compactly. Alone in the great hall they seemed to constitute a body of opinion knowing exactly what it wanted and knowing exactly how it proposed to get it. In the midst of a Russia of irresolution and of indecision they were clear and emphatic. They were ominous. They were the delegates from the Soldiers' and Workmens' Soviets." Here was the sense of unity, the feeling of resolve, that made it possible for the Bolsheviks to seize power three months later.[11]

The militants have still another advantage over the moderates. They are more determined, more persevering; some would say more ruthless. They are prepared to ignore pledges and forget promises. They change their tactics to fit changing conditions, even if this means a reversal of direction, an about-face in policy. To their opponents they seem faithless and unprincipled; yet that may not be altogether fair. They too have their principles, principles to which they remain consistently loyal. But these are different from the ones professed by the moderates. What the latter consider ends—individual liberty, political democracy, representative government, parliamentary authority—the former regard as only means. They are implements to be used for the attainment of a nobler aim, a higher purpose: the creation of a society without classes, without rich and poor, without oppressors and oppressed. To achieve that goal, a shift of tactics or a disregard of commitments or a violation of pledges is fully justifiable. The ultimate objective is too important to be risked for the sake of squeamish consistency. It must be attained, whatever the cost.

To Lenin, for instance, it was clear that as soon as the *ancien régime* falls, the left has to be prepared to take advantage of the weaknesses of its democratic rivals, even if this means entering into a spurious alliance with some of them. Writing in the spring of 1920, he argued in his critique of *"Left-Wing" Communism—An Infantile Disorder* that the best way to hasten the defeat of the moderates was by fostering their disputes and differences. "The petty-bourgeois democrats . . . inevitably vacillate between the bourgeoisie and the proletariat, between bourgeois democracy and the Soviet system, between reformism and revolutionism, between love for the workers and fear of the proletarian dictatorship." The proper tactics for the Communists should therefore consist in *"utilizing* these vacillations, not ignoring them." And utilizing them meant "concessions to elements that are turning towards the proletariat—in addition to fighting those who turn towards the bourgeoisie." As a result of these "correct tactics," not only had the Mensheviks begun to decline, but "stubbornly opportunist" groups were being isolated, and "the best of the workers and the best elements among the petty-bourgeois democrats are being brought into our camp." This was bound to be a "lengthy process," however, so that rash slogans like "no compromises, no manoeuvres" would only delay "the strengthening of the revolutionary proletariat's influence and the enlargement of its forces."

Since the enemies of the revolution remained strong despite the overthrow of the old order, Lenin maintained, the best strategy for dealing with them was to divide and rule:

> After the first socialist revolution of the proletariat, and the overthrow of the bourgeoisie in some country, the proletariat of that country remains *for a long time weaker* than the bourgeoisie, simply because of the latter's extensive international links, and also because of the spontaneous and continuous restoration and regeneration of capitalism and the bourgeoisie by the small commodity producers of the country which has overthrown the bourgeoisie. The more powerful enemy can be vanquished only by exerting the utmost effort, and by the most thorough, careful, attentive, skillful and *obligatory* use of any, even the smallest, rift between the enemies, any conflict of interests among the bourgeoisie of the various countries, and among the various groups or types of bourgeoisie within the various countries, and also by taking advantage of any, even the smallest, opportunity of winning a mass ally, even though this ally is temporary, vacillating, unstable, unreliable and conditional. Those who do not understand this reveal a failure to understand even the smallest grain of Marxism, of modern scientific socialism *in general.* Those who have not proved *in practice,* over a fairly considerable period of time and in fairly varied political situations, their ability to apply this truth in practice have not yet learned to help the revolutionary class in its struggle to emancipate all toiling humanity from the exploiters. And this applies equally to the period *before* and *after* the proletariat has won political power.

Accordingly, the defenders of the revolution must be not only brave but cunning, not only resolute but deceptive. The sanctity of their cause justifies any tactics.[12]

It is a combination of ends and means, in other words, a combination of purposes and methods, that accounts for the victory of the radicals in the revolution. They are more responsive and more resourceful than the moderates. They reflect the spirit of the times more accurately; they capture its fervor and exuberance. As a result, they rapidly increase their popular following at the expense of their democratic rivals. They may not always gain a majority, since the underlying discontent of the masses remains to a considerable extent diffuse and amorphous. It is inarticulate, undisciplined, focused largely on local injustices and private grievances. But the radicals do attract sufficient support among the lower classes to form a militant, resolute minority strong enough to defeat their opponents.

The steady leftward shift of public opinion following the fall of the *ancien régime* can be measured by the growth of the various Communist parties in the early years of the revolution. Some of the converts, to be sure, are only opportunists who sense which way the wind is blowing and are eager to end up on the victorious side. But others are won over by a sincere faith in a new and better social order based on equality and justice.

In January 1917, on the eve of the overthrow of czarism, the Bolsheviks had a membership of less than 24,000, but by April the figure had climbed to 79,000, and by August to roughly 200,000. Only after they seized power three months later, however, did the period of mass conversion begin. In March 1918 there were 390,000 members. By March 1919, a critical period in the civil war in Russia, the number had declined slightly to 350,000, but in March 1920 it reached 612,000, and in March 1921 733,000.

The figures for the Chinese Communist Party show the same general tendency. In April 1945, a few months before the defeat of Japan, it had 1,211,000 members. At first the total rose slowly, reaching 1,348,000 in the course of 1946. But then a sudden jump occurred to 2,200,000 at the beginning of 1947 and 2,759,000 at the end. By the middle of 1948 the membership reached 3,000,000. In October 1949, when the Communists finally achieved victory over the Kuomintang, the number was 4,488,000; in the middle of 1950 it was 5,000,000 and, at the end, 5,822,000.

Not enough is known about the growth of the Dang Lao Dong in North Vietnam; but the pattern was roughly similar. In 1946, when the struggle against the French was just beginning, the membership totaled no more than about 20,000. By 1948, after the revolutionary movement had demonstrated that it could hold its own against a technologically superior enemy, the figure rose to 168,000. And in 1960, six years after victory, the membership stood at 500,000. In Southeast Asia, then, as in Russia and China, there was first a steady growth in the strength of the far left, followed, as soon as the Communists gained power, by a massive expansion.[13]

Not long after the fall of the *ancien régime,* the radicals are thus firmly in control. Having succeeded in defeating the democrats, with whom they had been allied during the struggle against the old order, they acquire substantial popular support, establish a dictatorial form of government, and prepare for a fundamental reconstruction of polity and economy. During their rise to power they display flexibility combined with firmness, idealism with shrewdness, moderation with tenacity. In a time of uncertainty and confusion, they alone seem to have a clear political objective and the discipline needed to achieve it. Hence victory is essentially their reward for commitment and determination. Now they are in a position to start rebuilding the world.

The Passing of the Moderates

And what about the losers? What happens to those who have been rejected by the new order that they helped create? They become the first in a long succession of victims of a revolution whose coming they greeted with so much joy and hope. A few of them survive, to be sure, by deserting to the other side. They confess their error; they renounce their heresy; they promise to improve; they swear allegiance to the cause of radicalism. The victors are charitable and forgiving. After all, generosity to penitent moderates may encourage others to desert. The converts are therefore permitted to participate in the building of the new order; sometimes they are even given prestigious though never central positions in the administration of the state. Yet they are constantly under scrutiny, constantly under surveillance. Their earlier heterodoxy may be forgiven; but it is never forgotten. They must therefore always display special loyalty, special obedience, special zeal. Their acceptance by the radicals is purchased at a heavy psychological price.

Most moderates, however, watch their impending defeat in helpless despair. They continue to preach the virtues of freedom and democracy, toleration and individualism. They condemn coercion and dictatorship, cruelty and violence. But no one listens to them anymore. Soon they are forced to be silent or go into exile or suffer imprisonment. Their role in the revolutionary process is now finished.

Julius Martov, who had led the Mensheviks in Russia during the struggle against the czarist regime, confessed early in 1919 in an obscure periodical published in Kharkov that the course of the revolution had "cruelly shattered" all his "illusions." For "the 'Soviet State' has not established in any instance electiveness and recall of public officials and the commanding staff. It has not suppressed the professional police. It has not assimilated the courts in direct jurisdiction by the masses. It has not done away with social hierarchy in production. It has not lessened the total subjection of the local community to the power of the state." On the contrary, the new order, "in proportion to its evolution, . . . shows a tendency in the opposite direction. It shows a tendency toward intensified centralism of the State, a tendency toward the utmost possible strengthening of the principles of hierarchy and compulsion. It shows a tendency toward the development of a more specialized apparatus of repression than before. It shows a tendency toward the greater independence of the usually elective functions and the annihilation of the control of these functions by the elector masses. It shows a tendency toward the total freedom of the executive organisms from the tutelage of the electors." Martov perceived that "in the crucible of reality" the "power of the soviets" was turning into "soviet power," that is, "*a power that originally issued from the soviets* but has steadily become independent from the soviets."

The more he studied the course of political development under the Bolsheviks, the more convinced he became that the new order was beginning to display the same authoritarianism and oppressiveness that had characterized the old. But it was no longer safe to say so in Russia. In 1921 Martov was forced into exile once again, this time not by the czarist but by the Communist authorities. His final assessment of what was happening to the revolution appeared two years later, around the time of his death, in an émigré journal in Berlin. Here he argued that the Bolsheviks were now establishing the identical form of oligarchical rule that they had once denounced as the fatal weakness of all "democratic" revolutions led by the middle class. *"The idea that the 'Soviet system' is equal to a definitive break with all the former, bourgeois, forms of revolution, therefore, serves as a screen behind which—imposed by exterior factors and the inner conformation of the proletariat—there are again set in motion methods that have featured the bourgeois revolutions.* And those revolutions have always been accomplished by transferring the power of a 'conscious minority, supporting itself on an unconscious majority,' to another minority finding itself in an identical situation." Worst of all, it now seemed clear to him that the Communist regime in Russia was building its power on the same immoral principles on which czarism had based its authority: oppression, intimidation, intolerance, and elitism.

Fifty years later Truong Nhu Tang came to a similar conclusion regarding the new order in Southeast Asia. Like Martov, he had devoted his life to the cause of the revolution, ever since his student days when he met the charismatic Ho Chi Minh. His reward had been an important position in the revolutionary government formed by the National Liberation Front to lead the resistance against the Saigon regime. Yet his assumption had always been that someday South Vietnam would form an independent nation based on the principles of a humane and tolerant socialism, different from the rigid Communist orthodoxy practiced in the north. The overthrow of the Nguyen Van Thieu government in 1975 revealed how illusory these hopes had been. The tough, shrewd bureaucrats in Hanoi had no intention of allowing the creation of an allied but separate Vietnamese state on their southern border. "They made it understood," Truong later recalled, "that the Vietnam of the future would be a single monolithic bloc, collectivist and totalitarian, in which all the traditions and culture of the South would be ground and molded by the political machine of the conquerors. . . . The [Provisional Revolutionary Government] and the National Liberation Front, whose program had embodied the desire of so many South Vietnamese to achieve a political solution to their troubles and reconciliation among a people devastated by three decades of civil war—this movement the Northern Party had considered all along as simply the last linkup it needed to achieve its own imperialistic revolution."

As soon as the old order had fallen, radicals from the north began to push aside the southern moderates who had made the victory possible. "Throughout the entire country, administration was in the hands of [communist] party cadres accustomed to taking their orders from the Politburo. These people felt quite comfortable disregarding directives emanating from the Southern government, especially those that seemed to them somehow deviant from the party line. Restrictions regarding who could arrest whom and for what reasons, restrictions about what could be done with the arrestees—such restraints, to their way of thinking, were clearly not in keeping with the requirements of the times."

The final step in the shotgun wedding of north and south was the convocation of a Political Conference for the Reunification of the Country in the fall of 1975. "Ostensibly called so that Northern and Southern representatives could exchange views on reunification, it was actually intended only to ratify the reunification program already decided on by the leadership." Truong had been one of the delegates: "I had the privilege of voting 'yes.' (In Vietnamese such a gathering is called a 'yes conference.') To my colleagues and me, it was like being among the unfallen dead, watching a farce strangely gotten up for our benefit." The outcome was foreordained. "Delegate after delegate, called on to express 'views,' employed [the phrase 'total support'] lavishly: total support for unification as fast as possible . . . total support for the establishment of socialism in the South . . . total support for forgoing the now unnecessary phase of 'national, democratic revolution.'" The conference voted unanimously to hold countrywide elections for a unified national assembly to ratify the establishment of a consolidated Vietnamese state.

All of this was too much for Truong. In 1978, three years after the fall of Nguyen Van Thieu, he followed him into exile. Here he finally poured out his grief over the tragic disappointment of the hopes of a lifetime:

Vietnam has indeed freed itself from its former colonial masters. But the national liberation that the revolution achieved was not the only liberation for which it was fought. . . . Many of us also believed we were fighting for the human dignity of our people, not just a *national* revolution, but a *national* and *democratic* revolution ... that would have insured free political and cultural expression among the variety of ethnic groups, religions, and regions—and among the commonwealth of individuals—that make up the nation.

But the national democratic revolution itself became a casualty, choked by the arrogance of power among those who were responsible for the nation's fate. Instead of national reconciliation and independence, Ho Chi Minh's successors have given us a country devouring its own and beholden once again to foreigners, though now it is the Soviets rather than the Americans. In the process, the lives that so many gave to create a new nation are now no more than ashes cast aside. That betrayal of faith will burden the souls of Vietnam's revolutionary leaders—even as surely as their rigid ideology and bellicose foreign policies have mortgaged the country's future.

In Cuba, Huber Matos learned even more painfully what happens to moderates in a revolution. A prominent guerrilla leader, he had been appointed after victory to the position of military commander of Camaguey Province. But the drift of the new government to the left led him to submit his resignation in the fall of 1959. In a letter to Castro he wrote: "I believe that, having to choose between accommodating myself or getting out of the way in order not to do damage, it is honorable and revolutionary that I go." Castro disagreed. Matos was arrested and sentenced to twenty years in prison. Only after his release and departure from Cuba in 1979 could he openly mourn what had happened to the revolution in words almost identical with those used by Truong Nhu Tang:

> We fought the Revolution with the commitment of complete freedom for our country, true independence, and national sovereignty for the Cuban people. It was clear in 1959 that the direction Castro was giving the Revolution would not lead to independence and sovereignty. ... The revolutionary motto was "Liberty or Death," and my view was that liberty encompasses *everything* that we call political freedom: the right to think and to express your opinion without having to adjust to a *padron*, the possibility of pluralism, and everything else that is generally accepted to be the universal rights of mankind. Liberty, freedom, that came first; we

wanted a democratic revolution. If we had a truly democratic revolution, the direction of the government would have had to be democratic too, without everything being left to one man, with no one being free to question his decisions.

Told by an American acquaintance that there had once been an attempt in South Vietnam to create a "third force" between right and left, Matos asked what had happened to its supporters following the Communist victory. "They left," he was informed, "or went to prison, or were put under house arrest. Some of them are now living in the United States and France, and some are now dead." This sounded only too familiar. "Huber Matos nodded, raising and lowering first his right hand, then his left: 'Like us, first Batista, then Castro.'" Such is the eternal lament of those caught in the middle during a revolution, too idealistic to support the old order, too scrupulous to accept the new, destined to be defeated and destroyed by a triumphant radical dictatorship.[14]

CHAPTER 6

The Revolutionary Faith

The overthrow of the old order leads to a sudden outburst of popular energies and talents. Ordinary men and women, people who had been leading obscure lives of toil and drudgery, now begin to play an important role in public affairs. The exceptional times in which they live make them exceptional as well. Radical conspirators struggling against the futility of political exile become wielders of power; left-wing intellectuals emerge from their studies to head cabinet ministries; sons of peasants learn to lead armies; workers in factories and mines are elevated to economic planners. Normal expectations become illusory; conventional assumptions and calculations prove misleading.

In the galvanizing atmosphere of the new order, those who had been dull plodders under the *ancien régime* start to display a remarkable capacity for leadership and organization. At first they appear bewildered by the complexities of government, but soon they learn to adjust, to improvise, to innovate. The unusual circumstances in which they find themselves force them to devise unusual tactics. Their opponents are confident that they will inevitably fail. How can such inexperience, such obvious clumsiness and amateurishness, lead to anything but disaster? Yet in fact the revolution demonstrates the superficiality of conventional logic. It demonstrates that those who had been regarded as fit only for menial toil are in fact capable of planning, organizing, fighting, and winning.

Not only the leaders of the new order reveal unexpected abilities. There are countless others, the rank and file, people previously concerned only with earning a meager livelihood, who suddenly display extraordinary dedication and sacrifice. They form volunteer organizations to distribute food and clothing, they attend mass meetings to support the revolution, they enlist in militia units fighting against the *ancien régime*, they serve on surveillance committees to ferret out reactionaries. They make possible the victory of the new order. Without expectation of economic reward or political preferment, they perform the countless small tasks of administration required for a radical reconstruction of polity and economy. What inspires them is the vision of human redemption, of a social system under which mankind will become better, nobler, more compassionate, more loving. Those who make the revolution insist that they are merely obeying the inexorable laws of dialectical materialism, that they are expressing the underlying forces of change and progress in society. But that is only a pseudoscientific facade for their real motivation. At heart they seek spiritual salvation.

Radicalism as
Moral Regeneration

Is it too much to suggest that the revolutionary movement is essentially ethical in nature, and that its ultimate goal is the moral regeneration of mankind? A close resemblance exists between its motives and goals and those of a religious faith capable of inspiring belief in the redemption of humanity. There is the same outpouring of popular enthusiasm, the same awakening of dormant power, the same unshakable confidence in ultimate victory. And there is the same spiritual passion that inspired Christianity in the age of the Crusades, the same heroic militancy that spread Mohammedanism from the Mediterranean to the Pacific. The parallels between the secular faith of revolution and the transcendent faith of religion are too obvious to be fortuitous. They seem to derive from similar psychological needs and impulses.

First of all, each has its eschatology, its vision of the ultimate destiny of mankind. The battle that they are waging is not for some narrow gain, some temporal advantage. It is for the triumph of good over evil. The cosmic struggle for human salvation, moreover, is now approaching its end; society stands at Armageddon. The war against the forces of darkness is almost over. "'Tis the final conflict," according to the *Internationale,* the anthem of the revolutionary movement. The cruel sacrifices that it demands will soon be rewarded with an everlasting reign of peace and justice. As the new order marches into battle, it finds inspiration in the thought that it is fighting not only for the redemption of its own society, but for the poor and oppressed everywhere in the world.

Early in 1918, three months after they seized power, the Bolsheviks, facing the Carthaginian peace terms that the Germans presented at Brest-Litovsk, found strength in the conviction that the proletariat of Europe was on their side. The masses would turn against their capitalist masters to save the revolution in Russia. The Soviet press overflowed with stories, reports, rumors, and myths of an imminent insurrection against the *ancien régime* throughout the Continent. On January 22 *Pravda* announced on its front page that "the flow of the social conflagration has spread over Austria. Vienna is on the eve of important events. The triumph of the international socialist revolution is near." Three days later even more exciting news appeared. "The red flag of the communist revolution is raised in Europe. Soviets of workers' deputies have been set up in Vienna and Budapest. At Warsaw there is about to begin a general strike of the socialist proletariat. Here, too, the revolution has formed Soviets of workers . . . . Long live the international revolution! Long live the International Soviet of Workers' and Soldiers' Deputies!"

The more obvious it became that Russia could not resist the German demands, the louder became the assurances that the masses of Europe were on the march to help the Bolsheviks. "Revolutionary disturbances in Austria continue," reported *Pravda* on January 27. "In England revolutionary strikes are about to begin. The Paris workers are ready to greet the new international. In Spain there are new troubles. In Finland the laborers are storming the citadel of capitalism. *The international workers' revolution is going forward.* Its path is lighted by the beacon of the Great Socialist Soviet Republic in Russia. *Long live the world revolt of the proletariat! Long live the Soviets of Workers, Soldiers, and Peasants!*" And on February 1, as the political situation steadily deteriorated, *Pravda's* tone grew even more ecstatic. "The conflagration of the world proletarian revolution is spreading. *The German proletariat has risen. Berlin has a Soviet of workers' deputies.* The destruction of capitalism is inevitable. The sun of socialism is rising. The victory of an honest peace is assured. Hail the International Proletarian Revolution! Hail the International Workers' Republic of Soviets! Proletarians of all countries unite!"

In that atmosphere of hysteria and exaltation, with the boundary between reality and fantasy no longer clearly discernible, Lenin himself appeared to believe that the revolution in Russia would be saved by the intervention of the toiling masses of Europe. On February 5, 1918, addressing Bolshevik cadres on their way to the provinces to promote support for the new order, he declared that even though the ruling classes were trying to encircle and destroy the Soviet system, their defeat was inevitable. "Our revolution sprang from the war: but for the war, we would find the capitalists of the world banded and ranged against us. Their only worry is to prevent the sparks of our fire from falling on their roofs." History would show, however, how futile such efforts were. "You can't throw up a Chinese Wall around Russia. We have yet to hear of a workers' organization anywhere in the world that is not elated at our decrees on land, nationalization of the banks, etc."

To Lenin the example of the Bolshevik revolution was bound to inspire the proletariat of other nations. The lower classes would never allow their governments to crush the Communist movement. "We may be faced with a stiff fight in the future, but you should never forget, comrades, that in most countries the workers, oppressed by their capitalists, are already awakening, and the [counterrevolutionaries] of all countries, no matter how they rave, will never be able to consolidate their positions, even if they manage to get in a blow at Russia. Upon the other hand, our position is sound because we have the workers of all countries behind us."

How much of this was rhetoric and how much conviction? The Bolsheviks never hesitated to use hyperbole for sustaining morale. Some of what they said in the dark days of 1918 was no doubt propaganda. But some reflected a genuine belief in the universality of their cause. That belief may not have been enough to protect them against the rapacity of imperial Germany. They were forced to accept disastrous terms at Brest-Litovsk from which only the victory of the Allies eight months later saved them. Beset and isolated, they then had to face a ruinous civil war, foreign intervention, privation, hunger, and disease. And yet long after it became apparent that capitalism in Europe was still strong enough to retain its hold on wealth and power, they continued to insist that their revolution was only the prelude to Communist revolutions throughout the world. Sooner or later the workers of other nations were sure to follow the example of the Soviet Union.

"The victory of socialism in one country is not a self-sufficient task," wrote Stalin, a man not ordinarily given to chiliastic pronouncements, at the end of 1924. "The revolution which has been victorious in one country must regard itself not as a self-sufficient entity, but as an aid, as a means *for* hastening the victory of the proletariat in all countries. For the victory of the revolution in our country, in the present case Russia, is not only the product of the uneven development and progressive decay of imperialism; it is at the same time the beginning of and the pre-condition for the world revolution." Although by now their early millenarian fervor had cooled, the Bolsheviks continued to cling to the concept of general insurrection.[1]

Indeed, every Marxist movement is committed to internationalism; every Marxist movement is global in outlook and ecumenical in spirit. Its immediate goal may be the overthrow of an old order in a particular country at a particular period; but its ultimate objective transcends the boundaries of time, geography, history, and culture. Essentially what it seeks is the emancipation of mankind. In fact, the strength of radicalism derives to a considerable extent from the sense of universal struggle, of cosmic purpose. The cause of the revolution is at heart always the cause of oppressed, suffering humanity.

Che Guevara reflected this conviction in his speech of August 19, 1960, announcing that society had now come to the end of an epoch, "and not only here in Cuba." Throughout the world the capitalistic system, which was responsible for so much human suffering, faced defeat. The monopolies that it had created were being attacked and destroyed. The ideas of socialism, on the other hand, were "scoring new and important triumphs" every day. History had chosen Cuba for an important role in the liberation of man from injustice and oppression, he proclaimed. The country had "the proud and devoted duty" to become the pioneer in the New World of a movement of liberation that had begun earlier in Africa and Asia, "the other subjugated continents." It was a glorious destiny. But the Cuban revolution could fulfill its historic mission only as part of the coming world revolution.

The most eloquent, most moving expression of the fervor of the new order could be heard in Castro's speech of February 4, 1962, in the Plaza de la Revolución, the "Second Declaration of Havana," which the National General Assembly of the People of Cuba ordered translated into all major languages and distributed throughout the world. Here he identified the revolution in his own country with the deliverance of the poor and oppressed everywhere in Latin America:

> This toiling humanity, inhumanly exploited, these paupers, controlled by the whip and overseer, have not been reckoned with or have been little reckoned with. From the dawn of independence their fate has been the same: Indians, gauchos, mestizos, zambas, quadroons, whites without property or income, all this human mass which formed the ranks of the "nation," which never reaped any benefits, which fell by the millions, which was cut into bits, which won independence from the mother country for the bourgeoisie, which was shut out from its share of the rewards, which continued to occupy the lowest step on the ladder of social benefits, which continued to die of hunger, curable diseases and neglect, because for them there were never enough essentials of life— ordinary bread, a hospital bed, the medicine which cures, the hand which aids—their fate has been all the same.

But now that was about to change. The final conflict of revolutionary eschatology had already begun. "From one end of the continent to the other they are signaling with clarity that the hour has come—the hour of their redemption." For the vast nameless mass, "this America of color, somber, taciturn America, which all over the continent sings with the same sadness and disillusionment," was beginning to play a decisive role in determining its destiny. It was beginning to write its own history with its own blood; it was beginning to suffer and to die for it. "Because now in the fields and mountains of America, on its slopes and prairies and in its jungles, in the wilderness or in the traffic of cities, this world is beginning with full cause to erupt." Eager hands were stretched out, ready to die for what was justly theirs, ready to die for the rights which had been denied them for five hundred years. "Yes, now history will have to take the poor of America into account, the exploited and spurned of Latin America, who have decided to begin writing history for themselves for all time." At last their liberation had begun. "Already they can be seen on the roads, on foot, day after day, in endless marches of hundreds of kilometers to the governmental 'eminences' to obtain their rights."

To the electrified crowd gathered in the square before him, Castro described impassionedly the apocalyptic struggle for freedom and justice that Cuba had been chosen to lead. The impoverished peasants of the New World "can be seen armed with staves, sticks, machetes, in one direction and another, each day, occupying lands, sinking hooks into the land which belongs to them and defending it with their lives. They can be seen carrying signs, slogans, flags; letting them flap in the mountain or prairie winds." The outcome of this final conflict between good and evil was foreordained. "The wave of anger, of demands for justice, of claims for rights, which is beginning to sweep the lands of Latin America, will not stop. That wave will swell with every passing day. For that wave is composed of the greatest number, the majorities in every respect, those whose labor amasses the wealth and turns the wheels of history. Now, they are awakening from the long, brutalizing sleep to which they have been subjected."

The movement for human liberation that had begun in Russia forty-five years earlier, which had triumphed in China thirteen years before, was about to sweep across the New World under the leadership of Cuba. Was that not a glorious destiny? "This great humanity has said 'enough!' and begun to march. And their giant march will not be halted until they conquer true independence—for which they have vainly died more than once. Today, however, those who die will die like the Cubans at [the Bay of Pigs]. They will die for their own true and never-to-be-surrendered independence. *Patria o Muerte! Venceremos!*" To the thousands listening enraptured to Castro in the Plaza de la Revolución, the cause for which they were fighting was greater than the emancipation of Cuba. It was nothing less than the salvation of mankind.[2]

The quasi-religious nature of the revolutionary faith is apparent not only in its ecumenical scope but in its moral imperative. Although those who embrace it speak the language of materialism, although they claim they are merely expounding the scientific laws of capital accumulation and class conflict, at heart they are moralists. They are embarked on a spiritual quest; they strive to perfect human nature. They agree with the Scriptures that "man shall not live by bread alone." It is their sacred duty to help him become better and nobler, help him pursue moral values and seek ethical goals. Hence the ultimate purpose of the revolution is not simply to improve the standard of living of the masses by giving them more food, better housing, warmer clothing, or greater leisure. Those are merely the means by which human nature will be purified and ennobled. The material gains that the new order promises are meant to serve spiritual ends. Its final objective is salvation.

How else can the speech by Che Guevara "On Party Militancy," delivered on March 24, 1963, before an audience of textile workers, be interpreted? Addressing those who in his view had been an exploited proletariat under capitalism, he dwelt not on the economic progress that the revolution had made possible, but on its promise of moral redemption. "Material incentives are something left over from the past. They are something that we must accept but whose hold on the minds of the people we must gradually break as the revolutionary process goes forward." Personal gain, the sole motive for economic activity that the capitalistic system had provided, would be replaced under a Communist regime by a concern for collective well-being. "Material incentives will not play a part in the new society being created; they will die out as we advance. We must establish the conditions under which this type of motivation that is [still] operative today will increasingly lose its importance and be replaced by nonmaterial incentives such as the sense of duty and the new revolutionary way of thinking."

Two years later, while on an extended tour of Africa, Guevara reiterated his conviction that the success of the new order depended ultimately on the reshaping of human nature. "To build communism, a new man must be created simultaneously with the material base."

That the most doctrinaire, the most visionary leader of the Cuban revolution should be so ardently committed to the moral regeneration of mankind may not seem surprising. But Castro himself, though constantly grappling with the intractable everyday realities of government and administration, was equally convinced that only through a spiritual transformation could the material goals of the new order be attained. Speaking from the steps of the University of Havana on March 13, 1968, he emphasized that the problems of economics were in essence problems of ethics:

> We cannot encourage or even permit selfish attitudes among men if we don't want man to be guided by the instinct of selfishness, of individuality; by the wolf, the beast instinct; man as the enemy of man, the exploiter of man, the setter of snares for other men. The concept of socialism and communism, the concept of a higher society, implies a man devoid of those feelings; a man who has overcome such instincts at any cost; placing, above everything, his sense of solidarity and brotherhood among men. And this brings to mind the famous topic of incentives. For a long time they were theoretically discussed, and it appeared to be a question of method, but, in our opinion, it is a much more profound question. And we don't feel that the communist man can be developed by encouraging man's ambition, man's individualism, man's individual desires. If we are going to fail because we believe in man's ability, in his ability to improve, then we will fail, but we will never renounce our faith in mankind!

To the revolutionaries the spiritual salvation of humanity is so important that everything else must be risked for its sake, even the revolution itself.[3]

The Sacerdotal Function of the Party

The crucial task of transforming man and society is entrusted by the new order to a hieratic organization of true believers, a sacred brotherhood sworn to defend the faith, a secular priesthood. Its members, variously described as "militants" or "activists," "cadres," or "guerrillas," are the mainstay of the radical dictatorship. They are unquestioningly, wholeheartedly committed to its principles and policies.

What motivates them is not the reward of power, so important to the elite of the *ancien régime,* but the ideal of social justice and moral redemption. This is the source of their strength. This is what makes them so determined and incorruptible—so fanatical, their opponents would say. The success of the revolution depends on their unshakable belief in an idea. It demonstrates the extent to which moral conviction can sometimes prevail over material advantage, spiritual faith over hardheaded calculation. It explains the victory of the new order.

The size of the radical vanguard is never very large, at least not in the early years of the revolution. The selflessness that membership requires discourages those not prepared for total commitment. By the same token, those accorded admittance are expected to devote themselves to the cause with single-minded determination. Hence to the leaders of the new order the exclusivity of the revolutionary organization is an advantage to be retained and fostered. In an address in Tiflis in the summer of 1921 "On the Immediate Tasks of Communism in Georgia and Transcaucasia," Stalin emphasized the need for careful selection of the radical elite:

> Comrades, you must remember that our Party is the government party, that often whole groups of unreliable careerist elements, alien to the proletarian spirit, get into or try to get into the Party and carry into it the spirit of disintegration and conservatism. It is the vital task of the Communists to guard the party against such elements. We must remember once and for all that the strength and weight of a party, and especially of the Communist Party, do not depend so much on the quantity of members as on their quality, on their staunchness and devotion to the cause of the proletariat. The Russian Communist Party has all-in-all 700,000 members. I can assure you, comrades, that it could raise its membership to 7,000,000 if it wished to do so, and if it did not know that 700,000 staunch Communists constitute a much stronger force than 7,000,000 unwanted and good-for-nothing fellow-travellers. If Russia has withstood the onslaught of world imperialism, . . . this is due, among other things, to the existence of the united Communist Party, forged out of hard steel and tempered in battle, which has never gone out for quantity of members, but which has made its first concern the improvement of their quality. [Ferdinand Lassalle, founder of the socialist movement

in Germany,] was right when he said that the party becomes strong by purging itself of dross. On the other hand, there can be no doubt that the reason why the German Social-Democratic Party, for example, the biggest Social-Democratic Party in the world, proved to be a plaything in the hands of imperialism during the imperialist war and collapsed like a colossus with feet of clay after the war was that for years it had devoted itself to enlarging its organizations by admitting all sorts of petty-bourgeois trash, which killed its living spirit.

Thus, to preserve the staunchness and purity of its ranks, not to go out for quantity of Party members, systematically to improve the quality of the Party membership, to guard itself against an influx of intellectual, petty-bourgeois nationalist elements—such is the . . . immediate task of the Communist Party.[4]

In every radical elite, therefore, recurrent purges of the membership occur, especially after the initial period of struggle against the *ancien régime* has come to an end. For once it becomes clear that the revolution is going to prevail, there is a rush to the victorious side by trimmers and opportunists, by those whose loyalty to the new order rests on expediency rather than conviction. Indeed, the longer the radicals are in power, the more difficult it becomes to maintain their original militancy.

During the years of conflict, however, the revolutionary vanguard, like a religious order, remains sworn to poverty, chastity, and obedience, not only in theory but to a considerable extent in practice. Here is the most striking difference between the elite of the new order and of the old. To the latter, high political position should be made manifest in a display of wealth and power. Its members dress therefore in dashing uniforms resplendent with military decorations, or in the cutaway coats and striped trousers of international diplomacy, or at the least in expensive business suits. They travel in chauffeured limousines, whose sleekness attests to the importance of their office, or in special railroad cars, or in private airplanes. They mingle with high society at formal banquets, fancy balls, coming-out parties, and charity dances—social occasions from which the common run of humanity is carefully excluded. Their aloofness is not simply a reflection of vanity or superciliousness. It expresses a general attitude regarding the proper relationship between the strong and the weak, between those who rule and those who are ruled.

The elite of the new order, on the other hand, adopts a different way of life reflecting a different view of society. Its members seek to demonstrate their identity with the masses by the way they speak, dress, eat, and play. Their power may be just as arbitrary as that which the *ancien régime* formerly exercised. They may be just as ruthless, autocratic, oppressive, or cruel. But the principles for which they stand are fundamentally different, and their personal behavior is designed to underscore that difference.

Lenin always appeared in a rumpled suit and cloth cap, the uniform of the professional revolutionary. Mao wore the drab padded jacket and cotton trousers of the common man, indistinguishable in appearance from the rank and file that had helped put him in power. Castro continued to dress in the olive green of a guerrilla commander long after the fall of the old order, keeping alive the memory of the struggle against Batista, hoping to maintain the spirit of the Sierra Maestra. Their ostentatious abstemiousness was more than an expression of personal taste. It was a means of communication, a tacit language expressing an ideal and an ideology.

This austerity of the radical elite should not be dismissed as merely a public display of virtue. The leaders of the revolution embrace it even in domestic life, with their spouses and children, among their relatives and friends. To them secular asceticism reflects a commitment to the cause, a faith in suffering humanity. Self-denial is a way of expressing their determination to create a better world.

After their victory in 1917, the Bolsheviks continued to lead lives of Spartan simplicity. Members of the Council of People's Commissars, the supreme governing body under the new order, received a monthly salary of 500 rubles, with an additional 100 for every dependent. Since the purchasing power of the currency had fallen to about 5 percent of its prewar value, the earnings of government leaders were at best modest. The housing provided for them was simple as well; they were to get no more than 1 room for each member of the family.

To be sure, the standard of living of a prominent official could not be measured entirely by the size of the salary he received. A good deal depended on the apartment allotted to him, on the supplies available in the store from which he bought his rations, and on the resources of the restaurant where he took his meals. Yet as a rule the Bolsheviks adhered to the principle that they should not lead substantially better lives than the masses whom they were guiding in the struggle for a new social system. Especially Lenin himself, Felix Dzerzhinsky, head of dreaded Cheka, the secret police organization, and G. V. Chicherin, who became commissar for foreign affairs, acquired a reputation for austere living. By and large, although the heads of the Communist government in Russia did not share the hunger and privation that the man in the street had to endure during the civil war, the ethics of their ideology as well as the pressures of their work prevented major lapses into self-indulgence.[5]

In its sexual conduct the radical elite of the new order displays a similar abstemiousness. Those who are in power under the *ancien régime* generally have little hesitation about indulging in amatory promiscuity. They feel that it is a sign of manliness; it suggests mental as well as physical vigor. For them a casual lubricity is one of the perquisites of exercising power. They therefore often enter into extramarital liaisons, sometimes into several simultaneously, with women in all social classes, from members of high society to actresses, singers, dancers, and prostitutes. Their dissoluteness may provoke scandalized indignation among the lower classes, occasionally mixed with secret envy. But since a dominant motive for acquiring power in the declining years of the old order is personal gratification, licentiousness seems only one manifestation of the hedonism that has now become a chief reward of political authority.

All that changes after the revolution. To the new order the proper goal of government is not private satisfaction but public good. A streak of puritanism exists in the radical temper that demands the repression of individual appetite for the sake of collective redemption. This does not mean that most revolutionaries remain celibate, although some do. But casual liaisons are discouraged. The new order favors marital ties that, even without the sanction of conventional matrimonial rites, are at least as firm as those maintained under church auspices. A good radical is taught to avoid dissoluteness as a form of corrupting self-indulgence; he is urged to adhere to the principle of monogamy. Marriage must be regarded not as a compact, not as a bargain, but as a free union of two people, without regard for economic position or social status, based only on mutual love and respect. Hence divorce by voluntary consent is permissible under the new order; indeed, it occurs much more frequently than under the *ancien régime*. But blatant infidelity is incompatible with the private austerity that the revolutionary movement demands of its leaders. In most cases the prevailing attitude of the radical elite toward sexual behavior resembles bourgeois moralism rather than priestly celibacy.

Of all the revolutionary virtues, however, none is of greater importance than obedience. It ranks even higher than poverty or chastity. For the maintenance of discipline, the willingness to subordinate private judgment to collective decision, is the organizational foundation on which the new order rests. This does not mean that there is never a difference of opinion within the radical elite. On the contrary, long and heated debate generally precedes every major shift in policy or tactics. But once a decision has been reached, each member is required to support it loyally and wholeheartedly. Even those who had opposed it most vehemently must now accept it in spirit as well as deed. The difficulty of this intellectual self-denial makes it the ultimate test of revolutionary devotion. Those who cannot pass it are expelled from the party, however great their merit or valuable their service. They are charged with wilfulness and insubordination, factionalism and deviationism. The new order may forgive sybaritic taste or carnal appetite, but disagreement with established authority is unpardonable. Every revolutionary movement conducts therefore periodic purges of those who may have fought valiantly for the cause before victory, but who afterward are unable to deny their own judgment or conscience.

The most difficult struggle of the radical elite is thus not against the external enemy, against the counterrevolutionary who seeks to bring about the overthrow of the new order. It is rather against the enemy within, against the assertiveness of the individual personality that pleads and demands to be heard. Only those who succeed in repressing it are worthy of admission to the priesthood of the revolutionary faith. Their devotion is now beyond question; they will remain loyal through thick and thin. And yet their elevation is costly. It requires a conscious rejection of something profoundly instinctive, something inherently human. Of all the sacrifices that the new order demands of its followers, none is greater than this deliberate denial of the self.

That is why the radical elite is popularly regarded with the same awe and reverence that under the *ancien régime* had been displayed toward the clergy. Here too is a sacerdotal order whose members display a spirit of piety and devotion unattainable by ordinary men. They lead lives of holiness, seeking spiritual goals loftier than the mundane concerns of the multitude. Even those who do not fully understand or agree with what the revolutionary elite is trying to achieve generally treat its members with respect and deference. The willingness of the radicals to repress common human needs and yearnings arouses among the lower classes an uncomprehending admiration.

That feeling was clearly expressed in 1967 by a peasant in the Red River delta of North Vietnam, when talking about the role of the Communist vanguard. "I should love to become a Party member," he sighed, "but I'm not up to the required standards yet, so I'm just an ordinary [member of a farm cooperative]. It's hard to explain exactly what these standards are. You have to achieve good production figures; you have to play an active part in all that is going on; you have to do a lot for the community. The party workers are the cream of the village, the torchbearers—I don't belong among them yet." An unmistakable similarity is apparent in the attitude of the masses toward the leadership of the new order and the priesthood of the old. Both are venerated for their commitment to human redemption.[6]

The Specter of Capitalist Encirclement

To the true believer in the revolution, ultimate success is never in doubt. The laws of historical development as well as the aspirations of the human spirit assure its victory. But the road to that victory is long and arduous. The new order is invariably beset by enemies who are cunning, unscrupulous, and merciless. It must therefore always be vigilant and suspicious. It must always be on guard against plots and conspiracies. The triumph of the radical cause can be achieved only after a prolonged struggle between the forces of good and evil, light and darkness. Hence the ideological appeal of the revolutionary movement is constantly reinforced by a sense of danger that helps sustain its militancy and élan.

This is not to deny that the revolution is in fact threatened, especially in its early years, by powerful opponents at home and abroad. The privileged classes under the *ancien régime* do not become easily reconciled to their loss of power. They go on hoping and planning for the overthrow of the new order. Their efforts, moreover, are often aided by foreign governments that feel menaced by the spread of radicalism. But the leaders of the revolutionary movement begin to warn against capitalistic intervention well before it actually starts, and they continue long after it ends. For they sense that the fear of reactionary encirclement performs an important psychological function. Not only does it promote resolve and militancy, especially after the initial idealistic ardor of the revolution has started to flag, but it serves to explain the inability of the radical dictatorship to fulfill all the exciting promises, all the rosy expectations. There are important emotional reasons, in other words, quite apart from political or military realities, why the new order always insists that it is in grave danger.

Early in February 1918, while the new Bolshevik government was engaged in peace negotiations with the Central Powers at Brest-Litovsk, Lenin warned his followers of the perils that confronted them on every side. "All the bourgeoisie, the civil servants, the saboteurs are against you, for they know that if the people manage to share out among themselves this national wealth which had been in the hands of the capitalists and kulaks, they will rid Russia of the chaff and the drones. That is why they have mustered against the working people all their forces." The enemies of the revolution ranged from former czarist generals to "the saboteurs, the bribed vagrants, and those who are simply weary." They were the ones chiefly responsible for the economic difficulties that the new order had to face. "One day they bribe ignorant soldiers to raid wine and spirit warehouses; the next day they get railway officials to hold up freights or shipowners to hold up grain barges, etc., on their way to the capital." The sufferings of the Russian people were primarily their fault.

Later that same month the Council of People's Commissars charged that Germany's real goal was not territorial expansion or even economic domination but the overthrow of the revolution. "The German government . . . does not desire peace. German militarism is carrying out the orders of the capitalists of all countries and is aiming *to crush the Russian and Ukrainian workers and peasants, to give back the land to the landlords, factories and banks to the bankers, and to restore the monarchy.*" The Kaiser's generals were planning to restore "order" in Petrograd and Kiev. "*The Socialist Republic of the Soviets is in the greatest danger.* Until the time when the German proletariat rises and conquers, it is the sacred duty of the workers and peasants of Russia to defend the Republic of the Soviets against the hordes of the bourgeois-imperialist Germany."

By December 1920 the new order was sounding more confident. The resistance of the white armies and the intervention of the foreign powers were finally coming to an end. "We have now won in the sense that we stand on our own feet," Lenin declared. The enemies of the revolution "have been unable to defeat us in three years of war, although we are infinitely weak from the military and economic standpoint." Better yet, "our strength is growing, and very rapidly." Nevertheless, the revolutionary forces had to remain vigilant, for the hostility of the capitalistic world was unrelenting. "We stand between two foes . . . . We are surrounded by imperialist states which detest the Bolsheviks and are spending vast sums of money, using ideological means, the power of the press, and so on."

A year later, in December 1921, Lenin voiced even greater optimism in his address to the Ninth All-Russian Congress of Soviets. "A certain equilibrium has been created," he explained. "This is the objective political situation, quite independent of our victories, which proves that we have fathomed the depth of the contradictions connected with the imperialist war, and that we are gauging them more correctly than ever before and more correctly than other powers." But the dangers facing the new order had in no way diminished. "For our part, we must display the utmost caution. And the first precept of our policy, the first lesson . . . which must be learned by all workers and peasants, is to be on the alert, to remember that we are surrounded by people, classes, governments who openly express the utmost hatred for us. We must remember that we are always a hair's

breadth away from invasion." The new order should therefore remain on its guard at all times, constantly watchful, constantly
distrustful.

As late as June 1930, Stalin, now the undisputed master of the
Soviet Union, continued to warn against foreign plots and machinations. In a report to the sixteenth congress of the Communist party,
he spoke of the unceasing hostility of world capitalism. "We must
bear in mind the circumstance that the resistance of the moribund
classes in our country is not taking place in isolation from the outside world, but is receiving the support of the capitalist encirclement. Capitalist encirclement must not be regarded simply as a
geographical concept. Capitalist encirclement means that the
U.S.S.R. is surrounded by hostile class forces, which are ready to
support our class enemies within the U.S.S.R. morally, materially, by
means of a financial blockade and, if the opportunity offers, by military intervention."

This helped explain why the new order had been unable to make
more rapid progress in improving Russia's economy. "It has been
proved that the wrecking activities of our specialists, the anti-Soviet
activities of the *kulaks*, and the incendiarism and explosions at our
factories and installations are subsidized and inspired from abroad.
The imperialist world is not interested in the U.S.S.R. standing up
firmly and becoming able to overtake and outstrip the advanced capitalist countries. Hence, the assistance it renders the forces of the old
world in the U.S.S.R. Naturally, this circumstance, too, cannot serve
to facilitate our work of reconstruction." Thirteen years after the Bolsheviks seized power, they still felt threatened by the designs,
schemes, intrigues, and conspiracies of the sinister forces of reaction.[7]

In China the theme of capitalistic encirclement resounded in the
rhetoric of the revolution with the same regularity. As early as September 1949, even before the proclamation of the People's Republic,
Mao warned that the imperialistic foreign governments that had
supported the Kuomintang, the United States in particular, would
now try to overthrow the new order. "Our revolutionary work is not
completed, the People's War of Liberation and the people's revolutionary movement are still forging ahead, and we must keep up our
efforts. The imperialists and the domestic reactionaries will not take
their defeat lying down; they will fight to the last ditch." The

counterrevolutionaries were not only cunning but indefatigable. "After there is peace and order throughout the country, they are sure to engage in sabotage and create disturbances by one means or another, and every day and every minute they will try to stage a comeback. This is inevitable and beyond all doubt, and under no circumstances must we relax our vigilance."

In June 1950, three weeks before the outbreak of the Korean War, Mao reported to the Central Committee of the Communist party that the danger of capitalistic encirclement had not diminished since the victory of the new order a year earlier. There had been important successes, to be sure. "The Central People's Government of the People's Republic of China and local people's governments at all levels have been set up. The Soviet Union, the People's Democracies and a number of capitalist countries have successively established diplomatic relations with our country. Basically the war has ended on the mainland, and only Taiwan and Tibet remain to be liberated." Yet very serious problems remained. "In certain areas on the mainland the Kuomintang reactionaries have resorted to bandit guerrilla warfare and incited some backward elements against the People's Government." More than that, "they have organized many secret agents and spies to oppose our government and spread rumors among the people in an attempt to undermine the prestige of the Communist Party and the People's Government and to disrupt the unity and cooperation of the various nationalities, democratic parties and people's organizations." But worst of all, "these secret agents and spies are also engaged in sabotaging the people's economic undertakings, assassinating the personnel of the Party and government organizations, and collecting intelligence for the imperialists and the Kuomintang reactionaries."

It was clear that the forces of international capitalism controlled the opposition to the new order. "All these counter-revolutionary activities are directed from behind the scenes by imperialism, and particularly by U.S. imperialism. All these bandits, secret agents and spies are imperialist lackeys. In the [last] thirteen and a half months . . . the people's public security organs have uncovered large numbers of reactionary secret service groups and agents." This then was no time for overconfidence. A false sense of security would only open the gates to the exploiters and oppressors of the people.

As late as September 1953, two months after the conclusion of the armistice at Panmunjom ending the hostilities in Korea, Mao was still insisting that the revolution must remain on the alert. There was no telling when international capitalism would attack again. "The enemy may resume the war, and even if he doesn't, he is sure to make trouble in all sorts of ways, such as by sending in secret agents to carry out wrecking activities. He has set up a vast network of secret services in places like Taiwan, Hongkong and Japan." The government was not intimidated, to be sure. "We have gained experience in the movement to resist U.S. aggression and aid Korea, and so long as we mobilize the masses and rely on the people, we know how to cope with the enemy." But there must always be wariness, determination, and vigilance.[8]

In China as in Russia, the first warnings against capitalistic encirclement coincided with direct or indirect foreign intervention in the struggle for power. But in Cuba the condemnation of imperialistic aggression started at least two years before the invasion by counterrevolutionary rebel forces at the Bay of Pigs. Almost as soon as the new order has been established, its leaders began to accuse the United States of plotting to overthrow the government. The denunciations of American policy in the Caribbean became increasingly bold and defiant. Their burden was that domestic opposition to the regime in Cuba was being incited and directed by reactionary politicians in Washington.

This charge appeared prominently, for example, in Castro's address to the United Nations on September 26, 1960. It began with a complaint that the United States had thrown open its doors "to a gang of murderers who had left our country covered with blood." The followers of Batista, "who had murdered hundreds of defenseless peasants, who, for many years, never tired of torturing prisoners, who killed right and left—were received in that country with open arms." To the Cuban people that was shocking. "Why this unfriendly act on the part of the government of the United States toward Cuba? Why this act of hostility? At that time, we could not quite understand; now we see the reasons clearly."

American politicians and capitalists were bent on destroying the new order by hook or by crook. "The government of the United States considers it has the right to promote and encourage subversion in our country. The government of the United States is promoting the organization of subversive movements against the revolutionary government of Cuba, and we wish to denounce this fact." Specifically, American authorities were using the Swan Islands in the Caribbean, which had been taken illegally from Honduras, as a base for military operations against the Cuban revolution. "Violating international law and despoiling a friendly people of a part of its territory, the United States has established a powerful radio station on one of those islands, in violation of international radio agreements, and has placed it at the disposal of the war criminals and subversive groups supported in this country; furthermore, military training is being conducted on that island, in order to promote subversion and the landing of armed forces in our country." In short, "part of the territory of a friendly country, seized in a piratical manner by the United States government, is being used as a base for subversion and attacks against our territory." The only way to defeat the machinations of American imperialists was by vigilance, resolve, discipline, and militancy.[9]

How sincere are all these warnings against capitalistic encirclement? How genuine are the repeatedly expressed fears of foreign intervention? The leaders of the revolution no doubt believe what they are saying, at least most of it. For there are in fact powerful forces abroad that seek to overthrow the new order and replace it with a more conservative regime. In the feverish, hysterical atmosphere of a social upheaval, moreover, enemies seem to lurk in every shadow, conspirators whisper behind every door, reactionaries incite every dissent and protest. No rumor, no suspicion is too farfetched to be believed. And yet there is more to it than that. Those in power recognize that the sense of danger helps maintain radical fervor, helps sharpen militant zeal. Hence it becomes a powerful weapon in defense of the new order. Capitalistic encirclement is to revolutionary faith what besetting sin is to religious faith. It provides a test of devotion, a measure of grace. It helps separate the wicked from the virtuous, the hypocritical opportunists from the sincere believers. It constitutes a trial by ordeal at the conclusion of which lies salvation.

Sometimes the supporters of the new order admit that the danger of foreign intervention, whether real or imaginary, serves to sustain the élan of the revolution. After visiting Cuba in 1960, the French existentialist philosopher Jean-Paul Sartre, one of the most ardent panegyrists of the radical regime, observed with unexpected shrewdness that "if the United States didn't exist, the Cuban revolution would perhaps invent it." The prospect of an imperialist invasion seemed to make the radicals on the island even bolder and more determined. "It is the United States which preserves Cuba's freshness and originality. For the Cubans today find themselves facing the United States in the situation that the rebels found themselves in 1958 against the 50,000 men of Batista." Castro himself declared early in 1963 that the persistence of a reactionary threat was useful for the defense of the new order. "The revolution needs the enemy; the proletariat does not flee from the enemy; it needs the enemy. . . . The revolutionary needs for his development his antithesis, which is the counterrevolutionary."

That is why, long after the new order has become established, recognized, and accepted—long after the Allies withdrew from Russia, and Western aid to the Kuomintang stopped, and American support for the invasion at the Bay of Pigs ended—the memory of foreign intervention is assiduously kept alive in newspapers, books, plays, films, and classrooms. As the original fervent idealism of the radical regime begins to weaken, it becomes increasingly important to maintain its commitment by recalling past insurrectionary victories and warning against future imperialist plots.[10]

The Psychology of Retributive Justice

The revolutionary faith is further reinforced by emotions of a quite different sort. The new order seeks to gain popular support through the release of class resentments and social hostilities that had been forcibly repressed under the *ancien régime*. The enmity of those who have neither wealth nor power toward those who do, the bitterness of the poor toward the rich, of the weak toward the strong, is suddenly unleashed by a transformation in the structure of authority that the radical dictatorship initiates. A system of retributive justice becomes institutionalized by which the pent-up animosity of the propertyless toward the propertied is finally vented. This is not quite

the same thing as the systematic redistribution of political and economic power that is the usual outcome of a social revolution. Nor
does it really bear on the question of the guilt or innocence of those
who are charged with wrongdoing under the old order. Many of
them, perhaps most, may have committed the misdeeds of which
they stand accused; they may deserve the punishment that has been
imposed on them. But the point is that the way in which the radical
dictatorship deals with its class enemies is designed not simply to
conform to some abstract principle of revolutionary justice, but to
fulfill a mass yearning for vengeance, a demand for retaliation. By
gratifying the hunger of the lower classes for retribution against the
high and mighty, the new order seeks to win their loyalty.

As soon as he came to power, Lenin announced that the time had
arrived for the proletariat to settle old scores. "It is an internal war
that is now before us," he declared on February 5, 1918. "The bourgeoisie, its plundered goods hidden in its chests, is not worried and
thinks: 'We shall sit this out.' The people must ferret out the sharks
and make them disgorge . . . . If we are not to collapse, we must get
at them in their hideouts. It is not the police who must make them
disgorge—the police are dead and buried—the people themselves
must do this, and there is no other way of fighting them." He
quoted with approval an old Bolshevik who had tried to explain to
a Cossack what the new order was seeking to achieve. "The Cossack asked him: 'Is it true that you Bolsheviks plunder?' 'Yes, indeed,' said the old man, 'we plunder the plunder.'" Here was the
strategy that the revolution should follow. "We shall sink in this sea
unless we manage to extract from those coffers all that is stored in
them, all that has been amassed through plunder over the years of
ruthless criminal exploitation."

In the early days of the Russian revolution reprisal for the misdeeds of the *ancien régime* often took the form of a spontaneous
sacking of the estates of great landowners or a mass looting of the
residences of wealthy businessmen. But equally important was the
conspicuous humiliation and degradation of those who had once
been in a position of eminence. There was a grim satisfaction for the
lower classes of Petrograd in seeing well-dressed, well-bred men
and women forced to dig trenches for the defense of the capital
against the Germans. There was a gratifying sense of proletarian

power in the threat to send fifteen rich capitalists from Kharkov into the coal mines of the Donets Basin, unless they provided a million rubles to pay the workers of the city. There was a feeling of sweet revenge among the employees of a button factory in Moscow, when a labor committee took possession of the plant, and the former manager was sentenced to three months in prison for sabotage. Such were the psychological rewards that the new order offered those who had toiled and suffered under czarism.

Early in 1919, at a critical moment for the Bolshevik government, while counterrevolutionary forces seemed to grow and multiply on all sides, a lead article in *Pravda* rejoiced at the thought that however bad things might be for the proletariat, they were much worse for the oppressors of the proletariat:

> Where are the wealthy people, the fashionably dressed ladies, the luxurious restaurants, the magnificent mansions, the sumptuous apartments, the grand driveways, the lying newspapers, all the old, corrupt, "good" life? It has all been swept away. . . . You will no longer meet a gentleman on the street in a fur coat who is reading the [prewar liberal newspaper] *Russkie Vedomosti*. There is no *Russkie Vedomosti*. The gentleman has no fur coat, and indeed there is no gentleman. He is far away in the Ukraine or the Kuban, hanging on in hope of better days. Or else he has wasted away, grown thin, lost his gentlemanly appearance living on third-class rations.

In its struggle for survival, the new order had found a valuable asset in the joy of getting even.[11]

Mao, like Lenin, recognized from the outset that retributive justice could prove a powerful weapon in the arsenal of the revolution. To be sure, the vindictiveness of the masses would have to be directed and controlled. "The number of counterrevolutionaries to be killed must be kept within certain proportions," he warned his followers in the spring of 1951. "As for those whose crimes deserve capital punishment but who owe no blood debts and are not bitterly hated by the people or who have done serious but not extremely serious harm to the national interest, the policy to follow is to hand down the death sentence, grant a two-year reprieve and subject them to forced labor to see how they behave." Yet for the enemies of the new order who had aroused deep hatred among the masses there could be no mercy. "Those who owe blood debts or are guilty of other extremely serious crimes and have to be executed to assuage the people's anger and those who have caused extremely serious harm to the national interest must be unhesitatingly sentenced to death and executed without delay."

A few years later, in February 1957, Mao explained, almost apologetically, that the appeasement of popular resentments and passions had been unavoidable. To have tried to suppress them might have jeopardized the support of the lower classes. "After liberation, we rooted out a number of counterrevolutionaries. Some were sentenced to death for major crimes. This was absolutely necessary, it was the demand of the masses, and it was done to free them from long years of oppression by the counterrevolutionaries and all kinds of local tyrants, in other words, to liberate the productive forces. If we had not done so, the masses would not have been able to lift their heads." There had simply been no alternative.

What retributive justice meant in practice can be gathered from the account, pieced together in 1948 from interviews with eyewitnesses, of what had happened three years earlier in the village of Changchuang in Shansi province after its liberation from the Japanese by the Communist Eighth Route Army. Some 200 peasants from all over the district gathered in the square to sit in judgment on Wen Ch'i-yung and Shen Chi-mei, who had served as garrison commander and police chief respectively under the collaborationist regime during the occupation.

> Hundreds of accusations were made that day against the leading traitors and all those who worked with them. A . . . woman told how her son, Chin-mao, had been killed. When she came to the part where the police threw him, gagged and bound, into a well, she broke down and could not go on. Many in the crowd wept with her. Shen Ch'uan-te . . . charged the puppet regime with the death of his brother. . . . Many then spoke out and said it was Shen Chi-mei and the landlords who backed him that lay at the root of the disaster that had befallen them. Before the meeting ended, Commander Wen and Police Officer Shen were condemned to death. They were taken to an empty field at the edge of the village and there, in the sight of the fort they had done so much to build

and to defend, they were shot. While the dead Shen Chi-mei lay still warm on the ground where he fell, a [Communist] militiaman, Yu-hsing, stripped a sweater off his corpse. Someone else took off his shoes. They left the body to his relatives to bury as they would.

Similar instances of popular retaliation against the wealthy and powerful were common throughout China in the last stages of the civil war and immediately after the triumph of the new order. They helped establish a subtle psychological bond between the revolutionary government and the masses hungry for revenge.[12]

After Castro's victory in Cuba, the same outburst of popular vindictiveness was directed against those who had been supporters and beneficiaries of the *ancien régime*. Especially officials exercising authority under the Batista dictatorship were exposed to public disgrace and abasement, often in the form of summary trials before a revolutionary tribunal whose verdict was almost invariably death. On February 2, 1959, a correspondent for *Time* magazine reported, critically though not inaccurately, the proceedings against a hated military commander of the fallen government:

"Announcement!" shouted Rebel Major Humberto Sorí Marin from the concrete arena of the Havana Sports Palace. "This man is being tried for murder and robbery." The crowd of 15,000 roared its approval. "And he is an assassin," added Sorí Marin, chief of the three-man panel charged with deciding guilt or innocence. "You know what the sentiments of Fidel Castro are about this trial," he said, and thoughtfully told the spectators: "Do not throw pop bottles."

Thus one night last week began Fidel Castro's showpiece trial, first of a planned 1,000 trials in the Havana area, for a captured underling of exiled Dictator Fulgencio Batista. The defendant was Captain Jesús Sosa Blanco, 51, a brutal killer who commanded the Batista garrison at Holguin. Charged by Rebel Prosecutor Jorge Serguera with 56 murders, he faced certain conviction. He faced it with flair.

Dressed in a blue denim prison jacket, Sosa Blanco grinned at the crowd. He raised his manacled hands, postured like the villain of a rigged wrestling match. The mob yelled, "Kill him! Kill him!" "This is the Colosseum in Rome," jeered Sosa Blanco, when he got a turn at the microphone. "I met brave rebels in the mountains, not types like you here. All you do is talk."

All night long the trial went on: 45 witnesses offered facts, hearsay, gossip. "This is the worst criminal in the world!" screamed Maria Jacinta Gálvez Martinez. "He killed every member of the Argate family—my neighbors." Argelio Argate, 12, confirmed that Sosa Blanco "came and took my father away." A wrinkled woman named Tomasa Batista Castillo fought to get at the prisoner: "I begged you not to kill my husband, because of our eleven children. You said the rebels could raise them." A soldier of Sosa Blanco's said calmly that he had seen the prisoner shoot 17 defenseless farmers.

Sosa Blanco's lawyer, a regular army attorney, who had been cleared by the rebels of any Batista ties and appointed just before the trial began, pleaded eloquently for calm justice. He argued that there was no death penalty in Cuba when the crimes took place, that Captain Sosa Blanco was a soldier serving under orders in a civil war. He had not a single witness to call. At dawn, after 13 hours and when the crowd had thinned to 500, the tribunal returned the verdict: death.

Something here suggested a medieval trial for witchcraft or an inquisitorial auto-da-fé. The new order in Cuba had become an instrument of divine retributive justice, avenging the wronged, punishing the wrongdoers, venting the accumulated class grievances of the poor and oppressed.[13]

Revolutionary faith, like religious faith, is an amalgam of doctrines and ideals, warnings and fears, passions and animosities. It rests on a vision of human redemption, on the concept of a new order of society embodying freedom and justice. But there are also obstacles and hardships on the road to salvation; those who hope to be saved must be able to overcome them. Ultimately, the triumph of true religion will lead to a day of judgment, when the guilty will be condemned and the wicked punished. For the god of the revolution, like the god of the Scriptures, is a god of vengeance. All these various ideological and emotional elements produce in combination a faith that is capable, at least initially, of moving mountains. Armed with this faith, the new order defeats its foreign enemies, suppresses its domestic opponents, and proceeds to reconstruct polity and economy.

CHAPTER 7

The Heroic Decade
of the New Order

The first ten years following the establishment of the radical dictatorship are the most fruitful period of the revolution. Inspired by
its victory over the *ancien régime*, convinced of its mission to build a
community of virtue, the new order introduces a series of political
and economic reforms that completely transform the structure of
society. As one far-reaching government measure follows another,
the relationship between strong and weak, rich and poor, rulers
and ruled is fundamentally altered. A different social system
emerges.

This process encompasses several simultaneous changes. There is
a new distribution of property resulting from a new system of ownership. There is a rapid growth of elementary education which puts
an end to illiteracy among the lower classes. There is a concerted effort to broaden the social basis of higher learning by encouraging
the children of workers and peasants to enter the universities. Literature, theater, music, painting, and dance are made more accessible to
the masses, not only by lowering the cost of books and tickets, but
by encouraging the arts to deal with themes of everyday existence,
to create "proletarian culture," to embrace "socialist realism." There is
a substantial improvement in public health, a greater availability of
medical care, and a significant rise in national life expectancy. And
finally, there is a new sense of emotional satisfaction among the
lower classes, who come to feel that the government no longer
represents the interests of the well-to-do, that the welfare of the
common man is now a main concern of those in power, and that the

high and mighty are finally getting their comeuppance. All these reforms, following one another in rapid succession, represent the most important achievements of the revolution. They constitute its heroic decade.

The Collectivization of Ownership

The first important result of the establishment of the new order is an alteration in the distribution of property, especially landed property. Since social revolutions occur typically in rural societies, a change in the form of landownership becomes the most urgent task of the radical dictatorship. Although that task is eventually completed through the expropriation of the propertied classes by the government, the first step is generally the independent and spontaneous collective activity of the peasants themselves. As soon as the *ancien régime* falls, they stop paying rents, seize the large estates, take over the livestock and equipment of the landowners, and frequently loot and destroy their residences. Thereby they initiate the revolution in agrarian proprietorship.

This alteration of property relationships begins without official direction or approval. In fact, the authorities of the new order regard it with uneasiness; they try to gain control over it as soon as they can—or dare. For the outburst of popular violence directed against the old system can just as easily turn against the radical dictatorship itself. Anarchy and lawlessness are as much a threat to the revolutionary government as to the *ancien régime*.

That is why the new order seeks to suppress the spontaneous transformation of the system of landownership. Local records in Russia show that in the provinces of Tver and Ryazan, where Soviet authority was established immediately after the November revolution, the transfer of land to the peasants occurred in most cases "in an orderly manner." But in the more distant province of Tambov, where the Bolsheviks were unable to assert their power before the end of January 1918, "the liquidation of landlords' property took place to a considerable extent in the form of spontaneous sackings of the estates." To the radical dictatorship, popular violence, which before the victory of the revolution is a useful weapon against the *an-*

cien régime, becomes afterward a source of danger. For might not those who succeed on their own in rejecting the old system because of economic grievances be tempted in the future to reject the new one for the same reason? The revolutionary government cannot afford to tolerate the independent, uncontrolled redistribution of property initiated by the masses.

Hence one of the first tasks that the leaders of the new order undertake is the suppression of popular violence. Sometimes they achieve this end by appeals and pledges, by promising to satisfy the demands of the lower classes once law and order have been restored. Sometimes they make concessions or strike bargains, allowing workers and peasants to retain what they have seized, often assuring them of still greater gains to come, provided they now submit to the radical dictatorship. And sometimes, when all else fails, they rely on the ultimate source of every established authority, the same source on which the *ancien régime* had depended: armed force. Within a few months after coming to power, the new order generally succeeds in repressing spontaneous collective activity among the lower classes, assuming sole direction over the reconstruction of state and society.

This does not mean, however, that the revolutionary transformation of proprietorship becomes less harsh or ruthless. The creation of a new social system is always violent, always painful. The assumption by the radical dictatorship of exclusive control over economic reorganization makes the process more disciplined, more rational, but not more lenient or humane. Indeed, the officials of the new order are not as vacillating, not as erratic in their hostility toward the propertied classes as the masses. They seek not only to expropriate their political enemy, but to justify the expropriation by condemning him as wicked, immoral, cruel, and treacherous. In other words, the redistribution of property is invariably accompanied by a systematic incitement of collective hatred against those who had been at the top, and who now must pay for their misdeeds with personal abasement as well as economic deprivation.

After coming to power, the Bolsheviks showed little mercy to "counterrevolutionaries," who were frequently punished not for some specific offense but for their class origin. The ferocity of the new order was intensified by the knowledge of what its opponents would do if they emerged victorious. In 1918 an official report from Kazan province informed the government that "punitive expeditions have been sent into every county." Although most of the well-to-do inhabitants managed to get away, the revolutionary authorities had seized their possessions and distributed them among the lower classes. "In Kazan proper only seven or eight people have been shot by the tribunal. This is explained by the fact that the entire bourgeoisie, including the petty bourgeoisie, the priests, and the monks, fled from the city. Half of the city houses are deserted. The property of the fugitives is being confiscated for the benefit of the city poor." The expropriation of landlords and capitalists in Russia was thus accomplished in a manner designed to underscore the concern of the new order for the poor and oppressed.[1]

The fate of the propertied classes in North Vietnam was equally harsh. The redistribution of landownership during the 1950s was accompanied by a wave of conspicuous legalized violence directed against those who had formerly dominated the rural economy. The first step was the elimination of all residents of the village community who were considered "well-to-do" or labeled "reactionary." The land reform program turned next against the "rich" and "middle" peasants. In the end only "poor" farmers and landless laborers remained safe from condemnation and retribution. Throughout the countryside, revolutionary militants, the *can bo*, helped whip up popular hatred against those who had been members of the agrarian patriciate. Public denunciations and trials before "special people's tribunals" took place, while the execution of landlords became a common mass spectacle in many Vietnamese villages.

As for the condemned, they were portrayed as deserving all the punishment they got and more. They were not only exploiters and oppressors; they were fiends, demons. They had hanged a peasant from a tree; they had forced another to lick a spittoon or to eat cow dung or to swallow human excrement; they had burned down houses, drowned small children, poisoned village wells; they had plundered, raped, and killed. Could any penalty be severe enough for the crimes they committed?

In February 1956 the Communist newspaper *Nhan Dan* described in vivid detail some of the misdeeds of which the propertied classes were guilty:

At Nghia-Khe village, in the district of Bac-Ninh, landlords urged small children to steal documents and to throw stones at peasant meetings. In Lieu-Son, they persuaded a small child to set fire to a peasant's house. More cruelly, they gave a poisoned cake to some children in Lieu-Ha, almost killing them. In Van-Truong, they urged young Suu, aged thirteen, to persuade two other small girls to join her in committing suicide by jumping together into a pond; this was to create confusion in the village. In Duc-phong (Ha-Tinh province), they distributed playing cards amongst the children, so that the latter, absorbed in their game, allowed the buffaloes to ruin the crops.

How could even the most softhearted feel pity for such evildoers?

The land reform program was designed not only to achieve a redistribution of property, but to appease the hunger of the masses for retaliation against the well-to-do. "During 20 days more than 100,000 persons of all the social classes of Hanoi participated in the judgment of the landlords of villages surrounding the capital," reported the official *Voice of Vietnam* in December 1955. "The trial of cruel landlords drew more than 20,000 compatriots. Moreover, 35 delegations composed of 2,300 cadres, workers, soldiers, civil servants, and people of the capital are at present visiting the suburbs. Others are at Nam Dinh and Haiphong."

All in all, some 5,000 people are estimated to have been killed in the name of agrarian justice. Not even those who had joined the resistance movement and fought against the French were safe from the ferocity of agricultural reformism, if they happened to belong to the propertied classes. Many of them were executed, and 12,000 members of the Lao Dong Party itself, a figure subsequently confirmed by official sources, were put in prison. Late in 1956 a Hanoi periodical admitted that "people were arrested, jailed, interrogated, and cruelly tortured; people were executed or shot out of hand and their property confiscated. Innocent children of parents wrongly classified as landlords were starved to death." Another journal reported that "the countryside was full of altars and mourning widows wearing white turbans around their heads." To be sure, once the mass hysteria subsided, 12,000 peasants who had been "falsely accused" were released, and many victims of the mass executions were now declared innocent and given decent burial. But for most of those put to death as "landlords" there was neither posthumous remorse nor official rehabilitation. They became part of the price paid for a better society.[2]

Still, while the human cost of the redistribution of property is high, the economic result is profound and far-reaching. A system of private ownership that had endured for centuries is altered in the space of a few years to make way for state control over the means of production and transportation. As soon as they came to power, the Bolsheviks decreed the partition of the estates of the great landowners among the peasantry. The expropriation of industry, commerce, and finance took a little longer, but by the end of 1920 even small manufacturing establishments employing as few as six workers had become nationalized. In agriculture the first phase—and this seems to be typical of all revolutionary economies—is the distribution of confiscated land among the masses of the countryside, which leads to the creation of a sizable class of small, independent farmers. But this phase is sooner or later followed by the collectivization of husbandry, often through the use of coercion and force.

Thus in Russia, where ten years after the November revolution close to 80 percent of the population still lived on the soil, Stalin turned against the *kulaks*, the well-to-do villagers, defined as those owning means of production valued at more than 400 rubles and employing hired laborers for more than 50 days in the year, a category comprising about 4 percent of the peasantry. To insure the success of collectivization, at least 5,000,000 *kulaks* were deported between 1929 and 1931, about 1,000,000 of whom perished, while countless others succumbed in the next four years to the hardships of forced labor in the new industrial enterprises in the east to which they had been exiled. The famine of 1933, in large part a result of the new agricultural policy, claimed many more victims. But the final outcome was the creation of a new system of large-scale collectivized production controlled and directed by the Soviet regime.[3]

In China the new order moved more cautiously. Hoping to avoid the excesses of Stalin's policy, Mao tried to steer a middle course between rapid collectivization and agricultural gradualism. In June 1953, speaking before the Politburo of the Central Committee of the Communist party, he rejected as "a vague formulation" the proposal to "move from New Democracy towards socialism." He argued that "merely moving towards it means that the goal has not been reached." That was wrong. "The formulation sounds plausible but does not bear scrutiny." On the other hand, the recommendation to "sustain private property," which had been advanced to allay the fears of the "middle" peasants, was "not right" either. Instead, Mao advocated a "step-by-step transition" to socialism. The process was to be spread out "over fifteen years and over the twelve months in each year." It would seek a golden mean between too much and too little agrarian reformism. "We must oppose 'Left' and Right deviations and make a step-by-step transition until the whole process is completed."

In practice the policy of slow but steady property redistribution meant that by the end of 1952 the ownership of between 40 and 50 percent of all cultivated land, a total of more than 46,000,000 hectares, had changed hands. Though undoubtedly improving the economic position of the poorest peasants, it came nowhere near establishing equality of proprietorship. To be sure, the share of income going to the bottom 20 percent of the farm population almost doubled between the 1930s and 1952. But the share going to the top 10 percent, that is, to "landlords" and "rich" peasants, according to the classifications employed in the land reform program, diminished by only about a tenth. Almost all of the decline, moreover, appears to have occurred in the income of the "landlord" category, which comprised no more than 2.6 percent of all rural households. The members of this small group were estimated to have been left with about as much land as the "poor" peasants held after redistribution. The "middle" and "rich" peasants, on the other hand, continued to own substantially larger holdings and to earn incomes well above the average.

In the course of the next few years, however, the pattern of agricultural proprietorship changed again, after China decided to adopt the policy of collectivization that Russia had introduced almost three decades earlier. By the end of 1956, well ahead of Mao's announced timetable of fifteen years, a series of drastic new reforms had eliminated the private sector as a significant source of farm output and employment. More than 95 percent of the peasant households had been organized into agricultural producers' cooperatives, in effect putting an end to the private ownership of land, equipment, tools, and draft animals. Although not enough is known about the details of this transformation of the rural economy, it was accomplished by and large without the hardships and cruelties accompanying the Soviet program of collectivization. No violent resistance or armed repression occurred, no mass deportation, no famine. While in the Soviet Union farm production dropped about 20 percent between 1928 and 1932, in China it rose about 20 percent between 1953 and 1957. The final outcome of the reorganization of husbandry may have been the same, but the human cost was substantially lower.

In the collectivization of industry Mao promised to adopt the same middle-of-the-road policy he had pledged to follow in the collectivization of agriculture. On September 7, 1953, he assured a gathering of "representative personages from the democratic parties and industrial and commercial circles" that the new order sought cooperation with capitalistic enterprise, not confrontation. Far from being an obstacle or threat, "private industry and commerce are a big asset to the state and play a large part in the nation's economy and the people's livelihood. Not only do they provide the state with goods, but they can also accumulate capital and train cadres for the state."

Unfortunately, Mao complained, there were employers who remained selfish and greedy, just as there were employees who remained obdurate and unreasonable. Both would have to learn to be more willing to compromise. "Some capitalists keep themselves at a great distance from the state and have not changed their profits-before-everything mentality. Some workers are advancing too fast and won't allow the capitalists to make any profit at all." The government should teach all of them restraint and moderation. "We should try to educate these workers and capitalists and help them gradually (but the sooner the better) adapt themselves to our state policy, namely, to make China's private industry and commerce mainly serve the nation's economy and the people's livelihood and partly earn profits for the capitalists and in this way embark on the path of state capitalism." The new order would seek to convert the propertied classes, not suppress them. "It is necessary to go on educating the capitalists in patriotism, and to this end we should systematically cultivate a number of them who have a broader vision and are ready to lean towards the Communist Party and the People's

Government, so that most of the other capitalists may be convinced through them." Those listening to Mao found his words encouraging and reassuring, no doubt.

Yet even while he spoke, the end of the system of private enterprise in China was approaching. Its decline had accelerated during the "five-anti" campaign launched in the first half of 1952 to combat bribery of officials, evasion of taxes, theft of public assets, fraud in fulfilling government contracts, and the misuse or betrayal of the economic secrets of the state. The result was a sharp drop in the proportion of capitalistic production in the gross value of industrial output from 28.7 percent in 1951 to 17.1 in 1952 and 14.0 in 1953. The figures provide a measure of the scale of socialization at the very time when Mao was announcing soothingly that "private industry and commerce are a big asset to the state."

The final stage in the collectivization of industry and commerce came in the middle 1950s, when virtually all individually owned businesses were placed under the partial or complete control of government. The share of private enterprise in the total value of industrial production fell from 24.9 percent in 1954 to 0.1 in 1956. The share of private enterprise in the total value of retail trade fell as well, from 26.4 to 3.0 percent. To be sure, the number of independent industrial establishments diminished by only about a third, from 134,000 to 89,000, but the number of employees in those establishments dropped precipitously from 1,796,000 to 14,000. In the great majority of cases, the only worker in the remaining individually owned enterprises was the proprietor himself. In even less time than in Russia, the economy of China had become nationalized and collectivized.[4]

The pattern in North Vietnam was almost exactly the same. First came the phase of agrarian redistribution, initiated in 1954, which was designed to bring about greater equality in landownership. In the course of the next three years, the reform program accomplished the reapportionment of between about 700,000 and 800,000 hectares out of a total area of 1,500,000 hectares of arable soil. Estimates of the number of households gaining land or other property vary from 1,600,000 to 2,200,000, comprising roughly 8,000,000 to 9,000,000 people. Although some farmers got little, the average per capita holding of "landless" peasants was reported to have risen from 199 to 1,528 square meters, and that of "small" peasants from 455 to 1,431 square meters. Hence an average family of five appears to have obtained or retained approximately 7,500 square meters, three-quarters of a hectare. In addition, the government announced the redistribution of some 100,000 head of cattle and an unspecified amount of housing and equipment.

Yet sooner or later the new order turns against small peasant proprietorship which it introduced immediately after gaining power. For in the long run the existence of a large class of independent farmers is incompatible with the ideals and objectives of the radical dictatorship. It may prove not only a hindrance but a threat to the revolutionary state. A fragmented, individualized form of husbandry cannot provide the economic advantages of large-scale rationalized production. But worse still, from the viewpoint of a Communist regime, agrarian proprietorship, even small agrarian proprietorship, tends to breed a petty-bourgeois mentality, an anti-collectivist outlook. Here then is a potential danger that must be scotched.

No sooner, therefore, had the land reform program in North Vietnam been completed, than the government launched a campaign for agricultural collectivization. By the end of 1960 the country had 41,000 farm cooperatives which included 85 percent of the peasant families and 76 percent of the cultivated area. For the authorities in Hanoi, as for those in Moscow or Peking, the ultimate goal of the reorganization of ownership had become the creation of a nationalized, socialized economy centrally directed by the state.[5]

The War Against Illiteracy

As important as the redistribution of property by the new order is the redistribution of learning. Since after the revolution, education rather than wealth becomes the key to high political and social status, the acquisition of formal knowledge is the chief avenue of upward mobility. In no regard is the difference between the *ancien régime* and the radical dictatorship more striking, therefore, than in their attitude toward the instruction of the lower classes.

To the old order, mass literacy always seems a potential menace; it always poses a danger to established institutions and loyalties. Once the common man learns to read and write, will he not become dissatisfied with his lot in society? Will he not become infected with radical ideas? And will he then not try to improve his position by rebelliousness and subversion? The *ancien régime*, to be sure, is sometimes forced to introduce a system of elementary popular education, since economic modernization requires a literate labor force. A skilled worker in an industrial plant must be able to read instructions, he must understand diagrams, he must know how to add and subtract. And yet the old order generally tries to restrict the knowledge to which the masses have access to the bare minimum essential for their economic function. Too much learning will only encourage vain hopes and unrealizable ambitions.

The leaders of the revolution take an entirely different view of popular education. They charge the *ancien régime* with monopolizing learning in the same way it monopolizes wealth. If the masses are to throw off the yoke of their oppressor, they must learn to read and write, they must acquire an understanding of revolutionary ideas and ideals, they must gain an awareness of their collective interest in the struggle for economic existence. Hence unrestricted access to knowledge is the right of all men, not only those with property and power.

The new order, moreover, sees even more clearly than the old that popular education is essential for technological progress and economic growth. Without it the promise of material improvement in the position of the lower classes cannot be fulfilled. But there is still another calculation behind the commitment of the radical dictatorship to universal literacy. It recognizes that, with proper guidance, popular education need not become a threat to established authority. On the contrary, it can prove a means of support, a source of strength. By determining the content of learning, the government can use mass schooling to reinforce loyalty to the revolutionary regime. In other words, the new order differs from the old in its perception that not the restriction but the control of knowledge is the key to maintaining the status quo.

That is why as soon as the radical dictatorship comes to power, it launches a campaign to achieve universal literacy. In Russia a substantial improvement in elementary education had already occurred during the last decades of the czarist regime, but under the

Soviets the pace accelerated. From 1914–15 to 1927–28 the number of pupils between the ages of six and ten enrolled in primary schools increased 34 percent, from 7,390,144 to 9,910,407, while the number of pupils between the ages of eleven and thirteen enrolled in intermediate schools grew even more rapidly, 248 percent, from 382,618 to 1,331,646. The movement to increase popular literacy through elementary instruction among the young was reinforced, moreover, by the growth of adult education in evening classes, factory schools, and vocational institutions.

An extrapolation from the data provided by the censuses of 1926 and 1939 indicates that at the end of the First Five-Year Plan, roughly 1932–33, the literacy rate of the Soviet population aged nine and over reached 68 percent, compared with 51 percent six years earlier. In some of the more backward national republics, where the proportion of illiterates had been especially high, the improvement under the new order was dramatic. In Tadzhikistan the literacy rate went from 4 percent in 1926 to around 38 in 1932–33, while in Azerbaijan there was a jump from 25 to approximately 49 percent. Fifteen years after the November revolution, although illiteracy was still common in many parts of the Soviet Union, the progress that had already been made suggested that its complete elimination could probably be achieved within another decade or two.

In China over 90 percent of the population had been illiterate before the revolution. The percentage for women in rural districts was close to 100, and even among industrial workers no more than 20 to 40 percent could read. As soon as the Communists came to power, therefore, they introduced an ambitious program for the improvement of popular education. The number of pupils in primary schools rose from 30,000,000 in 1950 to between 64,000,000 and 66,000,000 in 1957. Yet eight years after the establishment of the People's Republic, Chou En-lai estimated that the rate of illiteracy was still 70 percent. As late as the middle 1950s almost half of the industrial work force could neither read nor write, and even in 1960 roughly 66 percent of the rural population and 24 percent of the urban population remained illiterate. Despite the vigorous efforts of the new order, the growth of literacy among the masses of China proved difficult, laborious, and slow.

In Cuba, on the other hand, where even under the *ancien régime* more than three-fourths of all adults could read, the elimination of illiteracy was relatively rapid. There was first of all an increase of 101 percent in the total enrollment in primary schools, from 717,417 pupils in 1958–59 to 1,444,395 in 1968–69. While the number of schools grew a little more slowly, 95 percent, from 7,567 to 14,726, the number of teachers almost tripled from 17,335 to 47,876, a rise of 276 percent.

This effort was supported, to an even greater extent than in Russia or China, by a massive campaign of adult schooling. The Castro regime declared 1961 to be "The Year of Education." Some 250,000 men, women, and children were mobilized for a period of eight months to serve as a vast instructional army, among them 100,000 pupils from secondary schools and 35,000 members of the teaching profession. Armed with 3,000,000 books and 100,000 paraffin lamps, they were sent out to all parts of the island to wage the battle for elementary education. In December the government proudly announced that the proportion of illiterates, officially estimated at 21 percent before the campaign, had now dropped to less than 4 percent of the entire population. Only around 270,000 adults were still unable to read. Cuba had become the first nation in Latin America to achieve virtually complete popular literacy.[6]

To the leaders of the new order, however, universal elementary education is more than a pedagogical reform or even an economic necessity. It is a moral obligation, an ideological imperative. They believe wholeheartedly that there are natural talents and abilities among the masses that the *ancien régime* had deliberately suppressed in order to maintain the domination of the ruling classes. It is therefore not only the policy but the duty of the revolutionary government to awaken the creative popular energies that had hitherto been allowed to lie dormant. The building of a new society will be impossible without the active participation of the people; they are the ultimate source of the strength that the radical dictatorship needs to attain its goal. Yet first the masses must learn to understand their historic mission; they must be taught to recognize the function they are destined to perform in the process of social reconstruction. Hence popular instruction is more than a token of progress or a sign of benevolence. It is the essential precondition for the success of the new order.

For that reason education must never become merely a means of satisfying private intellectual inquisitiveness. It always has a collective role, a communal purpose. The radical dictatorship has a right, even an obligation, to make education conform to its ideals and objectives. The system of instruction must guide and nurture, it must train and indoctrinate, it must shape the popular mind. How else will the common man, whose interests the new order is sworn to defend, know what to read? How else will he be able to tell what is progressive from what is reactionary, what is orthodox from what is heretical? Learning is never an intrinsic value, an independent good. It is always a social means of attaining a social end.

That is why the campaign that the new order wages to achieve mass education is accompanied by a disproportionately rapid growth in the volume of publication. Numerous books are published that are designed to make good literature available to the lower classes, improving their taste, refining their sensibility: novels, essays, plays, and poems. But greater still is the increase in polemical writings calculated to enlist popular literacy in the service of the revolution: newspapers, journals, pamphlets, and tracts. The rise in literacy is invariably outstripped by the rise in readership. Not only does the new order teach the masses to read; it encourages them, it urges them to read. Reading is of great importance to the radical dictatorship; reading implants ideas, it nourishes convictions. It is an invaluable tool for winning loyalty and inspiring devotion. Thus, though the number of newspapers in Russia rose only modestly from 859 in 1913 to 1,197 in 1928, an increase of 39 percent, more or less in keeping with the increase in literacy, the circulation of newspapers rose nearly 250 percent, from 2,700,000 to 9,400,000. Whereas for the old order mass education was a potential threat to established authority, for the new it is a powerful weapon in defense of the revolution.

Even the campaign to spread elementary instruction among the lower classes has an ideological dimension, a political function. The instructor's manual prepared in 1961 under the auspices of the Cuban ministry of education for the war against illiteracy contained 24 "themes of revolutionary orientation" on such topics as nationalization, imperialism, and racial discrimination. The first "theme," entitled "The Revolution," was headed by a quotation from Castro:

"Revolution means the destruction of privilege, the disappearance of exploitation, and the creation of a just society." The text itself elaborated on these points:

> People need revolution in order to develop and advance. When a nation is dominated by another, more powerful nation, only through revolution can it end foreign domination and establish its own government free from such domination.
>
> When the riches of a nation are in the hands of another nation, a revolution is needed to recover those riches.
>
> When the humble men and women of a country are without work, without land to cultivate, without education, they must revolt.
>
> When the work of the humble serves to enrich a small group of exploiters, then the humble must make a revolution so that the wealth produced by labor ceases to enrich the exploiters and remains in the hands of the working people.
>
> That is revolution: liberty, work, land, schooling, and respect for those who struggle and work. And to attain these things it is not enough to take up arms against tyranny; it is also necessary to make all those changes that are now being made in our country.

Thus to those holding revolutionary power the ability to read is never to be exercised purely in accordance with private taste or individual judgment. It should always be used socially to persuade, inspire, indoctrinate, and politicize.[7]

The Changing Function of Advanced Learning

Even more important to the new order than the growth of elementary schooling is the reconstruction of higher education. The level of literacy among the masses may have an important effect on the popular acceptance of the revolution. But the system of advanced learning provides it with the administrators and technicians whose expertise is essential for the creation of a better society. Under the radical dictatorship, therefore, as under the *ancien régime*, a university degree is the key to advancement and success. There is an im-

portant difference, however. Formerly the government sought to restrict the admission of students to higher education to members of
the propertied classes with a vested interest in the preservation of
the status quo. Now it throws open the gates of advanced learning to
the children of workers and peasants, those most likely to support
the cause of the revolution.

Hence the first effect of the reorganization of higher education by
the new order is a vast increase in the number of students. This reflects in part the resolve of the radical dictatorship to "democratize"
formal knowledge, transforming it from an instrument of class domination into a weapon for social change. But it is also in part a result
of the rapidly growing demand of the revolutionary government for
skilled organizers and administrators, for economists, managers,
engineers, scientists, and civil servants. The collectivization and
nationalization of the economy impose on the state the need for a
vastly enlarged bureaucratic apparatus capable of assuming those
functions of direction and management which the private sector had
formerly performed. The overthrow of the *ancien régime* is thus followed by a striking growth in higher education.

Indeed, the relative increase in the number of students enrolled in
institutions of advanced learning is significantly larger than the relative increase in the number of pupils attending elementary schools.
The statistical evidence on this point is unambiguous. Under every
revolutionary regime the expansion of higher education exceeds by
a substantial margin the expansion of elementary education. In Russia the enrollment in primary schools rose from 7,390,144 in 1914–15
to 9,910,407 in 1927–28, a growth of 34 percent. But the enrollment in
institutions of advanced learning rose during the same period from
112,000 to 159,800, a growth of 43 percent. And the increase in the
enrollment of upper vocational schools or "technicums," which specialized in the training of plant managers and factory experts, was
even more striking, 429 percent, from 35,800 to 189,400. Under the
new Soviet system, then, mass literacy was subordinated for the
time being to professional and technical expertise.

The pattern in China was by and large similar. The victory of the
revolution led to a rapid growth of elementary education, but the
growth of higher education was far more rapid. The number of pupils in primary schools rose by roughly 165 percent between 1949

and 1957, from something over 24,000,000 to something over 64,000,000. The number of students in the universities, on the other hand, rose by almost 240 percent, from 130,058 to 441,000. According to official figures, by the late 1950s enrollment in institutions of advanced learning was about 300 percent greater than in the best years of the Kuomintang regime, whereas enrollment in elementary education was 160 percent greater. The new order clearly needed trained economists and engineers more than literate workers and peasants.

In North Vietnam the demand for administrative and scientific personnel with university training was even greater than in Russia or China, since under the colonial system the access of native students to institutions of higher education had been restricted to the point of virtual exclusion. In 1939–40 there had been only 600 in all of Vietnam. By 1954, the year of the defeat of the *ancien régime*, the figure had risen to 915 for North Vietnam alone, not much more than before the Second World War. The number of pupils in elementary schools, on the other hand, though also relatively small, 592,095 for a population of over 20,000,000, was proportionately far greater than the tiny number of students attending a university. A swift expansion of enrollment in educational institutions offering specialized training thus became the first priority of a government impatient to collectivize, nationalize, and industrialize.

In the course of the following decade a dramatic increase occurred in both primary and advanced education, but the growth of higher learning far exceeded the growth of elementary instruction. While by 1964 the number of pupils in primary schools had reached 2,654,665, a rise of 348 percent in ten years, the number of students in the universities had climbed to 25,000, an extraordinary 2,600 percent. This rapid expansion of education, especially higher education, reflected the determination of the new order to reconstruct the polity and economy of North Vietnam after long years of alien domination.

In Cuba a proportionately far greater supply of university graduates existed, since under the *ancien régime* the propertied classes had easy access to institutions of higher learning. Hence the situation of the revolutionary government was more favorable than in North Vietnam. Yet here too a substantial increase in public expenditure for learning took place, particularly for advanced learning. The national budget for instruction and culture grew from a total of 74,200,000 dollars or 11.40 per capita in 1958 to a total of 270,400,000 dollars or 38.10 per capita in 1962, a rise of 264 percent.

The disparity in the rate of increase between elementary and higher education, however, was as pronounced in Cuba as in other revolutionary societies. The percentage of the total public expenditure for instruction that was devoted to primary schooling fell from 61.2 in 1952–53, under the Batista dictatorship, to 38.7 in 1962 after Castro's victory. The percentage going to the universities, on the other hand, more than doubled from 2.6 to 5.4. Whereas the growth in enrollment in primary schools between 1958–59 and 1968–69 was 101 percent, from 717,417 to 1,444,395, the growth in enrollment in advanced schools, those offering technical and professional as well as university training, was 245 percent between 1961–62 and 1968–69, from 31,858 to 110,049.

The overthrow of the *ancien régime* is thus followed as a rule by a swift expansion of education, especially in institutions of higher learning. For the attainment of the goals of the new order requires such a drastic reorganization of the political structure and economic system that only a substantial increase in administrative and scientific personnel can make it feasible.[8]

But the revolution changes more than the scope of higher education. It also changes its content and purpose; it changes its function. Under the *ancien régime* formal learning is to a large extent a mark of individual distinction, a badge of personal prominence. It serves to establish the intellectual superiority of those who can afford to attend a university. Precisely because it is so largely a symbol of rank and status, it tends to assume a recondite or esoteric character. It must not be debased by too much preoccupation with practicality, with something as commonplace as earning a living. Hence the dominant disciplines in the curriculum of higher education are the humanities—philosophy, classics, literature, and history—whose very lack of commercial usefulness sets them apart as lofty and edifying. Their study is a form of decorative display or conspicuous consumption of formal knowledge. Of the other fields of learning, only law and political science, which provide an avenue to high government positions, can compete with the humanities in value and prestige.

After the revolution, however, a different view of higher education emerges. Learning ceases to be a token of individual eminence and becomes an instrument of economic progress and social reform. Not abstract intellectuality but practical utility comes to determine the relative importance of the various fields of knowledge offered in the university curriculum. This means that those disciplines that were formerly looked down upon as materialistic and grubby—medicine, engineering, physics, chemistry, agriculture, forestry, and pedagogy—now become central in higher education. The skills they impart are indispensable for the collectivization of ownership, the growth of production, and the improvement of the standard of living. In other words, change in the values of formal learning logically reflects change in the values of the social system.

The humanities, to be sure, do not acquiesce meekly in their loss of status. They struggle to retain relevance in an increasingly egalitarian political environment; they try to adapt to the new civic faith of the revolutionary regime. They tone down their emphasis on private sensibility and individual fulfillment. They strive to demonstrate that they too embrace the ideals of the radical dictatorship. The classics begin to dwell on the class struggle in antiquity; philosophy increasingly traces the ramifications of the Marxian dialectic; literature turns more and more to the study of economic motivation and social significance in creative writing; and history underscores the achievements of the new order by trumpeting the iniquities of the old. But none of these efforts can reverse the shift in university instruction from intellectual to professional training. The goals pursued by the radical dictatorship make it inescapable.

The statistical data on China illuminate this process of educational change. During the period 1928–32, while the Chiang Kai-shek regime was consolidating its hold on power, the most popular fields of study in institutions of higher learning were law and political science with 38.2 percent of total enrollment. Next came literature and the arts with 21.8 percent. Lagging far behind were the technical, scientific, and professional disciplines: engineering with 10.2 percent, the natural sciences with 8.3, education with 7.8, economics and finance with 5.9, the health sciences with 4.0, and in last place, agriculture and forestry with 3.8 percent. Here was a curricular pattern characteristic of the *ancien régime*.

But by 1949–50, barely a year after the Communist victory, the distribution of student enrollment had already undergone a drastic change. Now law and political science accounted for no more than 6.3 percent of those attending institutions of higher learning, and literature and the arts for only 12.5. To the new order the most important disciplines were those that could provide technical expertise. Hence the big winners in the competition for enrollment were engineering with 26.0 percent, economics and finance with 16.7, the health sciences with 13.0, education with 10.6, and agriculture and forestry with 8.9. The natural sciences, on the other hand, suffered a modest but unexpected decline to 6.0, reflecting the growing emphasis of the revolutionary regime on practical study at the expense of theoretical research.

By 1957–58 the transformation of advanced learning in China was complete. Eight years after the proclamation of the People's Republic, curricular preference in higher education had assumed a form typical of every new order. Law and politics were now in last place with 2.1 percent of student enrollment, a precipitous fall from their leading position under the Kuomintang. Literature and the arts were not much better off with 5.4 percent, barely a fourth of their share a generation earlier. Now the dominant field in popularity as well as prestige was engineering, with 40.9 percent, followed at a considerable distance by education with 21.3. Then came the health sciences with 12.6, agriculture and forestry with 8.6, and the natural sciences with 6.2, roughly the same percentages as at the time of the Communist victory. The proportionate enrollment in economics and finance, on the other hand, had fluctuated erratically. In the late 1920s it accounted for 5.9 percent of the total. By the end of the civil war the figure had risen to 16.7 percent in response to an urgent need for managers, planners, and bureaucrats. But within a decade that need had been met, so that in 1957–58 the percentage dropped again to 2.9, the lowest in thirty years. The new order in China thus succeeded in altering the underlying function of higher education from individual development to collective social utility.

Educational statistics on Cuba, though not as detailed as the Chinese, reveal a similar course of development. Total enrollment in institutions of higher learning expanded during the first decade of the Castro government from 31,858 in 1958–59 to 110,049 in 1968–69, an increase of 245 percent. Yet here as well a sharp difference in the rate of growth was apparent between disciplines offering cultural enrichment and those providing technical or professional skill. The number of students at the universities, where law and the humanities had long dominated the curriculum, rose 57 percent, from 25,599 to 40,147. But the number of students in industrial colleges rose 379 percent, from 6,259 to 29,975. And while there had been no schools of agriculture in Cuba when Castro came to power, a decade later there were 37 with an enrollment of 36,812.

All in all, the number of students in schools providing advanced technical or professional training reached 69,902 in 1968–69, over 170 percent of the students in the universities, whereas in 1958–59 the number had been less than 7,000 and the percentage only 24. The share of the total public expenditure on education going to the universities, moreover, rose from 2.6 percent in 1952–53 to 5.4 in 1962, whereas the share going to institutions providing technical instruction rose from 3.8 percent to 14.9. Altogether, enrollment in the schools of technology in Cuba increased 300 percent in the first four years of the Castro regime. The same pronounced shift in the emphasis of advanced learning from personal cultivation to collective usefulness had taken place.[9]

The new order, however, seeks to alter not only the scope and purpose of higher education. It also tries to change its class basis, its social structure. Under the *ancien régime* there had been a deliberate attempt to limit access to organized formal knowledge. It had appeared self-evident that admission to a university ought to be restricted to those whose position in society provided assurance of their loyalty to the established system. The high cost of tuition and residence had the intended effect of excluding members of the lower classes. For to provide higher education to those destined to occupy a subordinate position in society would only arouse resentment; it would encourage subversive ideas and radical organizations. The result would be the rise of a disgruntled, overeducated intelligentsia hoping to improve its social status through revolution.

The old order is aware, to be sure, that there are many university students, including some from the best families, who denounce the political oppression, economic exploitation, and public corruption that the government tolerates. But this is dismissed as youthful indiscretion, romantic exuberance. Once the young rebels mature, once they achieve financial success, once they marry and settle down, they will become loyal supporters of the status quo. Their self-interest will take care of that. The danger to the existing system comes supposedly not from dissident patricians but from ambitious commoners whose attainments exceed their opportunities.

The new order takes an opposite view of the social role of higher education. Its ideology demands that knowledge like property ceases to be a monopoly of the well-to-do classes. Learning must become democratized and collectivized; it must become an instrument of revolutionary change. And that means that the class background of students receiving university training must reflect the new structure of society. Those in power acknowledge that under the *ancien régime* many well-to-do students had fought selflessly for its overthrow. But how reliable is support for the revolution based primarily on idealism and guilt? How strong, how firm? Would it not be better to create a new lower-class intelligentsia whose devotion to the new order derives not only from ideological conviction but material interest? Hence the radical dictatorship always seeks to alter the social basis of higher education in such a way as to proletarianize university enrollment.

Yet nowhere does the educational policy of the new order encounter greater resistance than in the attempt to transform the class structure of advanced learning. The campaign against illiteracy progresses more or less steadily, not as fast perhaps as the government might like, but fast enough to achieve universal elementary education within a generation. A decade after the revolution, moreover, student enrollment in institutions of higher learning is two, three, or four times what it had been before. The shift of emphasis in the university curriculum from law and the humanities to technology and the professions is swift and thorough. But the effort to proletarianize the social origin of those admitted to advanced learning meets stubborn opposition. The authorities try to overcome it by lowering academic requirements, by making entrance examinations easier, by providing special tutoring for lower-class applicants, and by establishing preferences and quotas for the children of workers and peasants. Still, progress remains slow and laborious.

The basic problem is that no amount of official prodding can compensate for the long-range effects of oppression and ignorance. The children of the lower classes come from an intellectually as well as materially impoverished background; they are rarely exposed at home to abstract ideas or analytical concepts. How are they then to compete effectively with those who have grown up in an environment of affluence and culture, encouraged from an early age to read, reason, reflect, and communicate? The only way to hasten the transformation of the social structure of advanced learning is by a drastic reduction of standards. But a revolutionary regime committed to economic and administrative reorganization cannot afford to dilute the training of those who are to be entrusted with the execution of its policies. The result of this dilemma is that long after the victory of the new order, a disproportionate number of students in higher education continues to be recruited from the nonproletarian strata of society, from families of businessmen, politicians, bureaucrats, technicians, intellectuals, and professionals.

The *ancien régime* in Russia had in its last years already begun to democratize the class structure of higher education, driven by a demand for trained personnel arising out of modernization and industrialization. Between 1880 and 1914 the percentage of university students from working-class families had grown from 12.4 to 24.3. In the course of the next decade, on the other hand, a period of war, revolution, and civil conflict, almost no change occurred in the social composition of enrollment at institutions of advanced learning. In 1927–28 the percentage of college and university students from working-class families was still only 25.4, almost the same as at the outbreak of the First World War.

But then came a concerted effort by the government to broaden the social foundation of higher education. The percentage of college and university students from working-class families rose to 30.3 in 1928–29, 35.2 in 1929–30, 46.4 in 1930–31, 51.4 in 1931–32, and 50.3 in 1932–33. The percentage in the technical colleges, which offered training for leading positions in industry and transportation, was even higher: 38.3 in 1927–28, 43.1 in 1928–29, 46.4 in 1929–30, 61.7 in 1930–31, 63.7 in 1931–32, and 64.6 in 1932–33.

Nevertheless, the grip of the elite groups within the social system proved stubborn. While the percentage of students from professional and white-collar families did decline from 51 in 1927–28 to 33 in 1932–33, still a disproportionately high ratio, in absolute terms there was actually an increase from 81,000 to 145,000 resulting from the general expansion of enrollment.

Even these figures represent an underestimation of the proportion of nonproletarian students, since the falsification of documents pertaining to social origin was quite common at a time when the authorities favored applicants from the lower classes. "About 30% of the first-year students [in the Second Moscow University] turned out to be persons deprived of voting rights," according to one contemporary report. Another complained about "how easy it is to get documents on social position from the village soviets and local executive committees, which give out endorsements that 'the bearer of this is a poor peasant' with criminal light-mindedness and irresponsibility to almost anyone, starting with middle peasants and ending with kulaks and merchants." Indeed, "the village soviets and local executive committees give statements to priests affirming that they are 'grain-sowers.'" More than ten years after the November revolution, higher education in the Soviet Union remained to a considerable extent a preserve of privileged strata within the social structure.

The proletarianization of organized knowledge in China progressed even more slowly, partly because the *ancien régime* had as a matter of policy rigidly restricted admission to advanced learning. To democratize the social basis of higher education seemed to both the imperial and the Kuomintang authorities highly dangerous. When the Communists came to power in 1949, therefore, much talk was heard about creating a new intelligentsia drawn from the people through a vigorous recruitment of the children of workers and peasants. But it soon became apparent that the maintenance of high academic standards could not be reconciled with relaxed admission policies. Moreover, there was a good deal of grumbling among the university students themselves, most of whom still came from bourgeois and landlord families, about the preference being given to five categories of applicants: workers and peasants, some members of the armed forces, the children of revolutionary martyrs, the national minorities, and the overseas Chinese.

The result was that as of September 1956, according to official statistics, no more than 34.29 percent of the undergraduates were of worker or peasant origin. Figures for graduate students in the colleges and universities as well as at the national Academy of Sciences were lower still, 17.46 and 5.92 percent respectively. Thus the proletarianization of the class basis of higher education proved even more difficult in China than in Russia. Indeed, no part of the program of social reorganization that every new order seeks to introduce proves as baffling, as difficult to achieve. In the competition for access to advanced learning, the advantage remains on the side of a managerial, technical, and intellectual elite.[10]

Health and Revolution

The campaign to democratize medical care, on the other hand, is generally a huge success. Not only is there an expansion of health services after the revolution, but their scope and distribution become broadened. To the *ancien régime* the problem of public health is of minor importance. Better still, there is no problem. The inequality in access to medical care seems as natural as the inequality in access to economic power or social influence. It is one of those hard but inescapable realities of the human condition. Nothing can be done about it. The state is no more able to provide health services for all than to provide fancy food or elegant clothing or comfortable housing for all. The disparity of material conditions is simply inevitable.

Hence medical training under the old order remains as restricted as other fields of advanced learning. The number of those admitted to the study of medicine is narrowly limited. More than that, they are recruited almost entirely from the well-to-do classes. The education they receive teaches them, at least implicitly, that their professional expertise may be properly used for personal advantage. It is a source of affluence, a badge of distinction. They come to regard it in the same way in which a banker regards his bank or a landowner his estate. Their ambition generally is to set up practice in some large city, cater to a wealthy clientele, and become part of fashionable society. As for the lower classes, especially in the rural districts, they must learn to cope with illness by means of herbs, teas, potions, incantations, and prayers. It is not only the shortage of medical care but its distribution that accounts for the inadequacy of health services under the *ancien régime*.

The revolution changes all that. Its leaders proclaim that health, like wealth and education, had hitherto been monopolized by the exploiters of the people. But now medical care must be democratized. Those who receive training as physicians should be taught that their skill ought to promote collective well-being, not private gain. Popular access to adequate health services becomes one of the highest priorities of the new order. This means first of all a rapid expansion of the enrollment in schools of medicine, so that within a few years the number of doctors and nurses triples or quadruples. Even more important, health professionals, now supported by government salaries rather than patient fees, are sent to remote villages where skilled medical treatment had previously been unknown. A new view of the state's responsibility for health services thus leads to a significant increase in their availability to the masses. By and large, the first thing to be successfully collectivized under the new order is not property or learning but medicine.

That is why the leaders of the revolution dwell so proudly on the improvement in health care that the radical dictatorship introduces. In 1960 Ho Chi Minh, commemorating the thirtieth anniversary of the Vietnamese Workers Party, contrasted the lack of medical services under the old order with their general availability under the new. At the outbreak of the Second World War, he pointed out, there had been only 54 hospitals in northern and central Vietnam, only 138 village health centers, 86 doctors, and 968 nurses. Now there were 138 hospitals in North Vietnam alone, 1,500 village health centers, 292 doctors, and 6,020 nurses. In addition, 169,000 medical workers were providing sanitary and public health care in the rural districts. Surely, this demonstrated that the revolutionary government had the interests of the common man at heart. "Our achievements to date are clear proof that it is the aim of socialism to abolish worry and poverty from the lives of the working people, to provide them with employment, to make them happy and prosperous. [And in return] it is the duty of the Party and the people to exert every effort to produce more, faster, better and with more economy."[11]

The new order has good reason to boast. Even tough critics of the revolution are forced to acknowledge its success in bringing about a major improvement in public health. When the civil war in China ended in 1949, the country had only 40,000 physicians trained in modern medicine and no more than 90,000 hospital beds. Yet to achieve a level of medical care comparable to that of the United States, the country would have needed more than 600,000 physicians and over 5,000,000 hospital beds. In the decade following the Communist victory, the government made considerable progress in narrowing the gap. By 1957, 860 new hospitals with a total of over 300,000 beds had been built, an increase of 234 percent. In the early 1960s, moreover, the schools of medicine began to graduate about 25,000 new doctors each year, so that the total number of physicians soon reached 150,000 and the number of medical assistants 170,000. Sixteen years after the establishment of the new order, the ministry of health announced triumphantly that every county in China now had at least one hospital.

The result was not only a sharp decline in the relative incidence of death but a major change in its medical cause. Under the *ancien régime* adverse material conditions had been to a considerable extent responsible for the high rate of mortality. Diseases resulting from malnutrition—pellagra, for example, scurvy, osteomalacia, beriberi, and nutritional edema—were common and widespread. There was a high incidence, moreover, of "social" maladies like venereal disease, opium addiction, and tuberculosis. Endemic or epidemic infectious illnesses, among them cholera, smallpox, typhoid fever, typhus, meningitis, encephalitis, plague, and leprosy, were rampant. And finally, many parts of the country suffered from infestations of schistosomiasis, hookworm, malaria, and other parasitic sicknesses.

After the revolution a remarkable change in public health began to take place. Alcoholism and drug addiction were effectively suppressed, infant mortality dropped, and life expectancy started to increase. Even more significant, a striking shift occurred in the leading causes of death from illnesses of malnutrition and infection to maladies of old age such as cancer and cerebrovascular disease. No achievement of the new order was more impressive than this rapid improvement in general medical well-being.

The statistical data on North Vietnam, though not nearly as detailed, point to comparable progress in public health. First of all, a steady expansion of primary medical care began. The number of physicians rose from 108 in 1955, following the victory over the French, to 312 in 1959. When the new order was established, the ratio of doctors to population was about 1 per 150,000. A decade later, in 1965, it was 1 per 8,700. The number of assistant doctors, those who had studied for five years instead of the seven required for a regular medical degree, increased from 363 to 1,660 between 1955 and 1959. There were 57 hospitals in 1955, 63 in 1959, and 83 in 1962; there were 4 infirmaries in 1955, 122 in 1959, and 277 in 1962. The number of hospital beds grew from 14,300 to 19,500 and then to 25,900. In less than a decade, the availability of primary medical care had at least doubled.

This improvement was reinforced by a rapid expansion of ancillary or supplemental services. There were 3,278 midwives and 104 pharmacists in 1955, but 6,511 and 334 in 1959. The number of dispensaries rose from 200 to 655. Before the new order there had been no systematic attempt to establish village health stations or mobile health units. Five years afterward there were respectively 1,335 and 123. In 1955 there had been one health officer for every 80,000 inhabitants, in 1965 one for every 1,850 inhabitants. The growth in auxiliary health care thus kept pace with the progress in basic medical service.

What helped make these advances appear impressive, however, was their low starting point. The colonial regime had done so little to promote the general health of the native population that under the new order even modest progress in absolute terms seemed remarkable. At the outbreak of the Second World War, there had been no more than 203 doctors and assistant doctors in all of Vietnam, north as well as south. There had been only 43 pharmacists and 307 midwives. Hospitals and infirmaries together numbered 109. The country did have 268 dispensaries, but no village health stations or mobile health units. While there is no figure for the number of hospital beds, it could not have exceeded the 19,500 in North Vietnam alone twenty years later. In other words, without minimizing the achievements of the new order, it was the inadequacy of health care under the *ancien régime* that made those achievements appear so extraordinary.

By the same token, the medical success of the revolution in Cuba seems less dramatic, partly because even under the old order the country had enjoyed a relatively high level of health services. According to the census of 1953, there were 6,201 physicians, and by 1958 the number was estimated to have risen to around 7,000. The ratio of doctors to population was thus approximately 1 to 1,000, the fifth highest in the Western Hemisphere, exceeded only by Argentina, the United States, Uruguay, and Canada.

After the fall of the Batista dictatorship, the new revolutionary government made a serious effort to increase further the availability of medical care. In a speech commemorating the seventeenth anniversary of his attack on the Moncada barracks, Castro emphasized the achievements of the new order in promoting the social welfare of the masses. "Public health services: In 1958 there were 8,209 workers in public health services. In 1969 the number increased to 87,646—87,646!" This was an even higher rate of growth than in the school system. "In 1958 there were 23,648 workers in public education. In 1969 this figure rose to 127,526." Did this not prove his commitment to the democratization of medicine?

Yet the figures were in part misleading; the achievements of the new order looked better on paper than in reality. Data on the personnel in public health before the revolution included only those employed by the government in such activities as sanitation, disease prevention, and registration of vital statistics. Data afterward covered everyone providing health care and medical treatment: doctors, nurses, technicians, hospital workers, and even staff members in the schools of medicine, categories that had previously not been counted because they belonged to the private sector. The numbers were simply not comparable.

This is not to deny the significant progress of the Castro regime in promoting medical care. Between 1958 and 1968 the budget of the ministry of public health rose from 22,000,000 to 263,000,000 pesos, a remarkable increase, even if much of it was a result of the nationalization of health services. The number of hospitals, clinics, and medical centers grew from 347 to 530, and the number of hospital beds from 36,141 to 42,561. Infantile paralysis, which had averaged about 300 cases annually before the revolution, was wiped out a few years afterward, thanks to a well-organized campaign of mass vaccination. There had been thousands of cases of malaria every year under the *ancien régime*, 3,519 as late as 1962. In 1967 there were only 7 and in 1968 none. The number of deaths from gastroenteritis, totaling 2,784 in 1958, fell more than 50 percent to 1,346, a decade later. These were impressive achievements.

Yet it is also apparent that in several important categories of health care little real progress was made. The rapid growth of the population from 5,724,200 in 1952 to 6,548,300 in 1958 and 7,799,600 in 1966 kept pace to a considerable extent with the rapid growth of medical service, so that by some of the standard measures of public health no significant improvement in relative terms was actually recorded.

The number of hospital beds per thousand inhabitants, for example, which had increased substantially under the *ancien régime*, from 4.5 in 1952 to 5.5 in 1958, declined slightly under the new order to 5.4 in 1966. The general mortality rate, after dropping rapidly during the Batista dictatorship from 5.8 per thousand inhabitants in 1953 to 4.9 in 1958, rose even more rapidly following its overthrow to 6.6 in 1959 and 7.3 in 1962, before declining again to 6.4 in 1967, a figure significantly higher than on the eve of the revolution. The infant mortality rate, though more stable than the general mortality rate, showed no improvement under the new order. Indeed, a slight deterioration occurred. The incidence, which had been 37.6 per 1,000 live births in 1953, fell to 33.7 in 1958, the last year of the *ancien régime*, but then began to climb steadily to 34.5 in 1959, 35.4 in 1960, and 37.2 in 1961, peaking in 1962 at 39.6. Thereafter the figure dropped again, becoming stabilized at 37.6 in 1963, 37.8 in 1964, 37.7 in 1965, and 37.6 in 1966, well above the level achieved by the old order just before its fall. The attempt of the Castro regime to expand health care in Cuba was thus less than an unqualified success.

Its real achievement lay in the distribution rather than the growth of medical service. Health under the *ancien régime* had been largely a commercial commodity bought and sold in the open market, its price determined by the laws of supply and demand. That meant that while the propertied classes enjoyed easy access to the benefits of modern medicine, for the masses, especially in the countryside, health care was at best inadequate and often unavailable.

The Castro government collectivized medical service by redefining its purpose and revolutionizing its ethos. Health ceased to be an individual concern and became a communal responsibility. Physicians, educated at government expense, were now taught to regard their profession not as an investment providing income but as a commitment to social progress. Nurses, therapists, dietitians, x-ray technicians, and ward attendants became public servants rather than private employees. Hospitals ceased to depend on the fees paid by patients, being supported instead by the revenues of the national treasury. The result was that for the first time adequate health care became available in small towns and isolated villages, where a doctor or an infirmary had once been a rarity. Hence the democratization of medicine which the revolution makes possible was, in Cuba even more than in China or North Vietnam, a result of the redistribution as well as the expansion of health care. But whatever the reason, the overthrow of the *ancien régime* led to a substantially greater availability of medical services to the lower classes.[12]

Popular Support
for the Radical Dictatorship

The first decade after the revolution is thus a period of exciting fundamental change. A transformation of property relationships takes place, leading to a transformation of class relationships. Under the new order the sharp differences in prestige and wealth that had characterized society under the *ancien régime* begin to diminish. They never disappear completely, but disparities in income and status become much less pronounced. The revolutionary government, moreover, makes a major effort to democratize and proletarianize learning, partly by introducing universal primary schooling, and partly by promoting the admission of students from worker and peasant families to institutions of higher education. Finally, health care, formerly the monopoly to a large extent of the well-to-do, becomes nationalized and collectivized, so that general morbidity starts to decline and life expectancy to rise. The result is that the lower classes are by and large better off than under the old order, and even more important, they feel themselves to be better off. The still vivid memory of conditions only a few years earlier, before the revolution, makes their life under the radical dictatorship seem by comparison more rewarding and hopeful.

This sense of greater well-being is not only a state of mind. It is in considerable part palpable and measurable. For to the leaders of the revolutionary government nothing is more important than raising the standard of living of the lower classes, on whose support they depend ideologically as well as politically. In Cuba, for example, the total public expenditure budget increased by 408 percent between 1957–58 and 1962, from 365,000,000 to 1,854,000,000 pesos. The most rapid rates of growth were recorded in the category of economic development, 1,462 percent, from 45,000,000 to 703,000,000 pesos, partly a result of the program of nationalization, and in the category of social and cultural development, 481 percent, from 98,000,000 to 569,000,000 pesos. Of the expenditure in 1962 for social and cultural development, moreover, 238,000,000 pesos went for education, 175,000,000 for social security, 89,000,000 for public health, 33,000,000 for science and culture, 21,000,000 for social assistance, and 14,000,000 for sport and recreation.

Increases in the other categories of the public expenditure budget were much more modest. The appropriation for the military rose by 163 percent, from 94,000,000 to 247,000,000 pesos; for administration by 135 percent, from 83,000,000 to 195,000,000; for the public debt by 190 percent, from 40,000,000 to 116,000,000; and for miscellaneous purposes by a relatively steep 380 percent, but in absolute terms by a mere 19,000,000 pesos, from 5,000,000 to 24,000,000. This pattern of expenditure growth is typical of the new order in its early period, reflecting the effort of the revolutionary government to improve general living conditions.

The result is a significant advance in the economic and social position of the lower classes. Even in the Soviet Union, devastated by almost a decade of military conflict and civil war, a remarkable recovery took place in the late 1920s. Immediately after the revolution the expropriation of the great landowners had increased substantially the holdings of the peasantry, while the early social legislation of the Bolsheviks had eliminated most of the industrial abuses tolerated by the czarist government. Now the return of political stability and the encouragement of individual initiative under the New Economic Policy led to a revival in agriculture as well as industry, so that prewar levels of production were not only regained but in some cases surpassed. The real earnings of factory workers began to equal and even exceed the norms reached under the *ancien régime*. And then there was the low cost of housing, the cheap price of food, the universal primary schooling, the free medical care, the paid leaves and vacations. All of this helped generate a feeling among the masses that under the new order their standard of living was not only improving but would go on improving.

In China, where the victory of the Communists marked the end rather than the beginning of civil war, the evidence of an advance in the economic position of the lower classes was even stronger. To start with, a rapid growth occurred in the earnings of the urban proletariat. Nominal wages of workers and white-collar employees rose 17.5 percent between 1949–50 and 1952, and another 7.4 percent between 1952 and 1957. The increase in real wages was equally impressive: 21.2 percent between 1949–50 and 1952, and 6.0 percent between 1952 and 1957. Urban housing improved significantly, moreover, with the construction by the state of almost 100,000,000 square meters of new residential space for industrial and clerical workers. What other Chinese government had done as much for the masses?

Not only the population of the cities benefited from the economic policies of the new order. The income of the peasantry rose about 20 percent between 1949 and 1957, a result of expanding production and modest improvement in the terms of exchange between agricultural and manufactured goods. The clearest sign of a rising standard of living, however, was the remarkable advance in public health. Life expectancy, one of the most reliable measures of material conditions, rose in China from thirty-six years in 1950 to fifty-seven in 1957, fifteen years above the average for low-income countries. For the lower classes the new order represented a major improvement over the *ancien régime*.

But the psychological satisfactions that the revolution provides are as important as the economic gains. The resort hotels in the Crimea and hunting lodges in the Caucasus that had once catered to an aristocratic clientele became transformed into recreation centers for coal miners and deserving *kolkhozniks*. The international trading companies by which Western businessmen had grown rich at the expense of Chinese producers and consumers were expropriated, while the foreign social clubs from which natives had been rigorously excluded were closed. They had been an affront to national dignity; they had reflected the weakness and obsequiousness of the *ancien régime*. Now the common man could feel that he was at last master in his own house. In Havana the fashionable residences of the well-to-do along the Malecón, the graceful avenue overlooking the beach and the sea, were divided into apartments for lower-class families. Where once the Cuban elite had lived in splendid exclusivity, drying laundry flapped from the balconies, housewives gathered in hallways to chat and gossip, and laughing children, many of them conspicuously black, played noisily on the sidewalk.

These are all symbolic statements, they are tacit public declarations of the resolve of the new order to champion the poor and oppressed. They provide the masses with intangible emotional gratification, they nourish among them a sense of self-esteem that is as important as the rising standard of living. They wordlessly express the commitment of the radical dictatorship to the welfare of those who toil.[13]

Hence the first decade after the revolution is the period when it enjoys the greatest, the most genuine, the most spontaneous popular support. There are those, to be sure, who are opposed to the new order from the beginning. Sometimes they are quite numerous; sometimes they may even be in a majority, though that would be hard to prove. But there is also in the early years a widespread faith in the radical dictatorship, a mass enthusiasm for its policies and goals. Never again will it be regarded by the lower classes with the same high hope, confidence, and optimism.

Admittedly, hard statistical evidence to support such a conclusion is difficult to find. Even in its early years the revolutionary government does little to encourage objective attempts to measure public opinion. Only those who for reasons of conviction or expediency embrace the new order feel free to express their views openly. Critics and doubters learn very soon that it is best to dissemble, equivocate, evade, or keep quiet. And yet reports by foreign observers—most of them, to be sure, based on subjective impressions, on conversations, interviews, and anecdotes—attest to a broad popular acceptance of the radical dictatorship.

Alexander Wicksteed, for example, a British Quaker who came to Russia after the revolution to live under the new egalitarian social system, had little doubt regarding the popularity of the Communist regime. "I may be wrong," he wrote in 1928, "but I feel convinced that if a plebiscite was taken of Moscow the result would be a very heavy majority in favour of the Government. In Leningrad it would be even larger, and this would apply to the industrial towns throughout the country. The great mass of the 'workers' and most of the best and most vigorous of the younger intelligentsia feel that the Dictatorship is fighting their battles and governing in their interests." Not even the suppression of dissenting opinion seemed to diminish the wide appeal of the new order. "As one of my students once expressed it to me, 'You must remember that it is *our* Russia that the secret police are defending.'" The views of Wicksteed, whose political leanings were clearly to the left, may not be altogether reliable. But many other foreign observers, more detached than he, agreed that widespread popular support for the Soviet system existed throughout the 1920s.

Still more persuasive are the findings of one of the few objective surveys of public opinion after the revolution conducted in 1960 in 34 Cuban cities, towns, and villages under the auspices of the American Institute for Social Research. What makes them all the more credible is that they were reported by an organization with little sympathy for the new order. The overwhelming majority of those surveyed supported the revolutionary regime, 43 percent expressing great fervor, and another 43 percent speaking at least favorably about it. Among its ardent supporters was a housewife who felt that "Fidel has the same ideas as Jesus Christ, our protector and guide," and a domestic servant who longed "to kiss the beard of Fidel Castro." Over two-thirds of the most enthusiastic believers in the new order had received either no schooling or only elementary schooling, while close to half were still in their twenties. No more than 10 percent of the 1,000 participants in the poll were clearly in opposition.

The reasons for Castro's popularity were obvious. All in all, 65 percent of the respondents felt that they were better off now than in the past, and 74 percent believed that they would be still better off in five years. Asked about their "national aspirations," 59 percent said that they sought "an improved or decent standard of living," 31 percent wanted "jobs for everyone," and 29 percent hoped for the "success of the revolution" and the "continuation of the present regime."

While almost a third favored the agrarian reform program, the "fight against ignorance and illiteracy" was mentioned by only 9 percent, "social justice" by 6 percent, and "honest government" by 5 percent. "Democratic government" and "protection of individual rights" were at the bottom of the list as well, with 5 percent each. Political and economic attitudes in Cuba thus conformed to the characteristic pattern of public opinion in a revolutionary society.[14]

In short, the creative popular energies and forces released by the struggle against the *ancien régime* seem to retain their vitality in the years directly following its overthrow. For about a decade there is the same uncomplaining willingness to endure hardships, the same unwavering readiness to make sacrifices. There is the same faith, moreover, in a more benevolent government, a more virtuous society. The ideals that made possible the victory of the new order help bring about a far-reaching reformation of polity and economy. And then a process of spiritual and intellectual debilitation or exhaustion sets in. The doctrines of class struggle gradually lose their appeal; the teachings of social justice cease to arouse and inspire. The revolution becomes increasingly institutionalized, bureaucratized, inflexible, and oppressive. The heroic decade of the new order comes to an end.

CHAPTER 8

The Institutionalization of Dictatorial Power

Although the new order relies from the outset on the political techniques of coercive force and mass indoctrination, it insists that the ultimate source of its authority is the will of the people. In this regard it resembles the old order. Yet important differences are apparent in the way the two define the concept of the will of the people. The *ancien régime* maintains that it represents the interests of all groups in society: the rich and the poor, the strong and the weak, the educated and the ignorant, the townsman and the villager, the capitalist and the worker, the landowner and the peasant. It claims that the established system transcends economic and social differences, that it embodies a collective purpose and a common goal. Although there may be a handful of dissidents who challenge its authority, they are only a disgruntled faction, a rebellious clique. Perhaps here and there, the government concedes, local authorities become a little arrogant, oppressive, inefficient, or corrupt. Perhaps they sometimes harass their critics, intimidate their opponents, or jail their enemies. But by and large the regime has the interests of all the people at heart; it rests on the unspoken assent of those it rules. Even without free elections, without opposition parties or muckraking newspapers, it provides justice for all, regardless of class or status.

The new order insists with equal conviction that it is the defender of the general well-being of society. It too claims to represent a collective purpose and a common goal. It too claims that without the cumbersome mechanism of party contests or electoral rivalries, it represents the popular will. But the people in whose name it professes to act do not include the oppressors, exploiters, and robbers of the people. Those who had battened on the misery of the masses must not be left free to go on deceiving and misleading them. Hence even in the days of the united front, the left maintains that only "democratic" forces can be allowed to share in the exercise of power. Those who are "reactionaries" or "exploiters" should be excluded from the political process.

Popular Will
and Democratic Government

In the late summer of 1917, while the Bolsheviks were still committed in theory to the convocation of a constituent assembly to decide the future of Russia, Lenin made it clear that for him democratic elections did not mean extending the franchise to bankers, industrialists, and landowners. "Democracy for the vast majority of the people, and suppression by force, i.e., exclusion from democracy, of the exploiters and oppressors of the people—this is the change democracy undergoes during the *transition* from capitalism to communism." Indeed, not until the forces of capitalism had been defeated and eliminated would democratic government become secure or, better still, unnecessary:

> Only in communist society, when the resistance of the capitalists has been completely crushed, when the capitalists have disappeared, when there are no classes (i.e., when there is no distinction between the members of society as regards their relation to the social means of production), *only* then "the state . . . ceases to exist," and "*it becomes possible to speak of freedom.*" Only then will a truly complete democracy become possible and be realized, a democracy without any exceptions whatever. And only then will democracy begin to *wither away*, owing to the simple fact that, freed from capitalist slavery, from the untold horrors, savagery, absurdities, and infamies of capitalist exploitation, people will gradually *become accustomed* to observing the elementary rules of social intercourse that have been known for centuries and repeated for thousands of years in copybook maxims. They will become accustomed to observing them without force, without coercion, without subordination, *without the special apparatus* for coercion called the state.

Until the traditional class system has been destroyed, however, until a "truly complete democracy" becomes possible, those who oppose the revolution must not be allowed to intrigue for the retention of power. The emancipation of the workers and peasants is more important than all the fine points of representative government. That is why Lenin urged the Central Committee of the Bolsheviks in October to prepare for an armed uprising against the provisional government before the election of a constituent assembly, especially since their party was not likely to win a majority at the polls. "It is senseless to wait for the Constituent Assembly that will obviously not be on our side," he argued, "for this will only make our task more involved." To reject now an expression of the popular will which the left had been advocating for more than a decade might seem inconsistent, but what did that matter when the outcome of the revolution was at stake?

At the end of the year, after the Bolsheviks had seized power and the elections to the Constituent Assembly had confirmed that three-fourths of the voters preferred one of the other parties, Lenin elaborated in public on what he had previously told the Central Committee in private. The will of the people could not be determined mechanistically, by conducting polls and counting ballots. It had to be interpreted in the light of political and social reality, in accordance with the logic of historical change. "Every direct or indirect attempt to consider the question of the Constituent Assembly from a formal, legal point of view, within the framework of ordinary bourgeois democracy and disregarding the class struggle and civil war, would be a betrayal of the proletariat's cause, and the adoption of the bourgeois standpoint." Not all of his followers, however, had understood the subtle distinction between arithmetical and dialectical democracy. "The revolutionary Social-Democrats are duty bound to warn all and sundry against this error, into which a few Bolshevik leaders, who have been unable to appreciate the significance of the [November] uprising and the tasks of the dictatorship of the proletariat, have strayed." Yet there was in truth something bewildering about the paradoxical doctrine that the majority misrepresented while the minority reflected the popular will.

On January 19, 1918, after the Bolsheviks dispersed the Constituent Assembly following its first and only meeting, Lenin explained in

greater detail why a freely elected representative body that yesterday had been described as progressive had today become reactionary. "Those who point out that we are now 'dissolving' the
Constituent Assembly although at one time we defended it are not
displaying a grain of sense, but are merely uttering pompous and
meaningless phrases. At one time, we considered the Constituent
Assembly to be better than czarism and the republic of Kerensky
with their famous organs of power; but as the Soviets emerged, they,
being revolutionary organizations of the whole people, naturally became incomparably superior to any parliament in the world."

According to Lenin, the tactics to be employed in the emancipation of the masses could not be dictated by outworn precedent or
rigid consistency. They had to respond to changes in the objective
political and social conditions:

> To hand over power to the Constituent Assembly would again be com-
> promising with the malignant bourgeoisie. The Russian Soviets place
> the interests of the working people far above the interests of a treacher-
> ous policy of compromise disguised in a new garb. . . . As long as the
> slogan "All power to the Constituent Assembly" conceals the slogan
> "Down with Soviet power," civil war is inevitable. For nothing in the
> world will make us give up Soviet power! . . . And when the Constitu-
> ent Assembly again revealed its readiness to postpone all the painfully
> urgent problems and tasks that were placed before it by the Soviets, we
> told the Constituent Assembly that they must not be postponed for one
> single moment. And by the will of Soviet power the Constituent As-
> sembly, which has refused to recognize the power of the people, is
> being dissolved.

Thus true popular sovereignty was represented by the soviets,
which the Bolsheviks controlled, rather than by the Constituent Assembly, which they did not.

Was all this simply leftist casuistry designed to disguise the determination to retain power at all costs? Not quite. The leaders of the
revolution believe what they say about the right of the governed to
determine the form of government. But to them the will of the people cannot be measured mechanically or statistically, by holding
elections and adding up votes. It cannot be ascertained by asking the

masses for their wishes under a system of authority that has methodically oppressed, exploited, and deceived them. The will of the people is rather what they would want if they really understood what their interests are, if they knew what is best for them. Once they have been liberated from capitalism, once they have been nourished and educated, they will be able to express their will directly in free and democratic elections. But in the meantime, what they want or rather what they should want is expressed best through the revolutionary movement, which must not hesitate to employ force against the few in order to achieve liberty for the many. Hence what appears to be democracy may actually be an instrument of reaction, while what appears to be repression may actually be a means of emancipation. Such is the doctrinal justification of the form of government established under the new order.[1]

The Rule of the Masses

The systematic disfranchisement of those groups in society whose class interests appear incompatible with the objectives of the revolution is more than a temporary measure adopted during the struggle for power. It becomes increasingly formalized and institutionalized, emerging finally as a permanent feature of the new order. At the end of 1919, although the tide had clearly begun to turn in favor of the Bolsheviks, Lenin was still emphasizing the importance of the dictatorship of the proletariat in creating a socialist society. "We say on the basis of the teachings of Marx and the experience of the Russian revolution: the proletariat must first overthrow the bourgeoisie and win *for itself* state power, and then use that state power, that is, the dictatorship of the proletariat, as an instrument of its class for the purpose of winning the sympathy of the majority of the working people." The growing success of the struggle for the emancipation of the masses had only increased the need for the organized repression of their enemies.

A year later, as the civil war and foreign intervention were drawing to a close, Stalin commemorated the third anniversary of the Bolshevik accession to power by dwelling once again on the need to maintain the dictatorship of the proletariat during the period of socialist reconstruction. "As to our policy towards internal enemies, it remains, and must remain, what it was in [the past], that is, a policy of crushing all the enemies of the proletariat. This policy cannot of course be called a policy of 'universal freedom'—in the era of the dictatorship of the proletariat there can be no universal freedom, that is, no freedom of speech, freedom of the press, etc., for our bourgeoisie." The revolution had to remain ruthless toward its enemies. "The sum and substance of our home policy is to grant maximum freedom to the proletarian sections of town and country, and to deny even minimum freedom to the remnants of the bourgeois class. That is the essence of our policy, which rests upon the dictatorship of the proletariat."

Fifteen years after the November uprising, Trotsky was still defending the use of dictatorial power in the liberation of the working class. His banishment from the Soviet Union had not shaken his conviction that the dissolution of the Constituent Assembly was historically justified. "Almost unnoticeably in the course of the events of the revolution, this chief democratic slogan [of a freely elected popular representation], which had for a decade and a half tinged with its color the heroic struggle of the masses, had grown pale and faded out, had become an empty shell, a form naked of content, a tradition and not a prospect." There was nothing mysterious about this process. "The development of the revolution had reached the point of a direct battle for power between the two basic classes of society, the bourgeoisie and the proletariat. A Constituent Assembly could give nothing either to the one or the other."

The petty-bourgeois reformers were in any case inherently incapable of playing more than "an auxiliary and secondary role" in this battle, Trotsky insisted. They were unable to seize and wield power. "Nevertheless in a Constituent Assembly the petty bourgeoisie might still win—and they actually did win as it turned out—a majority. And to what end? Only to the end of not knowing what to do with it." This revealed the bankruptcy of "formal democracy" in a major historical crisis. "Neither camp had yet renounced the name of the Constituent Assembly. But as a matter of fact the bourgeoisie had appealed from the Constituent Assembly to [the counter-revolutionary General L. G.] Kornilov, and the Bolsheviks to the Congress of Soviets." To the end of his life Trotsky failed to see any connection between the suppression of "formal democracy" in 1918 and his own expulsion from Russia a decade later. He remained in essential agreement with Stalin on the need to maintain the dictatorship of the proletariat. The two differed only regarding those against whom it ought to be directed.[2]

The Communists in China did not dwell with the same persistence on the importance of dictatorial power. They simply assumed it. How else could the masses, which had been oppressed and exploited by the propertied classes generation after generation, be emancipated? The disfranchisement of the enemies of the revolution was the obvious precondition for the building of a better society. The short-lived Chinese Soviet Republic in Kiangsi declared in its constitution of November 7, 1931, that "the workers, peasants, Red Army soldiers, and the entire toiling population shall have the right to elect their own deputies to give effect to their power." On the other hand, "all exploiting and counter-revolutionary elements" were to be "deprived of the right to elect deputies to participate in the government and to enjoy political freedom."

The rights of democracy were thus not universal in scope; they were always contingent on class origin and social function.

> The Soviet government of China guarantees to the workers, peasants, and toilers freedom of speech and the press as well as the right to assembly; it will be opposed to bourgeois and landlord democracy, but it is in favor of the democracy of the workers and peasant masses. It breaks down the economic and political prerogatives of the bourgeoisie and the landlords, in order to remove all obstacles placed by the reactionaries on the workers' and peasants' road to freedom.

The "toiling masses" were to receive from the "people's régime" free access to "printing shops, meeting halls, and similar establishments" as a "material basis for the realization of [their] rights and liberties." But the enemies of the people were to be treated differently. "Under the Soviet régime, all propaganda and other similar activities by reactionaries shall be suppressed and all exploiters be deprived of all political liberties." To give political freedom to those who would only use it to maintain their class predominance would be a betrayal of the revolution.

Even during the period of the united front, Mao made it clear that some groups in society must be denied the democratic rights to which the great majority of the people were entitled. "Everyone, except traitors, should have freedom of speech, publication, assembly, association, and of armed resistance in the anti-Japanese fight for national salvation," declared the "Ten Great Policies of the [Chinese Communist Party] for Anti-Japanese Resistance and National Salvation" of August 15, 1937. But who precisely were the "traitors" who ought to be deprived of the civic liberty to which all other citizens had a rightful claim? Were they simply those who had collaborated with the Japanese in the war against their own countrymen? Or were there others as well, those perhaps who had supported the domestic enemies of the people? For the time being, the Chinese Communists preferred not to elaborate on the meaning of treason. The hour had not yet come to start separating the sheep from the goats and the patriots from the renegades.

Yet after the victory of the new order, the delimitation of political freedom could no longer be postponed. The radical dictatorship began therefore to retreat step by step from the accommodating promises, explicit or implied, that had been made during the struggle against the *ancien régime*. The people were of course still to enjoy the rights of democracy, the rights of speech, assembly, representation, and dissent. But what about the enemies of the people, what about the landlords and capitalists, the counterrevolutionaries and reactionaries? Were those who had collaborated with native oppressors any better than those who had collaborated with foreign oppressors? Surely, it would be self-destructive to give freedom to the well-to-do, who would only exploit it to reestablish their class hegemony.

The clearest statement of the doctrine that the dictatorship of the proletariat was actually a higher form of democracy appeared in an article that Mao published in the spring of 1955. "What [has been called] 'uniformity of public opinion' actually means that counterrevolutionaries are not allowed to express counter-revolutionary views," he explained. "Our system does deprive all counterrevolutionaries of freedom of speech and allows this freedom only among the people. We allow opinions to be varied among the people, that is, there is freedom to criticize, to express different views and to advocate theism and atheism (*i.e.*, materialism)." But those trying to enslave the people should not be permitted to carry out their evil schemes. Did that really sound unreasonable?

Political freedom is not an unconditional good, Mao argued. Rather, it is an instrument of class justice, a means of social progress. "In any society and at any time, there are always two kinds of people and views, the advanced and the backward, that exist as opposites struggling with each other, with the advanced views invariably prevailing over the backward ones. . . . Society can progress only if what is advanced is given full play and prevails over what is backward." Hence a just government ought to promote truth and suppress error. "In an era in which classes and class struggle still exist both at home and abroad, the working class and the masses who have seized state power must suppress the resistance to the revolution put up by all counter-revolutionary classes, groups, and individuals, thwart their activities aimed at restoration and prohibit them from exploiting freedom of speech for counter-revolutionary purposes."

This did not mean in any true sense a restriction of civic liberty. Far from it. "Public opinion in our country is at once uniform and non-uniform. Among the people, both the advanced and the backward are free to use our newspapers, periodicals, forums, etc. to compete with each other, so that the former can educate the latter by the democratic method of persuasion and backward ideas and systems can be overcome." Whenever one contradiction was resolved, others would arise, and there would then be renewed competition among them. "In this way, society constantly progresses. The existence of contradictions means non-uniformity. The resolution of contradictions results in temporary uniformity, but new contradictions soon emerge, which means non-uniformity, and they, in turn, have to be resolved." Mao's faith in the give-and-take of ideas as the surest means of attaining political truth had a surprisingly Jeffersonian ring.

Still, there were limits to his commitment to conventional democracy. Freedom, he insisted, must be reserved for those who believe in freedom. To give it to those who will only try to subvert it would be irresponsible. It would open the gates to reaction and tyranny. The logic in this reasoning seemed to him self-evident. "As for the contradiction between the people and the counter-revolutionaries, that is matter of dictatorship over the counter-revolutionaries by the people under the leadership of the working class and the Communist Party. Here the dictatorial, not the democratic, method is used; in other words, the counter-revolutionaries must behave themselves and are not allowed to be unruly in word or deed. In this respect, it is not only public opinion that is uniform, but the law too."

A few muddleheaded doctrinaires had unfortunately been misled by deceptive phrases like "uniformity of public opinion" or "absence of public opinion" or "suppression of freedom," Mao conceded. "Don't [such phrases] sound awful? These people cannot distinguish clearly between two different categories, between what is within the ranks of the people and what is without." Since dictatorial power is always an inherent part of the political process, is it not better to let the progressive majority use that power against the reactionary minority, rather than the other way around? The choice between the two forms of political democracy, the bourgeois and the proletarian, was obvious.[3]

In North Vietnam the leaders of the new order spent even less time proving that the dictatorship of the proletariat reflected the will of the people. They simply acted as if it did; they took it for granted. To be sure, the constitution of November 9, 1946, which remained largely a dead letter during the years of struggle against the French, contained enough civic freedoms to satisfy the most fastidious middle-class democrat. All citizens were to enjoy "equal rights in the economic, political, and cultural fields." They were to be "equal before the law" and to have "equal opportunity to participate in the administration and in national construction." They would of course be protected in the exercise of freedom of speech, the press, assembly, religion, residence, and travel. They were not to be arrested "except under the law," and their homes were to be regarded as "inviolable." As for "the rights of property and possession," they were "guaranteed" to every citizen.

The constitutional provisions establishing democratic government were as generous as those protecting individual freedom. "The mode of election to all popular representative state bodies is first and primarily through universal suffrage by free, direct, and secret ballot." In addition, "all citizens have the right to recall their elected representatives" and "to decide on constitutional issues and all problems affecting the destiny of the nation." On the face of it, the commitment of the revolutionary movement in North Vietnam to political democracy seemed as firm as that of any government in Europe or America.

Yet the constitution of January 1, 1960, which went into effect after the victory of the new order, differed in subtle but crucial ways from the one adopted fourteen years earlier, while the outcome of the war against colonialism remained in doubt. To be sure, it still contained the same provisions guaranteeing the civil rights of all citizens. But toward the end of the section dealing with the "Fundamental Rights and Duties of the Citizen" appeared, almost as an afterthought, an article with an ominous ring. "The state forbids any person to use democratic freedoms to the detriment of the interests of the state and of the people." This prohibition, moreover, was repeated indirectly in the following article warning that "citizens of the Democratic Republic of Viet-Nam must abide by the Constitution and the law, uphold discipline at work, keep public order, and respect social ethics." The meaning was clear. The rights guaranteed to the people were not to be exercised in opposition to the regime that had established them. The freedoms of democracy were not to be used as weapons against democracy. Every North Vietnamese understood that.[4]

In Cuba there was not even an attempt to disguise dictatorial power behind a facade of constitutional liberty. Now that the old order had fallen, why reestablish the sham democracy which served only to conceal oppression and exploitation? The revolution would express the will of the people directly, not through parties, elections, and endless debates. Speaking on May Day 1961, Castro rejected the demand for a parliamentary system of government. The only ones supporting it, he charged, were Cuban conservatives and their sympathizers in the United States. "What elections did they want? The ones of the corrupt politicians who bought votes? Those elections in which a poor person had to turn over his ballot in return for work? Those fake elections that were just a means for the exploiting classes to stay in power? Those elections which were not a military coup?" The bourgeois concept of political freedom had nothing to offer the masses; it provided no solution to a society yearning for economic justice. "There are many pseudo-democracies in Latin America; what laws have they passed for the peasants? Where is nationalization of industry? Where is their agrarian reform?"

The new order would establish a different kind of democracy, a direct democracy, a proletarian democracy, a democracy without the factions, squabbles, arguments, and compromises that only obscure the real needs of the masses. "A revolution expressing the will of the people is an election every day, not every four years; it is a constant meeting with the people .... The old politicians could never have gathered as many votes as there are people [assembled here today] to support the Revolution. Revolution means a thoroughgoing change." Those opposing the new order hoped to return to the outworn forms of parliamentary representation that had provided the shadow of freedom without its substance. "What do they want? Elections with pictures on the lampposts. [But] the Revolution has exchanged the conception of pseudo-democracy for direct government by the people." The new order embodied a different, a more perfect form of civic liberty.

As for the old familiar game of party politics with its petty rivalries and intrigues, with its monotonous succession of legislative majorities as different as Tweedledum and Tweedledee, Cuba had no need for that. "Do the people now have time for elections? No! What were the political parties? Just an expression of class interests." The situation had changed completely, Castro insisted.

> Here there is just one class, the humble; that class is in power, and so it is not interested in the ambition of an exploiting minority to get back in power. Those people would have no chance at all in an election. The Revolution has no time to waste in such foolishness. There is no chance for the exploiting class to regain power. The people know that the Revolution expressed their will; the Revolution does not come to power with Yankee arms. It comes to power through the will of the people fighting against Yankee arms.

The cumbersome machinery of bourgeois democracy would only make the task of popular government more difficult.[5]

Although the new order claims at first that the disfranchisement of its opponents is only a temporary measure to provide time for the political reeducation of the masses, the dictatorial system becomes an enduring feature of every revolutionary government. For the danger that its leaders perceive in free elections lies less in the period following the overthrow of the *ancien régime* than in the distant future. The achievements of the new order in the early years are impressive enough to assure success at the polls even without official coercion. But what about later? What will happen if the revolutionary fervor of the masses begins to cool? What if the radical dictatorship proves unable to live up to all its promises of economic improvement and social progress? Should the reactionaries then be free to exploit its mistakes in order to stir up political opposition? Should the very survival of the revolution be made dependent on the vagaries of popular opinion and the secret ballot? The new order maintains its dictatorial rule permanently, because the truth that it represents is too important to be risked on the roulette wheel of a free electoral system.

Crushing the Class Enemy

The revolutionary regime is not content merely to disfranchise those opposed to its ideas and purposes, thereby excluding them from the political process. It seeks to suppress them, to crush them, to eliminate them physically. As a latent source of counterrevolution, they must be destroyed through exile, imprisonment, and execution. To tolerate them today on the condition that they remain submissive will only free them to engage in subversion tomorrow. They are a constant threat to the new order. The government therefore maintains an elaborate repressive apparatus designed to identify and constrain actual or potential opponents of the regime. It is generally most rigorous in the early years of the new order, when the opposition to the radical dictatorship is still strong, when there is still hope among many conservatives that the revolutionary regime can be overthrown. That is when the authorities are especially ruthless. As the government begins to feel more secure, as resistance to its rule weakens, the war against political dissidence becomes less intense as well. But the maintenance of a system of repression directed against those perceived as enemies of the revolution remains a feature of every new order.

Even before they come to power, the radicals occasionally avow their acceptance of coercive force as a legitimate instrument of revolutionary government. In 1901 Lenin, still the fiery young rebel, announced openly that systematic collective violence directed against czarism was an acceptable means of achieving the emancipation of the proletariat. "In principle we have never rejected, and cannot reject, terror." To be sure, the class struggle in Russia had not yet reached the stage where the forcible repression of the enemy was possible. The objective conditions for such a strategy were still lacking. "[Hence] terror, at the present time, is by no means suggested as an operation for the army in the field, an operation closely connected with and integrated into the entire system of struggle, but as an independent form of occasional attack unrelated to any army. Without a central body and with the weakness of local revolutionary organizations, this, in fact, is all that terror can be."

Lenin's rejection of the strategy of organized terror, however, was based on expediency rather than principle. The time was simply not ripe for it, he maintained. "We, therefore, declare emphatically that under the present conditions such a means of struggle is inopportune and unsuitable; that it diverts the most active fighters from their real task, the task which is most important from the standpoint of the interests of the movement as a whole; and that is disorganizes the forces, not of the government, but of the revolution." Still, that did not mean that the violent suppression of the opponents of the revolutionary movement would not be employed in the future, under more favorable circumstances. "Terror is one of the forms of military action that may be perfectly suitable and even essential at a definite juncture in the battle, given a definite state of the troops and the existence of definite conditions." For the time being, it would be self-defeating to try to overthrow czarism by systematic violence. But when sixteen years later the *ancien régime* collapsed, Lenin had little hesitation about employing banishment, incarceration, and execution to insure the victory of the Bolsheviks.[6]

Most leaders of the revolution, however, wait until the victory of the new order before justifying its use of coercive force. For example, not until his speech of April 25, 1956, "On the Ten Major Relationships" did Mao offer a detailed analysis of the role of official repression under a Communist regime. He began by portraying the Heavenly City of the revolutionary eschatology, in which the need for dictatorial rule would someday come to an end, in which the wolf would dwell with the lamb and the radical with the moderate. "The Communist Party and the democratic parties are all products of history. What emerges in history disappears in history. Therefore, the Communist Party will disappear one day, and so will the democratic parties. Is this disappearance so unpleasant? In my opinion, it will be very pleasant. I think it is just fine that one day we will be able to do away with the Communist Party and the dictatorship of the proletariat. Our task is to hasten their extinction." The ultimate goal of the new order was a society free of coercion, regimentation, violence, and conflict.

But the achievement of such a society was still a long way off. For the time being the revolution would have to continue to wage a bitter struggle against those determined to destroy its accomplishments. "At present we cannot do without the proletarian party and the dictatorship of the proletariat," Mao insisted, "and, what is more, it is imperative that they should be made still more powerful. Otherwise, we would not be able to suppress the counter-revolutionaries, resist the imperialists, and build socialism, or consolidate it when it is built." The new order must deal with its enemies severely. "The dictatorship of the proletariat cannot but be highly coercive." Now was no time for compromise or appeasement; only unremitting struggle could safeguard the revolution.

Not all opponents of the new order need to be put to death, Mao explained. Since there were varying degrees of guilt, the punishment should, insofar as possible, be made to fit the crime. "Counter-revolutionaries may be dealt with in these ways: execution, imprisonment, supervision, and leaving at large. Execution—everybody knows what that means. By imprisonment we mean putting counter-revolutionaries in jail and reforming them through labor. By supervision we mean leaving them in society to be reformed under the supervision of the masses. By leaving at large we mean that generally no arrest is made in those cases where it is marginal whether to make an arrest, or that those arrested are set free for good behavior." The treatment of the opponents of the new order was thus to vary with the circumstances. "It is essential that different counter-revolutionaries should be dealt with differently on the merits of each case."

And yet, according to Mao, even the most severe punishment imposed on the enemies of the radical dictatorship was justified. For while the revolution might be stern, it was never unfair. "Now let's take execution in particular. True, we executed a number of people during the . . . campaign to suppress counter-revolutionaries. But what sort of people were they? They were counter-revolutionaries who owed the masses many blood debts and were bitterly hated. In a great revolution embracing 600 million people, the masses would not have been able to rise if we had not killed off [the] local despots. . . . Had it not been for that campaign of suppression, the people would not have approved our present policy of leniency."

Mao denied that any similarity existed between the political purge in Russia during the 1930s, which Khrushchev had recently denounced, and the repression of opponents by the new order in China. One was irrational and despotic, designed to bolster the dictatorial power of a single man. The other was a judicious effort to promote the common good. "Now that some people have heard that Stalin wrongly put a number of people to death, they jump to the conclusion that we too were wrong in putting those counter-revolutionaries to death. This is a wrong view. It is of immediate significance today to affirm that it was absolutely right to execute those counter-revolutionaries." The difference between Mao's and Stalin's use of coercive force derived from the difference in their goal. The former had exercised it properly, the latter improperly.

In any case, to renounce political repression altogether because it was sometimes applied arbitrarily would leave the revolution paralyzed and defenseless. The enemies of the new order were cunning and tireless. They may have been defeated, but they had not been destroyed. "It should be affirmed that counter-revolutionaries still exist, although their number has greatly diminished," Mao warned. "The effort to clear out those who remain hidden must go on. It should be affirmed that there are still a small number of counter-revolutionaries carrying out counter-revolutionary sabotage of one kind or another. For example, they kill cattle, set fire to granaries, wreck factories, steal information, and put up reactionary posters." The defenders of the revolutionary regime must therefore be always alert, always suspicious. "It is wrong to say that counter-revolutionaries have been completely eliminated and that we can therefore lay our heads on our pillows and just drop off to sleep. As long as class struggle exists in China and in the world, we should never relax our vigilance. [The] counter-revolutionaries . . . are the mortal and immediate enemies of the people." In dealing with them, the government had to rely on dictatorial power. There was no other way.[7]

The Intensity
of Political Repression

Although the theoretical justification of coercive force usually comes after the victory of the new order, its practical application begins at once. As soon as the *ancien régime* collapses, a large-scale physical elimination of its political supporters occurs through expulsion, confinement, and execution. The cabinet ministers, military officers, leading bureaucrats, and police officials who had served the fallen government must pay the penalty of defeat. While in power, they had shown little mercy to their opponents, and now little mercy is shown to them. Then comes the turn of those who may not have held high office, but who were favorites and beneficiaries of the old order. Landlords, bankers, merchants, and industrialists are not only deprived of their wealth but punished for the collective sins of their social class. The more fortunate ones get off with public humiliation and drudgery at a menial job, while the others face exile, prison, or death. Soon after the overthrow of the *ancien régime*, those who had enjoyed its political and economic rewards are effectively crushed.

The radicals turn next against the moderates, with whom they had been allied during the struggle against the old order. As long as the outcome had remained in doubt, they declared repeatedly that the united front of all progressive political forces, bourgeois as well as proletarian, would be maintained after victory. But now that they are in power, their attitude changes. The new order begins to employ methods and pursue goals that middle-of-the-road reformers find unacceptable. Even some radical supporters of the new order become increasingly critical of the government for being too fast or too

slow, too rash or too timid. To the revolutionary authorities this disaffection represents a political danger that must be countered. As
soon as they settle accounts with their opponents on the right, they
declare war on their allies in the center and on the left. This conflict
is generally not as protracted or brutal as the one with the counter-
revolutionaries, but the choice before the losers is the same: surrender or destruction.

Even after the new order defeats all its opponents, whether conservative, moderate, or radical, the system of political coercion remains in force. It becomes an organized and institutionalized
instrument of the revolutionary regime for the defense of its authority. It stands as a constant warning to those who might be tempted to
question the government's claim to power. Occasionally some disgruntled politician or dissident publicist is arrested, tried, and punished for plotting against the state. But as a rule the chief purpose of
the repressive apparatus becomes the prevention rather than the
suppression of political opposition. Its leniency is thus a function of
its effectiveness.

This pattern in the development of coercive governmental force
can be seen clearly in Russia. No sooner were the Bolsheviks in
power, than they initiated a campaign of repression against those
who had been beneficiaries of the czarist regime. Ministers, gover-
nors, bureaucrats, generals, landowners, industrialists, financiers,
and merchants were executed or expropriated by the thousands.
Long before the adoption of formal legislation establishing a new
system of authority and proprietorship, the well-to-do classes were
crushed politically as well as economically.

Rival socialist parties, on the other hand, were at first tolerated, although their press faced periodic harassment through the suspen-
sion of publication or the withholding of newsprint. Even after the
Cheka, on December 31, 1917, arrested some of the leaders of the
Mensheviks and the Right Socialist Revolutionaries, the two groups
continued to be represented in the Central Executive Committee of
the Congress of Soviets. Not until June 14, 1918, were they finally expelled on the ground that they had engaged in counterrevolutionary
or at least antigovernment activities.

This meant that only the Left Socialist Revolutionaries now remained in the Central Executive Committee besides the triumphant

Bolsheviks. But they did not last much longer than the other dissident revolutionary parties. Their opposition to the Treaty of Brest-Litovsk made a break with the government inevitable. In the summer of 1918, after assassinating the German ambassador, they organized a brief abortive uprising. As a result, not only were most of their delegates to the fifth All-Russian Congress of Soviets arrested, but 13 were executed. To Lenin this was no more than just punishment for their betrayal of the revolution. "If anybody was well pleased with the action of the Left Socialist-Revolutionaries and rubbed his hands in glee," he declared in a newspaper interview, "it was only the whiteguards and the servitors of the imperialist bourgeoisie; whereas the worker and peasant masses have been rallying ever closer and more solidly around the Communist-Bolshevik Party, the authentic spokesman of the masses."

The Left Socialist Revolutionaries, however, did not accept their defeat meekly. Late in August they killed M. S. Uritsky, head of the Petrograd Cheka, and seriously wounded Lenin himself. The government replied by intensifying the repression of political dissent. The "red terror" now began to operate on a massive scale. Within a few months all noncommunist party organizations were crushed, although the Bolsheviks, under the pressure of civil war, continued to distinguish between "loyal" dissidents, who supported the regime against the whites, and "disloyal" ones, who were collaborating with the bourgeois reaction. On November 30, 1918, the "loyal" Mensheviks were readmitted to the Central Executive Committee of the Congress of Soviets, and on February 25, 1919, came the reinstatement of those Socialist Revolutionaries who were ready to repudiate "external and internal counterrevolution." Still, Lenin made it clear that the price of their rehabilitation was submission. "We certainly do not want to use force against the petty-bourgeois democrats," he announced before the eighth congress of the Russian Communist Party. "We say to them, 'You are not a serious enemy. Our enemy is the bourgeoisie. But if you join forces with them, we shall be obliged to apply the measures of the proletarian dictatorship to you, too.'"

As long as the civil war continued, the government grudgingly tolerated those noncommunist political groups that supported its struggle against the counterrevolution. Though subject to constant harassment, they still held occasional party conferences and sporadically published their newspapers and manifestos. As late as 1920 the Mensheviks managed to elect some delegates to local soviets, to control a few trade unions, and even to participate in the Congress of Soviets. But once the whites were defeated, the government abandoned its policy of halfhearted toleration toward the "loyal" opposition. *"The Mensheviks and Socialist-Revolutionaries have now learned to don the 'non-party' disguise,"* wrote Lenin in April 1921, a month after the suppression of the Kronstadt uprising. "We have no time for this 'opposition' at 'conferences' game. We are surrounded by the world bourgeoisie, who are watching for every sign of vacillation in order to bring back 'their own men,' and restore the landowners and the bourgeoisie. We will keep in prison the Mensheviks and Socialist-Revolutionaries, whether avowed or in 'non-party' guise."

By now there was no longer any need to keep up the pretense of legal dissent. Large numbers of Constitutional Democrats, Mensheviks, and Socialist Revolutionaries were shipped off into exile in the north, in Siberia, or in Central Asia. Only a few succeeded in winning a temporary reprieve by publicly renouncing any connections with the outlawed political organizations. All opposition to the new order was finally driven underground; the dominance of the Communist party had become complete.[8]

In China the human cost of insuring the victory of the revolution was even higher. Here too the deadliest application of coercive force came in the two or three years immediately following the downfall of the old order, when there was still considerable opposition to the government, especially among the well-to-do classes. According to some noncommunist sources, Mao instructed his followers to limit the number of political executions to 0.6 percent of the population in rural areas and 0.8 percent in urban districts. If so, those limits were frequently exceeded. At least 10,000 people were arrested in Shanghai during the single night of April 27, 1950. Exiled Nationalists claimed that the actual figure was between 25,000 and 30,000, and that the total for the period from April 27 to May 31 was 300,000. The number of executions was much smaller, but it was by no means inconsiderable: 376 in Nanking on April 29; 293 in Shanghai and 50 in Hangchow on April 30; 32 in Shanghai and 40 in Soochow on May 6; 221 in Peking on May 23; and 208 in Shanghai on May 31.

In addition, there must have been more than twice as many who were condemned to forced labor or whose death sentence was commuted to imprisonment. Chou En-lai gave a figure of 28,332 executions out of a total of 89,701 arrests in the space of ten months in the province of Kwangtung. Still, the proportion did not seem to him quite right; too many counterrevolutionaries, he felt, had been allowed to escape just punishment.

No comprehensive statistics have ever been published on the number of victims of the campaign of repression against actual or potential opponents of the new order. But at least a reasonable guess is possible. Reports from four of the six administrative regions into which China had been divided reveal that between October 1949 and October 1950 a total of 1,176,000 people were put to death in those areas. From January 1950 to November 1951 there were 322,000 executions in the Central-South region alone. Thus a total figure of 2,000,000 executions during the first three years of the People's Republic, accepted by some writers, seems rather low, while a figure of 5,000,000 suggested by others is probably too high. The actual number is in all likelihood about midway between the two.

Furthermore, for every person put to death there must have been close to 5 who received some lesser punishment. That at least is the conclusion implied in Chou En-lai's report of June 26, 1957, on "The Work of the Government," including "the suppression of counterrevolution." Of those arrested for opposing the revolution, 16.8 percent were condemned to death, "because they had committed heinous crimes and public wrath was extremely strong against them." The "overwhelming majority" had been executed between 1949 and 1952. Another 42.3 percent were sentenced to "reform through labor," 32 percent were "put under surveillance," and 8.9 percent were "given clemency after arrest," regaining their freedom on the completion of "some re-education."

All in all, Chou calculated, 57.4 percent of all "counterrevolutionaries" had now been freed "after undergoing reform through labor or after being shown clemency." They had thus received "the opportunity to lead a new life." As for the others, "they are still undergoing reform through labor or are still under public surveillance." Yet there was hope for them as well. "They too will be given the opportunity to lead a new life, if they atone for their crimes, abide by the law, and honestly go through the process of reform."

If Chou's figures are correct, 20,000,000 people in China must have suffered some form of punishment in the early years of the new order for demonstrable or presumptive opposition to the Communist government. This estimate corresponds closely to the number of those categorized by Mao as class enemies of the revolution in his talk on "Democratic Centralism" early in 1962. Here he defined the groups in society that were fundamentally hostile to the interests of the laboring masses. "Those whom the people's democratic dictatorship should repress are: landlords, rich peasants, counter-revolutionary elements, bad elements, and anti-communist rightists. The classes which the counter-revolutionary elements, bad elements, and anti-communist rightists represent are the landlord class and the reactionary bourgeoisie. These classes and bad people comprise about four or five percent of the population. These are the people we must compel to reform. They are the people whom the people's democratic dictatorship is directed against."

The 4 or 5 percent of the population described by Mao as class enemies of the revolution represented a total close to the roughly 20,000,000 people on whom the new order had imposed legal penalties ranging from execution to "some re-education." In other words, the great majority of those who had been political or economic beneficiaries of the *ancien régime* were punished in a variety of ways for having once belonged to the privileged strata of society.

Even after all opposition to the government had been suppressed, the system of coercive authority remained in force in China, a permanent monitory institution of the radical dictatorship. Its chief function, however, was no longer to insure the victory of the new order but to sustain its morale, to preserve its sense of commitment. Without the pressure of dictatorial power, the regime might be tempted to relax and sink into democratic reformism. That was the danger against which Mao warned his followers in the spring of 1963. "If classes and class struggle were forgotten and if the dictatorship of the proletariat were forgotten," he insisted, "then it would not be long, perhaps only several years or a decade, or several decades at most, before a counter-revolutionary restoration on a national scale would inevitably occur, the Marxist-Leninist party would undoubtedly become a revisionist party, a fascist party, and the whole of China would change its color. Comrades, please think it over. What a dangerous situation this would be!" Fourteen years after the Communist victory, political repression had become transformed from a weapon of class struggle into a safeguard of revolutionary militancy.[9]

The exercise of coercive force in Cuba was less severe because there the establishment of the new order had been less arduous. Compared to the long years of civil war in Russia or China, the struggle of the revolutionaries against the Batista dictatorship was relatively easy. As a result, their policy was to change the social structure primarily through legislative enactment rather than violent retaliation. On January 21, 1959, three weeks after the fall of the *ancien régime*, Castro pledged in a speech in front of the presidential palace that "the criminals we will shoot are not going to exceed 400." Seemingly, most Cubans, even those who belonged to the propertied classes, had little to fear from the recent change in government.

But the new order was not quite that generous. Even while Castro was speaking, the number of those shot by firing squads must already have exceeded 400, and two years later the total figure for political executions could not have been less than 2,000. By the summer of 1963, according to the estimate of a Cuban exile newsletter, 2,875 people had been put to death by order of the revolutionary tribunals, another 4,245 had been executed without a trial, and 2,962 had died fighting against the Castro forces. While these figures are no doubt inflated, the estimate a few years later by Jaime Caldevilla, a Spanish diplomat stationed in Havana, was not substantially different: 22,000 had been killed or had died in jail, while 2,000 more had drowned trying to escape. Thus a guess of about 10,000 executions in Cuba by the early 1970s seems reasonable. The number, even if proportionately far below the totals for other revolutionary regimes, is not inconsiderable.

The figure for political prisoners is naturally much higher, although here too calculations vary widely, depending in most cases on ideological predilection. Cuban émigrés have maintained that the total as of 1963 was 81,706: 63,440 in fortresses, jails, and prisons; 16,120 in "concentration camps"; and 2,146 in compounds and "other agencies of repression." But two years later Castro himself gave a figure only a fourth as large. In an interview with an American photo-journalist, he dismissed most of the estimates circulating abroad. "Although we usually do not give this kind of information, I am going to make an exception with you," he confided to Lee Lockwood. "I think there must be approximately twenty thousand. But this number comprises all those sentenced by revolutionary tribunals, including not only those sentenced on account of counter-revolutionary activities, but also those sentenced for offenses against the people during Batista's regime, as well as many cases that have nothing to do with political activities, such as embezzlement, theft, or assault, which because of their character were transferred to revolutionary tribunals." Still, according to Caldevilla, in 1969 there were 24,000 prisoners in "concentration camps," 7,000 in jail, 7,200 on "penal farms," and 17,231 under some other form of detention by the security police. All in all, a figure of between 40,000 and 50,000 political prisoners ten years after the revolution seems realistic, although the total number of those who had at one time or another been incarcerated must obviously have been much higher.

The proportion of the population punished by execution or imprisonment was thus not nearly as great in Cuba as in China. Yet the relative decline in the number of those who could be categorized on the basis of their social origin as potential opponents of the new order was roughly comparable. To put it another way, the elimination of the well-to-do as a force in national life occurred under the Castro government to about the same extent as under other revolutionary regimes. The means may have been different, but the results were the same. Whereas in Russia, China, and Vietnam death and incarceration were the chief weapons against the class enemy, in Cuba the authorities relied primarily on more or less voluntary emigration. Although the method was more humane, its effect was equally drastic.

According to official data, the net recorded surplus of departures over arrivals in international travel to and from Cuba was 217,000 between July 1, 1959, and June 30, 1962. This figure represents approximately 1 percent of the population annually, about the same percentage as was executed or imprisoned in China in the early years of the revolution. Since a substantial number of illegal departures had also taken place, the actual gross emigration must have been even greater than the official statistics reveal. The demographic losses were made up by the high birth rate, the return of Cubans exiled under the Batista government, and the influx of sympathizers and admirers from other countries in Latin America. But the political and social consequences of the exodus were profound. Those groups in society most bitterly opposed to the radical dictatorship were in effect expelled, mostly to the United States, where they continued to rage impotently against the revolution in their homeland.

To Castro, however, the use of coercive force seemed fully justified. Those executed had been mass murderers under the old order or counterrevolutionary traitors under the new. They had gotten what they deserved. To those who emigrated, good riddance. They had been exploiters and oppressors during the Batista regime; they had been lucky to get away with their lives. As for political prisoners, they were being treated humanely, they were being reeducated to lead useful, productive lives. Indeed, "at least half" of them, Castro claimed in the summer of 1965, were "in some form of rehabilitation plan."

Even on the Isle of Pines, he insisted, "where prisoners under sentence for the most serious crimes are kept," about 40 percent were being rehabilitated. Not only that, efforts were being made to provide them with economically useful skills. "We may possibly organize . . . two technological institutes, one for cattle raising and another for citrus fruits. It could happen that counterrevolutionary prisoners who go into prison with a relatively low level of education will leave with technical training and a job, even having graduated from the university, depending on their educational level when they were captured." The most hardened sinners were not beyond redemption. "I have no doubt that many of these men will come to be Revolutionaries." How could anyone call that harsh?

Besides, Castro went on, for Cuba the exercise of dictatorial power was an inescapable necessity. He gradually began to sound less genial, less benign, more like Lenin or Mao. "Unfortunately, we are going to have prisoners for counterrevolutionary reasons for many years to come. This is not easy to understand unless social and historical events are analyzed with scientific rigor, and above all unless the widespread support which the Revolution has among the people is kept in mind." The rhetoric of radical militancy now replaced the tone of the stern but kindly schoolmaster. "In a revolutionary process, there are no neutrals; there are only partisans of the revolution or enemies of it. In every great revolutionary process it has happened like this: in the French Revolution, in the Russian Revolution, in our Revolution. I'm not speaking of uprisings, but of processes in which great social changes take place, great class struggles involving millions of persons."

The new order really had no alternative; it had to rely on intimidation and repression. "We are in the middle of such a [class] struggle," according to Castro. "While it lasts, while the counterrevolution exists and . . . has . . . support—even though its force will grow weaker and weaker—the revolutionary tribunals will have to exist in order to punish those who undertake such activities against the Revolution." For although the dictatorship of the proletariat should always be fair and reasonable, it could not afford to be soft and indecisive. Only a firm, unyielding determination would insure its final victory.[10]

The Collectivization
of Coercive Authority

On the face of it, the exercise of repressive power by the new order seems indistinguishable from its exercise by the old. There is the same official apparatus of compulsion, the same political police, the same secret service, the same hunt for dissidents and subversives, the same surveillance of suspected opponents of the established system. The color of the uniforms and the ideology of those wearing them may be different, but the means employed to protect the status quo appear essentially the same. That was what troubled a devoted liberal like Derk Bodde, who was not unsympathetic to the revolution in China but found it hard to justify its adoption of coercive measures similar to those that he had criticized under the Kuomintang. In the fall of 1949, only a few days after the proclamation of the People's Republic, he expressed in his diary a growing concern about the political repressiveness of the new order:

There is a darker side [to the revolution] as well, and one which, because it is most immediately evident to the foreigner, will attract chief attention from the outside world. It is seen in the use of "special service" agents, now beginning to characterize Communist China, as it did Kuomintang China; the threat of force that underlies their moral blandishments; the effort to pigeonhole all individuals into occupational or social groups, partly, at least, in order to insure their easier control; the existence of a small inner group that "knows" and does the controlling, and a large outer mass that is told what to know and is the object of that control; the manipulation of the press, education, literature, and the arts for the advancement of a particular ideology.

All this seemed sadly familiar to Bodde. He discovered that, whether exercised by the *ancien régime* or the new order, coercive force remains central to the maintenance of the established system.[11]

Nor is there much to choose between the two forms of authority regarding their brutality. To be sure, each accuses the other of horrible crimes and atrocities. The victorious revolutionaries claim that their opponents had jailed, tortured, and killed thousands of innocent people suspected of insufficient enthusiasm for the status quo. The supporters of the *ancien régime*, in turn, charge the new order with punishing anyone, however harmless or guiltless, who had once belonged to the propertied and educated classes. To some extent, both are right. Minor differences may exist between them with respect to method and strategy. The old order tends perhaps to be more arbitrary, more random in its use of repressive force. It has less central direction and coordination; more is left to the whim or initiative of local authorities. But for that very reason the coercion is not as effective or pervasive. The new order, on the other hand, is by and large more rational, more disciplined in its application of political repression, so that in the long run it proves more efficient and relentless in crushing dissent. So many exceptions to this generalization can be found, however, that in practice it has little predictive value.

More demonstrable is the proposition that the degree of brutality exercised by the established system, whether conservative or radical, is a function of the degree of its insecurity. To put it another way, the intensity of coercive force diminishes when the government feels strong and stable, and increases when it feels weak and threatened. This means that the *ancien régime* is as a rule most repressive in its last years, as it faces growing resistance, whereas the revolutionary dictatorship is most repressive in its early years, while seeking to consolidate its power against foreign and domestic enemies. Once it has been firmly established, once it succeeds in crushing the political opposition, the new order becomes less ruthless. Yet the institutionalized system for enforcing civic conformity remains always on the lookout, in good times as well as bad, a permanent reminder that organized dissent will not be tolerated.

At least one fundamental difference is apparent, however, between the old order and the new in their use of repressive power. Under the *ancien régime* the right to enforce law and order always remains a monopoly of the authorities. They guard it jealously. The ordinary citizen should not concern himself with the suppression of crime or subversion. That ought to be left to the police. He should merely obey. To give the lower classes a role in punishing dissidents may embolden them to seek to participate in other functions of government as well. The new order, on the other hand, encourages the involvement of the masses in the enforcement of political conformity. In a sense, it collectivizes and democratizes the use of repression. By urging workers and peasants to play an active part in reprisals against supporters of the *ancien régime,* by allowing them to release their economic resentments and social hostilities through acts of retaliation against those who had been their betters, it reinforces popular support for the radical dictatorship. Mass participation in the reconstruction of the class system helps win converts to the cause of the revolution. It forges a bond of common interest between those who lead and those who follow in the transformation of society.

This planned, organized involvement of the lower classes in the struggle against opponents of the new order is most apparent in China. During the "Campaign for the Elimination of Counterrevolutionaries" from 1949 to 1952, those accused of political crimes were frequently tried before a jury of thousands and an audience of tens of thousands. Most of them were not judged individually, on the basis of what they had done or failed to do. Rather, a few "type cases" would be heard, and the same punishment would then be imposed on large numbers of prisoners who had never received a hearing. Prominent members of the Communist regime like P'eng Chen, the mayor of Peking, presided over some of these mass trials. Defendants receiving the death sentence would be immediately transported to the execution grounds, where they were shot through the head in the presence of a large crowd, including children, which was then invited to walk past the corpses of the enemies of the people.

Not all beneficiaries of the *ancien régime* were executed, to be sure. Many got off with a prison sentence, a public humiliation, or simply a good beating. Revolutionary justice, moreover, especially in the countryside, was often haphazard and inconsistent. But its social effect was everywhere the same; it led invariably to the elimination of the well-to-do as a significant force in the life of the community. The account by the chairman of the peasants association in Changchuang of what had happened there after the Communist takeover was typical of developments in countless villages throughout China:

When the final struggle began, Ching-ho [a landlord, the richest man in Changchuang] was faced not only with those hundred accusations but with many more. Old women who had never spoken in public before stood up to accuse him. . . . Altogether over 180 opinions were raised. Ching-ho had no answer to any of them. He stood there with bowed head. We asked him whether the accusations were false or true. He said they were all true. When the committee of our Association met to figure up what he owed, it came to 400 bags of milled grain, not coarse millet.

That evening all the people went to Ching-ho's courtyard to help take over his property. It was very cold that night so we built bonfires and the flames shot up toward the stars. It was very beautiful. We went to register his grain and altogether found but 200 bags of unmilled millet—only a quarter of what he owed us. Right then and there we decided to call another meeting. People all said he must have a lot of silver dollars—they thought of the wine plant, and the pigs he raised on the distillers' grains, and the North Temple Society and the Confucius Association.

We called him out of the house and asked him what he intended to do since the grain was not nearly enough. He said, "I have land and house."

"But all this is not enough," shouted the people. So then we began to beat him. Finally he said, "I have 40 silver dollars under the *k'ang*." We went in and dug it up. The money stirred up everyone. We beat him again. He told us where to find another hundred after that. But no one

believed that this was the end of his hoard. We beat him again and several militiamen began to heat an iron bar in one of the fires. Then
Ching-ho admitted that he had hid 110 silver dollars in militiaman Man-
hsi's uncle's home. . . .

Altogether we got $500 from Ching-ho that night. By that time the
sun was already rising in the eastern sky. We were all tired and hungry,
especially the militiamen who had called the people to the meeting, kept
guard on Ching-ho's house, and taken an active part in beating
Ching-ho and digging for the money. So we decided to eat all the things
that Ching-ho had prepared to pass the New Year—a whole crock of
dumplings stuffed with pork and peppers and other delicacies. He even
had shrimp.

All said, "In the past we never lived through a happy New Year because he always asked for his rent and interest then and cleaned our
houses bare. This time we'll eat what we like," and everyone ate his fill
and didn't even notice the cold.

For the lower classes participation in the exercise of dictatorial power
means above all a redistribution of property and status.[12]

Even after the reconstruction of the national economy has been
completed, the new order continues to maintain a collectivized form
of coercive authority. That is, it promotes the formation of an intricate network of voluntary neighborhood organizations, composed
of local residents, whose main function is to check on political beliefs and attitudes in each district, sometimes even in each street or
apartment building. Who displays banners and slogans on revolutionary holidays and who does not? Who goes to mass meetings and
demonstrations and who stays home? Who expresses support for
the regime and who prefers to keep his opinions to himself? Under
the radical dictatorship the masses join in the suppression of dissidence. To be sure, political surveillance is not the only task of the
local citizens committees. They also deal with a large variety of
other problems: housing, schooling, transportation, and public
health, for example. The enforcement of law and order, however, is
their primary duty. As for the members, they are motivated partly
by their devotion to the cause of the revolution, but partly also by
the sense of importance that comes from being able to tell others
what to do.

That the new order places great emphasis on popular participation in the exercise of coercive authority seems evident. As early as the spring of 1951, less than two years after the Communist victory in China, Mao ordered: "In the current great struggle to suppress counter-revolutionaries public security committees must be organized among the masses everywhere. Such committees should be elected by the people in every township in the countryside and in every department and organization, school, factory, and neighborhood in the cities." The members of each committee might number as few as 3 or as many as 11, but they should include "reliable non-Party patriots so as to make the committee a united front type of organization for safeguarding public security." Under the leadership of the police authorities, these committees were to have responsibility for "assisting the people's government in eliminating counter-revolutionaries, guarding against traitors and spies, and safeguarding our national and public security." Their establishment was therefore to be conducted with great care, in rural areas where agrarian reform had been completed as well as in cities where the suppression of "counter-revolutionaries" was well under way, "so as to prevent bad elements from seizing the opportunity to worm their way in."

Although the implementation of Mao's instructions began within a year, the "Organic Regulations of Urban Inhabitants' Committees" were not promulgated until the end of 1954. They defined the tasks of the committees as follows: "1. To undertake public welfare work for inhabitants; 2. To reflect views and demands of inhabitants to local people's councils or their deputed organs; 3. To mobilize inhabitants to respond to government calls and observe laws; 4. To direct mass security work; and 5. To mediate disputes among inhabitants." Every committee was to have jurisdiction over an area covering in general 100 to 600 households, but this in turn was subdivided among several "inhabitants' teams," not to exceed a total of 17, with jurisdiction over 15 to 40 households. The "inhabitants' committee" was to have between 7 and 17 members, 1 elected by each "inhabitants' team," as well as 1 chairman and 1 to 3 vice-chairmen co-opted from among the members.

In practice the functions that the inhabitants' committees were required to perform proved even more diverse than the "Organic Regulations" had envisaged. Not only did they justify the policies of the government to the masses, but they reported the views of the masses to the government. They exercised quasi-judicial authority in arbitrating family quarrels and neighborhood disputes. They assumed the role of an informal police force in investigating and suppressing criminal activity and political dissent. They accepted responsibility for such municipal services as public sanitation and fire prevention. They contributed to social welfare by providing relief to the needy and organizing local recreational activities. But basically they remained the prime agents of the regime for maintaining ideological control.

In Cuba less effort was made to disguise the repressive purpose of popular participation in dictatorial power. On September 28, 1960, Castro launched the "Committees for the Defense of the Revolution" in a speech before a crowd of tens of thousands gathered in front of the Presidential Palace. He left no doubt what their function would be:

> We are going to establish a system of collective vigilance; we are going to establish a system of revolutionary collective vigilance (Applause). And we are going to see whether the lackeys of imperialism are still able to operate among us. For in fact we have people throughout the city; there is not an apartment building in the city, there is not a dwelling, not a block, not a neighborhood, which is not amply represented [among those assembled] here (Applause). In response to the imperialist campaigns of aggression, we are going to set up a system of revolutionary collective vigilance, so that everyone will know everyone else on his block, what he does, what relationship he had with the tyranny [of the Batista regime], what he believes in, with whom he associates, and in what activities he engages. For if [the counterrevolutionaries] think they can defy the people, they will be greatly disappointed. For we will set up a Committee of Revolutionary Vigilance on every block. . . . When the masses of the people are organized, there is no imperialist, no lackey of the imperialists, no mercenaries of the imperialists, no tools of the imperialists who will be able to operate.

In the course of the next few years a vast surveillance system emerged in Cuba to ferret out the enemies of the people. The number of Committees for the Defense of the Revolution grew from

8,000 in April 1961 to around 110,000 in September 1964, while the membership rose from 70,000 to 2,000,000, almost two-thirds of them women, in a total population of roughly 8,000,000. The occupational background of those serving on the committees reflected the groups in Cuban society most favorable to the new order. Industrial and agricultural workers constituted 30.2 percent of all members in September 1963, housewives 26.4 percent, and white-collar employees 20.1. Peasant landowners, on the other hand, accounted for only 6.8 percent of the total, students for 5.6, professionals for 2.1, and small businessmen for 0.6.

As for their duties, the Committees for the Defense of the Revolution were made responsible for the assignment and distribution of ration cards; they assisted the health authorities in the campaign for the vaccination of children; they participated in the allocation of housing; they organized brigades of volunteer workers for harvesting; they helped wage the struggle against the black market; they organized educational courses and public meetings for "criticism" and "self-criticism"; they kept a sharp lookout for anyone who might suddenly start disposing of his furniture, as if preparing to leave the country; and they sought in general "to counteract all behavior detrimental to the social system." They became the chief instrument of civic surveillance under the radical dictatorship.

In North Vietnam a similar function was performed by the "Street and Inhabitant Protection Committees" established in 1957–58 as a means of politically integrating those strata of the population, ranging from adolescents to the elderly, which could not be easily absorbed into the Vietnamese Workers Party. Their general task was "to make known and popularize the government's decisions dealing with city affairs ... and to maintain order and public safety." In Hanoi alone, according to the state radio, there were 7,600 block chiefs, deputy chiefs, and committee members at the end of July 1958, roughly 1 for every 60 inhabitants, making sure that everyone showed up for elections, for spontaneous greetings to visiting dignitaries from Communist countries, for "Hate America Week," and for other demonstrations of loyalty to the regime. They were entrusted with the primary duty of achieving political conformity.[13]

To the new order popular participation in the exercise of coercive force is not only just but advantageous. Whereas the *ancien régime*

seeks to restrict access to repressive authority, the radical dictatorship collectivizes the maintenance of law and order. It recognizes
that the involvement of the masses in the enforcement of civic
acquiescence makes it not less but more efficient and rigorous.
Self-regulation provides greater effectiveness in the defense of the
established system than a narrow concentration of police power. The
democratization of dictatorial power only intensifies its oppressiveness.

Public Duties and Private Emotions

The popular exercise of coercive authority is not only a weapon
against the enemies of the revolution. It also provides an important
test of loyalty for those who claim to be its friends. Participation in
the apprehension, prosecution, and punishment of the opponents of
the new order becomes a measure of political reliability. Anyone
seeking to achieve a position of trust under the radical dictatorship is
expected to demonstrate his ideological commitment by unrelenting
hostility toward all counterrevolutionaries. Has he been active in his
neighborhood surveillance committee? Has he helped identify foes
of the regime? Has he attended the trials of reactionaries and traitors? Even more important, has he been willing to subordinate private feelings to public responsibilities, individual obligations to
collective duties? The establishment of the new order invariably creates divisions among members of the same class, the same profession, sometimes the same family. A true revolutionary must
therefore be prepared to disown his neighbors, friends, relatives, or
even parents who stand in the way of social progress and reconstruction. This is the ultimate test of devotion to the cause of the
people. Hence every radical dictatorship extols the sacrifice of filial
affection or parental love for the sake of a more just society.

The best-known example in the Soviet Union was the case of
Pavlik Morozov, a boy of fourteen, who in 1932 denounced his father, head of the local soviet in the village of Gerasimovka in the
Ural Mountains, for counterrevolutionary activity in secretly shield-
ing kulaks. In retaliation the youngster was murdered by a group of
peasants, among them his uncle, thereby becoming a martyr of the

revolution. The Palace of Culture of Young Pioneers in Moscow was named after him, and his birthplace established a museum dedicated to his memory. "In this timbered house," ran the inscription, "was held the court at which Pavlik unmasked his father who sheltered the *kulaks*. Here are the reliquaries dear to the heart of every inhabitant of Gerasimovka." His name became enshrined in countless articles, pamphlets, and books. "Millions of Soviet children," according to one of them, "will constantly strive to become as honest and dedicated sons of the great party as he was." Revolutionary sainthood was the reward for his martyrdom.

But the story of Pavlik Morozov is only one instance of the generational conflict between parents and children that the establishment of the new order often engenders. In 1934 there was the case of another youthful hero, Pronya Kolibin, thirteen years old, who received a great deal of publicity and applause for reporting to the authorities that his mother had been stealing grain. That same year the Soviet press also carried the story "Pioneer Sorokin" from the northern Caucasus region, who had his father arrested after discovering that he was filling his pockets by illegally appropriating part of the harvest. And in 1937, in a speech celebrating the twentieth anniversary of the founding of the secret police, A. I. Mikoyan, commissar for the food industry and member of the Politburo, praised a youngster of fourteen from the village of Poryabushki in the Pugachev district who had denounced his father. "Pioneer Kolya Schelgov knows what Soviet power is to him and to the whole people. When he saw that his own father was stealing socialist property, he told the NKVD."

In her memoirs the widow of the Russian poet O. E. Mandelstam, who spent the years before the Second World War in internal exile with her husband, described this repudiation of parents by children from a different perspective.

When we first arrived in Voronezh, we saw there the son of Stoletov, who wandered the streets, alone and half out of his mind, complaining that his father had turned out to be a "wrecker." [In fact,] neither M. nor I nor anybody else thought Stoletov's son really meant it—but there were sons who sincerely cursed their executed fathers. After M.'s death, when I lived for a time on the outskirts of Kalinin, I met there a few wives who for some reason had been banished rather than sent to camps. They had also sent here a boy of fourteen who was distantly related to Stalin. He was being looked after by an aunt who lived nearby—also in exile—and his former governess. For days the boy went on raving against his father and mother as renegades, traitors to the working class, and enemies of the people. He used a formula which had been instilled in him during his very careful upbringing: "Stalin is my father and I do not need another one," and he kept referring to the hero of all the Soviet schoolbooks, Pavlik Morozov, who had managed to denounce his parents in time. He was tormented by the thought that he had lost the chance of becoming a second Pavlik by likewise exposing the criminal activity of his parents. His aunt and governess were forced to listen in silence—they knew what the boy would do if they dared breathe a word.

The psychological cost of sacrificing familial loyalty to civic duty could be very high.[14]

In China even more than in the Soviet Union the denunciation of parents for counterrevolutionary activity became a common test of loyalty to the new order. Precisely because the national culture placed such heavy emphasis on devotion to the family, its rejection came to constitute persuasive evidence of revolutionary commitment. A Chinese intellectual who had supported the Communists during the civil war recalled afterward that following their victory "the way to get ahead . . . was to curse yourself, to claim that you were dirty, polluted, to attack other people—your family, parents, the foreigners—say you were polluted by them. Then you could be considered to be okay, reeducated." The price of forgiveness was confession and accusation.

A student at Peking University claimed after his escape to Hong Kong that he had at first hesitated to denounce his father. "Prior to these [self-criticism] meetings, I did not believe that family affiliation could be a mistake." But group pressure soon overcame his scruples. "The [government, party, and youth corps] kept emphasizing that attachment toward our families was selfish and wrong, since they had been against the welfare of the people. So I began to feel that by loving my family, I was neglecting my duty to my country." The example of his fellow students was especially important. "When I saw others criticizing their family happily, and I contrasted this with my own reluctance, I began to think that this must be due to my own selfishness."

He finally saw that the only way out was to submit. "I felt very confused and upset. . . . I knew that the matter must be settled—and that if I didn't do it well, the government would discover that I wasn't being frank enough and I would be in for trouble. I felt that if I could once and for all settle the turmoil in my mind, I would calm down and be able to feel that I had done my duty to my country." He knew, moreover, that he must now reveal what he was most ashamed of. "To me the only thing I wanted to conceal was that I came from a reactionary, bureaucratic family—so this was the thing to confess. . . . I told that my father had been a [Kuomintang] official, . . . that he had been a reactionary, a man who worked for the welfare of his class which was against the welfare of the people, . . . and that my attachment for my family was selfish and wrong." That at last gave him a sense of relief. "I had the feeling that what I did was right, because it was what the government required me to do, and that it was proper behavior."

The children of families prominent during the *ancien régime* were under special pressure to disown their parents. Lu Chih-wei, the former president of Yenching University in Peking, who had been dismissed for not displaying sufficient loyalty to the new order, was publicly condemned by his daughter at a student rally. "Now I want to denounce my father," she announced. "He did all in his power to deceive me and make loose my stand as a Chinese and to make me disloyal to the masses. . . . Lu Chih-wei, I have in the past considered you a 'noble scholar,' clever and capable." But that had changed. "Now I know you full well. You are a 100 percent claw of imperialism and a tool faithful to U.S. imperialism for its cultural aggression. You would not hesitate to betray the interest of the entire people just to satisfy your political ambition." His sins were unforgivable. "You have poisoned many youths and made politically obscure their vision about the future. . . . You have trained many pro-American elements for imperialism, and you have directly given shelter to the secret agents of U.S. imperialism. For this act of yours no Chinese will ever pardon you."

The son of the well-known philosopher and scholar Hu Shih was equally harsh in his denunciation. "In the old society, I considered my father as an 'aloof' and 'clean' good man," he wrote in a public statement. "Even after the liberation I felt deeply insulted whenever my father was being criticized." Now he knew better. "Today after my education in the Party, I begin to recognize his true qualities. I have come to know that he is [a] loyal element of the reactionary class and an enemy of the people. Politically, he has never been progressive." That had not always been clear. "In the past, I was subjected to a long period of enslavement education of the reactionaries, and I was ignorant about the policies of the people. . . . Today I realize the lenient policy of the People's government. It gives a chance to all those who have acted against the interests of the people to live down their past and start life anew, [but] only if they can come to realize their past misdeeds." Without contrition there could be no absolution. "[Until] my father returns to the people's arms, he will always remain a public enemy of the people, and an enemy of myself. Today in my determination to rebel against my own class, I feel it important to draw a line of demarcation between my father and myself." To the true revolutionary civic duty must always come before filial duty.[15]

Not all denunciations of family members were directed against parents. Sometimes they involved children, siblings, uncles, or cousins. Nor did they always deal with major transgressions against the regime. More commonly they reported some petty crime, some violation of a minor ordinance, regulation, or directive. The important thing was to display a willingness to subordinate private affection to public welfare. A few months after the victory of Ho Chi Minh's forces over the French, a North Vietnamese newspaper reported approvingly the story of a woman who had denounced her daughter to the authorities for black marketeering. "Although she loves her daughter very much, Mrs. T. told the police what the latter had done, because she knows that her daughter does harm to the entire population of Hanoi and is the cause of the increase in prices." The denial of the family, which is at the same time a denial of the self, becomes the ultimate proof of devotion to the welfare of the masses.[16]

Hence the new order regards the exercise of coercive force as more than an unavoidable hardship or sad necessity. It is rather the concrete, visible manifestation of a lofty purpose. It is the sword of justice and the shield of virtue; it is intrinsically good. The mystique of the revolution alters the collective perceptions of civic reality. Surveillance becomes vigilance, compulsion becomes reeducation, repression becomes redemption, and dictatorship becomes democracy. The new order changes not only the forms of political power and economic control. It also reshapes the dimensions of human emotion and social interaction.

CHAPTER 9

The Revival
of Social Elitism

No commandment in the revolutionary decalogue is more sacred
than equality in the distribution of property and power. Indeed, the
new order maintains that the oligarchical structure of wealth and
authority under the *ancien régime* was the prime justification for its
overthrow. Any social system that permits the rich to exploit the
poor or the strong to oppress the weak forfeits its claim to legitimacy.
While the masses had toiled and suffered, the privileged few had
prospered on their misery. Does a form of government that tolerates
such inequity deserve to survive? The basic cause of the downfall of
the old order had been the acceptance of social injustice and the
maintenance of class domination. Its fatal weakness had been elitism, the concentration of political and economic power in the hands
of a privileged patriciate more interested in private advantage than
in general welfare. Such is the standard political rhetoric of the radical dictatorship.

Radicalism and Administration

The new order is determined to change that. Domination by the few
must give way to rule by the many; democracy must replace oligarchy. But the attainment of that goal requires the destruction of the
social foundation of elitism. Hence the inequality in wealth that had
characterized the *ancien régime* should be eliminated as the source of
class exploitation. Equally important, the great difference in influ-

ence between those who control the government and those who obey it should come to an end. The revolution will no longer tolerate the traditional sharp distinction between rulers and ruled. Therefore the position of the bureaucracy, the group in society that is primarily responsible for the basic operations of the government, ought to be drastically altered. The state official will cease to be the master and become the servant of the people. Indeed, the need for a separate class of administrators will diminish and vanish, as the masses themselves assume the duties of a civil service. The equality of power is as important as the equality of wealth in the struggle against social elitism.

This is the position that Lenin took in the spring of 1917 after his return to Russia. In an article published early in May, he discussed the form of administration best suited to a revolutionary government. "Does the state need a bureaucracy of the usual type?" he asked. For the parties on the right and for the middle-of-the-road Constitutional Democrats the answer was "Most decidedly." How could it be otherwise? "Nine-tenths of them are the sons and brothers of landowners and capitalists. They must continue to remain a privileged and, in practice, permanent body of people." The Mensheviks and the Socialist Revolutionaries preferred to dodge the problem. Their view, according to Lenin, was: "It is hardly fitting to raise so hastily a question that was raised by the Paris Commune." Only the Bolsheviks, he insisted, took an unequivocal stand in opposition to traditional forms of state authority. To them it was clear that the state "certainly does not" need a bureaucracy of the sort maintained under the old order. "All officials and all and every kind of deputy must not only be elective, but displaceable at any moment. Their pay must not exceed that of a competent worker. They must be replaced (gradually) by the people's militia and its detachments." The bureaucratic apparatus of the state, like the state itself, would wither away in a society free of class domination.

Lenin's accession to power did not at first change his opinion regarding the need to abolish an institutionalized form of government administration. Addressing the seventh congress of the Russian Communist Party in March 1918, he maintained that the revolution would introduce a new system of state authority based on the direct participation of the masses. "[It] is theoretically regarded as indisputable," he assured his followers, "that Soviet power is a new type of state without a bureaucracy, without police, without a regular army, a state in which bourgeois democracy has been replaced by a new democracy, a democracy that brings to the fore the vanguard of the working people, gives them legislative and executive authority, makes them responsible for military defense, and creates state machinery that can re-educate the masses." His opposition to traditional bureaucracy derived from a recognition that differences in the possession of power, like differences in the possession of wealth, were bound to lead to social elitism. The maintenance of a separate caste of professional civil servants entrusted with state authority would therefore be a threat to the principle of equality. Only if the masses performed the functions of government themselves would they be safe against administrative oppression.[1]

The Bureaucratic Oligarchy

Yet while the leaders of the revolution perceive the elitist implications of an institutionalized system of administration, the practical problems of running a government make them increasingly dependent on it. In the end, the new order comes to rely on a class of professional bureaucrats even more than the old order had done. The attempt to create a collectivized economy imposes on the state a multitude of new functions that had formerly been performed by the private sector or that had not even existed. Someone has to supervise the redistribution of land, the nationalization of industry, the reorganization of commerce, the rationing of food, the improvement of education, and the expansion of health care. In other words, the establishment of the radical dictatorship leads not to a contraction but an expansion of the administrative apparatus. The withering away of the bureaucracy, like the withering away of the state, becomes more and more a remote prospect, a theoretical concept. Instead, a new class of professional administrators emerges, larger than the old, based on the possession of technical expertise, sharing a distinct professional outlook, and characterized by a sense of separate identity. Its ethos still emphasizes the advancement of the common welfare, but the growing distance of the bureaucratic caste from the masses of the population contains the seeds of social elitism.

The first step in this process is a vast increase in the size of the ruling party. As the traditional bureaucratic system disintegrates because of its opposition to the revolution and hostility to the new order, the radical dictatorship finds itself in urgent need of reliable followers willing to work for the realization of its goals. The result is a rapid growth of the administrative apparatus. In Russia the membership of the Communist party rose from 23,600 at the beginning of 1917 to 115,000 a year later. By January 1919 the figure reached 251,000, by January 1920 431,400, and by January 1921 576,000. Then came a temporary decline, as the leadership tried to purge the ranks of dissenters and opportunists, but after the middle of the decade there was a new period of expansion: 639,652 in 1926, 786,228 in 1927, 914, 307 in 1928, and 1,090,508 in 1929. The numbers continued to climb until the completion of the First Five-Year Plan. The membership reached 1,184,651 in 1930, 1,369,406 in 1931, 1,769,773 in 1932, and 2,203,951 in 1933. In the course of a decade and a half the Communist Party of the Soviet Union had grown a hundredfold.

In China the membership of the Communist party fluctuated more erratically during the first twenty years of its existence. To begin with, a rapid increase took place from 57 in 1921 and 123 in 1922 to 57,967 in the spring of 1927. After the break with the Kuomintang a few months later, the figure dropped to 10,000 at the end of the year and 40,000 in 1928. Then came a period of renewed growth from 122,318 in 1930 to about 300,000 in 1934, followed again by a decline to 40,000 in 1937 resulting partly from losses suffered during the "Long March." But the beginning of the conflict with Japan that same year led to a remarkable recovery: 800,000 members in 1940, 763,000 in 1941, 736,000 in 1942, and 853,000 in 1944.

The surrender of the Japanese government in the summer of 1945 led to a further rapid increase in the strength of the Communists. A few months before hostilities ended, they had reached a membership of 1,211,000, and the outbreak of the civil war in China brought the party even more recruits. Its size grew from 1,348,000 in 1946 to 2,759,000 at the end of 1947, 3,066,000 at the end of 1948, and 4,488,000 at the proclamation of the People's Republic in October 1949.

The victory of the new order helped to swell the flood of converts to Communism. During 1950 and 1951 the number remained more or less constant, fluctuating between 5,000,000 and 5,800,000, but in 1952 it reached 6,002,000, in 1953 6,612,000, in 1954 7,859,000, in 1955 9,393,000, in 1956 10,734,000, in 1957 12,720,000, in 1959 13,960,000, and in 1961 17,000,000. While in the Soviet Union the Communist party sixteen years after coming to power had a membership approaching 1.5 percent of the population, in China the Communist party twelve years after coming to power had a membership exceeding 2.5 percent of the population.[2]

Why the radical dictatorship promotes such an explosive growth of its administrative apparatus is obvious. Determined to impose new purposes on a confused, recalcitrant society, it is in pressing need of large numbers of supporters committed to the task of social reconstruction. But what motivates the millions who flock to the party after the fall of the *ancien régime*? Are they driven by principles and convictions, by the desire to help build a better world? Or do they act out of expediency, in the expectation that radical beliefs will bring them material rewards?

The answer appears to be that those joining the revolutionary movement are impelled by a variety of motives, mostly philanthropic in the early years of the new order, but increasingly utilitarian afterward. The radical dictatorship is at first able to inspire faith, especially among the young and idealistic, in its ability to regenerate human society. The importance of this faith should not be underestimated. It attracts large numbers of recruits to the party, men and women prepared to endure hardship and danger for the sake of a social ideal. The leadership, moreover, seeks initially to discourage "opportunists" and "careerists" by insisting that members can expect no advantage, only duty and responsibility. Thus during the civil war in Russia, a party congress restated the traditional view that those who join "have no privileges over other workers, they have only higher obligations." For the Bolsheviks it was axiomatic that the struggle for a better social system could be won only by committed revolutionaries ready to sacrifice themselves for the cause.

Yet from the beginning there are also those who enter the party in the anticipation of rewards. They believe in the basic principles of the revolution, to be sure; they subscribe in a general way to the doctrines of the radical dictatorship. But their public convictions are reinforced by private calculations. The longer the new order is in power, the rosier its prospects become, the larger grows the number of those who support it for reasons of expediency. And in fact party membership does become progressively more remunerative. Considerable prestige can be derived from a position of responsibility, not to mention the advantage of being close to governmental power: more food, better housing, finer dress, greater comfort. Nor should the improved chances of professional advancement be overlooked. The faithful follower of the regime can expect more rapid promotion not only in the bureaucracy but in industry, agriculture, education, science, and the arts. These considerations increasingly attract to the revolutionary movement members who accept its doctrines, but who are at least equally interested in its rewards.

The leaders of the new order are aware of the gradual erosion of ideological fervor among the rank and file. They therefore inveigh tirelessly against the "opportunists" and "careerists" who threaten to corrupt the party. Four years after the November revolution, Stalin denounced the "unreliable careerist elements," those members "alien to the proletarian spirit" who were infecting the Communist movement with "disintegration and conservatism." He argued that the effectiveness of the party depended not on the quantity but the quality of its followers, "on their staunchness and devotion to the cause of the proletariat." The organization could become strong only "by purging itself of dross," by rejecting "all sorts of petty-bourgeois trash." The task facing the Bolsheviks was "to preserve the staunchness and purity of [their] ranks."

The radical dictatorship, however, is not content merely to condemn the spread of opportunism. Periodic purges of the party are carried out to eliminate those more interested in their own advancement than in the welfare of the masses. In the Soviet Union the eighth congress of the Communist party in the spring of 1919 admitted that the open-door policy on recruitment had led to an influx of "careerists." The result was the decision to weed out those considered "unworthy" of membership, so that within six months the size of the organization shrank from 250,000 to 150,000. But during the "Party Week" late in 1919 roughly 200,000 new recruits were admitted, so that by the ninth congress in the spring of 1920 the total reached 612,000, and by the tenth congress a year later it was approaching 750,000.

The renewed growth of the party meant in turn a renewed threat to its ideological purity. That was why the leadership initiated a second purge late in 1921 and early 1922, not as severe as three years before, but severe enough to reduce the membership from a little over 650,000 to just under 500,000. Although this time a determined effort was also made to enforce stricter standards of admission, the need for bureaucratic expansion began to wear down the resistance against political opportunism. By the beginning of 1926 membership had almost regained the level reached before the purge, and in January 1927 it rose to a new high of 786,000.

In China statistics on the Communist party suggest a similar pattern of repeated but unsuccessful attempts to maintain ideological zeal by mass expulsions. Of the 4,500,000 members who had joined before 1949 only 3,400,000 were left in 1961, an annual attrition rate of 2 percent. While about half of the 1,100,000 who were no longer in the party had probably died, the rest had been purged. The annual attrition rate among those joining between 1950 and 1953 was even higher. Of the 2,100,000 members in this category only 1,700,000 were left in 1961, an average loss of 2.9 percent annually. While part of this decline was attributable to the casualties suffered during the Korean War, part resulted from large-scale expulsions from the party. The statistics on those who joined later in the decade are inconclusive, but scattered reports suggest a substantial decline in this group as well as in the aftermath of the "rectification" and "antibourgeois rightist" campaigns toward the end of the 1950s.

Admittedly, not all of those purged are considered guilty of opportunism. On the contrary, some are expelled for being too inflexible in their beliefs, too doctrinaire. They are slow to adapt to the twists and turns of the party line. They hesitate, they question, they argue. To the new order excessive zeal is even more of a danger than opportunism. Hence the periodic purges of the rank and file are increasingly directed against members too dogmatic to adjust to changes in official policy. As the regime is gradually forced to make concessions and accept compromises, the fundamentalist believers become a potential threat. They are always grumbling and complaining about the growing heterodoxy of the government. How long will it be before they start to organize and conspire? They must be purged.

On the other hand, the opportunists who pay lip service to the principles of the revolution can be quite useful to the new order, more useful than the radical zealots who believe in them blindly. They will remain loyal servants of the radical dictatorship as long as they are rewarded with a higher economic and social status. That is not too high a price to pay for the attainment of the government's goals. Within a decade after coming to power, the new order abandons its insistence on strict egalitarianism. It acquiesces in the reemergence of disparities in affluence and prestige, thereby laying the foundation for a new elite centered on the administrative apparatus. What else can it do? Neither exhortations nor expulsions prove effective in maintaining the fervor of the initial phase of the revolution. The new order, like the old, is increasingly forced to rely on a professional bureaucracy in which technical competence rather than ideological commitment is the key to advancement.

In turn, those who serve the radical dictatorship become bolder in advancing their demand for rewards. In the Soviet Union the revival of private enterprise under the New Economic Policy in the early 1920s encouraged the rank and file of the Communist party to start grumbling about the heavy burdens of membership. Complaints grew that those who belonged had to accept jobs selected by their superiors, whereas those who did not could choose for themselves. A party member had no time for his family. Even his wife had to "work like a horse" to maintain his reputation as a dedicated revolutionary. Moreover, a woman joining the party practically forfeited her chances of marriage because of the widespread belief that she would neglect her husband and children for the sake of the organization. Nor did the reaction against the requirement of self-sacrifice stop with complaints. A voluntary exodus from the party took place that in 1922 reached 10 percent of the membership in some areas. The new order had little choice. Although sermons urging selfless service to the masses continued to appear regularly, after the middle of the decade the struggle against "opportunism" was in effect abandoned. The administrative system had become permanently bureaucratized, professionalized, and institutionalized.[3]

What separates the emerging elite of the new order from the broad masses is social origin as well as social status. Before the Bolsheviks seized power, it had seemed obvious to Lenin that "all officials . . . must be replaced (gradually) by the people's militia and its detachments." Yet in fact the victory of the revolution creates a growing need for a professional bureaucracy that cannot be recruited entirely from the lower classes. In October 1919, 52 percent of the party members in Russia were workers in the sense that they had once been employed in industry, 15 percent were peasants, 18 percent were white-collar employees, and 14 percent were "intellectuals." In other words, almost a third were or had been clerks, officials, academics, or professionals, a number out of all proportion to their share in the population.

The leadership of the party, conscious of the anomaly of a proletarian organization with a substantially nonproletarian membership, sought to encourage the enlistment of recruits from factories and farms. But progress was slow. By 1921 the percentage of those classified as peasants had risen to 28, but the percentage of workers had dropped to 41, and worse still, the proportion of white-collar employees and "intellectuals" was almost the same as two years before, 31 percent. As of 1923, the situation had still not improved significantly. An official analysis of party membership published early that year showed that the proportion of workers had risen slightly, to 45 percent, and the proportion of peasants had dropped a little, to 26 percent, while the percentage of "others" remained disturbingly high at 29. To make the figures look better, the leadership decided to add those white-collar employees and "others" who had received only a primary education to the category of workers, thus claiming that "proletarian elements" now constituted two-thirds of the party. But there could be no disguising the fact that members of "bourgeois" origin remained a powerful force within the bureaucratic apparatus.

In China the proportion of "intellectuals" in the Communist party actually increased after the victory of the new order, at about the same rate as the representation of the urban proletariat and much more than the representation of the rural population. Although in 1949 about 80 percent of the members were peasants, by 1956 the percentage had dropped to 69.1, by 1957 to 66.8, and by 1961 to approximately 66. The proportion of industrial workers, on the other hand, rose from almost none in 1949 to 14 percent in 1956 and 15 percent in 1961. The percentage of "educated" members, defined as "teachers, students, engineers, technicians, and professional people," and categorized collectively as "intellectuals," grew at a comparable pace. They constituted probably no more than 5 percent in 1949, roughly the size of the party's administrative staff, but then their share rose to 11.7 percent in 1956, 14.8 percent in 1957, and 15 percent in 1961. Even more striking, while in 1956 1.4 percent of the peasants and 18 percent of the workers in China were members of the party, for "intellectuals" the percentage was close to 33. The avenue for advancement was clearly shifting from rural to urban areas and from manual to white-collar occupations.[4]

The percentage of workers and peasants in the party is even smaller than the official statistics of the new order indicate. First of all, those seeking admission to the revolutionary patriciate frequently try to conceal their bourgeois origin. In the Soviet Union during the early 1920s that was a frequent reason for expulsion from the organization. But more important was the deliberate manipulation of the data to inflate the proportion belonging to the lower classes. This usually took the form of defining a member's social origin not by the class background of his parents or by his current employment, but his occupation at the time of the revolution or his entry into the party. Thus in the fall of 1919, when the Russian Communist Party claimed that 52 percent of its members were workers, only 11 percent were currently employed in industry. And since many of those who were held managerial or administrative positions, the percentage actually engaged in manual labor was insignificant. On the other hand, 53 percent of the members were working in government offices, 27 percent were in the armed forces, and 8 percent were party or union officials.

By the beginning of 1928 the situation had improved, at least according to the figures published by the statistical department of the Central Committee; but the disparity between appearance and reality of the party's social composition remained substantial. Official statistics showed that 56.8 percent of the members were workers, 22.9 percent peasants, 18.3 white-collar employees, and 2 percent "others." Yet an analysis of the current occupations of the members produced a significantly different picture. Only 35.2 percent were actually working "at the bench" as wage earners. Of the 10.4 percent properly classifiable as peasants, no more than 1.2 percent were employed as agricultural laborers, while 9.2 percent were well-to-do farmers prosperous enough to afford hired help. Officials of all sorts, including those holding junior or part-time positions, accounted for the largest single category with 38.3 percent. Finally, members of the armed forces constituted 6.3 percent of the total and "others" 9.8 percent. Less than half of the membership, even excluding those serving in the army, was thus actually engaged in manual occupations.

As late as 1932 the nonproletarian element in the Communist party continued to account for more than a third of the members. On paper the organization was dominated by the urban and rural masses. Figures on the class composition of the membership determined by family background or original employment showed that 65.2 percent were workers, 26.9 percent were peasants, and only 7.9 percent were white-collar employees. But according to the data on their current occupations, 43.8 percent were workers, 18.5 percent were individual or collective farmers, and 37.6 percent were white-collar employees and "others." It is clear, furthermore, that many of those whose source of employment was given as industry or agriculture were in fact administrators, managers, overseers, and foremen far removed from the lathe or the plow.[5]

The leaders of the revolutionary regime, recognizing the growing stratification of the bureaucratic system, preach tirelessly about the need to collectivize and democratize the administration of state and party. How can there be a dictatorship of the proletariat without the participation of the proletariat? V.M. Molotov, one of Stalin's trusty right-hand men, complained in 1925 that "those who enter the party under the rubric of peasants are very often not peasant elements at all, but sometimes that very official group which is seeking to ease its way into the party." That was highly disturbing to a government committed in theory to social egalitarianism.

Three years later a party publication conceded that a serious decline had taken place in the proportion of bona fide workers and peasants in the organization. It spoke of "an exodus from the working class and—in lesser degree—from the peasantry into the state apparatus, into economic, trade union, social, and other work." Of the 638,000 members classified as workers and 217,000 as peasants, 184,000 and 56,000 respectively were in fact employed as "officials and social workers." On the other hand, although only 258,000 members were classified as officials, 440,000 actually held administrative jobs. Was not this disparity between the rhetoric and the practice of the new order likely to spread disillusionment among the masses?

The radical dictatorship, however, is not content simply to admonish and exhort. It makes repeated efforts to increase the representation of the lower classes in the administrative system. The purge of the Soviet party in 1921–22, for example, affected intellectuals more than workers and peasants, so that the combined percentage for the latter two categories rose from 47 to 53 in the industrial provinces and from 31 to 48 in the agricultural provinces. Two years later the "Lenin enrollment," which was expected to produce 200,000 new admissions, led in fact to about 240,000, increasing the total membership by over 50 percent. More important, since almost all of the newcomers were workers "from the bench," the representation of the industrial proletariat rose for the first time to well over half. Indeed, throughout the early years the leadership fought to increase the proportion of lower-class members, reaching, on paper at least, a high of 92 percent workers and peasants in 1932.

Yet, in the long run, the struggle against elitism, like the struggle against opportunism, ends in failure. The longer the radical dictatorship remains in power, the more dependent it grows on the bureaucracy. The administrative system ceases to be the servant and becomes the partner of the regime. And that means that ultimately professional expertise proves more useful in the attainment of power than social origin or ideological commitment. For the increase of industrial production and the expansion of agricultural output are too important to be entrusted to an inexperienced worker or peasant, however unexceptionable his class background or revolutionary zeal. As the new order begins to run out of ideological fervor, as it comes under growing pressure to improve the material well-being of the masses, technical proficiency becomes the chief requirement for advancement in the bureaucratic structure.

That is why the higher a position is within the administrative hierarchy, the less likely it is to be held by someone of lower-class origin. The process of rigidification, in other words, is most apparent at the upper levels of the state apparatus. An analysis in 1921 of close to 15,000 leading officials of the Communist party of the Soviet Union showed that barely a third were of proletarian background, although 41.0 percent of the total membership was classified as workers, 28.2 percent as peasants, and only 30.8 percent as white-collar employees and "others." According to a similar study published in 1925 of nearly 2,000 members appointed to important positions during the previous two years, 59.7 percent came from the "black-coated" category, which accounted for no more than 27.2 percent of the total membership, as opposed to 44.0 percent for workers and 28.8 for peasants. Nowhere was the contrast between egalitarian theory and elitist practice more glaring than at the top of the administrative pyramid.

Even the party members recruited from the lower classes soon become estranged from those they left behind in the factory or on the farm. They are assimilated by the bureaucratic organization which they are supposed to proletarianize and democratize. They develop a distinctive professional outlook, a separate collective ethos, an independent social identity. Their class origin cannot prevent their growing alienation from the broad masses. Molotov reported to the fourteenth congress of the Russian Communist Party in 1925 that although 58 percent of the members were described in the official statistics as workers, only 38 percent were actually "from the bench." The others, whatever their original form of employment, had become part of the administrative apparatus.

Indeed, the trend toward the bureaucratization of the rank and file was by now irresistible. A party census in the Soviet Union early in 1927 revealed that of all members classified as workers on the basis of their "social situation," less than half were still in manual occupations, while 29 percent had become officials of the government, the party, the trade unions, or other public organizations, 7 percent were in the armed forces, 5 percent were students, and 2.5 percent held minor office jobs. On the other hand, about 85 percent of the members classified as "intelligentsia and white-collar workers" were still employed as such, with only a very small proportion serving in the army or engaged in study. The recruitment policy of the party, instead of proletarianizing the bureaucracy, had only succeeded in bureaucratizing the proletariat.

The enlistment of the peasantry in the Communist party proved even more difficult. The government felt obliged both by its rhetoric and its ideology to encourage the participation of the rural working class in the administration of the state. But it was hard going. Their background, outlook, experience, and interest tended to make the Russian farmers unsympathetic to the collectivist ideals of the new order. Hence in a country where close to 80 percent of the population lived on the land, the proportion of party members categorized as peasants on the basis of their class origin never reached 30 percent, and on the basis of their current occupation the proportion was less than half of that. In 1925 the leadership was forced to admit that most of the recruits from agriculture had "entirely or to some extent broken with the peasant economy." Although official statistics claimed that 25 percent of the membership came from the land, no more than 8 percent lived exclusively by farming. In Leningrad province 11.3 percent of the members were classified as peasants, but by current occupation the percentage dropped to 1.4. While for the country at large 18.9 percent of the membership of the party's county, department, and city district committees was described as peasants, only 8.8 percent actually came "from the plough."

Efforts to "improve the social composition" by increasing recruitment in the agricultural labor force had little success. Many of those joining the party were not really peasants but workers living in farm communities. What motivated them, moreover, was expediency at least as much as principle. Only 10 percent of the membership in the rural districts had been in the party before the November revolution. A typical cell in the countryside during the 1920s consisted of between 4 and 6 members scattered among 3 or 4 villages several miles apart. Occasionally, therefore, entirely fictitious peasant organizations, created to help make the official statistics look better, would receive favorable mention in the party's reports for their meritorious but nonexistent achievements.

Even those villagers who joined were in most cases no longer employed in agriculture, and those who were tended to be the more successful and prosperous farmers. Early in 1929 an analysis of the party's composition showed that while members of the rural cells totaled 330,000, only 123,828 depended on farming for their livelihood. Worse still, the "proletarian elements" were only a small minority. A party member practicing husbandry usually belonged to the village patriciate. In the Russian Soviet Federated Socialist Republic only one-sixth of the peasant households had assets of more than 800 rubles, but for those headed by party members the figure was one-fourth. In the Ukraine the proportion of peasant members employing hired labor was twice as high as of peasant nonmembers. Landowning farmers constituted close to 13 percent of the membership of the party, whereas farm laborers and agricultural workers constituted only 2 percent. Despite all the efforts to encourage the enlistment of the rural proletariat in the administrative system, peasant participation remained not only low but heavily weighted in favor of the well-to-do groups in the village community.[6]

Sooner or later the new order is forced to accept the growing stratification of the bureaucratic structure. The struggle between technical proficiency and social egalitarianism invariably ends with the victory of the former. The regime does not openly admit defeat, to be sure. On the contrary, there are continuing exhortations to increase the participation of the lower classes in the task of social reconstruction, and even sporadic efforts to raise the percentage of workers and peasants in the Communist ranks. But nothing seems to arrest the transformation of the administrative apparatus into an exclusive bureaucratic caste. The statistical evidence is irrefutable. In 1929, 81.2 percent of all the recruits into the Communist party of the Soviet Union were workers, 17.1 percent were peasants, and only 1.7 percent were white-collar employees and members of the "intelligentsia." But a decade later, for the period from November 1936 to March 1939, the percentages were substantially different: 41.0 for workers, 15.2 for peasants, and 43.8 for white-collar employees and members of the "intelligentsia."

Statistics on the occupational composition of local organizations of the party underscored the abandonment under Stalin of the policy of proletarianization. The district committee of the Gorky region, for example, reported that of the 602 candidates for membership enrolled between November 1936 and November 1938, 208 were employed in engineering or technical enterprises, 312 were workers, and only 82 belonged to other categories. The Georgian organization announced at the party's eighteenth congress in March 1939 that 35.6 percent of the 26,000 members admitted since November 1, 1936, were workers, 18.3 percent were collective farmers, and 42.8 percent were white-collar employees. Its spokesman stressed the large number of agronomists, teachers, doctors, heads of village soviets, and chairmen of collective farms who had been enrolled. Similarly, the Azerbaijan organization announced that of the recent candidates for admission, 25.5 percent were workers, 30.0 percent were collective farmers, and 44.5 percent belonged to the "intelligentsia." These figures measured the growing social divergence between the party and the masses.

The official rhetoric of the new order began to reflect the emergent elitism of the bureaucratic apparatus as well. As early as June 1931, in an address to a conference of economic executives, Stalin dwelt on the need to create an efficient system of administration in the Soviet Union. "Our country has entered a phase of development in which the *working class must create its own industrial and technical intelligentsia*, one that is capable of upholding the interests of the working class in production as the interests of the ruling class." That of course did not mean the revival of class differences or social inequalities. "Our policy is by no means to transform the party into an exclusive caste. Our policy is to create an atmosphere of 'mutual confidence,' of 'mutual control' (*Lenin*) between party and nonparty workers." And yet the emergence of a new patriciate of experts and technicians was inevitable. "No ruling class has managed without its own intelligentsia. There are no grounds for believing that the working class of the U.S.S.R. can manage without its own industrial and technical intelligentsia."

Five years later, in a report "On the Draft Constitution of the U.S.S.R." presented in the fall of 1936 before a meeting of soviets, Stalin elaborated on this theme. "The intelligentsia [created by the revolution]," he expounded, "is no longer the old hidebound intelligentsia which tried to place itself above classes, but which actually, for the most part, served the landlords and the capitalists. Our Soviet intelligentsia is an entirely new intelligentsia, bound up by its very roots with the working class and the peasantry." For one thing, its social composition was altogether different. "People who come from the aristocracy and the bourgeoisie constitute but a small percentage of our Soviet intelligentsia; 80 to 90 per cent of the Soviet intelligentsia are people who have come from the working class, from the peasantry, or from other strata of the working population." But an even more important difference existed. "The very nature of the activities of the intelligentsia has changed. Formerly it had to serve the wealthy classes, for it had no alternative. Today it must serve the people, for there are no longer any exploiting classes. And that is precisely why it is now an equal member of Soviet society, in which, side by side with the workers and peasants, pulling together with them, it is engaged in building the new, classless, socialist society."

Still, Stalin's defense of the bureaucratization of the administrative system failed to silence criticism within the ranks of the Communist party. Hence early in 1939 he restated his position even more vigorously at the eighteenth congress. "During the period of Soviet development the intelligentsia has undergone a radical change both in its composition and status," he insisted. "It has come closer to the people and is honestly collaborating with the people, in which respect it differs fundamentally from the old, bourgeois intelligentsia." The reason was obvious. "Hundreds of thousands of young people coming from the ranks of the working class, the peasantry, and the working intelligentsia . . . radically changed the whole aspect of the intelligentsia, molding it in their own form and image. The remnants of the old intelligentsia were dissolved in the new, Soviet intelligentsia, the intelligentsia of the people. There thus arose a new, Soviet intelligentsia, intimately bound up with the people, and for the most part, ready to serve them faithfully and loyally." The revolution had found in this intelligentsia an effective tool for the building of a better society.

Barely two decades after Lenin had declared that "Soviet power is a new type of state without a bureaucracy [and] without police," a state in which "a new democracy . . . brings to the fore the vanguard of the working people, gives them legislative and executive authority, . . . and creates state machinery that can re-educate the masses," Stalin was justifying the establishment of a new Communist bureaucratic system that in its professional exclusiveness, economic advantage, and social eminence resembled the old czarist one. The harsh exigencies of political power had left him no alternative.[7]

The Managerial Oligarchy

Party officials and government bureaucrats are not the only members of the new revolutionary patriciate. They are joined by leading figures in science, scholarship, education, literature, art, and music. For a doctor or a journalist, a chemist or a historian, a painter or a composer, entering the party can mean important professional advantages. It can lead to a more rapid promotion, a more generous salary, a wider reputation, a greater influence. This does not mean that the members of the learned professions and fine arts who embrace the doctrines of the new order are motivated solely by the expectation of material rewards. Most of them believe, with varying degrees of conviction, in the ideals of the revolution. But their loyalty is reinforced by the knowledge that it will be suitably recompensed, that it will be remembered and commended by those in power. In culture as in administration, expediency becomes intermingled with principle in the avowal of political faith.

But more important than the cultural elite, second only to the bureaucratic oligarchy, is the managerial elite. The administrators, planners, directors, managers, engineers, and technicians, whose task is to improve production in industry and agriculture, gradually acquire an influence within the revolutionary patriciate comparable to that of government officials, party functionaries, police commissioners, and army officers. The longer the regime is in power, the more dependent it becomes on the administrative apparatus of the economy for the fulfillment of its promise of a better life for the masses. In the end bureaucracy and technocracy join to form a ruling aristocracy in a theoretically egalitarian society.

The social composition of the economic elite closely resembles that of the political elite. At first an attempt is made to proletarianize the administration of industry and agriculture, to create a new managerial class recruited primarily from the masses. But the need to raise production soon forces the radical dictatorship to subordinate social origin to technical competence. In Russia the victory of the revolution led initially to the wholesale promotion of workingmen and farmers to administrative positions in the economy. In 1922, according to a contemporary study of 159 industrial

enterprises, close to two-thirds of the managers had started out as
workers, peasants, or clerks without experience in business administration. Only 6 were skilled engineers. As for their schooling, 13
percent had received a higher education, 24 percent a secondary
education, and 63 percent no more than an elementary education.
The figures reflect the uncompromising proletarianization of the
economic bureaucracy which the Bolsheviks introduced immediately after coming to power.

But the same need to increase production that led to the New
Economic Policy soon revived the importance of technical expertise in industrial planning. As early as 1923 a study of 1,306 factory
managers showed that now only 39 percent were workers by class
origin. Most of the others belonged to the category of former employers or directors. The proportion of those with a higher education, moreover, had risen to 22.6 percent, the percentage for those
with a secondary education remained almost the same as in 1922,
24.9, and those with no more than an elementary education had
dropped to about half of the total, 52.5 percent. Even so, only 61.0
percent of the factory managers were rated as qualified for their positions, 30.3 were described as acceptable but "feeble," and 8.7 percent were clearly unqualified.

The new order was therefore forced to turn for help to those who,
whatever their class origin, had the training and experience to promote economic recovery. In many cases managers and engineers were
reappointed to the same positions they had held under the *ancien
régime*. By the late 1920s, 267,415 of the 963,232 members of the union
of soviet and trade employees, covering administrative institutions as
well as collective and cooperative economic enterprises, had been in
similar public or private employment in 1913. Nor were they now rele-
gated to minor branches of administration. Almost half of them, 47.7
percent, held jobs in collective or cooperative economic enterprises,
37.2 percent worked in various government ministries, and 5.9 percent were employed by public or cooperative credit institutions. Their
earlier accommodation to czarism had been forgiven. All that mattered was technical proficiency.

The government did return for a few years to a policy of proletarianization in the period of the First Five-Year Plan, promoting workers into administrative jobs or university classrooms on a massive

scale. During this "cultural revolution," large numbers were moved directly from the factory and the mine into industrial management and public administration, replacing "class enemies" purged from the state or trade-union bureaucracy. By late 1933 more than 140,000 of the 861,000 jobs in the elite category of "leading cadres and specialists" were filled by employees who in 1928 had been workers "at the bench." Between 1930 and 1933, furthermore, over 500,000 workers who had joined the Communist party moved from manual to white-collar occupations, while the number of workers outside the party receiving a similar promotion was roughly the same. The total of those getting white-collar jobs during the First Five-Year Plan was in all probability at least 1,500,000. By 1933, 59 percent of the members of the Communist party who were white-collar employees had entered the organization originally as workers and 22 percent as peasants. Thus for 800,000 men and women membership had meant upward mobility into the administrative system.

Yet this attempt to proletarianize the political and economic elite proved only a temporary interruption in the process of bureaucratic rigidification. Stalin's purge during the 1930s had the effect of reducing the membership of the Communist party by almost 50 percent. A new expansion did begin late in the decade, so that by 1940 the size of the organization had almost regained the peak reached in 1933. But a significant social transformation had taken place. The preference shown earlier to members of the urban and rural proletariat had come to an end. Those now favored for admission to the bureaucratic patriciate belonged primarily to the new intelligentsia. They were administrators, engineers, technicians, and "leading workers."

The growing exclusiveness of the managerial elite can be measured by the rising level of formal training required of the administrative and technical personnel. Although, as late as 1934, 50 percent of the factory directors in the Soviet Union had received no more than an elementary education, by 1936 the percentage had dropped to 40. At the same time, the proportion of factory directors who had at least some higher education rose from 26 to 46 percent. By the end of the decade the "red directors" promoted after the revolution from factory directly to management had largely disappeared from the administrative system. A sharp decline occurred also in the number of "red specialists" who, after receiving accelerated training during the First Five-Year Plan, had risen to positions of responsibility in industry. Their place was taken mostly by young engineers recently graduated from the universities and technical institutes. This new generation, though lacking the practical experience of its proletarian predecessors, had obtained a much more thorough training, so that it soon came to dominate key industries in the Soviet economy. For example, by 1939, 86 to 87 percent of the factory directors in defense production and ferrous metallurgy had received a higher education. The technological bureaucracy had now become largely inaccessible to the ordinary worker.

The ossification of the employment pattern emerges clearly from a study of 765 émigrés between the ages of twenty-one and forty in 1940 who left the Soviet Union during or soon after the Second World War. A comparison of their source of livelihood with that of their fathers shows a close correlation between family background and occupational status. Among those who in 1940 were professionals and administrators, the highest job category, 65 percent of the fathers had been in the same category, although no more than 2 percent of the entire labor force was employed in those occupations. By contrast, workers and collective farmers, who accounted for 33 and 50 percent of the labor force respectively, constituted only 14 and 4 percent of the fathers of those holding professional and administrative jobs.

At the other end of the occupational scale, 55 percent of the fathers of those classified in 1940 as "ordinary workers" were themselves "ordinary workers," while 29 percent were peasants. Only 7 percent had held professional or administrative jobs. The statistics for those employed as collective farmers in 1940 were equally lopsided. Almost a third of their fathers, 32 percent, had been peasants, while only 4 percent had belonged to the professional and administrative category. Thus within two decades after the Bolshevik victory, social mobility in the Soviet Union had become narrowly restricted.[8]

The same diminishing access to the managerial elite can be seen in China. The available statistical data are too meager to trace all the fluctuations in the process of occupational stratification. But there can be little doubt that here too admission to the technocratic patriciate was becoming highly selective, not as much as in the Soviet Union, but enough to establish a disproportionate representation of the nonproletarian groups in society.

This conclusion is supported by a study conducted in 1966 of the social origin of 30 enterprise directors in Chinese industry. The great majority were of lower-class background; 40 percent came from worker families and 33 percent from poor peasant families. But 10 percent were children of "middle" peasants, 7 percent were children of managers, administrators, and technicians, another 7 percent were children of "capitalists," and 3 percent were children of landlords. More than a fourth of the enterprise directors thus belonged by social origin to the propertied classes under the *ancien régime.*

The overrepresentation of nonproletarian occupational groups in the Chinese managerial elite appears even more strikingly in another study, conducted at the same time, of the class origin of 65 key industrial administrators below the rank of enterprise director. This group included vice-directors, chief engineers, department heads, and workshop directors. Here the proportion of technological bureaucrats belonging by family background to the propertied classes was close to half. A substantial part, 47 percent, came from worker families, but only 9 percent from poor peasant families. On the other hand, 11 percent of the fathers were classified as "middle" peasants, 4 percent as rich peasants, 20 percent as managers, administrators, and technicians, 7 percent as "capitalists," and 2 percent as landlords. What the figures suggest is that in making appointments to the most prominent positions in industrial management, the government gave preference to candidates of lower-class origin, although even in this category nonproletarian groups were heavily overrepresented. But at the administrative level immediately below the top, the relative advantage of candidates from propertied families was much more pronounced. In China as in the Soviet Union, proletarian access to positions of authority in the economy had become narrowly limited.[9]

The fusion of the bureaucratic and technocratic elites to form a new privileged caste takes place usually within the framework of the party. Here department heads and factory directors, bureau chiefs and industrial planners mingle, interact, socialize, and coalesce. What draws the members of the managerial patriciate to Communism is partly a belief in its goals and ideals. By controlling the system of professional training, the radical dictatorship is able to influence and indoctrinate the technological intelligentsia. But that is not all. Before long the government also begins to offer substantial material rewards to the bureaucrats in industry and agriculture who join the party.

According to statistics covering the major trusts and syndicates in the Soviet Union, while in 1922 only about 15 percent of the managerial personnel were members, a year later the percentage had risen to nearly 50. Biographical data on the leading administrators of 88 big trusts, moreover, show that, at the beginning of 1924, 91 percent of the presidents of the boards of directors in industry belonged to the party, although the percentage for all board members was no more than 48. Figures published at the same time regarding 639 large factories reveal that 48 percent of the directors but only 34 percent of the vice-directors were members. In the 18 largest factories, those employing at least 5,000 workers, all the directors were members, whereas for vice-directors the proportion was 31 percent. At the other end of the scale, just 7 percent of the clerical staff in the 88 big trusts belonged to the party.

The pattern is clear. The higher the level of industrial management, the greater the rate of party membership. Generally, acceptance by the Communist organization was the precondition for an appointment to a top managerial post, although occasionally membership was not conferred until after a promotion to leadership in the economy. In either case, for those eager to get ahead, it was obviously important to join the party, whether out of ideological conviction or for personal advantage or both.

Especially after the purge of the 1930s, the influx of the new technological intelligentsia into the Communist organization became massive. Not only were the members of this group—the young engineers, managers, economists, and scientists—indebted to the new order for the higher education they had received, but they found rich opportunity for advancement in the bureaucratic apparatus. The managerial elite thus began to exert a growing influence in the higher councils of the party, gaining control over important positions in its leadership. The radical dictatorship in turn became increasingly dependent on the professional technocrats who, in return for their privileged status, supported its policies. This was the basis of the new social patriciate that had emerged in the Soviet Union by the time of the Second World War.

The expanding role of the managerial elite in the affairs of the party aroused considerable criticism among the rank and file. Particularly the older generation, those who had joined in the heady days of insurrectionary fervor, began to grumble about the spread of opportunism within the membership. But there could be no turning back from the policy of deproletarianization. The technocratic praetorians had by now become too important for the maintenance of the new order.

In 1939 A.A. Zhdanov, party secretary in Leningrad, denounced those who opposed the influence of the managerial intelligentsia. "Our best [skilled workers]," he complained at the eighteenth congress, "once they become foremen or directors, that is, have been promoted to executive posts because of their abilities and services, find themselves, when applying to join the Party, in the position of second-rate people. . . . Antiquated requirements are clung to by retrograde people who are not anxious for the advancement of new and young forces." The result was a petty, spiteful anti-intellectualism in the ranks. "The antiquated standards furnish a pretext for the cultivation of retrograde, essentially anti-Marxist, anti-Leninist tendencies with regard to the new, Soviet intelligentsia, with regard to foremost people of the working class and the peasantry; they furnish a pretext for the cultivation of an attitude of disdain towards advanced people who because of their education or services have been promoted to leading posts." This hostility toward the managerial elite would have to change, he insisted.

The sharpest condemnation of those resisting the influence of bureaucrats and technocrats within the organization came from Stalin himself in his report to the eighteenth congress on the work of the Central Committee. "In spite of the fact that the position of the Party on the question of the Soviet intelligentsia is perfectly clear," he charged, "there are still current in our Party views hostile to the Soviet intelligentsia and incompatible with the Party position. As you know, those who hold these false views practice a disdainful and contemptuous attitude to the Soviet intelligentsia and regard it as an alien force, even as a force hostile to the working class and the peasantry." How could economic progress be achieved in the face of such stubborn anti-intellectual prejudice?

Stalin then launched into a tirade against the dogmatists who could not see that technical expertise was essential for the success of the revolution:

> It is . . . all the more astonishing and strange that after all [the] funda-
> mental changes in the status of the intelligentsia people should be found
> within our Party who attempt to apply the old theory, which was di-
> rected against the bourgeois intelligentsia, to our new, Soviet intelligent-
> sia, which is basically a socialist intelligentsia. These people, it appears,
> assert that workers and peasants who until recently were working in [ex-
> emplary] fashion in the factories and collective farms and who were then
> sent to the universities to be educated, thereby ceased to be real people
> and became second-rate people. So we are to conclude that education is
> a pernicious and dangerous thing. (*Laughter.*) We want all our workers
> and peasants to be cultured and educated, and we shall achieve this in
> time. But in the opinion of these queer comrades, this purpose harbors a
> grave danger; for after the workers and peasants become cultured and
> educated, they may face the danger of being classified as second-rate
> people. (*Loud laughter.*) The possibility is not precluded that these queer
> comrades may in time sink to the position of extolling backwardness, ig-
> norance, benightedness, and obscurantism. It would be quite in the na-
> ture of things. Theoretical vagaries have never led, and never can lead, to
> any good.

The same revolutionary leaders who had once denounced the elite of the *ancien régime*, were now extolling the elite of the new order.[10]

The Stratification of Learning

Underlying the reemergence of a social patriciate is the growing im-
portance of higher education as a requirement for the exercise of power. After the fall of the *ancien régime*, the leaders of the radical dictatorship maintain that there will no longer be any need for a separate, institutionalized bureaucratic caste. They profess an almost mystical faith in the ability of the proletariat to perform spontane-

ously the basic managerial functions essential for its well-being. They assert that those who really believe in the new order can move directly from factories or farms to government offices or party bureaus and then back again, as circumstances may require, without weakening the administration of state and economy. Conversely, they see in the creation of a class of professional bureaucrats the danger of a new social elite rising in defiance of the egalitarianism that the revolution is sworn to uphold.

Sooner or later, however, the radical dictatorship is compelled to abandon this belief in the innate capacity of the masses for self-administration. At first, in the early days of the new order, the chief requirement for many important bureaucratic positions is simply faith in the revolution. But that leads only to confusion and chaos, especially in the economy. Industrial production drops, agricultural output declines, commerce languishes, finance stagnates. Hence the radical dictatorship is compelled to acquiesce in the creation of a new bureaucracy, loyal to the new order yet separated from the masses by its occupational status and sacerdotal ethos. The government of the revolution, in other words, like the government of the *ancien régime*, becomes dependent on a class of professional administrators whose chief qualification is technical competence rather than ideological commitment.

The radical dictatorship seeks reassurance in the reflection that the new bureaucracy will no doubt be different from the old; it will be democratic in outlook and proletarian in composition. Admittedly, in order to insure effective performance, higher education will have to remain a requirement for admission to the administrative system, but higher education will now be available to all classes of society. Under the *ancien régime*, so the argument runs, entrance requirements for colleges and universities were designed to favor the rich and powerful. Children of lower-class families were deliberately excluded, partly by the social bigotry of academic administrators, but even more by the high cost of residence and tuition. That will change. Higher education will become open to every qualified student, regardless of class origin or social background. The only requirement for admission will be talent, achievement, and intellectual promise. Thus the new bureaucracy, unlike the old, will not constitute a privileged caste, it will not look down on the proletarian masses. It will instead promote the interests of ordinary working men and women.

Here is the basic miscalculation of the new order. It assumes that free competition for admission to higher education will lead to a proportionate representation within the intelligentsia of the various classes of society. But, in fact, equality in access to learning leads directly to inequality in access to power. Those who come from families with a tradition of academic learning, and that means primarily the well-to-do, have an insuperable advantage in intellectual achievement over those whose families had to devote all their energies to earning their daily bread. How can the child of a worker be expected to contend on even terms with the child of a physician, or the child of an agricultural laborer with the child of a civil servant? A system of higher education in which admission depends on academic performance inevitably favors the affluent and educated groups in the community. This effect of free competition in the world of learning can be avoided only by a policy of deliberate preference for students of proletarian origin. But since technical proficiency becomes increasingly important in the administrative apparatus of state and economy, intellectual promise rather than class background eventually emerges as the chief criterion for access to organized learning.

To illustrate, during the early years of the new order in Russia, the government encouraged the large-scale admission of workers and peasants into the Communist party regardless of their education. What mattered was revolutionary commitment and proletarian origin, not academic achievement. As the radical dictatorship became established and institutionalized, however, formal school training assumed progressively greater significance. In 1922 only 0.6 percent of the membership had received a higher education and only 6.3 percent a secondary education. By 1927 a modest but noticeable shift toward more schooling had taken place. Now the percentages were 0.8 and 7.9 respectively. And by 1939 the proportion of members with academic credentials had nearly tripled; 5.1 percent had received a higher education and 14.2 a secondary education. The longer the new order remained in power, the greater became its need for educated, professional bureaucrats.

The regime sought initially to achieve greater administrative efficiency without sacrificing the policy of academic proletarianization. Determined efforts were made throughout the 1920s to increase the proportion of lower-class students in colleges and universities. The most important was the establishment of *rabfaks*, preparatory schools attached to institutions of higher learning, which were designed to provide workers quickly with the equivalent of a secondary education so that they could then continue their training at a more advanced level. In 1925, for example, 8,000 of the 18,000 places available in the universities for entering students were set aside for *rabfak* graduates. Of the rest, almost 50 percent went to party, trade-union, and Communist youth organizations, another 10 percent to members of the working-class intelligentsia, and only 25 percent to the best secondary-school graduates. By 1928, 176 *rabfaks* with about 37,000 students were providing close to a third of all the entering students in institutions of advanced learning.

These efforts were reflected in the growing representation of the lower classes in the system of higher education. The proportion of members of worker families in the student body of schools offering university training rose from 17.8 percent in 1924–25 to 24.2 in 1926–27, 25.4 in 1927–28, 30.3 in 1928–29, 35.2 in 1929–30, 46.4 in 1930–31, and a high of 58.0 in 1931–32. The proportion of students from peasant families peaked a few years earlier, climbing from 23.1 percent in 1924–25 to 23.3 in 1926–27, and 23.9 in 1927–28. By contrast, the proportion of students from families in the nonmanual occupations diminished from 59.1 percent in 1924–25 to 52.5 in 1926–27, 50.7 in 1927–28, 47.3 in 1928–29, 43.9 in 1929–30, 34.3 in 1930–31, and 27.9, its lowest level, in 1931–32. The new order was seemingly determined to achieve a proportionate representation of the lower classes in higher education, whatever the cost.

The heaviest influx of students of plebian background came during the First Five-Year Plan, when secondary-school graduates from middle-class families found it extremely difficult to obtain a university education. Ignoring the grumblings of bourgeois professors and the lamentations of white-collar parents, the authorities admitted about 150,000 young workers and members of the Communist party to institutions of higher learning. Most of them chose to attend schools of engineering, since technical expertise rather than mastery of the humanities or the social sciences was becoming the chief qual-

ification for advancement in an industrializing society. An entire co-
hort of future Soviet leaders—including Nikita Khrushchev, Aleksei
Kosygin, and Leonid Brezhnev—received their higher education
during these years, many of them working as engineers before moving into the bureaucratic or managerial elite. They were intended to
constitute the nucleus of what would become a new proletarian
intelligentsia.[11]

After the First Five-Year Plan, however, the government discon-
tinued the hothouse cultivation of lower-class entry into higher education. It had proved costly, cumbersome, and, worst of all,
inefficient. In 1931, therefore, came the abandonment of the policy,
introduced seven years earlier, of including a large "core of workers,"
at first as much as 65 percent and later as much as 70 percent of the
total, among applicants admitted to the universities and schools of
technology. The campaign to proletarianize academic learning
ended at about the same time as the campaign to proletarianize the
administrative apparatus and the managerial system, and essentially
for the same reason. The regime was determined to achieve greater
technical proficiency even at the cost of social ossification.

The results could be seen in the statistics on the class composition
of the student body. The proportion of members of worker families,
which had reached 58.0 percent in 1931–32, started to drop steadily
to 50.3 percent in 1932–33, 47.9 in 1933–34, 45.0 in 1934–35, and 33.9
in 1937–38, less than it had been at the end of the 1920s. The percentage of students from peasant families began to decline even earlier.
After peaking at 23.9 in 1927–28, it dropped to 22.4 in 1928–29, 20.9 in
1929–30, 19.3 in 1930–31, and 14.1 in 1931–32, before rising to 16.9 in
1932–33, dropping to 14.6 in 1933–34, and then rising again to 16.2 in
1934–35 and 21.6 in 1937–38, still below the figure reached thirteen
years earlier. Conversely, the proportion of students from families in
nonmanual occupations, after touching bottom in 1931–32 with 27.9
percent, started to climb rapidly to 32.8 in 1932–33, 37.5 in 1933–34,
38.8 in 1934, and 44.5 in 1937–38, close to where it had been before
the First Five-Year Plan. By the end of the decade the professional
and white-collar groups, constituting less than one-fifth of the population, accounted for more than two-fifths of the student body in
higher education in the Soviet Union.[12]

The government sought to disguise this growing social stratification of academic learning. After 1938 it stopped publishing statistics on the class background of students. The figures had become something of an ideological embarrassment. The authorities continued to insist, nevertheless, that the new order was succeeding in proletarianizing knowledge. Stalin boasted in 1936 that "hundreds of thousands of young people [from the lower classes] entered the universities and technical colleges, from which they emerged to reinforce the attenuated ranks of the intelligentsia. They infused fresh blood into it and reanimated it in a new Soviet spirit." The structure of higher education had become democratized, he maintained, since "80 to 90 percent of the Soviet intelligentsia are people who have come from the working class, from the peasantry, or from other strata of the working population." How could anyone then complain about academic exclusivity or rigidification?

Yet in fact the proportion of students from worker and peasant families had never reached 80 to 90 percent. The highest figure, recorded in 1931–32, was 72.1 percent, and within two years after Stalin's remarks about the proletarianization of the intelligentsia, the percentage had dropped to 55.5 The social base of academic learning had become progressively narrower, resting more and more on the groups in society employed in nonmanual occupations. Even the university graduates from a proletarian background gradually ceased to identify with the masses from which they had ascended, combining instead with the white-collar intelligentsia to form a privileged academic elite. Higher education came to be largely dominated by an exclusive, self-contained, and self-perpetuating patriciate.

This conclusion is reinforced by a study of 880 émigrés born between 1905 and 1919 who left the Soviet Union around the period of the Second World War. A comparison of the level of education they had attained with the source of livelihood of their fathers reveals a close correlation between social origin and access to learning. No less than 43 percent of the college graduates had fathers in professional or administrative jobs, while another 29 percent had fathers in semiprofessional or white-collar jobs. Only 6 percent were children of ordinary workers and 5 percent of peasants. By contrast, in the group which had received no more than four years of schooling, only 5 percent of the fathers were in professional or administrative occupations and only 4 percent in semiprofessional or white-collar occupations, whereas 30 percent were ordinary workers and 58 percent peasants.

Clearly, the process of academic stratification was not the result of a deliberate policy. On the contrary, the authorities had diligently sought to democratize and proletarianize higher education through the preferential treatment of applicants from the lower classes. In the end, however, their efforts failed because it proved impossible to divorce the exercise of power from economic advantage, social ascendance, and educational superiority. Indeed, the ossification of the social structure of learning began almost as soon as the Bolsheviks emerged victorious in the civil war. By the spring of 1927 an obscure peasant delegate at a meeting in Moscow was complaining about the growing exclusivity of organized knowledge. "[The universities] used to be inaccessible to the poor, and now it is no different," he charged. "The son of a party man or someone with an official position can get into [an institution of higher learning], but if I don't have money or an official position, then my children will stay uneducated. And I have no money to pay. It's unjust." This open declaration of what everyone knew but no one acknowledged was irrefutable.[13]

The situation in China closely resembled that in the Soviet Union. The establishment of the People's Republic had been accompanied by solemn pledges to make learning accessible to the masses. There were slogans about "opening the doors of schools for peasants and workers," and about the "intellectualization of the proletariat" and "proletarianization of the intellectuals." Yet in practice the achievement of a representation of the lower classes in higher education commensurate with their numbers proved difficult. The percentage of students from worker and peasant families in the total enrollment of colleges and universities climbed laboriously from 19 in 1951–52 to 29 in 1955–56, 48 in 1958–59, and 67 in 1962–63. It soon became apparent that the proletarianization of academic life would take considerably longer than had been expected in the early days of the Communist victory.

Mao himself was forced to concede early in 1957 that progress toward a greater accessibility of learning was not as rapid as he had hoped. "According to a survey made in Peking," he admitted, "most college students are children of landlords, rich peasants, the bourgeoisie, and well-to-do middle peasants, while students from working-class and poor and lower-middle peasant families account for less than 20 percent. Probably this is roughly the case too in the rest of the country. This situation should change, but it will take time." The early assumption that free competition would provide equal opportunity in higher education was proving unfounded.

In order to increase lower-class participation in academic learning, the Chinese authorities were forced to adopt the same tactics that the Soviet authorities had employed a generation earlier. They began to give preferential treatment to students from worker and peasant families. Those who displayed a high degree of political commitment to the new order, moreover, could be exempted from taking the entrance examinations. For other categories of applicants even the requirement of a high-school diploma was frequently waived; for example, for active party cadres under thirty who had two years of secondary education, for demobilized soldiers, and for government workers who had engaged in revolutionary activity for at least three years under the Kuomintang. Special consideration was also given to the children of martyrs of the revolution, to the members of ethnic minorities, and to overseas Chinese. Of the 65,893 students entering college in 1952, almost half came from these special categories, the party cadres alone accounting for about 8,000.

To accelerate the proletarianization of learning, moreover, thousands of skilled workers were promoted directly to engineers and technicians, while thousands of peasants became farm experts holding positions in research institutes and agricultural colleges. By 1960 some 45,000 plebeian scientists by fiat had joined the Shanghai Scientific and Technical Association, constituting about half of the entire membership. They were extolled by the authorities as a new class of proletarian intellectuals who, unlike disaffected bourgeois scholars, would continue to engage in productive labor, would not treat their research as private property, and would never doubt that China could "leap forward with flying speed."[14]

Despite these efforts, students from professional and white-collar families continued to attend institutions of higher learning in disproportionately large numbers. Wherever admission to a college or university depended on performance on an entrance examination, the results invariably favored the sons and daughters of the upper strata of society: the old educated bourgeoisie, high party and governmental officials, intellectuals, managers, and technicians. They were also the ones who predominated in the system of secondary education that prepared students for professional training. A survey conducted in the middle 1970s among émigrés from Canton found that pupils from worker and peasant families were proportionately most numerous in the poorer junior middle schools, those with the lowest rate of subsequent admissions to a university. Many of them had been recently established in lower-class neighborhoods where no schools had previously existed. Here 42 percent of the pupils were children of workers or peasants, 20 percent were children of intellectuals, and no more than 8 percent were children of "revolutionary cadres."

In the best junior middle schools, on the other hand, those with the highest rate of admissions to more advanced education, only 11 percent of the pupils came from worker or peasant families, 32 percent from families of intellectuals, and 48 percent from families of "revolutionary cadres." In the best senior secondary schools, with the largest proportion of admissions to a college or university, where openings were fewest, standards highest, and applicants strongest, the distribution of social backgrounds was somewhat different, although the disparity between pupils from proletarian and nonproletarian families remained just as wide. Children of workers and peasants constituted 12 percent of the enrollment, while children of intellectuals accounted for 34 percent, children of "revolutionary cadres" for 27 percent, and children of lower middle-class families for 16 percent. The system of education in China thus remained largely segregated by occupation and status.

The suppressed resentment of a lower-class student against the intellectual elite that had come to dominate academic life exploded in a mimeographed leaflet which Ch'i Hsiang-tung, a young militant in the middle school attached to Tsinghua University in Peking, composed in the summer of 1966:

> For seventeen years our school has been ruled by the bourgeois class. We shall not tolerate this any longer! We shall overthrow it, seize power, or-

ganize the revolution of the class troops, forward the class-line, according to social status! In this great cultural revolution the children of workers, peasants, revolutionary [soldiers and martyrs], and of cadres are active, daring, astute, [and] determined in struggle, while the majority of those with evil family origin are bad eggs. On whom could one rely if not on the children of workers, peasants, revolutionary [soldiers and martyrs], and of cadres? Should one rely on the landlord and bourgeois class young gentlemen and young lady bastards? Should they ride the wind, when leftists are in an overwhelming majority? No! The leading power must be in the hands of the children of workers, peasants, revolutionary [soldiers and martyrs], and of cadres. . . . Landlord and bourgeois class young gentlemen and ladies, . . . you thought you could make use of the temporarily existing bourgeois education to climb higher up the ladder to become white experts, get into the university, join up with "professors, experts." Your heart was set on a small car, a little modern house, a white coat, a laboratory, . . . on enjoying comfort, affluence, a good reputation, a good salary. You thought that even if you were not as well off as before, you could be at ease and you would not be obliged to go to a village to suffer. And perhaps you could even build up a little political capital and get a little power. Then would come [a] "peaceful transformation," and you would be up again and honor your glorious forefathers. . . . [But] workers and peasants and the children of workers, peasants, revolutionary [soldiers and martyrs], and of cadres, whom you despised, will fill the posts in culture, science, and technique; your monopolies are broken. A new period is beginning in which workers, peasants, and soldiers take the doctrine into their [own] hands.

It was a cry of rage by a believer in the revolution who had discovered that an intellectual elite founded in the name of social equality can be as rigid and restrictive as one designed to perpetuate class domination.[15]

The Rise of a Revolutionary Aristocracy

Clearly, within a generation after the overthrow of the *ancien régime*, a new oligarchy becomes established under the radical dictatorship.

It differs from the old in that admission depends initially on talent and ambition rather than superior social status. Hence it is more flexible, more diverse and democratic, in its class composition, at least at first. Yet this oligarchy recruits from the outset a disproportionate share of its members from the professional, white-collar, and educated strata of society. The tendency toward deproletarianization becomes progressively more pronounced, as the new order begins to require a higher degree of training, expertise, and efficiency among those admitted to the exercise of power. Even the bureaucrats and managers who come from worker or peasant families gradually grow alienated from the masses whose interests they are in theory supposed to represent. They become more and more like the bureaucrats and managers from professional or white-collar families, adopting their style, manner, and outlook. In the end, those occupying leading positions in politics and economics come to form a distinct social elite separated from the plebeian classes by easier access to governmental authority and greater availability of material affluence. They even begin to assume the characteristics of a hereditary privileged caste, as the children of members acquire an increasing advantage in admission to the ruling patriciate over the children of nonmembers.

The new oligarchy remains outwardly different from the old in important respects. It is less ostentatious in displaying its superiority. It is more moderate in speech, more circumspect in conduct, not as haughty in dealing with subordinates and suppliants. It continues to pay lip service, moreover, to the egalitarian pieties of the radical ideology. But these differences pertain more to style and rhetoric than substance. At bottom the revolutionary aristocracy is as rigid and exclusive as the aristocracy of any other system of authority.

This progressive ossification of the social structure does not go unnoticed. Almost from the beginning those who continue to cling to the original ideals of the radical movement warn that the reemergence of a bureaucratic elite is incompatible with the creation of a classless society. Late in 1918 a Menshevik delegate at a conference dealing with the national economy of Russia charged that the administrative system of the new order was becoming as oppressive as that of the czarist regime. "There is no proletariat, there remains only the dictatorship, not of the proletariat, but of a vast bureaucratic machine holding in its grip dead factories and workshops," he maintained. "Thus we are creating a new bourgeoisie which will have no prejudices of culture and education, and will be like the old bourgeoisie only in its oppression of the working class. You are creating a bourgeoisie which knows no limits to persecution and exploitation."

By the beginning of 1923 it was no longer safe to say things like that openly in the Soviet Union. But a small underground group of leftist dissidents, the "Workers' Truth," published a manifesto addressed to "the revolutionary proletariat and all revolutionary elements that remain faithful to the struggling working class." It expressed bitter criticism of the social consequences of the New Economic Policy. "The working class ekes out a wretched existence, while the new bourgeoisie (responsible party workers, directors of factories, managers of trusts, presidents of executive committees, etc.) and [the profiteers] live in luxury and revive in our memory the picture of the life of the bourgeoisie of all ages." Was that what the proletariat had fought and died for during the revolution? "The soviet, party, and trade-union bureaucracy and the organizers of state capitalism live in material conditions sharply differentiated from the conditions of existence of the working class; their very material prosperity and the stability of their general position depend on the degree of exploitation, and of the submission to them, of the toiling masses. All this makes inevitable a contradiction of interests and a rift between the Communist Party and the working class." The only way to achieve the original egalitarian goals of the Bolsheviks was to return to the stern, puritan virtues of the struggle against czarist oppression.

More than forty years later, during the Cultural Revolution in China, which was largely a reaction against the growing rigidification of the social structure, an obscure member of the Red Guards circulated a similar statement calling for the revival of the radical ideals which had inspired the Communists in their conflict with the Kuomintang:

> Landlord and bourgeois class old and young gentlemen: In your eyes we [are] nothing particular. Your ancestors held that workers and peasants are born idiots. Yes, we are simple-minded, a) we do not know how

to be opportunist, how to be ambitious; b) we do not know how to flatter, to show off, to look only at externals; c) we are unable to accept your education, to read dead books. . . . To sum up, we are not interested in making a name for the individual and we continually repeat "revolution, communism," [which are] things that you people cannot grasp.

Are we really "silly idiots, nothing particular"? Old and young gentlemen, we tell you frankly, you all stink and you are nothing particular, just rotten trash. It is no wonder that we should want to oppress you! We detest you from our hearts! We hate you! . . . Old and young gentlemen, formerly you were in a privileged position, sat on our heads, and let your excrement fall on us to show that you were superior. Today . . . our parents want to be officials of the revolution, to dictate to counterrevolutionaries, and we want to follow the footsteps of our revolutionary fathers, follow Chairman Mao, and overthrow you, oppose you to the end!

A deep hostility toward social elitism resounds in the rhetoric of those who believe that by some bold act of defiance or sacrifice they can still protect the revolution against its protectors.[16]

Yet neither denunciations nor exhortations, neither purges nor recruitments can prevail in the long run against the advance of social stratification. The reemergence under the new order of substantial differences in income, education, status, and power reflects a profound human need. At first, in the early heroic days of the revolution, the hunger for personal recognition and distinction can be kept in check. For a brief period of time abstract principles and ideals appear capable of directing individual behavior. But the appetites of the ego, like those of the libido, cannot be permanently suppressed. Sooner or later the radical dictatorship finds itself forced to yield to private desires and yearnings. It has to start offering rewards, advantages, perquisites, and gratifications to those who serve its needs and defend its interests. The result is a widening gulf between the more and the less talented, ambitious, and opportunistic. The rise of oligarchical authority gradually becomes inexorable. In the end a new elite emerges in revolutionary society that in form, function, and ethos resembles the old.

CHAPTER 10

The Graying
of the Revolution

Within a few years after the downfall of the *ancien régime*, the cherished doctrines of the new order begin to lose their inspirational power. Once the enthusiasm aroused by the overthrow of established authority has cooled, the revolutionaries discover that building a better social system is far more complex than they imagined. For one thing, they had assumed that their success in defeating the old order would encourage sympathetic uprisings in other parts of the world, culminating in the destruction of capitalism and the establishment of a classless society. The revolution, in other words, was to be global in scope. The Bolsheviks believed that their cause would be aided by proletarian insurrections throughout Europe. The Communists in China felt confident that their example would be followed by the oppressed masses of Asia. The collapse of the Batista dictatorship in Cuba was heralded as the initial triumph of a revolutionary movement about to sweep across Latin America. Every radical dictatorship assumes at first that it is the vanguard of an insurrectionary army that will conquer the earth.

The revolution, moreover, would become progressively more popular and democratic. To be sure, the war against the old order might have to be waged at first by an organized, determined minority. The masses, brutalized and stupefied by centuries of oppression, would have to be led or perhaps driven into the struggle for their emancipation. There was no other way. In the fall of 1918 Karl Radek, one of the leading Bolshevik publicists, emphasized the need for a radical dictatorship as a temporary means of liberating the proletariat:

In no country can the revolution begin as an action of the majority. . . . Capitalism implies not merely a physical mastership over the means of production, but also a spiritual dominion over the masses of the people, and in the most developed capitalist countries, under the stress of misery and dire need, under the burden of [the] consequences of capitalism . . . , the whole body of the oppressed arises. [Yet] the most active are always the first to rise; it is a minority which carries out the revolution, the success of which depends on . . . whether this revolution corresponds with the historical development, with the interests of the masses of the people, who can shake off the rule of the class hitherto governing them. But first the creative and impulsive force of the revolution is required to rouse the great body of the people, to liberate them from their intellectual and spiritual slavishness under capitalism, and to lead them into a position where a defense of their interests can be made. It might fairly be said that every revolution is undertaken by the minority, that the majority only joins in during the course of the revolution and decides the victorious issue.[1]

But once the masses had been liberated "from their intellectual and spiritual slavishness under capitalism," the historic role of the minority would come to an end. The proletarian dictatorship would become transformed into a popular democracy with a higher degree of political and economic freedom than could be provided by bourgeois constitutionalism. For the so-called civic rights established under the more enlightened forms of capitalistic rule are of little value to the common man. What good is legal equality in the face of material inequality? What good is access to the ballot without access to wealth, education, and power? Only the revolution, by collectivizing the means of production and distribution, can insure liberty for all, The emancipation of the lower classes may require an initial period of dictatorial authority. Yet after the new order is secure, a true people's democracy will replace the sham capitalistic democracy. The temporary rule of a radical minority will then give way to a government resting on the will of the majority. Although the revolution may initially be forced to exercise repression against its adversaries, that is only a means of attaining liberty. Coercion is in reality the instrument of freedom.

Most important, the new order will put an end to economic privation and disparity. Under capitalism calculations of profit rather than welfare determine production. Hence the volume of output is deliberately restricted and manipulated to serve the interests of the propertied classes. The functioning of the economy is based not on the needs of the masses but on the dictates of the international market. To make matters worse, inequality in the distribution of wealth perpetuates inequality in the standard of living. While the few lead an existence of profligate abundance, the many toil, hunger, and suffer. Behind the mask of democracy that the *ancien régime* occasionally assumes lies a merciless economic tyranny.

The revolution will put an end to that. The expropriators will be expropriated; the malefactors will be punished; the oppressors will be crushed. Production will cease to be determined by a roll of the dice in the financial marketplace; it will become responsive to the needs of the people. The volume of output will no longer be restricted in order to maintain prices and profits. The general welfare will become recognized as the sole determinant of economic policy. Even more important, the distribution of goods will cease reflecting the inequality in wealth, power, and influence. It will be decided instead by the principles of social justice, by the doctrines of popular democracy. "From each according to his abilities, to each according to his needs," Marx urged in the *Critique of the Gotha Program.* The vision of a society capable of providing material comfort and economic equity for all inspires the revolutionary movement. In the euphoria produced by the fall of the *ancien régime,* its realization seems within easy reach.

The Demythologization
of the New Order

Yet once the revolution has to start grappling with the hard realities of political power, what had once seemed so easy becomes increasingly complex and confusing. One after another the doctrinal myths of the radical ideology start to lose their persuasiveness. The radical dictatorship is forced to compromise, to dissemble, to retreat. For one thing, international capitalism proves far more resilient and vigorous than had been anticipated. It may at first become confused or frightened by the early successes of the revolutionary movement. But it soon regains its confidence; it begins to rally its forces; it organizes a military and economic counteroffensive. Within a few years the enthusiasm for the new order among the lower classes of neighboring nations has cooled; the hope for sympathetic uprisings in nearby capitalistic countries has faded. The revolution now stands beleaguered and isolated.

The victory of the Bolsheviks in Russia, for example, was followed by the establishment of short-lived radical governments in Finland, Hungary, and Bavaria. But the proletariat of Western Europe failed to follow Lenin's summons to revolution, and the handful of Communist regimes among the secondary states in the east collapsed within a few months. Castro's triumph in Cuba encouraged left-wing guerrilla movements in other parts of Latin America, in Venezuela, Bolivia, and Uruguay. Nowhere were the revolutionaries able to gain power, however. Although the victorious struggle of the Communists in Vietnam led to the rise of radical dictatorships in Cambodia and Laos, elsewhere in Southeast Asia there seemed little inclination to follow their example. Thus soon after the overthrow of the *ancien régime*, it becomes apparent that for the time being the new order will have to survive on its own.

That is when the revolution begins to retreat from the universality of the insurrectionary conflict, from the belief that the defeat of the capitalistic system in one part of the world is bound to lead to its defeat in other parts. Instead, every radical dictatorship is forced, sooner or later, explicitly or implicitly, to adopt the policy of "socialism in one country."

In Russia the abandonment of the doctrine of globalism in the struggle for proletarian emancipation was led by Stalin. Within a few months after Lenin's death, he began to argue that the new order would have to adapt its political strategy to the long-term coexistence of Communism and capitalism. "Formerly, the victory of the revolution in one country was considered impossible," he wrote in the spring of 1924 in his *Foundations of Leninism*, "on the assumption that it would require the combined action of the proletarians of all or at least of a majority of the advanced countries to achieve victory over the bourgeoisie." But this point of view no longer accorded with the facts. "Now we must proceed from the possibility of such a victory, for the uneven and spasmodic character of the development of the various capitalist countries under the conditions of imperialism, the development within imperialism of catastrophic contradictions leading to inevitable wars, the growth of the revolutionary movement in all countries of the world—all this leads not only to the possibility, but also to the necessity of the victory of the proletariat in individual countries."

Seven months later, in December 1924, Stalin restated his position even more forcefully. Writing about *The October Revolution and the Tactics of the Russian Communists,* he insisted that "the universal theory of a simultaneous victory of the revolution in the principal countries of Europe, the theory that the victory of socialism in one country is impossible, has proved to be an artificial and untenable theory." The recent history of Russia had demonstrated that. "This theory is unacceptable not only as a scheme of development of the world revolution, for it contradicts obvious facts. It is still less acceptable as a slogan, for it fetters, rather than releases, the initiative of individual countries which, by reason of certain historical conditions, obtain the opportunity to break through the front of capital independently." The concept of "permanent revolution" would only deter a direct assault against class oppression in a single capitalistic state, no matter how favorable the circumstances. "For it . . . encourages passive waiting for the moment of the 'universal denouement'; for it cultivates among the proletarians of the different countries not the spirit of revolutionary determination, but the mood of Hamlet-like doubt over the question as to 'what if the others fail to back us up?'"

Stalin denied that the shift of emphasis to the consolidation of the new order in the Soviet Union would mean a renunciation of global revolution. Not at all. The victory of Communism in any state was bound to encourage Communism in every state. The emancipation of the Russian proletariat would hearten the world proletariat. The goal of the Bolsheviks would not change, only the means of attaining that goal. Socialism in one country would promote socialism in all countries.

"After consolidating its power and leading the peasantry in its wake," he expounded, "the proletariat of the victorious country can and must build a socialist society. But does this mean that it will thereby achieve the complete and final victory of socialism, i.e., does it mean that with the forces of only one country it can finally consolidate socialism and fully guarantee that country against intervention and, consequently, also against restoration? No, it does not." To achieve that, a victory of the revolution in at least several countries would be needed. "Therefore, the development and support of revolution in other countries is an essential task of the victorious revolution. Therefore, the revolution which has been victorious in one country must regard itself not as a self-sufficient entity, but as an aid, as a means for hastening the victory of the proletariat in other countries." There would be no abandonment of the international struggle. On the contrary, the victory of the revolution in Russia would be "the beginning of and the precondition for the world revolution."

Nevertheless, it was becoming clear that the overthrow of the capitalistic system as a whole was no longer an immediate prospect. The Bolsheviks had underestimated its resourcefulness and tenacity. Stalin conceded as much in his address to the Moscow branch of the Communist party in May 1925. "The new feature that has revealed itself lately, and which has laid its impress upon the international situation, is that the revolution in Europe has begun to ebb, that a certain lull has set in, which we call the temporary stabilization of capitalism, *while* at the same time the economic development and political might of the Soviet Union are increasing."

Yet, according to Stalin, this by no means signified "the beginning of the end of the world revolution, the start of the liquidation of the world proletarian revolution." After all, Lenin himself had declared that after the victory of the working class in Russia a new epoch of world revolution would begin, "an epoch replete with conflicts and wars, advances and retreats, victories and defeats, an epoch leading to the victory of the proletariat in the major capitalist countries." Here was the key to understanding the temporary standstill between capitalism and communism. "The epoch of world revolution is a new stage of the revolution, a whole strategic period, perhaps even a number of decades. During this period there can and must be ebbs and flows of the revolution." But the final outcome could never be in doubt.

Still, even Stalin had to admit that the rejection of the concept of "permanent revolution" was bound to have a serious effect on the morale of the new order. As the prospect for ultimate victory receded into the future, its followers were likely to start succumbing to fears and misgivings, to discouragement and defeatism. In June 1925 he dealt with this problem in his reply to a question which had been submitted to him: "What dangers are there of our Party degenerating as a result of the stabilization of capitalism, if this stabilization lasts a long time?" He made no effort to disguise the gravity of the situation. "Such dangers, as possible and even real dangers, undoubtedly exist. They face us quite apart from stabilization. Stabilization merely makes them more palpable." They included "a) the danger of losing the socialist perspective in our work of building up our country, and the danger of liquidationism connected with it; b) the danger of losing the international revolutionary perspective, and the danger of nationalism connected with it; c) the danger of a decline of party leadership and the possibility connected with it of the Party's conversion into an appendage of the state apparatus."

For Stalin it was evident that these dangers could be overcome. All that was needed was determination, firmness, courage, and faith. But among many believers in the new order, the growing isolation and rigidification of the revolution, its transformation from a worldwide insurrectionary movement into a solitary fortress under siege, engenders a feeling of apprehension and foreboding. Their faith in "permanent revolution" is eroded by the reality of permanent stalemate, of a long war of attrition in whose course the differences between the combatants slowly diminish. The demythologization of the radical dictatorship thus begins with the discovery that idealism, dedication, courage, and sacrifice are not enough to create a better world. The final victory of the new order keeps receding. How much more hunger and privation will it require, how much more suffering and bloodshed? Perhaps the New Jerusalem will always remain beyond the reach of weak, imperfect man. Perhaps the deliverance of humanity will prove too difficult and elusive; perhaps it will never be attained. The belief in the imminent redemption of society begins to give way to doubts and fears.[2]

More serious is the perception that the new popular democracy that the revolution has promised is only a theoretical ideal whose realization lies in the distant future. For after the defeat of the *ancien régime,* the new order continues to rely on the same methods of intimidation and repression that the old order had employed. Police agents go on arresting dissidents; political prisons remain full of subversives; firing squads are busy executing saboteurs and traitors. Indeed, with the passage of time the system of repression becomes better organized and more efficient. The ends that it serves may be different, but the means that it applies are the same as those of traditional forms of authority.

Worse still, the instrumentalities of political coercion are increasingly directed against friends and allies of the revolution. At first the radical dictatorship seeks to eliminate only those who had been prominent supporters of the *ancien régime:* cabinet ministers, leading bureaucrats, police officials, landowners, bankers, industrialists, and merchants. But that is only the beginning. Soon it turns against political groups that had also opposed the old order, but for different reasons and for different objectives. Liberals, democrats, socialists, and anarchists discover that to those in power they are no better than the conservatives, monarchists, clericalists, and jingoists against whom they had once fought. Finally, the repressive apparatus begins to check on the members of the ruling minority itself, to weed out those who may be weakening in their loyalty, who seem to be succumbing to doubt or dissent. In the end everyone, however devoted to the revolutionary cause, learns to be on guard, to dissemble, pretend, conceal, and distrust. The belief that the radical dictatorship is simply a temporary means of achieving democracy yields to a pervasive attitude of political wariness and conformity.

But most disillusioning is the inability of the new order to live up to the promise of material welfare and equality for the masses. In the beginning its fulfillment seems imminent. The economy has ceased to be controlled by the rapacity of the propertied classes. The people will now be able to apply their productive energies to the satisfaction of their needs. Will this not inevitably lead to an increase in output? Will not the workers and peasants, knowing that they can at last enjoy the fruits of their labor, redouble their efforts? The wealth that had once been monopolized by the exploiters will hereafter go to those who have produced it. And the result will be a new economy of mass consumption and mass affluence. It all seems so logical, so obvious. Nothing inspires the supporters of the revolution more than the vision of an equitable social system capable of providing security for all.

The economic achievements of the new order prove disappointing, however. This is not to deny that the standard of living of the masses rises after the revolution, especially for those at the bottom of the social scale, those least skilled and most exploited. Yet progress remains slow and laborious. At first the position of the lower classes improves substantially as a result of the expropriation of the well-to-do, through the partition of large estates, for example, or the conversion of wealthy mansions into housing for the poor. But then comes a slowdown; further advances become laborious and intermittent. Apologists for the new order point out, not without some justice, that workers and peasants are better off than they had been a decade or two earlier under the *ancien régime*. Still, the actual accomplishments of the revolution are overwhelmed by the tide of rising expectations released by the establishment of the new order. The gap between what had been anticipated and what is accomplished remains vast.

In China, for instance, the real wages of workers rose immediately after the revolution by an impressive 21.2 percent annually between 1949–50 and 1952. During the next five years, from 1952 to 1957, there was a smaller but still substantial growth of 6 percent annually. But during the next period from 1957 to 1963, the increase turned into a decline averaging 2.1 percent annually. And finally, in the period from 1963 to 1972 real wages began to rise again, but at a much slower pace, no more than 1.9 percent annually. Indeed, for the entire two decades from 1952 to 1972 the average yearly growth of real wages was a disappointing 1.9 percent.

Despite the scarcity and unreliability of economic statistics on Cuba, the situation there appears quite similar to China's. Right after the revolution consumption increased at the expense of investment, but this benign policy of the new order was soon reversed and, by the middle 1960s, living conditions worsened drastically as the consequence of a decline in production and rise in investment. According to data published by the Cuban Central Planning Board, the gross national product in 1967, measured in constant prices, was 2 percent below 1962, a year of recession, and 14 percent below 1965, a year of relative prosperity. The growth of per capita gross national product, measured in current prices, was equally disappointing. After averaging about 2 percent in 1950–58, under the Batista dictatorship, it rose modestly in 1959–60, immediately after the revolution, stayed about the same in 1961, declined sharply by at least 10 percent in 1962, touched bottom in 1963, rose by roughly 6 percent in 1964, remained stable in 1965, and then dropped once more, this time by 6 percent, in 1966. Measured in constant prices, per capita gross national product increased annually by 1 percent in 1950–58 and decreased annually by 0.5 percent in 1962–66. The figures paint the picture of a stumbling, stagnating economy.[3]

The material achievements of the new order are as a rule sufficient to prevent out-and-out destitution. Indeed, such manifestations of mass privation as pauperism, homelessness, and petty crime generally diminish after the revolution. And yet the establishment of the radical dictatorship is occasionally followed by a severe shortage of the bare necessities of life. In 1988, for example, more than a decade after the victory of the revolution in Vietnam, the government acknowledged that serious malnutrition threatened the nation because of a drop in food production and a rise in birth rate. Emergency food aid from the United States would be welcome. "We are not yet starving," announced Vu Khoan, an assistant minister in the foreign office, "but food at the moment is the most acute problem we face." He drew a bleak picture of the economic situation. Agriculture was producing only about 620 pounds of food per capita annually, a drop from 748 pounds in 1985, partly because population was growing by 2 to 2.5 percent annually. Per capita gross national product, moreover, had fallen to roughly 100 dollars annually. Large collective farms were being broken up into smaller holdings because of the lack of tractors and other mechanized equipment. Even if there were more tractors, he explained, they would have to sit idle for lack of fuel. It was a portrait of economic disaster.

Widespread hunger under the new order is rare, however. Much more common is a chronic shortage of consumer goods, a constant insufficiency of clothing, housing, and transportation. Here supply never seems to catch up with demand. Conditions are especially hard for young people wishing to marry and establish their own households. They often face frustration and disappointment. In Moscow in 1923, although the amount of per capita living space was slightly larger than in 1912, overcrowding remained a harsh reality of everyday life. More than half the residents of the city lived in apartments with two occupants for each room and a third lived in apartments with three to five occupants for each room, while less than a tenth enjoyed the luxury of a room entirely for themselves.

To provide housing for their labor force, many enterprises established factory barracks to which especially the younger workers, a large number of them recent arrivals in the city, were often assigned. In 1928 a Soviet newspaper described one such barracks in dismal detail:

> The long narrow room has only one window, which cannot be opened. Some of the panes are broken and the holes plugged with dirty rags. Near the doorway is an oven which serves not only for heating but for cooking as well. The chimney spans the entire length of the room from the doorway to the window. The smell of fumes, of socks hung to dry, fills the room. It is impossible to breathe in the closeness of the air. Along the walls are crude beds covered with dirty straw ticks and rags, alive with lice and bugs. The beds have almost no space between them. The floor is strewn with cigarette butts and rubbish. About two hundred workers are housed here, men and women, married and single, old and young—all herded together. There are no partitions, and the most intimate acts are performed under the very eyes of other inhabitants. Each family has one bed. On one bed a man, a wife, and three children live, a baby occupies the "second floor"—a cot hanging over the bed. The same toilet is used by men and women.

Such were the living conditions of a large part of the working class of Russia eleven years after the Bolsheviks rose to power.[4]

Why is the gap between vision and reality so wide? Why is an economy committed to the general welfare so much less productive than one based on personal gain? Some of the reasons are admittedly beyond the control of the new order. Its apologists point to the devastation and chaos that are the frequent aftermath of the struggle to overthrow the *ancien régime*. They dwell, moreover, on the military intervention and economic boycott directed against the radical dictatorship by hostile foreign governments. The material hardships that the new order has to endure, they claim, are primarily the fault of an antagonistic capitalist world.

There is something in that, but it is only part of the story. Long after the new order has consolidated its hold on power, long after foreign military and economic intervention has come to an end, production continues to sputter and falter. More crucial than the ruthlessness of the opponents of the revolution is the inexperience and doctrinairism of its supporters. They are convinced that the overthrow of capitalism and the replacement of private property with public ownership are enough to create an economy of abundance. Without practical training in business administration, without firsthand knowledge of the problems of industrial and agricultural management, they believe that they can establish a more fruitful economic system by a stroke of the pen. They therefore embark on risky experiments like "war communism" or the "great leap forward," confident of their ability to translate radical theory into economic reality.

The consequences of their dogmatism are often disastrous. In the fall of 1962 even Che Guevara had to admit that his hopes regarding the effect of the revolution on the material welfare of the Cuban masses had not yet been realized. "We did the best we could, but there were difficulties. There were many errors in the administrative part of the executive body. Enormous mistakes were made by the new administrators of enterprises, whose responsibilities were too great." The building of a better society had seemed so much simpler during the guerrilla struggle in the Sierra Maestra.

The most important reason for economic stagnation under the new order, however, is a decline in the productivity of labor. The rhetoric condemning the exploitation of the proletariat that had helped undermine the *ancien régime* comes back to haunt the revolution. The radical dictatorship hesitates to employ the same financial threats, the same material pressures on which the old order had relied to enforce discipline in the work force. And yet, since the economy is now based on the principle of collective ownership, individual initiative and accountability rapidly erode. The result is a sharp drop in efficiency and output.

In Moscow after the revolution many workers would habitually arrive at the factory late; worse still, absenteeism became common. There was drinking, cardplaying, and merrymaking on the job. Sometimes employees would damage the equipment, whether through inadvertence or by design. In 1908 the average worker had spent the equivalent of 320 eight-hour days in the shop; by 1920 the total diminished to 219. Not counting vacations, he now missed 60 days of work, 15 because of organizational activity and 45 because of illness or unexcused absence. In addition, 8 days were lost due to shutdowns of the workplace. In some branches of manufacture the situation was even worse. Thus in the metal industry the average worker stayed away from the job 84 days. The assumption that the collectivization of the economy would lead directly to an increase in production proved unfounded. From the beginning, the new order had to cope with truancy, malingering, inefficiency, and indiscipline in the work force.

The demoralization of labor contributed in turn to a general deterioration in living conditions. The inadequacy of housing, for example, was aggravated by poor maintenance and management. Harold H. Fisher, who had been in Russia in the early 1920s, described the quarters assigned to the American Relief Administration in Moscow in what had once been the home of a wealthy Armenian family:

> The condition of this building was representative of a great number of the larger residences . . . that had been nationalized and used by the government for either offices or housing purposes. . . . The central heating plant, since no one was responsible for it, had long since ceased to function and the occupants of the house had kept warm by setting up stoves in their rooms, making holes in the walls, where necessary, for stovepipes. The water system was also useless, and a large area of the cellar was under two feet of water. The rooms were indescribably filthy, particularly the bathrooms, which had been used for every purpose but bathing. An inspection of the cellar revealed not only the wreck of the heating plant, but that some of the occupants of the house were following agricultural pursuits, either to piece out their own food supply or as a business venture. Here was an indiscriminate collection of pigs, poultry, and rabbits, whose living conditions, like those of their owners, left much to be desired.

A decade later the situation had not improved a great deal. Even important officials were now beginning to complain. In 1931 L.M. Kaganovich, member of the Politburo and head of the Moscow organization of the party, criticized the neglect of basic building maintenance in the Soviet capital. At one address the residents had reported to him that "when the house was taken over by the [housing] trust, it began to fall into disrepair. One of the courtyards was turned into a dumpheap. The broken gates were not repaired. The furnaceman, a drunkard who did nothing whatever, was rewarded for economizing fuel. The house was practically not heated at all and the occupants froze. The majority of the tenants had never once seen the manager of the housing trust."

At another address conditions were not much better, according to Kaganovich. Here too "bureaucracy in management" was rampant. "The house is falling into disrepair. Garbage is not removed. The water tap in the apartment of [one of the tenants] became damaged. His wife went to the manager's office at 8 A.M. and was told that 'we begin work at noon.' All the time the water was flowing from the tap. She came again at noon and they gave her a repair order, but the plumber never came. Two days later a neighboring plumber, a friend of the family, repaired the tap." What was everybody's property had come to be regarded as nobody's property.[5]

To the leaders of the new order nothing is more disappointing than the discovery that the emancipation of the proletariat does not promote greater idealism, dedication, productivity, and happiness. On the contrary, for a large part of the labor force the fall of the *ancien régime* simply leads to idleness, inefficiency, negligence, and disorganization. Sometimes the radical dictatorship openly expresses its disillusionment with those for whose sake the revolution had been fought. In the spring of 1988 Nguyen Co Thach, the foreign minister of Vietnam, admitted to an American visitor "that it was a fallacy of Communism that everything could be provided by the state, and that this was the reason that Vietnamese leaders had been forced to consider some capitalistic policies." The revolution had been too visionary, too impractical. "We were very romantic. . . . We wanted happiness for all the people. But happiness must be [achieved] by the people, and we have made the people lazy." He acknowledged sadly that the leaders of the new order might have been too optimistic about the creation of a better economic system.

Still, upbraiding the masses does little to increase output. The government is therefore forced to take more drastic measures. It starts by sermonizing, exhorting, encouraging, and pleading. Cannot the lower classes see that they will now be able to reap the fruits of their labor, that they will no longer be enriching their exploiters but insuring their own future? This is followed by various social and psychological pressures. Those who fail to perform satisfactorily are condemned as "shirkers" and "parasites." Those who do exceptionally well, on the other hand, earn praise and recognition; they become "experts," "specialists," "cadres," and "Stakhanovites"; they receive compliments, medals, bonuses, and vacations. But in the end the new order has to start employing the same methods of material reward and punishment for which it had once denounced the *ancien régime*. The promise that after the overthrow of capitalism every member of society would receive support "according to his needs" is replaced by the warning that "he who does not work, neither shall he eat." That means in practice a return to a system of financial remuneration comparable in diversity and disparateness to that maintained under private ownership. The ideal of economic equality becomes subordinated to the need for economic efficiency.

Those who oppose this turnabout, who cling to the pristine egalitarianism of the revolutionary ideology, come to be criticized as dogmatists, formalists, obstructionists, or visionaries. During the First Five-Year Plan, whose success depended largely on increasing the productivity of the work force, Stalin urged greater differentiation in the distribution of rewards in Soviet industry:

What is the cause of the fluidity of manpower? The cause is the wrong structure of wages, the wrong wage scales, the "Leftist" practice of wage equalization. In a number of factories wage scales are drawn up in such a way as to practically wipe out the difference between skilled and unskilled labor, between heavy and light work. The consequence of wage equalization is that the unskilled worker lacks the incentive to become a skilled worker and is thus deprived of the prospect of advancement; as a result he feels himself a "visitor" in the factory, working only temporarily so as "to earn a little money" and then go off to "try his luck" in some other place. The consequence of wage equalization is that the skilled worker is obliged to go from factory to factory until he finds one where his skill is properly appreciated.

He sounded almost like a defender of free enterprise.

To Stalin it was clear, moreover, that the rapid turnover of labor would continue as long as financial rewards in the work force were not diversified. "In order to put an end to this evil we must abolish wage equalization and discard the old wage scales. In order to put an end to this evil we must draw up wage scales that will take into account the difference between skilled and unskilled labor, between heavy and light work. We cannot tolerate a situation where a rolling-mill worker in the iron and steel industry earns no more than a sweeper. We cannot tolerate a situation where a railway locomotive driver earns only as much as a copying clerk."

Marx and Lenin, he went on, had understood that differences between skilled and unskilled labor would have to continue even under socialism, even after class distinctions had been abolished. Only under Communism would they disappear. Hence in the Soviet Union, which was still in the socialist stage of revolutionary development, wages should be paid "according to work performed and not according to needs." But the equalitarians among industrial managers and union officials did not agree with this view; they seemed to believe that under the Soviet system differences in the financial rewards of labor should be eliminated at once. "Who is right, Marx and Lenin or the equalitarians?" There could be no doubt. But if Marx and Lenin were right, "whoever draws up wage scales on the 'principle' of wage equalization, without taking into account the differences between skilled and unskilled labor, breaks with Marxism, breaks with Leninism."

The implications of this conclusion for the system of compensation were obvious. "In every branch of industry, in every factory, in every shop," Stalin argued, "there is a leading group of more or less skilled workers who first and foremost must be retained if we really want to ensure a constant labor force in the factories. These leading groups of workers are the principal link in production." By retaining them, an industrial enterprise would be better able to retain the rest of its labor force as well and thus put an end to the constant turnover of manpower. "But how can we retain them in the factories? We can retain them only by promoting them to higher positions, by raising the level of their wages, by introducing a system of wages that will give the worker his due according to qualification." Soviet industry, in other words, should begin introducing greater distinctions between the skilled and the unskilled, the more and the less qualified, the better and the worse paid.

This would not mean the reestablishment of distinct social castes or classes, Stalin maintained. It would provide rather an inducement to the less efficient employee to improve his performance, to increase his output. It would provide him with an opportunity to raise his standard of living. "What does promoting [skilled workers] to higher positions and raising their wage level mean?" he asked. "It means, apart from everything else, opening up prospects for the unskilled worker and giving him an incentive to rise higher, to rise to the category of a skilled worker. You know yourselves that we now need hundreds of thousands and even millions of skilled workers. But in order to build up cadres of skilled workers, we must provide an incentive for the unskilled workers, provide for them a prospect of advancement, of rising to a higher position." The more vigorously this was done, the better, for there was no other way of ending the continual turnover in the work force. "To economize in this matter would be criminal, it would be going against the interests of our socialist industry."

The principle of social equality, which had helped inspire the Bolshevik revolution, was thus in effect abandoned within a few years after the establishment of the new order. It was forced to yield to the imperatives of greater economic efficiency. The ideal of an egalitarian society was not publicly renounced, to be sure. It remained central to the official ideology. But its realization was postponed; it was consigned to the distant realm of communist eschatology. For the time being, during the socialist phase of revolutionary development, material rewards and punishments similar to those applied under capitalism would have to remain in force. "In the U.S.S.R.," the Soviet constitution of 1936 proclaimed, "the principle of socialism is realized: 'From each according to his ability, to each according to his work,'" rather than Marx's "according to his needs." The vision of a new social order without distinctions

of wealth or status had succumbed to the material demands of production and distribution.[6]

Disappointments and Defections

The steady erosion of the central doctrinal myths of the new order—
world revolution, political democracy, and social equality—
engenders a mood of disillusionment among many of its allies and
supporters. What had appeared so easy turns out to be very difficult; what had seemed readily attainable proves elusive and baffling. Once the fervor inspired by the fall of the *ancien régime*
dissipates, familiar human faults and weaknesses gradually reappear. People begin once more to bargain, scheme, haggle, and exploit. The facade of selfless dedication to the common welfare
remains in place, but behind it a furtive yet pervasive concern for
private gain becomes apparent. The distance between theory and
practice, ideology and reality widens. And as the perception spreads
that the creation of a just society lies beyond mortal reach, that traditional social disparities are too deep-seated to be overcome by rhetoric and idealism, a feeling of disenchantment starts growing, not
only among the masses, but even among revolutionaries who had
risked their lives for a better world.

The first to turn against the new order are the moderates, who
had participated in the struggle against the *ancien régime*, but who
had from the outset questioned the policies adopted after its overthrow. The Menshevik leader Julius Martov greeted the fall of czarism as the opening of an era of political democracy and social
progress for Russia. The Bolshevik seizure of power eight months
later filled him with foreboding, however, and what happened in
the next two years seemed to confirm his fears. In an essay on "The
Ideology of 'Sovietism'" published in 1919, he voiced his disillusionment. The radical dictatorship had failed to introduce the
"electiveness and recall of public officials"; it had failed to suppress
the arbitrary power of the police; it had failed to put an end to "social
hierarchy in production"; it had failed to mitigate the "total subjection of the local community" to the central government. In fact, conditions had gotten worse. A tendency was now apparent toward

greater centralization by the state, toward a reinforcement of the "principles of hierarchy and compulsion," toward the growth of "a more specialized apparatus of repression." The masses had lost all control over the government; those in power did whatever they pleased. The authority derived from the people had become independent of the people. Was that what the revolution had been fought for?[7]

More serious is the defection of those who had started out as supporters of the radical dictatorship, but had gradually become alienated by its policies and tactics. Disenchantment spreads not only among the rank and file of the party, but among those who had been leaders in the battle against the old order. C.G. Rakovsky had played a crucial role in establishing Bolshevik control over the Ukraine during the civil war. By the late 1920s, however, he became increasingly critical of the Soviet regime. Banished to Astrakhan for his insubordination, he wrote there an analysis of "the 'professional dangers' of power," expressing disappointment with the direction taken by the revolution. The new order, it seemed to him, was beginning to resemble the old.

To start with, the ideological fervor of the Bolshevik movement had become dissipated. "The working class and the party—not now *physically* but *morally*—are no longer what they were ten years ago. I do not exaggerate when I say that the militant of 1917 would have difficulty in recognizing himself in the militant of 1928. A profound change has taken place in the anatomy and the physiology of the working class."

The overthrow of capitalism had been expected to bring about the liberation of the entire proletariat, of the "semi-vagabonds" as well as the skilled and well-paid workers. Indeed, members of the lowest strata of the labor force had been most bitterly opposed to the *ancien régime*. "The semi-vagabond elements made the bourgeoisie and the capitalist state responsible for their situation; they [believed] that the revolution [would] bring a change in their condition." But in fact there had been no improvement. "These people are now far from satisfied; their situation has been ameliorated little if at all. They are beginning to consider Soviet power, and that part of the working class working in industry, with hostility. They are especially becoming enemies of the functionaries of the soviets, of the party, and of the trade unions. They can sometimes be heard speaking of the summit of the working class as the 'new nobility.'"

To Rakovsky the decline in the idealism of the new order had led to a revival of economic and social inequality. He spoke disapprovingly of "the differentiation which power has introduced into the bosom of the proletariat." To put it more broadly, "the function has modified the organism itself; that is to say that the psychology of those who are charged with the diverse tasks of direction in the administration and the economy of the state has changed to such a point that, not only objectively but subjectively, not only materially but also morally, they have ceased to be a part of this very same working class." For example, "a factory director playing the satrap in spite of the fact that he is a communist, in spite of his proletarian origin, in spite of the fact that he was a factory worker a few years ago, will not become in the eyes of the workers the epitome of the best qualities of the proletariat."

Clearly, the new order had gone astray. "What has happened to the spirit of revolutionary activity of the party and of our proletariat?" Rakovsky wondered. "Where has their revolutionary initiative gone? Where [have] their ideological interests, their revolutionary values, their proletarian pride . . . gone? . . . There is so much apathy, weakness, pusillanimity, opportunism, and so many other things that I could add. . . . How is it that those who have a worthy revolutionary past, whose present honesty cannot be held in doubt, who have given proof of their attachment to the revolution on more than one occasion, can have been transformed into pitiable bureaucrats?" Perhaps no more was to be expected of those who had started out as members of the bourgeoisie or petty bourgeoisie, of the "intellectuals" or "'individuals' in general." But "how can we explain a similar phenomenon in respect of the working class? Many comrades have noted the fact of its passivity and cannot hide their feeling of disillusion."

Everything was supposed to be so different, so much nobler, so much better. "According to the conception of Lenin and of us all, the task of the party leaders consists precisely in keeping the party and the working class from the corruption of privileges, of favors, of special rights inherent in power. . . . At the same time, we had the hope that the party leadership would [create] a new, truly worker and

peasant apparatus, new, truly proletarian trade unions, a new morality of daily life." Alas, the Bolsheviks had not opposed vigorously
enough the "nefarious influence" of the New Economic Policy and
the "temptations of the ideology and morality of the bourgeoisie."
The outcome had been disastrous. Now the duty of a true revolutionary was to criticize the mistakes of the regime "frankly, clearly,
and in a loud and intelligible voice." No more dissimulation. "The
apparatus of the party has not accomplished [its] task. It has shown
. . . the most complete incompetence; it has become bankrupt; it is
insolvent. We have been convinced for a long time . . . that the leadership of the party was advancing on a most perilous road." And
worse still, "it continues to follow this road."

Every revolution produces its Rakovskys; every revolution ends
up disappointing those who had been among its most idealistic followers. Huber Matos provides a good illustration. He had played a
prominent role in the struggle against the *ancien régime* in Cuba, but
after its overthrow his hopes had gradually turned into bitter disillusionment. "I differed from Fidel Castro," he explained following his
release from political imprisonment many years later, "because the
original objective of our Revolution was 'Freedom or Death.' Once
Castro had power, he began to kill freedom."

Most of those who had opposed the Batista government, Matos
maintained, were committed to "complete freedom for our country,"
to "true independence and national sovereignty for the Cuban people." But the radical dictatorship had other plans. To him liberty had
meant political freedom, the right to think and to speak without fear
of retaliation by those in power. It had meant a diversity of opinions,
policies, and parties. It had meant "everything . . . that is generally
accepted to be the universal rights of mankind." In short, "we
wanted a democratic revolution" under which "the direction of the
government would have had to be democratic too." Instead, the new
order had established a political tyranny, "everything being left to
one man, with no one being free to question his decisions."

After going into exile in 1978, Truong Nhu Tang, who had been
minister of justice in the provisional revolutionary government of
South Vietnam, expressed a similar disenchantment. His country
had thrown off the yoke of colonialism, to be sure. Yet national independence had not been the only goal of the struggle for liberation.

"Many of us also believed we were fighting for the human dignity of our people, not just a *national* revolution, but a *national* and *democratic* revolution." Victory was supposed to safeguard the rights of the various ethnic groups, religious faiths, and geographical regions constituting the nation as well as the liberties of all its members.

Still, that was not how things had turned out. The "national democratic revolution" had faltered; it had been corrupted by the "arrogance of power" of those in authority. The successors of Ho Chi Minh, instead of achieving reconciliation and independence, had created an oppressive system of government "devouring its own." They remained dependent on foreigners, "though now it is the Soviets rather than the Americans." As for those who had sacrificed their lives to help build a better society, their ashes had been thrown on the political rubbish heap of the new order. "That betrayal of faith will burden the souls of Vietnam's revolutionary leaders—even as surely as their rigid ideology and bellicose foreign policies have mortgaged the country's future."

All disillusioned revolutionaries, whatever their differences in language or style, end up sounding alike.[8]

The mood of disenchantment even affects the leaders of the radical dictatorship. They too begin to sense that things are not going the way they had hoped or expected. Yet there is a fundamental difference between the critics and the defenders of the new order. The former maintain that the revolution has failed the people; the latter feel that the people have failed the revolution. They have not lived up to its lofty ideals; they have not appreciated what was being done for them; they have yielded to selfish impulses and temptations; they have remained indifferent to the great historic mission entrusted to them. Those in power never say it in so many words, but in their rhetoric can be detected an undercurrent of bitterness and disappointment.

In an interview in 1968 with the French writer André Malraux, for instance, Mao criticized the Soviets for having underestimated the corruptibility of human nature. "Victory is the mother of many illusions" he argued. "The truth is that if the contradictions due to victory are less painful than the old ones, . . . they are almost as deep. Humanity left to its own devices does not necessarily reestablish capitalism . . . , but it does reestablish inequality. The forces tending toward the creation of new classes are powerful." Hence the struggle against the backsliding of the masses had to be relentless.

In Castro's speeches disappointment with the inability of the revolution to transform basic popular attitudes, motives, and aspirations was even more apparent. In 1963 he characterized the years since the overthrow of the *ancien régime* as "the era of spoiled children, of tolerating things around here, of mistakes, of infantilisms." Now that the people had gained liberty, why did they use it so ineffectually, so irresponsibly?

In 1967, commemorating the ill-fated assault against the Moncada barracks during the Batista dictatorship, he acknowledged that seizing power is not the hardest part of the revolution. Knowing what to do with it is much harder. "The most difficult task is the one we are engaged in today; the task of building a new country on the basis of an underdeveloped economy; the task of creating a new consciousness, a new man, on the basis of ideas that had prevailed in our society for centuries."

Victory in the battle against the old order had been only a prelude to further battles, further sacrifices, Castro went on. "The attack on Moncada can be said to have been the first attack on one of the many fortresses to be taken." Other strongholds of the *ancien régime* continued to offer resistance. "Among them were the Moncada of illiteracy, ... the Moncada of ignorance, the Moncada of inexperience, the Moncada of underdevelopment, the Moncada of a shortage of technicians, the Moncada of a shortage of resources in all fields." But the bitterest struggle of all was for the possession of man's soul. "Another and more difficult Moncada was left to be taken—that was the Moncada of old ideas. And that Moncada of old ideas, of old, selfish feelings, of old ways of thinking and looking at things and solving problems has still not been completely taken." The task of reforming human nature remained endless.

In 1970, addressing a trade-union meeting in Havana, Castro finally admitted that he might have been too optimistic about the ability of the revolution to alter the mentality of the masses. "Perhaps our greatest idealism lies in having believed that a society that had barely begun to live in a world that for thousands of years had lived under the law of 'an eye for an eye and a tooth for a tooth,' the law of the survival of the fittest, the law of egoism, the law of deceit and the law of exploitation could, all of a sudden, be turned into a society in which everybody behaved in an ethical, moral way." More than a decade after seizing power, he was forced to recognize that the creation of a just social order would take far longer than he had imagined in the flush of victory. The new order would have to go on demanding new efforts, new struggles, new sacrifices, new martyrs.[9]

The Corruptions of Power

The realization that the revolution is becoming stabilized and rigidified, that economic and social equality is receding farther into the future, leads to the spread of expediency among those in positions of authority. The readiness of the supporters of the new order to subordinate private interest to public welfare, individual ambition to collective purpose, begins to erode. Officially the government continues to demand self-denial and self-sacrifice of the functionaries whom it entrusts with power. It goes on preaching the virtues of humility, simplicity, dedication, and unselfishness. But in fact it winks at the growth of perquisites and privileges within the bureaucratic apparatus. Since the idealism of the early years of the revolution has now largely dissipated, it has to start offering material rewards to those who help execute its policies. In other words, it is forced to accept the widening gulf between the radical elite and the proletarian masses.

The most obvious evidence of that acceptance is the disparity in the standard of living. Carlos Franqui, who had served as editor of the official newspaper of Castro's political organization, recalled years later that shortly after the fall of the Batista regime "the Urban Reform people handed me the keys to my new house [which had formerly belonged to a wealthy Cuban family]. I'd be a hypocrite if I were to say I didn't like what I found—swimming pool, books, nice furniture, garden, air conditioning—but at the same time I felt guilty."

Other important officials were treated even more generously. "When a certain commandante-minister got married, he was given a house in the [fashionable] Miramar district, a new car, assorted whiskies, dishes, and perfume for the blushing bride. . . . As an old veteran of Prague and Moscow remarked, 'only the best for the proletariat.' We were all more or less caught up in that cynical sentence."

Franqui remembered in particular the house occupied by Manuel Piñeyro, "second in command of Security, the man in charge of revolution in Latin America." It was surrounded by an extensive tract of land, "a farm right in the city," complete with "chickens, pigs, ducks—all taken care of by army personnel," a striking example of "conspicuous consumption by a new [ruling] class." This seemed incredible to him. "In a city where everything was rationed, where scarcity was the order of the day, where the socialist police had forbidden citizens to keep pigs or chickens in their houses, a chief of police was doing it right out in the open. I remembered that Fidel had denounced Batista's officers for using soldiers as farm laborers, and now both the army and the police were doing the same thing. . . . Was I seeing the past, the present, or the future?"

Another manifestation of growing social inequality is the expansion of the civil service. Material rewards are so much greater in administration than production that a massive influx of labor into the bureaucratic apparatus takes place after the revolution. Admittedly, some of it reflects the diminished role of the private sector in the economy. As the government increasingly assumes the managerial functions formerly performed by capitalistic entrepreneurship, its demand for additional personnel begins to intensify. And because many of the new employees lack administrative training and experience, proportionately more of them are needed than under the *ancien régime*. But equally important is the higher income, security, and status that the civil service can provide. Since entry into the bureaucracy is now the chief avenue of upward mobility, the movement of manpower into public employment becomes almost irresistible.

Some leaders of the revolution complain quite openly about the increasingly cumbersome administrative system, but they are unable to do much about it. They have become in a sense captives of their own creation. Now they can only criticize and grumble. In an article published in 1962, Che Guevara acknowledged the failure of the new order to check the growth of bureaucratism in Cuba. "We . . . made large and costly errors in the political apparatus, which little by little was becoming a peaceful and cozy bureaucracy. It was virtually seen as a springboard for promotions and for bureaucratic positions of varying importance, and was totally cut off from the masses."

In 1967, at a ceremony in honor of Cuban steel workers, Castro was equally critical. "The capitalists had a lot of bureaucracy, and we have not eradicated it; we have, on occasion, increased it." That was not entirely the fault of the new order, however. "Everybody's life-long dream in an underdeveloped country was to land an office job. Very few people in our country ever studied to be lathe operators. Tens of thousands studied typing, shorthand, and other clerical subjects. Naturally, we have inherited this mass." As a result, the government was now stuck with the problem of trying to streamline a bloated and unwieldy administrative system.[10]

The inflation of the bureaucracy is also a major cause of its inefficiency. It leads to the growth and multiplication of rules and regulations, paperwork and red tape, all in the name of rational planning and scientific management. Initiative becomes risky, independence dangerous. The system encourages rigid adherence to the letter of official directives. Even government leaders often complain of growing routinization in the civil service. Reporting in 1934 to the seventeenth congress of the Soviet Communist party, Kaganovich deplored the fearful avoidance by many functionaries of personal responsibility for the execution of policy. "Formal paper measures are useless; you receive a report, scribble an order, and [think you are] finished. Sometimes an order from above is received, it is slightly paraphrased and sent down to the next link, and they send it down still lower. And so the red tape is spun out." At this point Stalin interjected: "And then the document is put in the files." Kaganovich agreed with alacrity. "Quite right, and then the document is put in the files."

Some thirty years later Castro, speaking before a working-class audience in Havana, complained of the same punctiliousness and bureaucratization:

There are factories, production units, where a capitalist owner employed three or four office employees, and we have twenty-five or forty (SHOUTS AND APPLAUSE). Why? We have to go to the root of the problem. The problem of forms has, at the same time, been a cause and an excuse. These blanks have created the need for paper work. The forms are one of the causes, [since] there are elements that dedicate themselves to abstractions, to creating paper work. . . . There were thousands here who felt they were organizational experts, thousands who dedicated themselves to making up forms, forms which clutter up files, forms which are never used, useless forms which serve no purpose. Therefore, in the struggle against bureaucracy, we must also struggle for the rationalization and reduction of these forms to the bare minimum.

Yet inefficiency is not the only weakness of the swollen administrative apparatus created by the new order. Even more serious is the patronage and favoritism, the logrolling and wire-pulling, that frequently determine admission to positions of authority. In a society in which talent is supposed to be the key to advancement, in which demonstrated ability rather than private influence is on paper the sole criterion of merit, personal contacts and loyalties continue to play a major role. Whom you know often proves more important than what you know.

Speaking in 1937 before the Central Committee, Stalin attacked the cronyism that had become commonplace in the Soviet system of administration. "Most frequently, workers are selected not according to objective criteria, but according to accidental, subjective, narrow, and provincial criteria. Most frequently so-called acquaintances are chosen, personal friends, fellow townsmen, people who have shown personal devotion, masters of eulogies to their patrons, irrespective of whether they are suitable from a political and a businesslike standpoint." The result was bound to be harmful to the public interest. "Instead of a leading group of responsible workers, a family group, a company, is formed, the members of which try to live peacefully, not to offend each other, not to wash their dirty linen in public, to eulogize each other, and from time to time to send inane and nauseating reports to [higher authorities] about [their] successes."

Stalin gave some illuminating examples of patronage in the bureaucratic apparatus. "Take . . . Comrades Mirzoyan and Vainov. The former is secretary of the regional Party organization in Kazakstan;

the latter is secretary of the Yaroslav regional party organization. These people are not the most backward workers in our midst." Yet by what criteria did they select their administrative staffs? "The former dragged along with him from Azerbaijan and the Urals, where he formerly worked, into Kazakstan thirty or forty of his 'own' people, and placed them in responsible positions in Kazakstan. The latter dragged along with him from the Donbas, where he formerly worked, to Yaroslav a dozen or so of his 'own' people also, and also placed them in responsible positions. Consequently, Comrade Mirzoyan has his own crew. Comrade Vainov also has his." The obvious purpose was the establishment of a personal satrapy. "These comrades evidently . . . wanted to create for themselves conditions which [would] give them a certain independence both of the local people and of the Central Committee of the party."

In China the political leadership was generally more restrained in condemning the spread of bossism and patronage. But in 1983 the Central Committee adopted a resolution expressing grave concern about the selfish, corrupt behavior of many of those in positions of influence. "At present some Party members and Party cadres have completely forgotten that the Party's aim is to serve the people wholeheartedly. Instead of correctly using the authority and the opportunities given to them by the Party and the people to work for the well-being of the masses, they seek benefits for themselves, or for a handful of people close to them, in every possible way." The outcome was the alienation of the workers and peasants. "These unhealthy tendencies and degenerate phenomena . . . have severely damaged the image of the Party in the minds of the people." The achievements of the revolution were being undermined by selfishness and favoritism within the administrative system.

But the most blatant weakness of the bureaucracy is its growing venality. Although in theory still committed to selfless service for the welfare of the people, it becomes in practice more and more susceptible to bribery. Its corruptibility is most apparent at the lower levels of administration. A suitable gift to an office supervisor may hasten the issuance of a permit or license. An attractive present to a police officer can lead to forgiveness for minor irregularities or transgressions. A tempting offer to a health official, preferably in hard capitalistic currency, will insure quicker and better medical care. But the sale of favors is not confined to the rank and file of the civil service. In 1964 Mao spoke openly of its spread to the higher echelons. "At present, you can buy a . . . branch secretary [of the Communist party] for a few packs of cigarettes, not to mention marrying a daughter to him." The seductions of power are sometimes too much even for those at the top of the bureaucratic ladder.[11]

The Corruptions of Powerlessness

The disparity within the revolutionary patriciate between theory and practice, between rhetoric and conduct, furthers the spread of disillusionment and demoralization among the masses. They too begin to engage in activities incompatible with the moral imperatives of the new order, activities that are dubious or improper or even illegal. They too try to get ahead by tricks and stratagems, by furtive deals and secret arrangements, by subordinating public good to private advantage. These violations of the new morality are a form of indirect protest against the inequalities and dissimulations of the radical dictatorship. The transgressors may continue to pay lip service to its ideals; they may even go on adhering in the abstract to its doctrines. But by their personal conduct they reveal an inner rejection of the official ethos. And while the authorities are aware of this spread of moral deviance, they can do little beyond suppressing organized or systematic expressions of its existence.

The most obvious manifestation of popular alienation from the radical canon of ethics is the black market. In theory the economy of the new order is governed by rules designed to maintain a rough equality in the standard of living. But in practice there are in every revolutionary society forms of economic activity, conducted in violation of the law, that promote free commerce and intensify social disparity. In the early chaotic days of radical dictatorship, the black market serves to alleviate the material hardships caused by the struggle against the *ancien régime*. Nevertheless, even after the new order achieves victory and stability, underground economic activity continues both to supplement and to rival the official system of production. Indeed, it becomes increasingly open, established, accepted, and institutionalized. It emerges in the end as a permanent feature of the revolution, a source of support and yet an admission of defeat.

Castro himself was forced in 1971 to acknowledge the existence of a black market in Cuba, although he portrayed its activities as only minor lapses from revolutionary grace. "You are all aware of the fact that prices have remained frozen in our country for who knows how many years," he declared at a May Day rally.

> Now, then, [this is] the material base for the black market, that phenomenon that promotes vice in a chain-like fashion, ranging from the person who goes to the countryside to buy produce from a farmer at exorbitant prices to the person who encourages stealing so that he can later sell the stolen goods in the black market. [It] also encouraged loafing, since there were some individuals who . . . made a living by acting as stand-ins for others in shopping lines, charging 10 pesos for each performance. And there are others who steal.

Still, these were no more than the natural growing pains of an economy in transition from capitalist acquisitiveness to socialist egalitarianism, according to Castro. "In our country, money is becoming more and more a means of distribution. There will be a day when distribution will no longer be dependent on the ration book. That day will come eventually, but not now. . . . This can only happen when we have an abundance of all those essential products so that distribution, no longer based on the ration book, will reach everyone." In the meantime the masses must work, struggle, endure, and be patient.

The American sinologist Orville Schell was much more graphic in describing the black market in China in 1983. While dining at the Jinjin Restaurant in Peking, he noticed two young men on the other side of the room "wolfing down plates of food and bottles of beer." They were *liumang*, roughly translatable as "hooligans" or "hoodlums." Their meal must have cost 10 or 12 yuan, about a fifth of an average factory worker's salary. After dinner he caught the eye of one of them. Cocking his head and grinning drowsily, the black marketeer called out: "Hey, foreign friend! Let's have some beer together." Schell walked over to their table.

As I sat down, Liumang No. 1 clamped a cigarette between his teeth and poured me some beer. After a few amenities, I asked them how they could afford such an expensive dinner.

"We get things for people," replied Liumang No. 2, his speech slightly slurred by the effect of the beer.

"We can get you anything you want," added Liumang No. 1 jauntily.

"What kinds of things?"

"Anything you want," repeated No. 1. "Clothes from Hong Kong, tape recorders, cameras, watches, televisions, radios."

"We can even get you women," said No. 2, leaning forward and lowering his voice to a conspiratorial whisper.

"Could you get fifty bottles of Qingdao beer?" I asked.

"Hey! No problem," replied Liumang No. 1, blowing a cloud of cigarette smoke out over my head. "When do you want them?"

"What does it take?" I asked.

"Money. Cold cash—that's the only thing that counts these days," Liumang No. 2 said.

He smiled and reached out with his chopsticks to pick up a roast peanut from the dish of hors d'oeuvres, a self-assured, successful entrepreneur thriving under the new order in China.[12]

Prostitution is another of those stubborn illegalities that the radical dictatorship has to learn to tolerate. Before the revolution it had been a source of bitter and inflammatory denunciations of the *ancien régime*. By maintaining an exploitative economic system, the government was allegedly forcing lower-class women to sell themselves, to submit to the degradation of white slavery. Only its overthrow could put an end to commercialized vice. After the victory of the new order, however, a rapid revival of the traffic in sex takes place, more circumspect than before, but widespread and flourishing. The authorities try to explain it away as a temporary aberration, the result of material hardships occasioned by the revolutionary struggle. Yet prostitution remains a permanent feature of life under the new order. Indeed, the longer the radical dictatorship is in power, the more accepted and established becomes the commerce in flesh.

After the Bolshevik revolution, for example, many orphaned young girls turned to prostitution. More than a fourth of the streetwalkers arrested in Moscow in 1927 were under eighteen; there were even twelve-year-olds among them. Some practiced the trade to earn a living, others to support a drug habit. Almost three-fourths of those picked up by the police in 1924 used narcotics regularly. Prostitutes solicited customers openly in several parts of the city, especially around Tverskaia Square and Trubny Square. In the former the sidewalks swarmed with teen-age streetwalkers, while in the latter the trade was a little more discreet. Patrons would stroll through the corridors of several large tenements in which, next to the doors, appeared photographs of available female occupants in poses of provocative undress. But these women at least had a bed. Others practiced their profession in hallways, alleys, and backyards, or on lawns and park benches.

Still, vice under the new order was not always tawdry or squalid. There were also establishments that in czarist days would have won the approval of the most finicky aristocratic playboy or tired businessman. The journalist Walter Duranty, who spent two decades in the Soviet Union, described an elegant restaurant called simply "Bar," not far from the Savoy Hotel, that in 1922 "blossomed out with small private dining rooms in sheds in a backyard." It also acquired upstairs premises by remodeling an abandoned building, and then "an era of naughtiness" began. "At first clients who took a girl friend or two to one of the private dining rooms would receive a modest hint from the waiter that there were rooms upstairs if they were in no hurry to go home. Then 'Bar' started a cabaret, and it was understood that the artists were ready to solace the evening of a lonely [profiteer] and would doubtless not refuse to spend the night with him."

By the end of the year the place was doing a roaring business as "a snappy restaurant, night club, and brothel all in one." The sale of wine and beer had just become legal, but here vodka and liquors were available as well. "In the winter . . . they went further, and cocaine and heroin were to be had, for a price, by clients in the know." Members of the American colony in Moscow tended to avoid the restaurant because "one of our number had been robbed there in a tough and flagrant way, which indicated all too obviously police connivance and 'protection.'" Yet many others, well-to-do Russians as well as foreigners, found solace there amid the pervasive drabness of life under the Bolsheviks. For those with money, illicit pleasures were available under the new order almost as easily as under the old.

The revolutionary authorities in Cuba were no more successful than those in the Soviet Union in stamping out prostitution. In 1968 Castro denounced the corruption of young womanhood in Havana in the same tone of virtuous indignation that he had once directed against the immorality of the Batista regime.

In our capital . . . a strange "phenomenon" has developed . . . among groups of young people and some who are not so young. . . . We began seeing several groups, hundreds of youngsters in different groups, influenced among other things by imperialist propaganda, who began to make a public display of their moral degradation. And so, for example, they began to live in a very extravagant way, to meet in certain streets of the city, in the area of La Rampa in front of the Hotel Capri. And what do you think they did there? Some engaged in corrupting 14- and 15-year-old girls and in promoting prostitution among 14-, 15-, and 16-year-old girls, serving as panderers for foreigners visiting Cuba, for sailors of ships from capitalist countries who were lodged in the area. And these individuals had the nerve to do business with those people and sell them girls who were practically children, right in the heart of the revolutionary capital which has eradicated the disgusting social canker of prostitution . . . common in a capitalist society.

To those who could remember the old days before the revolution, Castro's description must have sounded quite familiar.

Two decades later, as China was preparing to celebrate the fortieth anniversary of the establishment of the People's Republic, Edward A. Gargan reported in the *New York Times* on the spread of prostitution in that country as well. Under the headline "Newest Economics Revives the Oldest Profession," he wrote: "In dark hotel bars along China's coast, young women in tight dresses and carefully coiffed hair wiggle their ankles as they linger for hours over a single Coke. Nearby, young men in ostentatious jewelry look for clients to whom they can offer the women's services. Prostitution in China is back and flourishing."

The article went on to describe conditions in the port city of Foochow, where "that profession once obliterated by the Communists in China has reappeared and is now an entrenched facet of urban life." Here the commerce in sex had become as commonplace as in Moscow or Havana:

> A young man in his 20's strolled into the bar fingering a gold watch on his left wrist, his eyes massaging the room the way a furrier fingers a pelt. He pivoted slightly on his stacked heels, cruised to a table and slithered into a lounge chair.
>
> "Girls?" he whispered as he stared intently away from the subjects of his inquiry. "Do you want girls?"
>
> "How much?" came the reply.
>
> Slowly and nonchalantly he lifted two fingers from the table, a tapered two-inch-long thumbnail tapping the glass surface twice. "Two hundred."
>
> "You can take the girls to your room now," he said, his voice low. "If they check, just swear at them and don't open your door under any circumstances. But I think they won't check."

This was not quite as blatant as the wide-open peddling of vice under the Kuomintang, but it was clearly moving in that direction.[13]

The most common form of implicit rebellion against the established values of the new order, however, is unconventionality rather than illegality—in other words, the rejection, especially by the young, of official pieties and orthodoxies. Before the revolution youthful defiance of authority finds expression in the repudiation of bourgeois attitudes and customs; afterward it finds expression in their cultivation. There is a curious irony in that. As long as the *ancien régime* remains in power, children of the elite frequently dress, speak, behave, and live in ways designed to scandalize their elders. Thereby they voice their disapproval of the system responsible for their superior social status. But once the *ancien régime* falls, the tables are turned. The children of the revolutionary patriciate now come to constitute a new *jeunesse dorée*, flaunting their affluence and modishness, scorning the egalitarian preachments of the new order, and openly imitating the fads and fashions of capitalistic society. Their conduct reflects a growing skepticism regarding the pious radical rhetoric of established authority.

In 1956 an official youth publication in the Soviet Union indignantly condemned these corrupt backsliders from revolutionary idealism. "If he is Boris, he calls himself Bob, and if he is Ivan, he calls himself John. He lives off his parents and 'burns' his money in restaurants. Sometimes he is registered as a student, but he 'despises' cramming and crammers and therefore does not study. He 'adores' everything foreign and is ready to give his right arm for a fashionable [phonograph] record." All right-thinking young people were warned to shun his example.

Similarly, in 1968 a radio broadcast in Havana deplored the passion for bourgeois styles and customs that a growing part of Cuban youth was beginning to display:

> The young boys think that the new man is one who wears short pants. One sees how these ill-mannered brats talk back to their parents and how they act in their homes, on the streets, and in the schools. They are disrespectful and use improper language. . . . Perhaps not so many of them have taken up their little guitars after Fidel spoke about them, but there are many left. They wear tighter pants every day, and they let their bangs grow longer until they look like girls. We could say that these are the new men of a bankrupt universe. They are the ones who like to sing and dance to modern music. . . . What do they call modern music? A Yankee rhythm which is imported so that they can dance their epileptic dances? They themselves say that they are sick, and they are. They need to be cured. They need a radical cure. The coffee plantations are waiting.
>
> The miniskirt, a type of urban bikini, is another of the styles we import with the greatest shamelessness. It is a temptation in the middle of the street. . . . Is that the new world? Is that the human being of the coming third world so heralded by the intellectuals? No! . . . Lack of respect and lack of raiment are not qualities which will denote the new man.

When it comes to reproving rebellious youth, all systems of authority, whether radical or traditionalist, sound alike.

After Mao's death in 1976, the same complaints could be heard about the growing indifference of young people to revolutionary teachings in China, about their adoption of foreign tastes and manners, about their interest in bourgeois pastimes and amusements. "What is happening is that the government now says it wants to learn from the West," a troubled schoolteacher confided to the American journalist Fox Butterfield. "By that it means Western science and technology and the rule of law. But when young people see it is fashionable to copy the West, what they imitate is all the superficial things, sunglasses, long hair, bell-bottom pants, dating in high school."

A letter from a scandalized reader published in the *Peking Daily* said the same thing more directly and critically. "Seeing the behavior of certain young people, we older workers are worried. These young people have not thoroughly studied literature, Marxism-Leninism, and Mao Tse-tung Thought. Instead of devoting themselves to work, these young people prefer to wear pornographic bell-bottom trousers, spend hours getting their hair permed, and excite themselves doing foreign dances. Such behavior really should not be permissible."

This pervasive condemnation of youthful unconventionality does not derive simply from differences in age, experience, or way of life. It also reflects a recognition that disregard for the usages and proprieties of the new order represents a symbolic rejection of its beliefs and doctrines.[14]

Within a generation after its establishment, the radical dictatorship thus begins to show the same signs of senescence and ossification, formalism and rigidity, that had characterized the *ancien régime* prior to its fall. The same widening gulf appears between word and deed, theory and practice, official rhetoric and unofficial behavior. Outwardly a world of difference seems to separate the new order from the old, but beneath the surface important similarities gradually emerge. While the structure of proprietorship changes, distinctions in affluence and status remain. The elite that arises under the radical dictatorship is at first more open and accessible; its social foundation is initially more democratic. But with time it too becomes exclusive and inflexible, stratified and rigid. Social differences, which are briefly suppressed by the revolution, soon reappear in a form less ostentatious than before, but substantial enough to maintain the hierarchical structure of the community. Even the ethical teachings and moral values of the new order calcify into a rigorous orthodoxy. The radical dictatorship starts displaying all the classic symptoms of age and exhaustion.

From the Communist Manifesto *to* Animal Farm

Most of the great revolutionary leaders of the twentieth century are now dead. They rest in embalmed splendor in mausoleums erected in their memory by the regimes they helped establish—Lenin in Red Square in Moscow, Mao in T'ien An Men Square in Peking, Ho Chi Minh in Ba Dinh Square in Hanoi. They are viewed daily by reverent throngs standing patiently in line to honor the tutelary deities of the new order. Foreign visitors are invited to make a pilgrimage to these sanctuaries as well, but they must remember to display a proper veneration. Anyone with his hands in his pockets or folded behind his back will be sternly reprimanded by one of the military guards, in spotless uniform and white gloves, whose task is to maintain decorum among the worshipers. Hands must be kept respectfully at the side in the presence of a dead radical saint.

But those who rest embalmed and preserved on their catafalques, like the pharaohs of ancient Egypt, also symbolize the revolution in ways their disciples had not intended. For beneath the serene expression and lifelike appearance lies a corpse; under the flowers and decorations and inscriptions reposes a dead body. The system of authority erected by the founders of the new order resembles them in its lack of spirit and vitality. Although the institutions introduced by the revolution are still there, they no longer command inner faith or respect. They no longer have the capacity to inspire, arouse, hearten, or excite. The words that had once moved the masses, the ideas that had once impelled them to heroic deeds, are now reduced to platitudes. They may still command ceremonial agreement or pious submission, but they no longer possess creative vigor. The new order, like its founders, lies lifeless on a catafalque.

The revolution resembles some great religious movement in its ability to transcend briefly the ordinary limitations of the human condition. For a decade or two the power of belief is able to inspire large numbers of people to actions of which they would under normal circumstances have been incapable. Like some great religious movement, moreover, the revolution rests on an inspiring vision of human destiny, on a cosmic epic of sin and grace, fall and redemption. Its victory represents the triumph of spiritual forces over the material limitations of everyday existence.

At the heart of the revolutionary faith lies a complex of ideas expressed in their most exciting form in the *Manifesto of the Communist Party*, a masterpiece of radical eloquence published by Karl Marx and Friedrich Engels early in 1848. Prophets of a new secular religion, they foretold the coming of a new age in which man would cease oppressing man, justice would govern every human institution, and happiness would become the birthright of all. But this goal could not be achieved without a struggle. Domination by a propertied elite would have to be replaced, violently, if need be, by the rule of the propertyless masses. "The first step in the revolution by the working class is to raise the proletariat to the position of ruling class, to win the battle of democracy." Only then would the meek inherit the earth and the pure in heart see God.

The overthrow of the old order, Marx and Engels preached, was bound to lead to a just redistribution of property and wealth. "The proletariat will use its political supremacy to wrest by degrees all capital from the bourgeoisie, to centralize all instruments of production in the hands of the State, *i.e.*, of the proletariat organized as the ruling class, and to increase the total of productive forces as rapidly as possible." Admittedly, the reconstruction of the economic system would require the use of force. How else could the resistance of the propertied classes be overcome? "In the beginning this cannot be effected except by means of despotic inroads on the rights of property and on the conditions of bourgeois production, by means of measures therefore which appear economically insufficient and untenable, but which in the course of the movement outstrip themselves, necessitate further inroads upon the old social order, and are unavoidable as a means of entirely revolutionizing the mode of production."

The ultimate goal of the revolution, however, is not oppression but freedom, not dictatorship but democracy. "The Communists . . . labor everywhere for the union and agreement of the democratic parties of all countries," proclaims the *Manifesto*. Indeed, once economic oppression has come to an end, the need for political oppression will come to an end as well. "When . . . class distinctions have disappeared and all production has been concentrated in the hands of a vast association of the whole nation, the public power will lose its political character." After the proletariat has become the ruling class and has swept away the old conditions of production, "then it will, along with these conditions, have swept away the conditions for the existence of class antagonisms and of classes generally, and will thereby have abolished its own supremacy as a class." In other words, "in place of the old bourgeois society with its classes and class antagonisms, we shall have an association in which the free development of each is the condition for the free development of all."

The revolution, moreover, will establish a just and harmonious system of relations among peoples. Once the source of economic exploitation has been removed, the source of armed conflict will vanish as well. "United action, of the leading civilized countries at least, is one of the first conditions for the emancipation of the proletariat." Social strife, Marx and Engels argued, is at the root of military strife. The elimination of the cause will therefore lead logically to the elimination of the effect. "In proportion as the exploitation of one individual by another is put an end to, the exploitation of one nation by another will also be put an end to. In proportion as the antagonism between classes within the nation vanishes, the hostility of one nation to another will come to an end." The victory of the revolution would introduce a new era in the history of mankind, an era of peace, justice, freedom, and virtue.

A hundred years later a disillusioned radical, a writer who once fought for the revolutionary cause in the Spanish Civil War, published a mordant political fable portraying what had happened to that noble dream of Marx and Engels. In *Animal Farm* George Orwell described a rebellion of the barnyard creatures, led by the pigs, against their two-legged masters. Their goal had been the establishment of an ideal community without oppression or exploitation. But in time a new porcine elite had emerged that became as tyrannical as the old human patriciate. When some neighboring farmers arrive for a friendly game of cards with the pigs, the other animals gaze bewildered through the windows of the house, no longer able to distinguish between liberators and oppressors:

Yes, a violent quarrel was in progress. There were shoutings, bangings on the table, sharp suspicious glances, furious denials. The source of the trouble appeared to be that [one of the pigs] and Mr. Pilkington had each played an ace of spades simultaneously. Twelve voices were shouting in anger, and they were all alike. No question, now, what had happened to the faces of the pigs. The creatures outside looked from pig to man, and from man to pig, and from pig to man again; but already it was impossible to say which was which.

To Orwell the new order ends up sooner or later indistinguishable from the old.[15]

How fair is this conclusion? Does the radical dictatorship in fact become eventually identical with the *ancien régime?* Perhaps not entirely; perhaps Orwell exaggerates. Disparity in wealth does diminish after the revolution, especially in the early years; access to power broadens; education becomes more democratic; health care grows more available. And yet it is also true that with the passage of time striking similarities begin to appear; the system ossifies and rigidifies; economic differences sharpen, social distinctions solidify, educational opportunities dwindle. The old and the new may never become exactly the same, but they start to resemble one another more and more.

It is clear, moreover, that social revolution is not a necessary condition of social progress. An improvement in the material position of the lower classes, sometimes a dramatic improvement, can take place without the violent overthrow of the established system of power and wealth. The standard of living of the masses in the Federal Republic of Germany or in Japan or in South Korea is in no way inferior to the standard of living in the Soviet Union or in the People's Republic of China or in Vietnam. Indeed, a system of private property can under favorable circumstances provide a much higher level of general economic well-being than a collectivized organization of production.

But are there not some conditions under which only mass insurrection can put an end to an irremediably corrupt and oppressive system of authority? Would the Russia of Nicholas II or the China of Chiang Kai-shek or the Cuba of Fulgencio Batista have ever been prodded by peaceful means into a commitment to economic welfare and social justice? Maybe not, though the answer can be no more than speculation. In any case, a society that adopts revolutionary means to serve progressive ends should have no illusions about their long-range effect. An enormous gulf stretches between the theory and reality of the new order, between its aspiration and achievement, its word and deed, its benefit and cost. Trying to change the human condition is a little like trying to change the human appearance. The prospect of correcting blemishes and deformities, of achieving love, harmony, and happiness by some radical surgical procedure, some drastic process of reconstruction, appears irresistible. Yet those contemplating it might recall Pascal's warning three hundred years ago: "Man is neither angel nor brute; and the misfortune is that he who would act the angel acts the brute."

BIBLIOGRAPHICAL ESSAY

———————◆▬—————————

The scholarly literature dealing with the nature and pattern of revolutionary movements, though vast, is to a large extent so abstruse as to be almost unintelligible to the layman. After reviewing it, Lawrence Stone concluded in his "Theories of Revolution," *World Politics*, XVIII (1965–66) that some of the writings of contemporary social scientists "are ingenious feats of verbal juggling in an esoteric language, performed around the totem pole of an abstract model, surrounded as far as the eye can see by the arid wastes of terminological definitions and mathematical formulae." The criticism is not without justification. Yet at least two works are not only readable and illuminating but essential for an understanding of modern revolutions. Edmund Wilson, *To the Finland Station: A Study in the Writing and Acting of History* (New York, 1940) is a brilliant study of the radical tradition and the rise of socialism in Europe during the last two hundred years. Crane Brinton, *The Anatomy of Revolution* (New York, 1938), on the other hand, seeks to find a revolutionary archetype by comparing the English, the American, the French, and the Russian Revolutions. These two books are a must.

Other works, some of them quite old, provide sharp insights and penetrating observations as well. For example, Alexis de Tocqueville's classic *L'ancien régime et la révolution* (Paris, 1856), which has appeared in English in numerous translations, deals primarily with the decline and fall of the old order in France during the eighteenth century. But what it has to say is highly pertinent for an understanding of every *ancien régime* on the eve of its overthrow. Similarly, the views expressed by Engels in his letter of April 23, 1885, to the Russian socialist Vera Zasulich about the way every revolution assumes forms that its makers had neither foreseen nor intended remain relevant a century after his death. This letter has been republished in many collections, in Karl Marx and Frederick Engels, *Selected Correspondence, 1846–1895* (New York, 1942), for instance.

In studying any particular revolutionary movement, the logical starting point is the speeches and writings of its most prominent leaders. These often provide the key to an understanding of their strategies and objectives. In the case of Russia, V. I. Lenin, *Collected Works*, 45 vols. (Moscow, 1963–70) is indispensable for the early years of the Bolshevik regime. After that there is J. V. Stalin, *Works*, 13 vols. (Moscow, 1952–55), which does not go beyond early 1934, however. Hence for the last two decades of the Soviet dictator's career the reader has to rely on individual reprints of his most important statements—almost all of them translated into the major European languages—such as Joseph Stalin, *Mastering Bolshevism* (New York, 1937). What the two top men had to say should be supplemented with the views expressed by the leading figures of the second rank; for example, L. M. Kaganovich, *Socialist Reconstruction of Moscow and Other Cities in the U.S.S.R.* (New York, 1931), J. Stalin, V. M. Molotov, L. M. Kaganovich, K. E. Voroshilov, V. V. Kuibyshev, G. K. Orjonikidze, and D. Z. Manuilsky, *Socialism Victorious* (New York, 1935), and *The Land of Socialism Today and Tomorrow: Reports and Speeches at the Eighteenth Congress of the Communist Party of the Soviet Union (Bolsheviks), March 10–21, 1939* (Moscow, 1939). For the policies and programs of the radical dictatorship in Russia, the reader might also look at the *Resolutions and Decisions of the Communist Party of the Soviet Union*, ed. Robert H. McNeal, 5 vols. (Toronto and Buffalo, 1974–82).

The opinions of the defenders of the new order should be balanced by those of its critics, both domestic and foreign. Here the most important work is Leon Trotsky, *The History of the Russian Revolution*, 3 vols. (New York, 1932). The author, whose role in the establishment of the Bolshevik regime was second only to Lenin's, not only deals with developments in Russia after the fall of czarism, but also offers sharp insights into the nature of the revolutionary process itself. Christian Rakovsky, *Selected Writings on Opposition in the*

USSR, 1922–30, ed. Gus Fagan (London and New York, 1980) presents the views of a disillusioned Bolshevik who paid with imprisonment and death for his belief that the Stalin dictatorship was betraying the ideals of the revolution. Julius Martov, the most prominent leader of the Mensheviks, voiced his disappointment with what was happening in Russia even earlier in a series of articles and essays, some of which appear in English translation as *The State and the Socialist Revolution* (New York, 1938). Of the numerous eyewitness accounts by non-Russian observers, Walter Duranty, *I Write as I Please* (New York, 1935), highly favorable to the Soviet system without being blind to some of its shortcomings, is among the more interesting.

While there are many general histories of the Russian Revolution, the most detailed and erudite is Edward Hallett Carr, *A History of Soviet Russia*, 10 vols. in 14 (London, 1950–78), which carries the story down to the end of the 1920s. Another important work, William Henry Chamberlin, *The Russian Revolution, 1917–1931*, 2 vols. (New York, 1935), though less exhaustive, is more successful in capturing the sense of upheaval and excitement during the revolutionary era. The scholarly literature on various aspects of the Soviet Union is enormous, but two studies deserve special mention. Leonard Schapiro, *The Communist Party of the Soviet Union*, 2d ed. (London, 1970) and Merle Fainsod, *How Russia Is Ruled*, rev. ed. (Cambridge, Mass., 1963) are indispensable for a comprehension of the structure of power under the new order. In addition, T. H. Rigby, *Communist Party Membership in the U.S.S.R., 1917–1967* (Princeton, N.J., 1968) contains useful statistical data on the growth of the bureaucratic apparatus following the victory of the revolution.

Some of the more specialized monographic works should be looked at as well for the insight they provide into broader issues. Regarding the question of foreign financial control over the economy of czarist Russia, see the scholarly and informative book by John P. McKay, *Pioneers for Profit: Foreign Entrepreneurship and Russian Industrialization, 1885–1913* (Chicago and London, 1970). Sheila Fitzpatrick, *Education and Social Mobility in the Soviet Union, 1921–34* (Cambridge, London, New York, and Melbourne, 1979) is a penetrating study of the way in which higher learning helped create a new social elite under the Bolshevik regime. A related subject, the unsuccessful attempt to establish an egalitarian system of university edu-

cation, is treated on a smaller scale but with equal perceptiveness by
James C. McClelland, "Proletarianizing the Student Body: The Soviet Experience during the New Economic Policy," *Past & Present*,
no. 80 (1978). An interesting collective profile of the leadership of the
Soviet Union during the 1920s, focusing on its social background and
political experience, can be found in Jerome Davis, "A Study of One
Hundred and Sixty-three Outstanding Communist Leaders," published as part of the *Studies in Quantitative and Cultural Sociology: Papers Presented at the Twenty-fourth General Meeting of the American
Sociological Society, Held at Washington, D. C., December 27–30, 1929*
(Chicago, 1930).

Finally, although not enough is known about everyday life in Russia between the two world wars, several illuminating studies, based
to a considerable extent on indirect evidence, have appeared.
William J. Chase, *Workers, Society, and the Soviet State: Labor and Life
in Moscow, 1918–1929* (Urbana, Ill., and Chicago, 1987) presents a fas-
cinating portrait of social conditions in the Soviet capital during the
first decade of the new order. For a critical but not unfair analysis of
the regime's agricultural policies, especially the program of forced
consolidation carried out in the early 1930s, see M. Lewin, *Russian
Peasants and Soviet Power: A Study of Collectivization* (Evanston,
1968). Robert Conquest, *The Harvest of Sorrow: Soviet Collectivization
and the Terror-Famine* (New York and Oxford, 1986) deals with the
same subject, but is even harsher in its attack on Stalin's treatment
of the peasantry. Alex Inkeles, *Public Opinion in Soviet Russia: A
Study in Mass Persuasion* (Cambridge, Mass., 1958) examines the
techniques employed by the radical dictatorship to shape popular
beliefs and attitudes. The growing stratification and rigidification of
the social system is portrayed in Alex Inkeles and Raymond Bauer,
The Soviet Citizen: Daily Life in a Totalitarian Society (Cambridge,
Mass., 1959), a highly informative work based on interviews obtained from nearly 3,000 émigrés from Russia who left during or
soon after the Second World War.

For the revolution in China, the indispensable source is the *Selected Works of Mao Tse-tung*, 5 vols. (Peking, 1961–77). It contains
the most important statements on policy and objective by the
leader of the Chinese Communist Party from the middle 1920s on.
Unfortunately, it does not go beyond 1957, so that for the last

nineteen years of his life it has to be supplemented with various other collections, all of them rather thin, such as *Mao Tse-tung Unrehearsed: Talks and Letters, 1956–71*, ed. Stuart Schram (Harmondsworth, Ringwood, and Markham, 1974). Furthermore, there is a useful edition of major documents and statements by Mao and his followers during the three decades preceding their triumph, published under the title *A Documentary History of Chinese Communism*, ed. Conrad Brandt, Benjamin Schwartz, and John K. Fairbank (Cambridge, Mass., 1952). For the first ten years or so of the new order, two handy collections of government decrees and official declarations have appeared: *The Chinese Communist Regime: Documents and Commentary*, ed. Theodore H. E. Chen (New York, Washington, and London, 1967) and *Communist China, 1955–1959: Policy Documents with Analysis*, ed. Robert R. Bowie and John K. Fairbank (Cambridge, Mass., 1972).

The accounts by foreign eyewitnesses are on the whole quite illuminating though by no means always reliable. For example, Edgar Snow, *Red Star over China* (New York, 1938), highly favorable to the Communists, created a sensation when first published, but today seems a little starry-eyed and Pollyannaish. On the other hand, A. Doak Barnett, *China on the Eve of Communist Takeover* (New York, Washington, and London, 1963), which contains reports by an American journalist stationed in China during 1947–49, and Derk Bodde, *Peking Diary: A Year of Revolution* (New York, 1950), the observations of a sinologist who lived in the Far East during the same period, have held up remarkably well. Both depict vividly the mood of confusion, resentment, and disaffection, especially among the educated classes, in the last years of the Kuomintang regime.

The best general history of China since the Communist rise to power is without doubt Maurice Meisner, *China and After: A History of the People's Republic* (New York and London, 1986), which is not only informative and readable but highly perceptive. Some of the older books, however, deserve to be looked at as well, especially Jacques Guillermaz, *The Chinese Communist Party in Power, 1949–1976* (Boulder, 1976) and Jürgen Domes, *The Internal Politics of China, 1949–72* (New York and Washington, 1973). For the triumph of the new order after the Second World War, see Suzanne Pepper, *Civil War in China: The Political Struggle, 1945–1949* (Berkeley, Los Angeles, and London, 1978). The role played in public affairs by young people pursuing a higher education under the Kuomintang has been examined in an interesting monograph by John Israel, *Student Nationalism in China, 1927–1937* (Stanford, 1966).

Concerning China's economic development in the last decades of the empire and during the Nationalist period, there are two excellent articles by Albert Feuerwerker, both in *The Cambridge History of China*, 15 vols. (Cambridge, 1978–). The first, "Economic Trends in the Late Ch'ing Empire, 1870–1911," appears in volume XI, and the second, "Economic Trends, 1912–49," in volume XII. For the years after Mao's victory, the best treatment is Carl Riskin, *China's Political Economy: The Quest for Development since 1949* (New York, 1987), which has now largely superseded such well-known earlier works as Yuan-li Wu, *The Economy of Communist China, 1949–1972* (New York, Washington, and London, 1965). At least some of the more important specialized studies of China's economy under the new order should also be mentioned. Barry M. Richman, *Industrial Society in Communist China* (New York, 1969), written by an expert in business administration, is based in part on firsthand observation. Franz Schurmann, *Ideology and Organization in Communist China*, 2d ed. (Berkeley and Los Angeles, 1968) analyzes from a sociologist's point of view the principles of control and management adopted by the People's Republic. Finally, Christopher Howe, "Labour Organization and Incentives in Industry, before and after the Cultural Revolution," in *Authority, Participation and Cultural Change in China*, ed. Stuart R. Schram (Cambridge, 1973) provides useful data on the standard of living of industrial workers following the establishment of the Communist regime.

An interesting comparative study of the political leaderships of the Nationalists and the Communists may be found in Robert C. North and Ithiel de Sola Pool, *Kuomintang and Chinese Communist Elites* (Stanford, 1952), which concludes that the two were quite similar in their social background. Other perceptive analyses, somewhat narrower in scope, of the origin and experience of those in power under the People's Republic are Chao Kuo-chün, "Leadership in the Chinese Communist Party," *Annals of the American Academy of Political and Social Science*, CCCXXI (1959) and Donald W. Klein, "The 'Next Generation' of Chinese Communist Leaders,"

China Quarterly, no. 12 (1962). The subject of John Wilson, *Leadership in Communist China* (Ithaca, N.Y., 1963) is not only the Communist party's concept of authority, but also its class composition and numerical growth.

The way in which power is exercised under the new order has been examined in a number of important monographs. Lyman P. Van Slyke, *Enemies and Friends: The United Front in Chinese Communist History* (Stanford, 1967), looks at how the radicals wooed, used, and then discarded the moderates, all in the name of Marxian principle. Their efforts to shape and direct public opinion are analyzed in Franklin W. Houn, *To Change a Nation: Propaganda and Indoctrination in Communist China* (Glencoe, Ill., 1961). On a similar subject, the educational policies pursued by the government of the People's Republic, nearly all the general histories provide at least some statistical information. But in addition see two first-rate articles, one by Suzanne Pepper, "Education for the New Order" in volume XIV of *The Cambridge History of China*, which covers the period through the middle 1950s, and the other by Immanuel C. Y. Hsu, "The Reorganisation of Higher Education in Communist China, 1949–61," *China Quarterly*, no. 19 (1964), which deals with developments down to the end of the decade.

For the grimmer aspects of the radical dictatorship, there is Anne F. Thurston, *Enemies of the People* (New York, 1987), a portrayal of the brutalities endured by those who were or appeared to be less than enthusiastic about the People's Republic. It is based on the personal accounts of about 50 Chinese, many of whom had suffered abuse for alleged disaffection during the Cultural Revolution, but some also during the early years of the Communist government. The way in which the fall of the *ancien régime* affected life in the countryside is depicted in William Hinton, *Fanshen: A Documentary of Revolution in a Chinese Village* (New York and London, 1966), a study of a small farming community in Shansi province after the Japanese were driven out in 1945 by the Communist Eighth Route Army. It is one of the few works to rely on interviews with eyewitnesses in portraying the impact of the new order on the everyday existence of the rural masses.

Finally, the observations of Westerners who visited China after 1949 can be quite illuminating, often for what they reveal about Occidental intellectuals rather than the People's Republic. Basil Davidson, for instance, a British publicist and novelist who traveled to the Far East in the early 1950s at the invitation of the Chinese government, described his impressions in *Daybreak in China* (London, 1953), proclaiming that he had finally found "people who believe that humanity can grow in stature and self-belief until wars and famine, pestilence, and hatred, may eventually become things entirely of the past." Similarly, the French philosopher Simone de Beauvoir, who made her pilgrimage to Peking a few years later, returned deeply impressed by the leaders of the new China. "They have this inimitable naturalness you scarcely find anywhere save among the Chinese," she wrote in her *Long March* (Cleveland and New York, 1958), "a naturalness which perhaps comes from their profound ties with the peasantry and with the soil." The future seemed to her bright with the promise of a better life for the masses of the Far East.

By the early 1980s, however, a less idealized, more hardheaded view of the People's Republic began to emerge among foreign visitors. China gradually ceased to be regarded as the embodiment of civic virtue and social justice. Thus both Fox Butterfield, *China: Alive in the Bitter Sea* (New York, 1982), written by an experienced reporter for the *New York Times*, and Orville Schell, *To Get Rich Is Glorious: China in the Eighties* (New York, 1984), the work of a recognized authority on the Far East, depicted not only the improvements and achievements of the new order but also its errors and corruptions.

The body of information on the revolution in Cuba is surprisingly large, considering the modest size of the country and its population. First of all, most of the major statements by Castro have been translated into English, quite an accomplishment, since he has talked, lectured, preached, and sermonized indefatigably for more than thirty years. For his pronouncements prior to seizing power in 1959, there is the *Selected Works of Fidel Castro*, ed. Rolando E. Bonachea and Nelson P. Valdés (Cambridge, Mass., and London, 1972). For the years after 1965, an even more complete source may be found in the weekly English edition of *Granma*, the official organ of the Central Committee of the Cuban Communist Party, published in Havana, which contains the text of virtually every important speech Castro has made. For the period between 1959 and 1965, on the other hand, serious gaps exist. There are a few meager collections such as *Fidel Castro Speaks*, ed. Martin Kenner and James Petras (New York, 1969) and Fidel Castro, *Speeches*, ed. Michael Taber, 3 vols. (New York, London, and Sydney, 1981–85); but the chances of finding a particular statement in any one of them are slim. It would be better to look at some of the leading Cuban newspapers like the well-known militant *Hoy* or the organ of Castro's political organizations, *Revolución*, both published in the capital city.

Of the other revolutionary leaders, only Che Guevara has been considered important enough to justify a translation into English, under the title *Venceremos!: The Speeches and Writings of Ernesto Che Guevara*, ed. John Gerassi (New York, 1968). But the new order in Cuba, like the one in China, has also attracted the uncritical admiration of many Western intellectuals. Some of them were veteran dissidents who had spent a lifetime opposing the political system in their own country. The American publicist and essayist Scott Nearing, for example, spoke approvingly in his *Making of a Radical: A Political Autobiography* (New York, Evanston, San Francisco, and London, 1972) about "Castro's spectacular success in challenging Washington's power monopoly in the western hemisphere," while the writer and historian Waldo Frank, who had once extolled Stalin, now extolled Castro in his *Cuba: Prophetic Island* (New York, 1961), expressing surprise that "this . . . man is called a dictator, even a Communist dictator. It seems unreal."

The French existentialist philosopher Jean-Paul Sartre, some twenty years younger than Nearing and Frank, was even more enthusiastic. His *Sartre on Cuba* (New York, 1961) is an ardent panegyric about the merits and accomplishments of the Cuban Revolution. And he was followed in turn by the youngest generation of foreign supporters of the Castro regime, men and women still in their thirties or forties, who saw in the new Cuba a rejection of the materialistic values of their own society. They included people like the sociologist C. Wright Mills, *Listen, Yankee: The Revolution in Cuba* (New York, Toronto, and London, 1960), the novelist Norman Mailer, *The Presidential Papers* (New York, 1963), and the cultural critic Susan Sontag, "Some Thoughts on the Right Way (for Us) to Love the Cuban Revolution," *Ramparts*, April 1969, to whom it seemed "as if the whole country [Cuba] is high on some beneficent kind of speed." Still, not every sympathizer with the Castro regime has been uncritical. K. S. Karol, *Guerrillas in Power: The Course of the Cuban Revolution* (New York, 1970), one of the most perceptive eye-witness accounts, was written by a left-wing European journalist who remained favorable to the revolution without ignoring its faults and failures.

The polemical literature hostile to the Cuban Revolution, though not nearly as voluminous, should not be ignored either. It includes, to start with, out-and-out apologias for the *ancien régime*. Fulgencio Batista himself wrote in exile two works, *Cuba Betrayed* (New York, Washington, and Hollywood, 1962) and *The Growth and Decline of the Cuban Republic* (New York, 1964), insisting that charges of atrocities leveled against his government were largely fabrications by left-ist enemies of law and order. More persuasive are the views of those who started out as supporters of the revolution, but then turned against it because of its excesses; for example, Theodore Jacquenay, "Face to Face with Huber Matos," *Worldview*, April 1980, and Carlos Franqui, *Family Portrait with Fidel: A Memoir* (New York, 1984). And finally there are the recollections of those who, without playing a significant political role, suffered persecution and imprisonment for expressing disapproval of the radical dictatorship, recollections such as *Against All Hope: The Prison Memoirs of Armando Valladares* (New York, 1986).

Among the best general accounts of recent Cuban history are Hugh Thomas, *Cuba: The Pursuit of Freedom* (New York, Evanston, San Francisco, and London, 1971), very detailed though not always easy reading, and Jorge I. Domínguez, *Cuba: Order and Revolution* (Cambridge, Mass., and London, 1978), less extensive but for the pe-riod since 1959 more informative. Some of the older books that, de-spite their political predilections, offer an interesting perspective on the new order include Boris Goldenberg, *The Cuban Revolution and Latin America* (New York and Washington, 1965), the work of a disil-lusioned Marxist who had lived in Cuba, and Theodore Draper, *Castroism: Theory and Practice* (New York, Washington, and London, 1965), sharply critical of the new order for its failure to institute polit-ical democracy. The sociologist Lowry Nelson has published two significant studies of living conditions in Cuba, the first, *Rural Cuba*

(Minneapolis, 1950), describing the situation under the *ancien régime*, and the second, *Cuba: The Measure of a Revolution* (Minneapolis, 1972), analyzing the accomplishments as well as shortcomings of the radical dictatorship. Sound accounts of Castro's struggle for power are presented by Ramón L. Bonachea and Marta San Martín, *The Cuban Insurrection, 1952–1959* (New Brunswick, N.J., 1974) and, on a smaller scale, by Marta San Martín and Ramón L. Bonachea, "The Military Dimensions of the Cuban Revolution," in *Cuban Communism*, ed. Irving Louis Horowitz, 6th ed. (New Brunswick, N.J., and Oxford, 1987).

A collection of thoughtful essays on various aspects of the new order—"The Economic and Social Background" by Dudley Seers, "Agriculture" by Andrés Bianchi, "Education" by Richard Jolly, and "Industry" by Max Nolff—may be found in *Cuba: The Economic and Social Revolution*, ed. Dudley Seers (Chapel Hill, N.C., 1964). Richard R. Fagen, *The Transformation of Political Culture in Cuba* (Stanford, 1969), is a cautiously sympathetic account of the way in which the government in Havana has sought to mobilize public opinion behind its policies. For popular views of the revolution, one of the few reliable studies is Lloyd A. Free, *Attitudes of the Cuban People Toward the Castro Regime in the Late Spring of 1960* (Princeton, N.J., 1960), which concludes that a large majority still supported the new order a year after its establishment.

There are several useful works dealing with the economy of Cuba both before and after the revolution. On the period of the Batista dictatorship, important statistical information may be found in the United Nations, Department of Economic and Social Affairs, *Economic Survey of Latin America, 1957* (New York, 1959). For figures on the country's output and earnings under the *ancien régime*, see also Harry T. Oshima, "A New Estimate of the National Income and Product of Cuba in 1953," *Food Research Institute Studies*, II (1961). An interesting study of the Cuban standard of living before 1959 in comparison with the other nations of Latin America is presented by Roger Vekemans and J. L. Segundo, "Essay of a Socio-Economic Typology of the Latin American Countries," in *Social Aspects of Economic Development in Latin America*, ed. Egbert de Vries and José Medina Echavarría (Paris, 1963). Carmelo Mesa-Lago, *Cuba in the 1970s: Pragmatism and Institutionalization* (Albuquerque, 1974) is very informative on the economic and administrative changes introduced during the first decade and a half of the new order. The same author has published in addition a perceptive article on the "Availability and Reliability of Statistics in Socialist Cuba," *Latin American Research Review*, IV, no. 2 (1969).

What has been written about the revolution in Vietnam seems by contrast meager and uneven, partly because so much scholarly attention has been focused on a single problem: the involvement of the United States in the region. Almost every other aspect of the situation in Southeast Asia cries out for further study. Even Ho Chi Minh, *Selected Works*, 4 vols. (Hanoi, 1960–62), which covers almost forty years in the life of the most important political figure of the new order, is thin and disappointing. It consists largely of revolutionary sermons, lectures, and exhortations, rarely touching on broader questions of radical theory or policy.

The other leaders of the Vietnamese Revolution sound equally uninspired. Vo Nguyen Giap, the brain behind the successful armed struggle against first the French and then the Americans, does not generally go beyond strategy and tactics in his *Military Art of People's War: Selected Writings*, ed. Russell Stetler (New York and London, 1970). Similarly, Truong Chinh, member of the Politburo of North Vietnam and chairman of the standing committee of its National Assembly, spouts radical platitudes about heroic defenders of the people and despicable lackeys of imperialism in such speeches as *March Ahead with the Party's Banner* (Hanoi, 1963) and *Forward along the Path Charted by K. Marx* (Hanoi, 1969). The very titles are a warning to the reader. One of the few dissenting voices can be heard in Truong Nhu Tang, *A Vietcong Memoir* (San Diego, New York, and London, 1985), the moving autobiography of a member of a well-to-do Vietnamese family who devoted his life to the revolution, only to be forced into exile after its victory because he could not accept the harsh policies of the new order.

The writings of contemporary foreign observers are by and large not very enlightening either. Most of them seem to have misunderstood the nature of the revolutionary movement against the French. Thus Harold R. Isaacs, *No Peace for Asia* (New York, 1947) maintained that the Viet Minh was a coalition of moderates and radicals united in a common struggle for freedom and democracy, while to

Ellen Hammer it was clear, according to her article on "Indochina" published in *The State of Asia: A Contemporary Survey*, ed. Lawrence K. Rosinger (New York, 1951), that the Vietnamese Revolution sought nothing more than economic progress, social justice, and political liberty.

As the uprising in Southeast Asia turned from a struggle against France into a struggle against the United States, many Western intellectuals began to express the same enthusiastic approval of North Vietnam that they had once displayed toward Russia, China, and Cuba. After returning from her *Trip to Hanoi* (New York, 1968), Susan Sontag declared that "North Vietnam, while definitely no Shangri-La, is a truly remarkable country," and that "the North Vietnamese is an extraordinary human being." What she admired most was that "the Vietnamese are 'whole' human beings, not 'split' as we are." Even the writer and literary critic Mary McCarthy, not ordinarily given to effusions about exotic revolutionism, found Pham Van Dong, the prime minister of North Vietnam, almost irresistible. He was "a man of magnetic allure, thin, with deep-set brilliant eyes," she recalled in *Hanoi* (New York, 1968). The "passion and directness" of his discourse matched "something fiery, but also melancholy, in those coaly eyes." During her conversation with him, "he used none of the prevailing political clichés." Among the handful of foreign observers critical of the new order was the British novelist Graham Greene, who maintained in his "Last Act in Indo-China," *New Republic*, May 16, 1955, that the united front in North Vietnam only provided the facade for an out-and-out radical dictatorship.

Of the older general histories of the revolutionary movement in Southeast Asia, those by two writers remain standard in the field. Joseph Buttinger, *Vietnam: A Dragon Embattled*, 2 vols. (New York, Washington, and London, 1967) is thorough and reliable though a little ponderous and plodding. The works of Bernard B. Fall, on the other hand—especially *The Viet-Minh Regime: Government and Administration in the Democratic Republic of Viet-Nam*, rev. ed. (New York, 1956), *Le Viet-Minh: La République Démocratique de Viet-Nam, 1945–1960* (Paris, 1960), and *The Two Viet-Nams: A Political and Military Analysis*, 2d ed. (New York, Washington, and London, 1967)—are sharp and perceptive, even if the author's aversion to the radical dictatorship leads him occasionally to questionable conclusions. More sympathetic toward the Hanoi government is Jean Chesneaux, *The Vietnamese Nation: Contribution to a History* (Sydney, 1966). P. J. Honey, *Communism in North Vietnam: Its Role in the Sino-Soviet Dispute* (Cambridge, Mass., 1963), is an informative study of the Ho Chi Minh regime. Among the more recent general works, the best is William J. Duiker, *The Communist Road to Power in Vietnam* (Boulder, 1981), which emphasizes military and diplomatic developments. For the period following the triumph of the new order, see also Carlyle A. Thayer and David G. Marr, *Vietnam since 1975: Two Views from Australia* (Brisbane, 1982).

The economy of Southeast Asia under French rule is the subject of two solid studies, both written before the Second World War: Yves Henry, *Économie agricole de l' Indochine* (Hanoi, 1932) and Charles Robequain, *The Economic Development of French Indo-China* (London, New York, and Toronto, 1944). There is a wealth of statistical information on the economic development of Vietnam under the old as well as the new order in Hoang Van Chi, *From Colonialism to Communism: A Case History of North Vietnam* (New York and London, 1964), although this book has been criticized for its undisguised hostility toward Hanoi. On the important question of agrarian reform, while J. Price Gittinger, "Communist Land Policy in North Viet Nam," *Far Eastern Survey*, XXVIII (1959) is still useful, at least some of its conclusions must now be modified in the light of the findings presented by Edwin E. Moise, *Land Reform in China and North Vietnam: Consolidating the Revolution at the Village Level* (Chapel Hill, N.C., and London, 1983). Gérard Chaliand, *The Peasants of North Vietnam* (Hardmondsworth, Baltimore, and Ringwood, 1969) is an informative examination of rural life under the radical dictatorship written by a sympathizer.

Too little is known about the social structure of the revolutionary movement in Vietnam, but at least some data may be found in Special Operations Research Office, *Case Studies in Insurgency and Revolutionary Warfare: Vietnam, 1941–1954* (Washington, 1964) as well as in Eric R. Wolf, *Peasant Wars of the Twentieth Century* (New York, Evanston, and London, 1968). The nature of the military and political struggle in Southeast Asia has been studied by George K. Tanham, *Communist Revolutionary Warfare: From the Vietminh to the*

Viet Cong, rev. ed. (New York, Washington, and London, 1967). For the united-front strategy which the radicals pursued during their rise to power, see first George Ginsburgs, "Local Government and Administration in North Vietnam, 1945–1954," *China Quarterly,* no. 10 (1962) and then George McTurnan Kahin and John W. Lewis, *The United States in Vietnam,* rev. ed. (New York, 1969).

NOTES

CHAPTER 1

1. Leon Trotsky, *The History of the Russian Revolution*, 3 vols. (New York, 1932), II, xi.

2. B. R. Mitchell, *European Historical Statistics, 1750–1970* (London and Basingstoke, 1975), 262, 355, 364, 394, 399, 401.

3. United Nations, Department of Economic and Social Affairs, *Economic Survey of Latin America, 1957* (New York, 1959), 177–178, 181, 185.

4. Alexander Gerschenkron, "Agrarian Policies and Industrialization: Russia, 1861–1917," in *The Cambridge Economic History of Europe*, 7 vols. (Cambridge, 1941–78), VI, 742, 776; Witt Bowden, Michael Karpovich, and Abbott Payson Usher, *An Economic History of Europe since 1750* (New York, 1937), 602, 604; Oron J. Hale, *The Great Illusion, 1900–1914* (New York, Evanston, and London, 1971), 47; Isaac Deutscher, "The Russian Revolution," in *The New Cambridge Modern History*, 12 vols. (Cambridge, 1960–1970), XII, 387; D. Mackenzie Wallace, *Russia* (New York, 1877), 517; Folke Dovring, *Land and Labor in Europe in the Twentieth Century: A Comparative Survey of Recent Agrarian History*, 3d ed. (The Hague, 1965), 259.

5. Yves Henry, *Économie agricole de l'Indochine* (Hanoi, 1932), 108–109, 182–183,210–213; Hoang Van Chi, *From Colonialism to Communism: A Case History of North Vietnam* (New York and London, 1964), 149.

6. James Mavor, *An Economic History of Russia*, 2 vols. (London, Toronto, and New York, 1914), II, 356–357.

7. Arcadius Kahan, "Social Structure, Public Policy, and the Development of Education and the Economy in Czarist Russia," in *Education and Economic Development*, ed. C. Arnold Anderson and Mary Jean Bowman (Chicago, 1963), 367–368; William H. E. Johnson, *Russia's Educational Heritage* (Pittsburgh, 1950), 192–193, 195, 287, 290; George F. Kennan, "The Breakdown of the Tsarist Autocracy," in *Revolutionary Russia*, ed. Richard Pipes (Cambridge, Mass., 1968), 5; Nicholas Hans, *History of Russian Educational Policy (1701–1917)* (London, 1931), 236.

8. Roger Vekemans and J. L. Segundo, "Essay of a Socio-Economic Typology of the Latin American Countries," in *Social Aspects of Economic Development in*

Latin America, ed. Egbert de Vries and José Medina Echavarría (Paris, 1963), 83–84, 88–93; Boris Goldenberg, *The Cuban Revolution and Latin America* (New York and Washington, 1965), 120; Theodore Draper, *Castroism: Theory and Practice* (New York, Washington, and London, 1965), 77, 79, 104; Richard R. Fagen, *The Transformation of Political Culture in Cuba* (Stanford, 1969), 23; Harry T. Oshima, "A New Estimate of the National Income and Product of Cuba in 1953," *Food Research Institute Studies*, II (1961), 214.

9. Kazimierz Waliszewski, *Le Roman d'une impératrice: Catherine II de Russie d'après ses mémoires, sa correspondance et les documents inédits des archives d'état (Paris, 1893), 494.

10. Albert Feuerwerker, "Economic Trends in the Late Ch'ing Empire, 1870–1911," in *The Cambridge History of China*, 15 vols. (Cambridge, 1978–), XI, 2, 25, 34, 38, 57–58.

11. Karl C. Thalheim, "Russia's Economic Development," in *Russia Enters the Twentieth Century, 1894–1917*, ed. Erwin Oberländer, George Katkov, Nikolaus Poppe, and Georg von Rauch (New York, 1971), 89–90, 318; B. R. Mitchell, *Historical Statistics*, 355, 357; Harry T. Willets, "The Agrarian Problem," in *Russia Enters the Twentieth Century*, ed. E. Oberländer, G. Katkov, N. Poppe, and G. von Rauch, 133; A. Kahan, "Social Structure," 367.

12. Charles Robequain, *The Economic Development of French Indo-China* (London, New York, and Toronto, 1944), 21, 80–81, 83, 85–86, 220, 244, 278–279, 303, 310, 344; Jean Chesneaux, *The Vietnamese Nation: Contribution to a History* (Sydney, 1966), 110–111, 113, 115; Joseph Buttinger, *Vietnam: A Dragon Embattled*, 2 vols. (New York, Washington, and London, 1967), I, 193, 198.

13. Lowry Nelson, *Rural Cuba* (Minneapolis, 1950), 4–5, 95–97, 103.

14. V. I. Lenin, *Collected Works*, 45 vols. (Moscow, 1963–70), XXXI, 84–85.

CHAPTER 2

1. L. Trotsky, *Russian Revolution*, I, 357, II, 250.

2. *Selected Works of Mao Tse-tung*. 5 vols. (Peking, 1961–77), III, 118–119.

3. V. I. Lenin, *Works*, V, 375, 383–385, 459–460, 464, 472–473; Karl Kautsky, "Die Revision des Programms der Sozialdemokratie in Oesterreich," *Neue Zeit*, II/I (1901–02), 79–80.

4. Leonard Schapiro, *The Communist Party of the Soviet Union*, 2d ed. (London, 1970), 172–173; Jerome Davis, "A Study of One Hundred and Sixty-three Outstanding Communist Leaders," in *Studies in Quantitative and Cultural Sociology: Papers Presented at the Twenty-fourth General Meeting of the American Sociological Society, Held at Washington, D.C., December 27–30, 1929* (Chicago, 1930), 46–50.

5. Robert C. North and Ithiel de Sola Pool, *Kuomintang and Chinese Communist Elites* (Stanford, 1952), 3, 46–47, 50–52, 63–64; John Wilson Lewis, *Leadership in Communist China* (Ithaca, N.Y., 1963), 110–111.

6. *Venceremos!: The Speeches and Writings of Ernesto Che Guevara*, ed. John Gerassi (New York, 1968), 116; Eric R. Wolf, *Peasant Wars of the Twentieth Century* (New York, Evanston, and London, 1969), 269; Theodore Draper, "Castro's Cuba: A Revolution Betrayed?" *Encounter*, March 1961, 19–20.

7. Special Operations Research Office, *Case Studies in Insurgency and Revolution-*

ary Warfare: Vietnam, 1941–1954 (Washington, 1964), 10; Bernard Fall, *Le Viet-Minh: La République Démocratique du Viet-Nam, 1945–1960* (Paris, 1960), 151, 173; Truong Chinh, *March Ahead under the Party's Banner* (Hanoi, 1963), 44; E. R. Wolf, *Peasant Wars*, 200–202.

8. Crane Brinton, *The Anatomy of Revolution* (New York, 1938), 52, 56.

9. Truong Nhu Tang, *A Vietcong Memoir* (San Diego, New York, and London, 1985), 22, 260.

10. *Oeuvres, papiers et correspondances d'Alexis de Tocqueville*, ed. J.-P. Mayer, 13 vols. (Paris, 1951–77), II/I, 223.

11. Suzanne Pepper, *Civil War in China: The Political Struggle, 1945–1949* (Berkeley, Los Angeles, and London, 1978), 132; A. Doak Barnett, *China on the Eve of Communist Takeover* (New York, Washington, and London, 1963), 22; Derk Bodde, *Peking Diary: A Year of Revolution* (New York, 1950), 23–24.

12. C. Brinton, *Anatomy of Revolution*, 60.

13. Li Po-yuan, "Modern Times or a Brief History of Enlightenment," *Renditions: A Chinese-English Translation Magazine*, II (1974), 127–128; Ku Chieh-kang, *The Autobiography of a Chinese Historian* (Leyden, 1931), 28; Harold Z. Schiffrin, *Sun Yat-sen and the Origins of the Chinese Revolution* (Berkeley and Los Angeles, 1968), 144; Charlotte Furth, "Intellectual Change: From the Reform Movement to the May Fourth Movement, 1895–1920," in *Cambridge History of China*, XII, 402.

14. *The Complete Poetical Works of William Wordsworth*, 10 vols. (Boston and New York, 1904), III, 132, 230–231, 263.

CHAPTER 3

1. Fulgencio Batista, *Cuba Betrayed* (New York, Washington, and Hollywood, 1962), 40–41; idem, *The Growth and Decline of the Cuban Republic* (New York, 1964), 47, 263–264.

2. Pedro A. Barrera Pérez, "Por que et ejercito no derrato a Castro," *Bohemia Libre*, August 6, 1961, 29, August 13, 1961, 25, 80.

3. F. Batista, *Cuba Betrayed*, 170; idem, *Growth and Decline*, 47–48; B. Goldenberg, *Cuban Revolution*, 144.

4. Ho Chi Minh, *Selected Works*, 4 vols. (Hanoi, 1960–62), I, 98, 122, II, 113–114, 121, IV, 37–38.

5. S. Pepper, *Civil War in China*, 52, 54–57; Thurston Griggs, *Americans in China: Some Chinese Views* (Washington, 1948), 7–8, 11–12.

6. Ramón L. Bonachea and Marta San Martín, *The Cuban Insurrection, 1952–1959* (New Brunswick, N. J., 1974), 33–34.

7. "A Secret Memorandum of Sergei Witte on the Industrialization of Imperial Russia," ed. T. H. von Laue, *Journal of Modern History*, XXVI (1954), 66; V. I. Lenin, *Works*, V, 333–334, XXII, 231–232; J. V. Stalin, *Works*, 13 vols. (Moscow, 1952–55), VI, 77–78; L. Trotsky, *Russian Revolution*, I, 10–11, 16–17.

8. "Secret Memorandum of Witte," ed. T. H. von Laue, 70; Fred V. Carstensen, "Foreign Participation in Russian Economic Life: Notes on British Enterprise, 1865–1914," in *Entrepreneurship in Imperial Russia and the Soviet Union*, ed. Gregory Guroff and Fred V. Carstensen (Princeton, N.J., 1983), 146; John P. Mckay, *Pioneers for Profit: Foreign Entrepreneurship and Russian Industrializa-*

tion, 1885–1913 (Chicago and London, 1970), 26–28, 33; Peter I. Lyashchenko, *History of the National Economy of Russia to the 1917 Revolution* (New York, 1949), 714–716.

9. Albert Feuerwerker, "Economic Trends, 1912–49," in *Cambridge History of China*, XII, 58–60, 116–117; idem, "The Foreign Presence in China," in ibid., 192–193, 199, 202–203.

10. B. Goldenberg, *Cuban Revolution*, 140–141; L. Nelson, *Rural Cuba*, 96; Dudley Seers, "The Economic and Social Background," in *Cuba: The Economic and Social Revolution*, ed. Dudley Seers (Chapel Hill, N.C., 1964), 16; T. Draper, *Castroism*, 109.

11. Edward Hallett Carr, *A History of Soviet Russia*, 10 vols. in 14 (London, 1950–78), I, 28, 72–73, 86–87.

12. *A Documentary History of Chinese Communism*, ed. Conrad Brandt, Benjamin Schwartz, and John K. Fairbank (Cambridge, Mass., 1952), 63–64; Edgar Snow, *Red Star over China* (New York, 1938), 388; *Selected Works of Mao*, II, 438, III, 234–235.

13. Bernard B. Fall, *The Viet-Minh Regime: Government and Administration in the Democratic Republic of Viet-Nam*, rev. ed. (New York, 1956), 157; George Ginsburgs, "Local Government and Administration in North Vietnam, 1945–1954," *China Quarterly*, no. 10 (1962), 198; Truong Nhu Tang, *Vietcong Memoir*, 324, 330.

14. *Selected Works of Fidel Castro*, ed. Rolando E. Bonachea and Nelson P. Valdés (Cambridge, Mass., and London, 1972), 346, 366, 387–388.

15. V. I. Lenin, *Works*, IX, 247, 296; *Selected Works of Mao*, II, 438, III, 234; *Venceremos!: Speeches and Writings of Guevara*, ed. J. Gerassi, 76–77.

CHAPTER 4

1. *Resolutions and Decisions of the Communist Party of the Soviet Union*, ed. Robert H. McNeal, 5 vols. (Toronto and Buffalo, 1974–82), I, 45, 50, 106, 151; V. I. Lenin, *Works*, IX, 49–50, XXI, 33.

2. *Documentary History of Chinese Communism*, ed. C. Brandt, B. Schwartz, and J. K. Fairbank, 64–65; *Selected Works of Mao*, I, 168–169, II, 438, III, 231.

3. *Selected Works of Castro*, ed. R. E. Bonachea and N. P. Valdés, 346–347, 366, 370, 388.

4. Lawrence K. Rosinger, "France and the Future of Indo-China," *Foreign Policy Reports*, XXI (1945–46), 59, 64; Ellen Hammer, "Indochina," in *The State of Asia: A Contemporary Survey*, ed. Lawrence K. Rosinger (New York, 1951), 232.

5. *Documentary History of Chinese Communism*, ed. C. Brandt, B. Schwartz, and J. K. Fairbank, 220.

6. *Selected Works of Mao*, II, 329, IV, 150; *Selected Works of Castro*, ed. R. E. Bonachea and N. P. Valdés, 387–388; George McTurnan Kahin and John W. Lewis, *The United States in Vietnam*, rev. ed. (New York, 1969), 458–463.

7. George K. Tanham, *Communist Revolutionary Warfare: From the Vietminh to the Viet Cong*, rev. ed. (New York, Washington, and London, 1967), 58; John Israel, *Student Nationalism in China, 1927–1937* (Stanford, 1966), 5, 7.

8. A. D. Barnett, *China on the Eve*, 22, 46, 50–51; S. Pepper, *Civil War in China*, 225–

226; V. I. Lenin, *Works*, VII, 354–355, 386–387, 389, 401; *Selected Works of Mao*, II, 321–322.

9. H. N. Brailsford, "Russia in Transition," *New Republic*, October 9, 1915, 252–253.

10. E. Snow, *Red Star*, 211, 437, 449–450.

11. Harold R. Isaacs, *No Peace for Asia* (New York, 1947), 147, 170–171.

12. *New York Times*, February 24, 25, and 26, 1957.

13. Michael Gasster, "The Republican Revolutionary Movement," in *Cambridge History of China*, XI, 524–525; Vidya Prakash Dutt, "The First Week of Revolution: The Wuchang Uprising," in *China in Revolution: The First Phase, 1900–1913*, ed. Mary Clabaugh Wright (New Haven and London, 1968), 404, 408, 412–413; Great Britain, *Parliamentary Papers: House of Commons* (1912–13), CXXI (*Accounts and Papers, LXXIII*), no. 6148, "Correspondence respecting the Affairs of China," 21–22.

14. William Henry Chamberlin, *The Russian Revolution, 1917–1931*, 2 vols. (New York, 1935), I, 74, 85.

15. R. L. Bonachea and M. San Martín, *Cuban Insurrection*, 104, 184; Marta San Martín and Ramón L. Bonachea, "The Military Dimensions of the Cuban Revolution," in *Cuban Communism*, ed. Irving Louis Horowitz, 6th ed. (New Brunswick, N.J. and Oxford, 1987), 38; B. Goldenberg, *Cuban Revolution*, 144.

16. J. Buttinger, *Vietnam*, I, 235–237.

CHAPTER 5

1. Karl Marx and Frederick Engels, *Selected Correspondence, 1846–1895* (New York, 1942), 437–438.

2. L. Trotsky, *Russian Revolution*, I, 357, II, vii.

3. V. I. Lenin, *Works*, XXIV, 22, XXVI, 170.

4. *Selected Works of Mao*, V, 24–25, 30–31, 35, 48, 77, 296–297.

5. Herbert L. Matthews, "Now Castro Faces the Harder Fight," *New York Times Magazine*, March 8, 1959, 71–73; *New York Times*, July 16, 1959.

6. *Fidel Castro Speaks*, ed. Martin Kenner and James Petras (New York, 1969), 60, 74, 87; Fidel Castro, *Speeches*, ed. Michael Taber, 3 vols. (New York, London, and Sydney, 1981–85), II, 65–66.

7. Lyman P. Van Slyke, *Enemies and Friends: The United Front in Chinese Communist History* (Stanford, 1967), 209–210; Jacques Guillermaz, *The Chinese Communist Party in Power, 1949–1976* (Boulder, Col., 1976), 14–15, 144; Donald W. Klein, "The 'Next Generation' of Chinese Communist Leaders," *China Quarterly*, no. 12 (1962), 72; idem, "The State Council and the Cultural Revolution," in *Party Leadership and Revolutionary Power in China*, ed. John Wilson Lewis (Cambridge, 1970), 362; A. Doak Barnett, "Profile of Red China," *Foreign Policy Reports*, February 15, 1950, 235; idem, "China's 'People's Democratic Dictatorship': Recent Trends in Communist China," *AUFS Reports: East Asia Series*, IV, no. 2 (1955), 15–16.

8. B. B. Fall, *The Viet-Minh Regime*, 11; idem, *The Two Viet-Nams: A Political and Military Analysis*, 2d ed. (New York, Washington, and London, 1967), 101, 133; P. J. Honey, *Communism in North Vietnam: Its Role in the Sino-Soviet Dispute* (Cambridge, Mass., 1963), 16; Graham Greene, "Last Act in Indo-China," *New*

Republic, May 16, 1955, 11; Jacques Arnault, *Du colonialisme au socialisme* (Paris, 1966), 230.

9. *Selected Works of Castro*, ed. R. E. Bonachea and N. P. Valdés, 347, 388; F. Castro, *Speeches*, ed. M. Taber, II, 32–33, 38; Alfredo Gomez, "The Political Situation in Cuba," *Political Affairs* (October 1954), 54; R. L. Bonachea and M. San Martín, *Cuban Insurrection*, 59–60, 221; K. S. Karol, *Guerrillas in Power: The Course of the Cuban Revolution* (New York, 1970), 234.

10. *Venceremos!: Speeches and Writings of Guevara*, ed. J. Gerassi, 114–115.

11. William Hard, *Raymond Robins' Own Story* (New York and London, 1920), 14.

12 V. I. Lenin, *Works*, XXXI, 70–71, 75.

13. L. Shapiro, *The Communist Party*, 172–173; T. H. Rigby, *Communist Party Membership in the U.S.S.R., 1917–1967* (Princeton, N.J., 1968), 52; Franz Schurmann, *Ideology and Organization in Communist China*, 2d ed. (Berkeley and Los Angeles, 1968), 129–130; Bernard B. Fall, "Power and Pressure Groups in North Vietnam," *China Quarterly*, no. 9 (1962), 41.

14. J. Martov, *The State and the Socialist Revolution* (New York, 1938), 38–39, 56; Truong Nhu Tang, *Vietcong Memoir*, 268, 282, 284–285, 309–310; *New York Times*, November 17, 1975; Theodore Jacqueney, "Face to Face with Huber Matos, *Worldview*, April 1980, 5, 7.

CHAPTER 6

1. *The Bolshevik Revolution, 1917–1918: Documents and Materials*, ed. James Bunyan and H. H. Fisher (Stanford, 1934), 505–506; V. I. Lenin, *Works*, XXVI, 513; J. V. Stalin, *Works*, VI, 415.

2. *Venceremos! Speeches and Writings of Guevara*, ed. J. Gerassi, 114–115; *Fidel Castro Speaks*, ed. M. Kenner and J. Petras, 116–117.

3. *Venceremos! Speeches and Writings of Guevara*, ed. J. Gerassi, 243, 391; *Fidel Castro Speaks*, ed. M. Kenner and J. Petras, 309.

4. J. V. Stalin, *Works*, V, 100–101.

5. W. H. Chamberlin, *Russian Revolution*, I, 360, 484.

6. Gérard Chaliand, *The Peasants of North Vietnam* (Harmondsworth, Baltimore, and Ringwood, 1969), 140–141.

7. V. I. Lenin, *Works*, XXVI, 514, XXXI, 441, XXXIII, 147–148; *Bolshevik Revolution*, ed. J. Bunyan and H. H. Fisher, 516; J. V. Stalin, *Works*, XII, 311–312.

8. *Selected Works of Mao*, V, 17, 27, 117.

9. *Fidel Castro Speaks*, ed. M. Kenner and J. Petras, 9, 28–29.

10. Jean-Paul Sartre, *Sartre on Cuba* (New York, 1961), 113; *Hoy* (Havana), February 23, 1963.

11. V. I. Lenin, *Works*, XXVI, 515–516; E. H. Carr, *History of Soviet Russia*, I, 152, 159, II, 70; *Pravda* (Moscow), January 1, 1919.

12. *Selected Works of Mao*, V, 51, 397; William Hinton, *Fanshen: A Documentary of Revolution in a Chinese Village* (New York and London, 1966), 116–117.

13. *Time*, February 2, 1959, 28.

CHAPTER 7

1. E. H. Carr, *History of Soviet Russia*, I, 168, II, 38, n. 1.

2. Ellen Hammer, *Vietnam Yesterday and Today* (New York, 1966), 239; Hoang Van Chi, *Colonialism to Communism*, 186; B. B. Fall, *The Viet-Minh Regime*, 133; Edwin E. Moise, *Land Reform in China and North Vietnam: Consolidating the Revolution at the Village Level* (Chapel Hill, N.C., and London, 1983), 222; J. Price Gittinger, "Communist Land Policy in North Viet Nam," *Far Eastern Survey*, XXVIII (1959), 118.

3. M. Lewin, *Russian Peasants and Soviet Power: A Study of Collectivization* (Evanston, 1968), 21; Hugh Seton-Watson, *The Pattern of Communist Revolution: A Historical Analysis* (London, 1953), 157, n. 1, 159.

4. *Selected Works of Mao*, V, 94, 113; Nicholas R. Lardy, "Economic Recovery and the 1st Five-Year Plan," in *Cambridge History of China*, XIV, 153, 156–157; Jürgen Domes, *The Internal Politics of China, 1949–1972* (New York and Washington, 1973), 38; Yuan-li Wu, *The Economy of Communist China* (New York, Washington, and London, 1965), 75; Barry M. Richman, *Industrial Society in Communist China* (New York, 1969), 899.

5. J. P. Gittinger, "Communist Land Policy," 119; J. Chesneaux, *Vietnamese Nation*, 214.

6. Sheila Fitzpatrick, *Education and Social Mobility in the Soviet Union, 1921–34* (Cambridge, London, New York, and Melbourne, 1979), 62, 176; Alex Inkeles, "Soviet Nationality Policy in Perspective," *Problems of Communism*, IX, no. 3 (1960), 32; B. M. Richman, *Industrial Society*, 134; J. Guillermaz, *Chinese Communist Party*, 149; Suzanne Pepper, "Education for the New Order," in *Cambridge History of China*, XIV, 211; K. S. Karol, *Guerrillas in Power*, 595; Richard Jolly, "Education," in *Cuba*, ed. D. Seers, 192; B. Goldenberg, *Cuban Revolution*, 217.

7. Alex Inkeles, *Public Opinion in Soviet Russia: A Study in Mass Persuasion* (Cambridge, Mass., 1958), 144; R. R. Fagen, *Transformation of Political Culture*, 39–40.

8. S. Fitzpatrick, *Education and Social Mobility*, 62; J. Domes, *Internal Politics of China*, 72; J. Guillermaz, *The Chinese Communist Party*, 147; Lê Châu, *Le Viet Nam socialiste: une économie de transition* (Paris, 1966), 290; B. B. Fall, *The Two Viet-Nams*, 185; R. Jolly, "Education," 183, 185; K. S. Karol, *Guerrillas in Power*, 595–596.

9. Immanuel C. Y. Hsu, "The Reorganisation of Higher Education in Communist China, 1949–61," *China Quarterly*, no. 19 (1964), 148; K. S. Karol, *Guerrillas in Power*, 596; R. Jolly, "Education," 185, 222.

10. W. H. E. Johnson, *Russian Heritage*, 290; S. Fitzpatrick, *Education and Social Mobility*, 188, 197; S. Pepper, "Education for the New Order," 216–217.

11. Ho Chi Minh, *Works*, IV, 440.

12. Victor W. Sidel, "Medicine and Public Health," in *China's Developmental Experience*, ed. Michel Oksenberg (New York, 1973), 110–113, 118–119; Maurice Meisner, *Mao's China and After: A History of the People's Republic* (New York and London, 1986), 285; Lê Châu, *Le Viet Nam socialiste*, 286; G. Chaliand, *Peasants of North Vietnam*, 50; Lowry Nelson, *Cuba: The Measure of a Revolution* (Minneapolis, 1972), 112–113, 189–191; *Granma* (Havana), English ed., August 2, 1970, 2; K. S. Karol, *Guerrillas in Power*, 597.

13. D. Seers, "Economic and Social Background," 41; Christopher Howe, "Labour

Organization and Incentives in Industry, before and after the Cultural Revolution," in *Authority, Participation and Cultural Change in China*, ed. Stuart R. Schram (Cambridge, 1973), 238; N. R. Lardy, "Economic Recovery," 156.

14. Alexander Wicksteed, *Life under the Soviets* (London, 1928), 188; Lloyd A. Free, *Attitudes of the Cuban People toward the Castro Regime in the Late Spring of 1960* (Princeton, N.J., 1960), 1–3, 6–8, 24.

CHAPTER 8

1. V. I. Lenin, *Works*, XXV, 467, XXVI, 189, 382–383, 439–441.

2. Ibid., XXX, 263; J. V. Stalin, *Works*, IV, 402; L. Trotsky, *Russian Revolution*, III, 86–87.

3. *Documentary History of Chinese Communism*, ed. C. Brandt, B. Schwartz, and J. K. Fairbank, 220, 222–223, 243; *Selected Works of Mao*, V, 172–173.

4. B. B. Fall, *The Viet-Minh Regime*, 157–158; idem, *The Two Viet-Nams*, 423–424.

5. *Fidel Castro Speaks*, ed. M. Kenner and J. Petras, 85–86.

6. V. I. Lenin, *Works*, V, 19.

7. *Selected Works of Mao*, V, 297–299.

8. Merle Fainsod, *How Russia Is Ruled*, rev. ed. (Cambridge, Mass., 1963), 135–137; V. I. Lenin, *Works*, XXVII, 535, XXIX, 151, XXXII, 361–362.

9. J. Guillermaz, *The Chinese Communist Party*, 21–22, 24; M. Meisner, *Mao's China*, 81; J. Domes, *Internal Politics of China*, 51; *Communist China, 1955–1959: Policy Documents with Analysis*, ed. Robert R. Bowie and John K. Fairbank (Cambridge, Mass., 1972), 303–304; *Mao Tse-tung Unrehearsed: Talks and Letters, 1956–71*, ed. Stuart Schram (Harmondsworth, Ringwood, and Markham, 1974), 169–170; *Selected Works of Lin Piao* (Hong Kong, 1970), 27.

10. *Revolución* (Havana), January 22, 1959; B. Goldenberg, *Cuban Revolution*, 209; *Cuban Information Service*, June 1, 1963, 9–10; Hugh Thomas, *Cuba: The Pursuit of Freedom* (New York, Evanston, San Francisco, and London, 1971), 1460; Lee Lockwood, *Castro's Cuba, Cuba's Fidel* (New York, 1967), 205–207; D. Seers, "Economic and Social Background," 32.

11. D. Bodde, *Peking Diary*, 260–261.

12. J. Guillermaz, *The Chinese Communist Party*, 21–22; W. Hinton, *Fanshen*, 137–138.

13. *Selected Works of Mao*, V, 52; *The Chinese Communist Regime: Documents and Commentary*, ed. Theodore H. E. Chen (New York, Washington, and London, 1967), 109–110; M. Meisner, *Mao's China*, 89–90; *Hoy* (Havana), September 29, 1960; R. R. Fagen, *Transformation of Political Culture*, 69, 77, 83; B. Goldenberg, *Cuban Revolution*, 270–271; H. Thomas, *Cuba*, 1322, 1457; B. B. Fall, *The Two Viet-Nams*, 181–182.

14. *New York Times*, October 3, 1932; Robert Conquest, *The Harvest of Sorrow: Soviet Collectivization and the Terror-Famine* (New York, 1986), 295; Katerina Clark, "Utopian Anthropology as a Context for Stalinist Literature," in *Stalinism: Essays in Historical Interpretation*, ed. Robert C. Tucker (New York, 1977), 181; Nadezhda Mandelstam, *Hope Against Hope: A Memoir* (New York, 1978), 212–213.

15. Anne F. Thurston, *Enemies of the People* (New York, 1987), 58; Robert J. Lifton, *Thought Reform and the Psychology of Totalism: A Study of "Brainwashing" in*

China (New York, 1961), 323–324; *Chinese Communist Education: Records of the First Decade*, ed. Stewart Fraser (Nashville, 1965), 136, 139–140; *Hongkong Standard*, September 24, 1950.

16. B. Fall, *Le Viet-Minh*, 106.

CHAPTER 9

1. V. I. Lenin, *Works*, XXIV, 100, XXVIII, 133.

2. M. Fainsod, *How Russia Is Ruled*, 249; F. Schurman, *Ideology and Organization*, 129–130; J. W. Lewis, *Leadership in China*, 116.

3. E. H. Carr, *History of Soviet Russia*, I, 207, VI, 195–196; J. V. Stalin, *Works*, V, 100–101; L. Schapiro, *The Communist Party*, 235; M. Fainsod, *How Russia Is Ruled*, 249; J. W. Lewis, *Leadership in China*, 112–113.

4. V. I. Lenin, *Works*, XXIV, 100; L. Schapiro, *The Communist Party*, 238–239; J. M. H. Lindbeck, "Transformations in the Chinese Communist Party," in *Soviet and Chinese Communism: Similarities and Differences*, ed. Donald W. Treadgold (Seattle and London, 1967), 89–91; Gordon A. Bennett, "Elite and Society in China: A Summary of Research and Interpretation," in *Elites in the People's Republic of China*, ed. Robert A. Scalapino (Seattle and London, 1972), 7.

5. L. Schapiro, *The Communist Party*, 237–238, 316; T. H. Rigby, *Communist Party Membership*, 116.

6. E. H. Carr, *History of Soviet Russia*, I, 207, IV, 354, V, 92, VI, 181–82, XI, 181; T. H. Rigby, *Communist Party Membership*, 116, 164; L. Schapiro, *The Communist Party*, 241, 316–317; M. Fainsod, *How Russia Is Ruled*, 250; M. Lewin, *Russian Peasants*, 119–122.

7. T. H. Rigby, *Communist Party Membership*, 223; M. Fainsod, *How Russia Is Ruled*, 263, n. 29; Joseph Stalin, *Selected Writings* (New York, 1942), 212–214, 384, 475–476; V. I. Lenin, *Works*, XXVII, 133.

8. Pitirim A. Sorokin, *The Sociology of Revolution* (New York, 1925), 241–242, 271–272; S. N. Prokopovitch, *The Economic Condition of Soviet Russia* (London, 1924), 41; E. H. Carr, *History of Soviet Russia*, XI, 304; Sheila Fitzpatrick, *The Russian Revolution, 1917–1932* (Oxford and New York, 1984), 133–134; idem, *Education and Social Mobility*, 241; M. Fainsod, *How Russia Is Ruled*, 268, 505–506; Alex Inkeles and Raymond A Bauer, *The Soviet Citizen: Daily Life in a Totalitarian Society* (Cambridge, Mass., 1959), 81.

9. B. M. Richman, *Industrial Society*, 296–297.

10. E. H. Carr, *History of Soviet Russia*, IV, 40–41, V, 109–110; M. Fainsod, *How Russia Is Ruled*, 505–506; *The Land of Socialism Today and Tomorrow: Reports and Speeches at the Eighteenth Congress of the Communist Party of the Soviet Union (Bolsheviks), March 10–21, 1939* (Moscow, 1939), 51, 53, 181, 183.

11. T. H. Rigby, *Communist Party Membership*, 401; Gail Warshofsky Lapidus, "Socialism and Modernity: Education, Industrialization, and Social Change in the USSR," in *The Dynamics of Soviet Policy*, ed. Paul Cocks, Robert V. Daniels, and Nancy Whittier Heer (Cambridge, Mass., and London, 1976), 203; James C. McClelland, "Proletarianizing the Student Body: The Soviet Experience during the New Economic Policy," *Past & Present*, no. 80 (1978), 124; S. Fitzpatrick, *Russian Revolution*, 134.

12. Boris Meissner, "Social Change in Bolshevik Russia," in *Social Change in the So-*

viet Union: Russia's Path toward an Industrial Society, ed. Boris Meissner (Notre Dame, Ind., and London, *1972*), *43–44*; J. C. McClelland, "Proletarianizing the Student Body," 124; S. Fitzpatrick, *Education and Social Mobility.* 235–236.

13. S. Fitzpatrick, *Education and Social Mobility*, 58, 235; J. Stalin, *Selected Writings*, 384, 476; J. C. McClelland, "Proletarianizing the Student Body," 124; A. Inkeles and R. A. Bauer, *The Soviet Citizen*, *142*.

14. C. T. Hu, "Communist Education: Theory and Practice," *China Quarterly*, no. 10 (1962), 90; B. M. Richman, *Industrial Society*, 298; *Selected Works of Mao*, V, 353; I. C. Y. Hsu, "Reorganisation of Higher Education," 148; Suzanne Pepper, "New Directions in Education," in *Cambridge History of China*, XIV, 410–411.

15. M. Meisner, *Mao's China*, 136; S. Pepper, "New Directions," 423; *China News Analysis*, November 11, 1966, 2, 4.

16. E. H. Carr, *History of Soviet Russia*, II, 184, IV, 79–80; *China News Analysis*, November 11, 1966, 3.

CHAPTER 10

1. Karl Radek, *The Development of Socialism from Science to Practice* (Glasgow, 1920), 17.

2. J. V. Stalin, *Works*, VI, 109–111, 414–415, VII, 91–92, 165–166.

3. S. Howe, "Labour Organization and Incentives in Industry," 238; Carmelo Mesa-Lago, "Availability and Reliability of Statistics in Socialist Cuba," *Latin American Research Review*, IV, no. 2 (1969), 51; idem, *Cuba in the 1970s: Pragmatism and Institutionalization* (Albuquerque, 1974), 52–53.

4. *New York Times*, April 7, 1988; William J. Chase, *Workers, Society, and the Soviet State: Labor and Life in Moscow, 1918–1929* (Urbana, Ill., and Chicago, 1987), 185, 191.

5. *Venceremos!: Speeches and Writings of Guevara*, ed. J. Gerassi, 205; W. J. Chase, *Workers, Society, and the Soviet State*, 36; H. H. Fisher, *The Famine in Soviet Russia, 1919–1923: The Operations of the American Relief Administration* (New York, 1927), 75; L. M. Kaganovich, *Socialist Reconstruction of Moscow and Other Cities in the U.S.S.R.* (New York, 1931), 26.

6. *New York Times*, April 7, 1988; J. V. Stalin, *Works*, XIII, 58–60.

7. J. Martov, *State and Socialist Revolution*, 18–19.

8. Christian Rakovsky, *Selected Writings on Opposition in the USSR, 1923–30*, ed., Gus Fagan (London and New York, 1980), 129–130, 132, 134; T. Jacqueney, "Face to Face," 7; Truong Nhu Tang, *Vietcong Memoir*, 309–310.

9. André Malraux, "'I Am Alone with the Masses—Waiting': Forty Years of Mao and Communism," *Atlantic* (November 1968), 118–119; *Revolución* (Havana), October 22, 1963; *Granma* (Havana), English ed., July 30, 1967, 2, September 20, 1970, 9.

10. Carlos Franqui, *Family Portrait with Fidel: A Memoir* (New York, 1984), 118, 203–204, 223–224; *Venceremos!: Speeches and Writings of Guevara*, ed. J. Gerassi, 205; *Granma* (Havana), English ed., February 26, 1967, 3, 5.

11. J. Stalin, V. M. Molotov, L. M. Kaganovich, K. E. Voroshilov, V. V. Kuibyshev, G. K. Orjonikidze, and D. Z. Manuilsky, *Socialism Victorious* (New York, 1935), 179; *Granma* (Havana), English ed., February 26, 1967, 3; Joseph Stalin *Mastering Bolshevism* (New York, 1937), 44–46; Orville Schell, *To Get Rich Is Glorious:*

China in the Eighties (New York, 1984), 86; *Mao Tse-tung Unrehearsed*, ed. S. Schram, 217.

12. *Granma* (Havana), English ed., May 16, 1971, 6; O. Schell, *To Get Rich*, 18–19.

13. W. J. Chase, *Workers, Society, and the Soviet State*, 195; Walter Duranty, *I Write as I Please* (New York, 1935), 146–148; *Granma* (Havana), English ed., September 29, 1968, 5; *New York Times*, September 17, 1988.

14. Allen Kassof, "Youth Organizations and the Adjustment of Soviet Adolescents" in *The Transformation of Russian Society: Aspects of Social Change since 1861*, ed. Cyril E. Black (Cambridge, Mass., 1960), 494; Foreign Broadcast Information Service, *Daily Report*, March 7, 1968, HHHH 3–4; Fox Butterfield, *China: Alive in the Bitter Sea* (New York, 1982), 193; O. Schell, *To Get Rich*, 144.

15. Karl Marx and Frederick Engels, *Selected Works*, 3 vols. (Moscow, 1969–70), I, 125–127, 137; George Orwell, *Animal Farm* (New York, 1946), 118.

INDEX

DATE DUE
